The Evangelical Quadrilateral

The Evangelical Quadrilateral

Volume 1

Characterizing the British Gospel Movement

David W. Bebbington

BAYLOR UNIVERSITY PRESS

© 2021 by Baylor University Press
Waco, Texas 76798

All Rights Reserved. No part of this publication may be reproduced, stored in a retrieval system, or transmitted, in any form or by any means, electronic, mechanical, photocopying, recording, or otherwise, without the prior permission in writing of Baylor University Press.

Cover and book design by Kasey McBeath
Cover art: Shutterstock/clivewa

The Library of Congress has cataloged this book under ISBN 978-1-4813-1378-0.
Library of Congress Control Number: 2021936430

Paperback ISBN: 978-1-4813-1378-0
Printed case ISBN: 978-1-4813-1443-5

CONTENTS

Preface		vii
Credits		ix
Introduction: The Parameters of Evangelical Identity		1
I	The Character and Culture of Evangelicals	27
	1 The Nature of Evangelical Identity	29
	2 Revival and Enlightenment in Eighteenth-Century England	43
	3 Gospel and Culture in British Evangelicalism	57
	4 Evangelicalism and Cultural Diffusion	75
II	Evangelicals, Americans and the Wider World	93
	5 The Legacy of Jonathan Edwards in Britain	95
	6 Dwight L. Moody and Transatlantic Evangelicalism	115
	7 Global Evangelicalism in the Nineteenth Century	133
III	Evangelicals, Doctrine and Experience	153
	8 The Advent Hope in British Evangelicalism since 1800	155
	9 Evangelical Conversion, *c.* 1740–*c.* 1850	167
	10 Holiness in the Evangelical Tradition	193
	11 The Deathbed Piety of Evangelical Nonconformists in the Nineteenth Century	209
IV	Evangelicals, History and Science	235
	12 Calvin and British Evangelicalism in the Nineteenth and Twentieth Centuries	237

		13 The Evangelical Discovery of History	267
		14 Science and Evangelical Theology in Britain from Wesley to Orr	301
V	Evangelicals into the Twenty-First Century		327
		15 Evangelical Trends, 1959–2009	329
		16 Evangelicals and Public Worship, 1965–2005	347

Index   371

PREFACE

The Evangelical Quadrilateral that gives these books their name is a phrase describing a way of characterizing the Evangelical movement. The quadrilateral was outlined in my book *Evangelicalism in Modern Britain* (1989), to which these volumes are complementary, and since that time has become widely used. Evangelical Christians, according to the quadrilateral, are those who specially emphasize the four elements of the Bible, the cross, conversion and activism. That idea is amplified in the reprinted papers collected in these two volumes. In volume 1 the quadrilateral is discussed in the introduction, in volume 2 it is expounded briefly in chapter 4 and throughout these pages its features recur frequently.

The chapters consist of previously published articles now standardized in presentation and very lightly amended. Cross-references to other chapters have been inserted but publications subsequent to the original printing of the articles have not been added. The introductions survey the main literature in the field that has appeared more recently. The original places of publication of the articles collected here are indicated in the list of credits below.

In these papers the word "Evangelical" is used with an initial capital letter to describe those associated with the movement whatever their denominational affiliation. The alternative usage, of confining "Evangelical" to members of the Church of England, is helpful in providing a parallel with the terms "High Church" and "Broad Church" when referring to the parties within the Church. It can be misleading, however, in suggesting that those outside the Church of England were not Evangelicals in the same sense as those within. So here a capital letter has been adopted for any type of "Evangelical."

I much appreciate the extensive work of preparation for these two volumes by my graduate assistant during the fall semester 2019 at Baylor University, Kaitlyn Waynen, who in addition produced the indexes. I am also very grateful to those who have looked through sections of this book: Andrew Atherstone, Eileen Bebbington, Neil Dickson, Robert Pope and Martin Wellings. My warm thanks go to Jay Brown of the University of Edinburgh, who, in addition to many other kindnesses over the years, has carefully read the whole of the text. None of these people, of course, shares any responsibility for the resulting books. I should like to dedicate the two volumes to friends who over the decades have encouraged and directed me in the parallel field of American Evangelical history, successive holders of the Francis A. McAnaney Chair of History at the University of Notre Dame, Indiana, George M. Marsden and Mark A. Noll.

David Bebbington
Stirling
September 2020

CREDITS

Chapter 1: "Towards an Evangelical Identity," in *For Such a Time as This: Perspectives on Evangelicalism, Past, Present and Future*, ed. Steve Brady and Harold Rowdon (London: Scripture Union, 1996), 37–48.

Chapter 2: "Revival and Enlightenment in Eighteenth-Century England," in *On Revival: A Critical Examination*, ed. Andrew Walker and Kristin Aune (Carlisle: Paternoster Press, 2003), 71–85. Used with the permission of Authentic Media (www.authentic.media.co.uk), the current publishers of Paternoster titles.

Chapter 3: "Evangelicalism and British Culture," in *Culture, Spirituality and the Brethren*, ed. Neil T. R. Dickson and T. J. Marinello (Troon, Ayrshire: Brethren Archivists and Historians Network, 2014), 25–38.

Chapter 4: "Evangelicalism and Cultural Diffusion," in *British Evangelical Identities Past and Present*, vol. 1: *Aspects of the History and Sociology of Evangelicalism in Britain and Ireland*, ed. Mark Smith (Milton Keynes: Paternoster Press, 2008), 18–34. Used with the permission of Authentic Media (www.authentic.media.co.uk), the current publishers of Paternoster titles.

Chapter 5: "The Legacy of Jonathan Edwards in Britain," in *The Global Edwards: Papers from the Jonathan Edwards Congress Held in Melbourne, August 2015* (Eugene, OR: Wipf and Stock, 2017), 1–21.

Chapter 6: "Moody as a Transatlantic Evangelical," in *Mr Moody and the Evangelical Tradition*, ed. Timothy George (London: T&T Clark International, 2004), 75–92. Used by permission of Bloomsbury Publishing Plc.

Chapter 7: "The Context of Methodist Missions: Global Evangelicalism in the Nineteenth Century," *Proceedings of the Wesley Historical Society* 59:6 (2014), 227–44.

Chapter 8: "The Advent Hope in British Evangelicalism since 1800," *The Scottish Journal of Religious Studies* 9:2 (1988), 103–14.

Chapter 9: "Evangelical Conversion, c. 1740–1850," *Scottish Bulletin of Evangelical Theology* 18:2 (2000), 102–27.

Chapter 10: "Holiness in the Evangelical Tradition," in *Holiness Past and Present*, ed. Stephen C. Barton (London: T&T Clark, 2003), 298–315. Used by permission of Bloomsbury Publishing Plc.

Chapter 11: "The Deathbed Piety of Victorian Evangelical Nonconformists," in *Heart Religion: Evangelical Piety in England and Ireland, 1690–1850*, ed. John Coffey (Oxford: Oxford University Press, 2016), 201–23. © Oxford University Press 2016. Reproduced with permission of the Licensor through PLSclear.

Chapter 12: "Calvin and British Evangelicalism in the Nineteenth and Twentieth Centuries," in *Calvin and His Influence, 1509–2009*, ed. Irena Backus and Philip Benedict (New York: Oxford University Press, 2011), 282–305.

Chapter 13: "The Evangelical Discovery of History," in *The Church on its Past*, ed. Peter D. Clarke and Charlotte Methuen, *Studies in Church History*, vol. 49 (Woodbridge, Suffolk: Boydell Press, 2013), 330–64. Used by permission of the Ecclesiastical History Society.

Chapter 14: "Science and Evangelical Theology in Britain from Wesley to Orr," in *Evangelicals and Science in Historical Perspective*, ed. David N. Livingstone, D. G. Hart and Mark A. Noll (New York: Oxford University Press, 1999), 120–44.

Chapter 15: "Evangelical Trends, 1959–2009," *Anvil* 26:2 (2009), 93–106.

Chapter 16: "Evangelicals and Public Worship, 1965–2005," *Evangelical Quarterly* 79:1 (2007), 3–22.

INTRODUCTION

The Parameters of Evangelical Identity

William Gaskell, the minister of Cross Street Unitarian Chapel, Manchester, but better known to posterity as the husband of the novelist Elizabeth Gaskell, preached a sermon on 9 June 1847. It was delivered before his denomination's West Riding Tract Society in the Westgate Chapel at Wakefield in Yorkshire. The subject of the sermon, subsequently published at the request of the committee of the society, was "Some Evil Tendencies of the Popular Theology." It was an eloquent denunciation of Evangelical religion, what Gaskell called "Orthodoxy." He found the very notion of orthodoxy abhorrent because it repressed religious inquiry and so tended "to clog and fetter the mind in the pursuit of the highest truth." It destroyed, in the preacher's view, the true idea of God as Father, depicting him instead as a being who was "so hard, so unpitying, so unforgiving." It presented human nature as corrupt and so incapable of any "holy ambition" before "miraculous conversion." It taught a false doctrine of the atonement according to which a Redeemer sets sinners free from the power of guilt "while they look on without effort." And it upheld a view of future punishment as a "work of pure vengeance." Such a theology might have satisfied "our Calvinistic puritan forefathers," but it would not do for Gaskell's contemporaries in the enlightened England of the nineteenth century. They should not uphold a system that "makes belief in a few mysterious dogmas the passport to heaven, in place of a heavenly spirit."[1] For Gaskell the "mysterious dogmas" of Evangelical Christianity contrasted sharply with his own milder Unitarian opinions, but by calling it "popular" he was bearing testimony to its pervasive power in his day. Evangelical religion was a profoundly important force in modern Britain.

---

1 William Gaskell, *Some Evil Tendencies of the Popular Theology* (Wakefield: Printed by Nichols and Sons, 1847), quoted at 3, 6, 9, 10, 11, 14, 4.

The history of the movement was recounted in my book called *Evangelicalism in Modern Britain: A History from the 1730s to the 1980s* (1989). Although there were complaints about aspects of the volume—sometimes that it neglected providence or Wales—many kind reviewers acknowledged its value as an analysis of the movement over the centuries.[2] Both before and after the appearance of the book I have published a range of articles on facets of the same subject. One of the earliest, published in 1983, was an overview of the gospel movement during the nineteenth century.[3] The topic was chosen because that was a major theme of a course I taught at the University of Stirling on "Church, State and Society in Nineteenth-Century Britain." A second article published in the same year, on "Evangelicals and Reform," reflected another root of my concern with the subject.[4] An interest in the political role of adherents of the movement had emerged from my Ph.D. project on the place of the Nonconformists of England and Wales in public affairs at the end of the nineteenth and start of the twentieth centuries. That research, published in revised form as *The Nonconformist Conscience* (1982), had shown that to a remarkable extent the political style of the chapels was conditioned by their Evangelical beliefs.[5] Since there was no existing history of the Evangelical movement as a whole, it seemed sensible to provide one and *Evangelicalism in Modern Britain* was the outcome. The richness of the field, together with requests from various audiences for papers, encouraged the production of associated articles. Thirty-two of them are gathered in this and its companion volume. They will be referred to by volume and chapter, so that "1:1" means volume 1, chapter 1, and "2:7" means volume 2, chapter 7. The papers in the first volume consider themes that affected Evangelicals in general, the issues that influenced their common identity; the chapters in the other examine particular sections of Evangelicalism, its sects,

2   Timothy Larsen, "The Reception Given *Evangelicalism in Modern Britain* since its Publication in 1989," in *The Emergence of Evangelicalism: Exploring Historical Continuities*, ed. Michael A. G. Haykin and Kenneth J. Stewart (Nottingham: Apollos, 2008), 21–36, at 22. Some of the weightier criticisms are discussed below. Perhaps it should be noted that, although the reverse of the title page says that the book appeared in 1989, it was actually on the market before the end of 1988.
3   David W. Bebbington, "The Gospel in the Nineteenth Century," *Vox Evangelica* 13 (1983), 19–28.
4   David W. Bebbington, "Evangelicals and Reform: An Analysis of Mass Socio-Political Action," *Third Way* 6:5 (1983), 10–13.
5   David W. Bebbington, *The Nonconformist Conscience: Chapel and Politics, 1870–1914* (London: Allen & Unwin, 1982). A previous article on the sociopolitical engagement of an Evangelical was "Politics and Philanthropy: The Social Concern and Political Activity of Lord Shaftesbury," *Third Way* 1:15 (1977), 13–16.

denominations and churches. Although there is necessarily some crossover, the first volume is centrally concerned with the Evangelical movement as a whole, the second with its variety. The collection equally reflects the unity and the diversity of the movement.

The Evangelical Quadrilateral

The 1983 article on "The Gospel in the Nineteenth Century" was the published form of the Laing Lecture for 1982 at London Bible College. Already in this lecture the characteristics held in common by Evangelicals constituted the theme:

> First, they were conversionist. They believed that people needed to have their lives changed by receiving the gospel. Secondly, they were activist. They insisted that true Christians must put effort into spreading the gospel. Thirdly, they were biblicist. They regarded the Bible as the sole source of the gospel. And fourth, they were crucicentric. They saw the doctrine of the cross as the focus of the gospel.[6]

Each of these attributes was illustrated in some detail. The same fourfold pattern was subsequently taken up in the first chapter of *Evangelicalism in Modern Britain*, where it is called "a quadrilateral of priorities that formed the basis of Evangelicalism."[7] Consequently the formula gradually became known as "the Evangelical quadrilateral," or even "the Bebbington quadrilateral," forming a succinct way of describing the main features that have been consistently emphasized in the movement. In this first volume of the collected essays the nature of the quadrilateral is set out in the first chapter, but it is a theme that runs through all the papers collected here, whether explicitly or implicitly. The fourfold pattern has proved sufficiently elastic to grasp the protean shape of the movement over time. What is more surprising, since it was conceived in relation to Britain alone, is that it has turned out to be a fair method of characterizing Evangelicals over space too. Thus the National Association of Evangelicals in the United States has long used it as a method of identifying the adherents of the movement.[8] The fourfold pattern has even become widely used beyond the bounds of the English-speaking world. A book on Evangelical political activity in Switzerland published in 2014, for example, stated that the fourfold description "*a rencontré un vif succès dans les cercles académiques,*

---

6   Bebbington, "Gospel in the Nineteenth Century," 19.
7   David W. Bebbington, *Evangelicalism in Modern Britain: A History from the 1730s to the 1980s* (London: Unwin Hyman, 1989), 3.
8   https://www.nae.net/what-is-an-evangelical/, accessed 25 June 2020.

mais aussi dans les milieux évangéliques."[9] It is gratifying that the quadrilateral has become acceptable to scholars and Evangelicals alike in many parts of the world. Although in the present two volumes the papers are largely confined to the British experience, they address issues that have affected global Evangelicalism. The quadrilateral has become a widely deployed tool in the analysis of the movement worldwide.

It will be helpful here to review the component parts of the quadrilateral, noting some of the advances in their study since *Evangelicalism in Modern Britain*, whether by other authors or by the present writer. This first volume of the collection opens with a chapter setting out the four points, beginning with biblicism. Although it has been settled throughout Evangelicalism that the Bible is fundamental for devotional life and doctrinal authority, debates about its status have often divided the movement. One of the most salient disputes, an early Fundamentalist controversy, is analyzed in 2:7 in this collection. There the acceptance of biblical criticism was challenged by conservatives in Wesleyan Methodism as subversive of the faith. The chapter reveals much of what appeared to be at stake between traditionalists and progressives in the Evangelical community as a whole in the early years of the twentieth century, so supplementing the argument of *Evangelicalism in Modern Britain* about the growing polarization of that era. That book, however, has been shown to underestimate the extent of belief in the inerrancy of scripture in the period down to the mid-nineteenth century.[10] Yet it remains important to note that, as the book suggests, there was a shift to stronger views of inspiration around the middle years of the century. More Evangelicals began to believe that the Bible was authoritative in fields beyond the religious, in matters of philosophy and science.[11] Evangelicals were just one of the sections of Victorian society who revered the Bible, but their devotion to it was second to none. The respect paid to the scriptures even by atheists and agnostics was in fact an indication of the permeation of Victorian Britain by the assumptions of Evangelicals.[12] The Authorized Version in particular owed much of its status—and even its title as the "Authorized Version"—to the dissemination of the scriptures by the British

---

9   Philippe Gonzalez, *Que ton règne vienne: Des évangéliques tentés par le pouvoir absolu* (Geneva: Labor et Fides, 2014), 30.
10 Kenneth J. Stewart, "The Evangelical Doctrine of Scripture, 1650–1850: A Re-Examination of David Bebbington's Theory," in *Emergence of Evangelicalism*, ed. Haykin and Stewart, 394–413.
11 David W. Bebbington, "Response," in *Emergence of Evangelicalism*, ed. Haykin and Stewart, 417–32, at 423–24.
12 Timothy Larsen, *A People of One Book: The Bible and the Victorians* (Oxford: Oxford University Press, 2011).

and Foreign Bible Society, initially and for long an Evangelical organization.[13] Publications since the appearance of *Evangelicalism in Modern Britain* in 1989 have done nothing to question the contention that Evangelicals have habitually insisted that the Bible was central to their faith.

Another constant feature of Evangelical religion has been a concentration on the cross of Christ. The atonement has been treated as the heart of the doctrine of salvation, essential for the message to be proclaimed effectively. Hence, again, the subject has been the occasion of much debate. The Evangelicals of the eighteenth century argued over whether, as Calvinists held, Christ died for a specific number, the elect, or whether, as the Arminians believed, he died for all. The varying opinions of Baptists on the subject are traced from the eighteenth century down to the start of the twenty-first in 2:11. The final coverage in the chapter is of a fierce controversy resulting from the dissatisfaction of Steve Chalke, a prominent figure in the Evangelical Alliance, with the idea of penal substitution. That doctrine, the conviction that Christ bore the penalty for the sin of human beings in their place, has been widely regarded as the main version of atonement theory accepted by Evangelicals. The discussions generated some weighty theological writing, largely designed to defend the doctrine.[14] None doubted that the atonement was the kernel of the Christian faith. The prominence of the doctrine under Evangelical influence in the early nineteenth century led Boyd Hilton in 1988 to label the period "The Age of Atonement." His book of that title, published immediately before *Evangelicalism in Modern Britain*, mounted a persuasive case that the doctrine was so salient that it shaped social theory and economic policy during the period.[15] Even if Evangelical teaching became less formative of government practice in subsequent years, the implications of the doctrine for later public life have been drawn out in other ways. I have suggested in particular that the focus on the atonement ensured that sin remained central to the worldview of

---

13 David W. Bebbington, "The King James Bible in Britain from the Late Eighteenth Century," in *The King James Bible and the World It Made*, ed. David Lyle Jeffrey (Waco, TX: Baylor University Press, 2011), 49–69, at 52–54.
14 *Pierced for Our Transgressions: Rediscovering the Glory of Penal Substitution*, ed. Steve Jeffery, Mike Ovey and Andrew Sach (Nottingham: InterVarsity Press, 2007); Stephen R. Holmes, *The Wondrous Cross: Atonement and Penal Substitution in the Bible and History* (Milton Keynes: Paternoster Press, 2007); *The Atonement Debate: Papers from the London Symposium on the Theology of the Atonement*, ed. Derek Tidball, David Hilborn and Justin Thacker (Grand Rapids, MI: Zondervan, 2008).
15 Boyd Hilton, *The Age of Atonement: The Influence of Evangelicalism on Social and Economic Thought, 1785–1865* (Oxford: Clarendon Press, 1988).

Evangelicals and so helped to mold their attitudes to empire in the late nineteenth century and into the twentieth.[16] The doctrine of the cross has always been crucial for Evangelicals.

Conversion has been a third mark of Evangelicals in general. A chapter here, 1:9, sets out detailed evidence for the experience over the period from the middle of the eighteenth to the middle of the nineteenth century. Although the coverage of the chapter is limited to the main denominations of Nonconformists and so omits Anglicans, who were less inclined to expect sudden conversions, it does show the wide variety of paths taken by Evangelicals on their way to Christian commitment. The experience is also touched on in several other papers, such as the ones on Methodist spirituality and Henry Drummond, 2:4 and 2:14. The subject has been illuminated since 1989 by Bruce Hindmarsh, whose book on *The Evangelical Conversion Narrative* (2005) points out the significance of his subject for the rise of individual consciousness in the modern era. The volume illustrates the momentous place of conversion in the lives of those who were caught up in the early days of the eighteenth-century revival. The Anglican clergyman William Grimshaw who assisted John Wesley in his itinerant ministry, for instance, claimed that converts possessed justification, assurance, union with Christ and hope of eternal life. "All this," he wrote, "they *experience* and *feel* in the Heart."[17] The book explicitly endorses the contention that conversionism was a hallmark of Evangelicals.[18] Other publications have reinforced the prominence of conversion in Evangelical teaching and experience. The papers in *George Whitefield: Life, Context and Legacy*, edited by Geordan Hammond and David Ceri Jones, repeatedly bring out the centrality of the new birth in Whitefield's message.[19] The subject has been less thoroughly treated for later periods, but the decay of conversion in Methodism, as its Evangelical temper began to dissolve, has been noted by Kenneth Brown in his study of the Nonconformist ministry.[20]

---

16 David W. Bebbington, "Atonement, Sin and Empire, 1880–1914," in *The Imperial Horizons of British Protestant Missions, 1880–1914*, ed. Andrew Porter (Grand Rapids, MI: Eerdmans, 2003), 14–31.

17 William Grimshaw, *An Answer to a Sermon Lately Published against the Methodists by the Rev. Mr George White* (Preston, 1749), 28, quoted by D. Bruce Hindmarsh, *The Evangelical Conversion Narrative: Spiritual Autobiography in Early Modern England* (Oxford: Oxford University Press, 2005), 90.

18 Hindmarsh, *Evangelical Conversion Narrative*, 325.

19 *George Whitefield: Life, Context and Legacy*, ed. Geordan Hammond and David Ceri Jones (Oxford: Oxford University Press, 2016).

20 Kenneth D. Brown, *A Social History of the Nonconformist Ministry in England and Wales, 1800–1930* (Oxford: Clarendon Press, 1988), 52–53.

As conversionism was lost, so Evangelical identity fell into abeyance. Here again was an essential feature of the movement.

The fourth characteristic, activism, was even more varied, extending beyond evangelism to social concern and political agitation. The evangelistic core is the subject of chapters in this collection on Dwight L. Moody, the American gospel preacher, and on changes in the Wesleyan Methodist home mission strategy (1:6 and 2:5). Elsewhere social concern is illustrated by the role of the Wesleyan minister Hugh Price Hughes and political agitation by a study of Baptist attitudes to the state (2:6 and 2:12). Other papers that I have written, but which are not reproduced here, address topics in these fields: on the long-term Nonconformist conscience and on nineteenth-century political agitation, on twentieth-century Nonconformist evangelism and Evangelical social concern, and on the relation of Evangelical theology to social engagement.[21] This is the area where most other writing has taken place. Evangelistic activity is the main theme of Mark Noll's book *The Rise of Evangelicalism* (2004), which synthesizes British and American material on the eighteenth-century revival.[22] One of the most revealing other works on evangelistic endeavor was Mark Smith's *Religion in Industrial Society* (1994), a study of the Lancashire towns of Oldham and Saddleworth between 1740 and 1865 which brings out that there was "An Evangelical Consensus" (as one chapter is called) about the imperative to spread the gospel.[23] For concern about the problems of society, the biography of Hugh Price Hughes by Christopher Oldstone-Moore provides a perceptive case study of the social gospel.[24] Dominic Erdozain has shown the steady transfer of focus within the Young Men's Christian Association from direct

---

21 David W. Bebbington, "Conscience and Politics," in *Free Churches and Society: The Nonconformist Contribution to Social Welfare*, ed. Lesley Husselbee and Paul Ballard (London: Continuum, 2012), 45–64; "The Dissenting Political Upsurge of 1833–34," in *Modern Christianity and Cultural Aspirations*, ed. David W. Bebbington and Timothy Larsen (London: Sheffield Academic Press, 2003), 224–45; "Evangelism and Spirituality in Twentieth-Century Protestant Nonconformity," in *Protestant Nonconformity in the Twentieth Century*, ed. Alan P. F. Sell and Anthony R. Cross (Carlisle: Paternoster Press, 2003), 184–215; "The Decline and Resurgence of Evangelical Social Concern, 1918-1980," in *Evangelical Faith and Public Zeal: Evangelicals and Society in Britain, 1780-1980*, ed. John Wolffe (London: SPCK, 1995), 175–97; "Evangelicals, Theology and Social Transformation," in *Movement for Change: Evangelicals and Social Transformation*, ed. David Hilborn (Carlisle: Paternoster Press, 2004), 1–19.
22 Mark A. Noll, *The Rise of Evangelicalism: The Age of Edwards, Whitefield and the Wesleys*, A History of Evangelicalism (Leicester: InterVarsity Press, 2004).
23 Mark Smith, *Religion in Industrial Society: Oldham and Saddleworth, 1740-1865* (Oxford: Clarendon Press, 1994).
24 Christopher Oldstone-Moore, *Hugh Price Hughes: Founder of a New Methodism, Conscience of a New Nonconformity* (Cardiff: University of Wales Press, 1999).

gospel work to catering for the recreational needs of its clientele, a process, he contends, of voluntary secularization.[25] In the political field perhaps the most important studies have been Timothy Larsen's *Friends of Religious Equality* (1999), on the political outlook of mid-nineteenth-century Nonconformists, and Gareth Atkins' *Converting Britannia* (2019), an account of the permeation of British public life by Anglican Evangelicals in the age of William Wilberforce.[26] Both stress the Evangelical impetus to be up and doing. Like so much other writing, they confirm that activism was at the heart of the movement.

Cultural Affinities

The quadrilateral therefore has been widely endorsed as a characterization of the Evangelicals. Alongside it, however, another key dimension of the case mounted in *Evangelicalism in Modern Britain* was the contention that the movement was in touch with the main currents flowing through Western civilization. Evangelicals, for all their efforts to reproduce the pristine gospel of the first century, were bound up in the cultural settings of the eighteenth to twentieth centuries. Historians in the later twentieth century were only slowly learning from anthropologists to use the word "culture" to describe the nexus of attitudes surrounding human beings in any society. High culture, the world of art, music and literature, was being joined by popular culture, the folkways, traditional customs and novel enthusiasms of the masses, as subjects for study.[27] *Evangelicalism in Modern Britain* tried to relate the movement committed to the eternal gospel to the flux of the culture in which it was embedded. That is equally true of the essays in these volumes. "Gospel and Culture in British Evangelicalism," 1:3, sets out the broad analysis that informs many of the other chapters. It brings forward evidence that the Evangelical movement was drastically affected by the successive waves of Western civilization, the Enlightenment, Romanticism and Expressionism (otherwise called cultural Modernism). These intellectual moods, providing frameworks for understanding the world, originated as features of high culture but gradually percolated down to wider proportions of the population and so deeply influenced those sitting in the pews. The process of diffusion is discussed in 1:4, where the preponderant

---

25 Dominic Erdozain, *The Problem of Pleasure: Sport, Recreation and the Crisis of Victorian Religion* (Woodbridge, Suffolk: Boydell Press, 2010).
26 Timothy Larsen, *Friends of Religious Equality: Nonconformist Politics in Mid-Victorian England* (Woodbridge, Suffolk: Boydell Press, 1999); Gareth Atkins, *Converting Britannia: Evangelicals and British Public Life, 1770–1840* (Woodbridge, Suffolk: Boydell Press, 2019).
27 Doreen Rosman had led the way in the study of high culture with her *Evangelicals and Culture* (London: Croom Helm, 1984).

flow of influence from the elite to the masses is qualified as well as expounded. Two other essays which I have written but which are not included in these volumes illustrate the way in which cultural diffusion affected Victorian Nonconformity in England and Methodism throughout the world.[28] Both give more space to popular culture, which could often prove resistant to influences spreading down from above, than does *Evangelicalism in Modern Britain*. Nevertheless what most requires discussion here is the sequence of the successive phases of Enlightenment, Romanticism and Expressionism.

The alignment of Evangelicalism with the Enlightenment seemed to many readers a startling element in the argument of *Evangelicalism in Modern Britain*. It had been conventional wisdom that the Evangelical Revival was a reaction against the secularizing rationalism of "enlightened" thinkers. Voltaire and the other French *philosophes*, together with such writers in the English-speaking world as the Deist John Toland, the skeptic David Hume and the radical Tom Paine, were the acknowledged enemies of vital religion. How could these figures and Evangelicals be on the same side? When, however, the premises of the participants in the revival are examined, they turn out to have shared much common ground with the protagonists of the Enlightenment. Wesley and his contemporary revival leaders believed in reason just as much as those who dismissed religion altogether. They favored experiment and they were outstandingly optimistic; they were moderate and ethical in emphasis; and they were pragmatic in method and classical in taste. All these common characteristics are discussed in 1:2, which makes out the same case as the book. This line of argument, however, can be criticized for treating the Enlightenment as too much of a monolith. Its assumptions are attributed to all the progressive thinkers of the period, whereas much of the literature published since 1989 has stressed the variation in the ideas of the era. Jonathan Israel in particular has pointed to a contrast between a moderate and a radical Enlightenment, with the thought of the philosopher Spinoza stimulating many of the more radical tendencies.[29] The distinction between the two types of Enlightenment, however, can actually be seen to have reinforced the argument of *Evangelicalism in Modern Britain*. The Evangelical movement could not tolerate the hostility

---

28 David W. Bebbington, "Gospel and Culture in Victorian Nonconformity," in *Culture and the Nonconformist Tradition*, ed. Jane Shaw and Alan Kreider (Cardiff: University of Wales Press, 1999), 43–62; "Methodism and Culture," in *The Oxford Handbook of Methodist Studies*, ed. William J. Abraham and James E. Kirby (Oxford: Oxford University Press, 2009), 712–29.

29 Jonathan I. Israel, *Radical Enlightenment: Philosophy and the Making of Modernity, 1650–1750* (Oxford: Oxford University Press, 2001), spec. 11–12.

to the Christian faith of the radical Enlightenment but could share the quest for assured knowledge of the moderate version. The issue of whether early Evangelicalism shared the novel intellectual approaches of the eighteenth century has been carefully evaluated by Bruce Hindmarsh, who concludes that it was a form of traditional Christian spirituality that emerged "highly responsive to the conditions of the modern world."[30] Although Hindmarsh stresses the traditional element more than my own book did in 1989, the indebtedness of the early Evangelicals to the atmosphere of Enlightenment is clear in his pages.

The revolution in outlook represented by Romanticism altered most features of intellectual life during the nineteenth century, supplanting and often denigrating attitudes characteristic of the previous hundred years. Although the legacy of the Enlightenment continued to grow in influence long into the Victorian years, its successor was beginning to advance in its rear. The term "Romantic" is used here for a set of preferences—for example, of will and imagination over bare reason—rather than for an era. The conventional usage among literary historians ends the Romantic period in around 1830 so that it is separated from the Victorian years that followed. Here, however, it is recognized that motifs such as a taste for the heroic and a love for the mediaeval that took root during the initial Romantic phase before 1830 continued to spread in society during the rest of the century and came to full flower only in the twentieth. The Romantic impact on Evangelicalism is discussed in 1:3 and two of its chief symptoms, premillennial eschatology and teaching about holiness by faith, are discussed in 1:8 and 1:10. The efflorescence of Evangelicalism with a Romantic turn in the twentieth century is at the heart of the analysis of the Brethren movement in 2:13. Again, the case mounted in *Evangelicalism in Modern Britain* and here can be called into question for taking Romanticism to be a single entity whereas in reality it gloried in pluriformity. There was certainly great variety in the Romantic phenomenon, but it is contended here that there was sufficient similarity between its fundamental premises to see it as a cluster of attitudes that could drastically affect religion. Many of the attitudes were gathered together by Edward Irving, an early nineteenth-century Romantic pioneer whose life has attracted continuing fascination.[31] Two books in particular have demonstrated the longer-term Romantic permeation of the Evangelical

---

30 D. Bruce Hindmarsh, *The Spirit of Early Evangelicalism: True Religion in a Modern World* (Oxford: Oxford University Press, 2018), 276.

31 Peter Elliott, *Edward Irving: Romantic Theology in Crisis* (Milton Keynes: Paternoster Press, 2013); Nicholas J. C. Tucker, "Edward Irving and Romanticism" (Unpublished Ph.D. dissertation, University of Stirling, 2018). See also below, nn. 71, 72.

world. Mark Hopkins showed in *Nonconformity's Romantic Generation* (2004) how the frame of mind associated with the new cultural movement swayed theologians of conservative as well as liberal tendency in the second half of the nineteenth century.[32] Subsequently Michael Watts, in volume 3 of *The Dissenters* (published posthumously in 2015), depicted the Romantic impulse, and especially its foregrounding of the immanence of God, as the primary solvent of Evangelical belief among Nonconformists in the same period.[33] Both books echoed the contention of *Evangelicalism in Modern Britain* about the transformative impact of Romanticism on the Evangelical movement.

In the twentieth century another cultural wave slowly spread across the Western world. In literary history its initial onset is usually called "Modernism," which is why that word is used for the fresh trend in *Evangelicalism in Modern Britain*. The use of the term, however, risks confusing the phenomenon with the contemporary tendency in Roman Catholicism as well as Protestantism towards liberal teaching more in accordance with the spirit of the age. Cultural Modernism was distinct from theological Modernism and so it is probably preferable to call it "Expressionism," a word more commonly used in Germany to describe the cultural indications, especially in poetry and painting, identified with Modernism.[34] In the present volume the relation of Expressionism to the Evangelical movement is considered in 1:3. As early as the 1930s the Oxford Group, a highly effective evangelistic body discussed in 2:15, showed marks of Expressionism, which are more fully analyzed in *Evangelicalism in Modern Britain* than here. Subsequently its chief vehicle within Evangelicalism was to be charismatic renewal, the subject of 2:16. In the 1960s the attitudes of Expressionism, once confined to the avant garde, became the common possession of the youth culture. The Evangelicals open to renewal took on Expressionist characteristics, most obviously a willingness to express their inner feelings openly in public worship, a topic considered in 1:16. Mathew Guest has demonstrated in a study of St Michael-le-Belfrey, York, for some years the premier charismatic Anglican congregation in the North of England, that what he calls "expressivism" was typical of its corporate life.[35] Similarly Rob Warner has argued that in the 1990s adherents of one

---

32 Mark Hopkins, *Nonconformity's Romantic Generation: Evangelical and Liberal Theologies in Victorian England* (Carlisle: Paternoster Press, 2004).
33 Michael R. Watts, *The Dissenters*, vol. 3: *The Crisis and Conscience of Nonconformity* (Oxford: Clarendon Press, 2015), spec. chap. 1.
34 The word is so used in *Evangelicalism in Modern Britain*, at 234 and 241.
35 Mathew Guest, *Evangelical Identity and Contemporary Culture: A Congregational Study in Innovation* (Milton Keynes: Paternoster Press, 2007), spec. 194.

section of English Evangelicals, predominantly charismatic, were so committed to conversionism and activism that they were willing to diverge from the other section which was biblicist and crucicentric. It was a cultural polarization.[36] Both these authors tend to support the case mounted in *Evangelicalism in Modern Britain* and here that, just as Evangelicals had been deeply affected by the Enlightenment and Romanticism, so they were powerfully influenced by the Expressionism of the twentieth century.

Challenges

The image of Evangelicalism presented in my book of 1989 has been challenged in several ways. Most fundamental have been complaints that the fourfold characterization of the movement is an inadequate statement of its priorities. That case was mounted by several speakers at two conferences held in the United States on the twenty-fifth anniversary of the publication of the book, at the American Society of Church History in Washington, D.C., in January 2014 and at the Conference on Faith and History at Pepperdine University the following September. Two contributors, Thomas Kidd and Darren Dochuk, regretted that other factors had not been given equal status to the four specified in the quadrilateral.[37] Both held that the ministry of the Holy Spirit was as noticeable a feature of Evangelicalism as biblicism, crucicentrism, conversionism and activism. However, while that claim may reflect the realities of the periods in which the two historians have specialized, the eighteenth and later twentieth centuries, in between was a long stretch of time when that cannot be substantiated. Nor do Darren Dochuk's further proposals of fellowship and premillennialism carry conviction. The first is the opposite of what others have advanced as an Evangelical characteristic, individualism,[38] which suggests that neither does justice to the internal variety of the movement. The second, which is considered as a candidate for being a normative characteristic of the movement in 1:1, cannot be so because premillennial teaching was repudiated by many Evangelicals. After the conferences this author remained convinced that no other characteristic needed to be added to the items in the quadrilateral.

---

36   Rob Warner, *Reinventing English Evangelicalism, 1966–2001: A Theological and Sociological Study* (Milton Keynes: Paternoster Press, 2007).
37   Thomas S. Kidd, "The Bebbington Quadrilateral and the Work of the Holy Spirit," and Darren Dochuk, "Revisiting Bebbington's Classic Rendering of Modern Evangelicalism at Points of New Departure," in *Evangelicals: Who They Have Been, Are Now and Could Be*, ed. Mark A. Noll, David W. Bebbington and George M. Marsden (Grand Rapids, MI: Eerdmans, 2019), 136–41, 147–58.
38   Mark Hutchinson and John Wolffe, *A Short History of Global Evangelicalism* (Cambridge: Cambridge University Press, 2012), 19.

At other times further qualities have been considered as additional hallmarks of Evangelical faith—sinfulness and revivalism, for example—but they have been recognized as being implicit in conversionism and activism.[39] Again anti-Catholicism and a primitivist reproduction of New Testament Christianity have been proposed by Linford D. Fisher as additional Evangelical markers. Neither suggestion, however, fits the requirement that it has been universally *emphasized* by Evangelical groups. Nor does Fisher's contention that the word has been so contested over time that it defies consistent characterization carry conviction because the four points do turn out to have been salient aspects of an ongoing movement.[40] Its edges may often have been fuzzy, its boundaries normally disputed, but an Evangelical entity existed. The author sees no reason to drop the quadrilateral.

A second challenge to the argument of *Evangelicalism in Modern Britain* relates to timing. Many Evangelicals have cherished their roots in the Reformation. E. J. Poole-Connor's history of *Evangelicalism in England* (1951), in adopting that perspective, allocates five of its ten chapters to the story down to the end of the sixteenth century and adds two more on the seventeenth.[41] *Evangelicalism in Modern Britain*, by contrast, posits that the Evangelical movement began only with the revival of the eighteenth century. That seemed unfair to some who wished to emphasize the continuity of Evangelicalism with the earlier Reformed tradition. In 2008 a volume called *The Emergence of Evangelicalism* (*The Advent of Evangelicalism* in the United States) appeared containing several chapters contending that there was far more consistency between Evangelicals and the Puritans who preceded them than my book indicated. Other chapters nevertheless tended to back the case for the novelty of the Evangelical movement and I was allowed to write a concluding response. It pointed out that the original book of 1989 had tried to give weight to the continuities with the past in the Evangelical Revival as well as to the elements of innovation. The response conceded that a greater measure of activism sometimes prevailed in the seventeenth century than *Evangelicalism in Modern Britain* had allowed. It also recognized that a stronger doctrine of assurance—a believer's confidence of being numbered among the saved—was at times professed by Puritans and that early Evangelicals often spoke more like Puritans about assurance than is delineated in the book. There was a higher degree of continuity over the

---

39 Hutchinson and Wolffe, *Short History*, 16.
40 Linford D. Fisher, "Evangelicals and Unevangelicals: The Contested History of a Word," in *Evangelicals*, ed. Noll, Bebbington and Marsden, 188–213.
41 Edward J. Poole-Connor, *Evangelicalism in England* (London: Fellowship of Independent Evangelical Churches, 1951).

doctrine of assurance than the book had proposed. Nevertheless the response continued to maintain that there was generally less doubt among Evangelicals than among their predecessors about their salvation. There were also other major discontinuities, such as the rise of Methodism, that made the Evangelical Revival a revolutionary stage in the trajectory of Protestantism.[42] The case that Evangelicalism, notwithstanding its immense inheritance from the Reformation, was in large measure a novel phenomenon in the early eighteenth century was substantially sustained.

The perspective of *Evangelicalism in Modern Britain*, in the third place, can be challenged on the grounds that it is too insular. Reg Ward's book *The Protestant Evangelical Awakening* (1992), supplemented by his *Early Evangelicalism: A Global Intellectual History, 1670–1789* (2006), brought out the close interconnections between continental movements and the stirrings of revival in the English-speaking world. Silesian preachers, Salzburger *emigrés* and Moravian revivalists prepared the way for the emergence of Evangelicalism in Britain and America.[43] The debt to continental Pietism and Moravianism is acknowledged in my book, but its dimensions are underestimated. Furthermore Andrew Kloes has shown that German parallels with the growing Evangelical movement in Britain were flourishing in the early nineteenth century to a greater degree than had previously been thought.[44] The worldwide Evangelical movement has also come more sharply into focus since the publication of my book, with Mark Hutchinson and John Wolffe's *A Short History of Global Evangelicalism* (2012) and Donald M. Lewis and Richard V. Pierard's *Global Evangelicalism* (2014) providing valuable overviews.[45] In the present two volumes there is more recognition that Britain formed part of an international network than is there in the book of 1989. A chapter on "Global Evangelicalism in the Nineteenth Century," 1:7, places Britain within that context and 2:13 does the same for the Brethren, one of the component denominations of the movement. Elsewhere I have sketched something of the formative part in global Evangelicalism played by Britain, but most of my writing on international affairs has concentrated on comparisons

---

42 Bebbington, "Response."
43 William Reginald Ward, *The Protestant Evangelical Awakening* (Cambridge: Cambridge University Press, 1992); *Early Evangelicalism: A Global Intellectual History, 1670–1789* (Cambridge: Cambridge University Press, 2006).
44 Andrew Kloes, *The German Awakening: Protestant Renewal after the Enlightenment, 1815–1848* (New York: Oxford University Press, 2019).
45 Hutchinson and Wolffe, *Short History*; *Global Evangelicalism: Theology, History and Culture in Regional Perspective*, ed. Donald M. Lewis and Richard V. Pierard (Downers Grove, IL: IVP Academic, 2014).

with American Evangelicalism.⁴⁶ A five-volume series on English-speaking Evangelicalism, including my contribution on the later nineteenth century, tries to show the connectedness of developments across the world, but with special attention to Anglo-American parallels.⁴⁷ That book is supplemented by a couple of the articles reprinted here, 1:5 and 1:6, showing the remarkable degree of influence exercised by the Americans Jonathan Edwards and Dwight L. Moody over Britain's movement.⁴⁸ Greater attention to the international context has been a main theme of my coverage of Evangelical history since the book of 1989.

A fourth challenge to the representation of the British movement in the book is the neglect of a crucial aspect of international Evangelicalism, the missionary dimension. Enthusiasm for foreign missions flowed in the lifeblood of Evangelicals, but a decision was taken to omit them from *Evangelicalism in Modern Britain* in order to make the material more manageable. In 1989 the academic study of missions was not yet strongly developed. The most important figure in stimulating higher scholarly standards in mission studies was Andrew

46 David W. Bebbington, "Of This Train, England Is the Engine: British Evangelicalism and Globalization in the Long Nineteenth Century," in *A Global Faith: Essays on Evangelicalism and Globalization*, ed. Mark Hutchinson and Ogbu Kalu (Sydney: Centre for the Study of Australian Christianity, 1998), 122–39; "Evangelicalism in Its Settings: The British and American Movements since 1940," in *Evangelicalism: Comparative Studies of Popular Protestantism in North America, the British Isles and Beyond, 1700-1990*, ed. Mark A. Noll, David W. Bebbington and George A. Rawlyk (New York: Oxford University Press, 1994), 365–88; "Evangelicalism in Modern Britain and America: A Comparison," in *Amazing Grace: Evangelicalism in Australia, Britain, Canada and the United States*, ed. George A. Rawlyk and Mark A. Noll (Grand Rapids, MI: Baker Books and Montreal and Kingston: McGill-Queen's University Press, 1994), 183–212; "Evangelicalism and Secularization in Britain and America from the Eighteenth Century to the Present," in *Secularization and Religious Innovation in the North Atlantic World*, ed. David Hempton and Hugh McLeod (Oxford: Oxford University Press, 2017), 65–79. There is also a comparison with Canada: "Canadian Evangelicalism: A View from Britain," in *Aspects of the Canadian Evangelical Experience*, ed. George A. Rawlyk (Montreal and Kingston: McGill-Queen's University Press, 1997), 38–54.
47 David W. Bebbington, *The Dominance of Evangelicalism: The Age of Spurgeon and Moody*, A History of Evangelicalism (Leicester: InterVarsity Press, 2005).
48 On Edwards, there are also David W. Bebbington, "Remembered around the World: The International Scope of Jonathan Edwards' Legacy," in *Jonathan Edwards at Home and Abroad: Historical Memories, Cultural Movements, Global Horizons*, ed. David W. Kling and Douglas A. Sweeney (Columbia, SC: University of South Carolina Press, 2003), 177–200; "The Reputation of Edwards Abroad," in *The Cambridge Companion to Jonathan Edwards*, ed. Stephen Stein (Cambridge: Cambridge University Press, 2007), 239–61.

Walls, who, after serving in Sierra Leone and Nigeria, created at the University of Aberdeen a Centre for the Study of Christianity in the Non-Western World. His essays, collected as *The Missionary Movement in World History* (1996) and *The Cross-Cultural Process in Christian History* (2002), together with the periodicals he edited and the Centre as it moved to the University of Edinburgh, began to transform missionary history into an academic discipline.[49] The process was continued by two large-scale international research ventures, the North Atlantic Missiology Project (from 1996) and Currents in World Christianity (from 1999), run by Brian Stanley, from 2009 one of Walls' successors at Edinburgh.[50] The vast legacy of Evangelical missions in global Christianity is evident in Stanley's major book, *Christianity in the Twentieth Century: A World History* (2018).[51] The relation of missions to imperial history, a theme to which Stanley also contributed, was taken up by others, notably by Catherine Hall and Andrew Porter, and the weighty scholarship produced in the field had the effect of placing the subject of missionary history within a mainstream historiographical channel.[52] A volume edited by Porter contained a previously mentioned essay of mine on "Atonement, Sin and Empire, 1880–1914" that attempted to illuminate the connection between the central concerns of Evangelicals and their changing stance on the question of imperialism.[53] Another essay I wrote showed the importance of missionary organizations in the British version of the Fundamentalist crisis around 1920.[54] These contributions served as minor tributes to the principle that the role of missions had become an inescapable feature of British history.

---

49   Andrew F. Walls, *The Missionary Movement in Christian History: Studies in the Transmission of the Faith* (Maryknoll, NY: Orbis Books, 1996); *The Cross-Cultural Process in Christian History: Studies in the Transmission and Appropriation of Faith* (Maryknoll, NY: Orbis Books, 2002).

50   On Walls and Stanley, see David W. Bebbington, "Andrew Walls, Brian Stanley, Dana Robert, Mark Noll and Global Evangelicalism," in *Making Evangelical History: Faith, Scholarship and the Evangelical Past*, ed. Andrew Atherstone and David Ceri Jones (Abingdon, Oxfordshire: Routledge, 2019), 257–74.

51   Brian Stanley, *Christianity in the Twentieth Century: A World History* (Princeton, NJ: Princeton University Press, 2018).

52   Brian Stanley, *The Bible and the Flag: Protestant Missions and British Imperialism in the Nineteenth and Twentieth Centuries* (Leicester: Apollos, 1990); Catherine Hall, *Civilising Subjects: Metropole and Colony in the English Imagination, 1830–1867* (Cambridge: Polity Press, 2002); Andrew Porter, *Religion versus Empire? British Protestant Missionaries and Overseas Expansion, 1700–1914* (Manchester: Manchester University Press, 2004).

53   Bebbington, "Atonement, Sin and Empire."

54   David W. Bebbington, "Missionary Controversy and the Polarising Tendency in Twentieth-Century British Protestantism," *Anvil* 13:2 (1996), 141–57.

A further major historiographical transformation in the late twentieth century was the rise of women's history. This change had made sufficient progress by 1989 for more on the female role in the Evangelical movement to have been included in the book and its relative paucity was a fifth criticism that was made at the time. Women do appear, but there are relatively few of them; and discussion of their part in the movement is included, but only in fairly short passages. It has been suggested that one paragraph, on arguments about women in ministry in the early twentieth century, attributes too little agency to the topic in polarizing liberals and conservatives against each other within the movement.[55] Since 1989 there has been a good deal of writing about Evangelical women. Following on Deborah Valenze's book on the subject, Janice Holmes and Jennifer Lloyd have demonstrated that women played a prominent part in Methodism.[56] Linda Wilson has analyzed the faith and practice of mid-nineteenth-century Evangelical Nonconformists, fruitfully comparing women's experience with that of men.[57] There have been biographies of significant figures such as Josephine Butler and Christabel Pankhurst.[58] And Callum Brown has argued that Evangelical women inculcated the values that shaped British Christian identity over successive generations down to the 1960s.[59] I had contributed in 1983 a minor piece reviewing the divided state of earlier Evangelical opinion on women's ministry as the question of female ordination was becoming the subject of serious debate in the Church of England.[60] After the appearance of *Evangelicalism in Modern Britain*, I offered evidence on aspects of women's spirituality in two of the articles republished here (1:9 and

---

55 Bebbington, *Evangelicalism in Modern Britain*, 206–7; Sarah Williams, "Feminism and the English Free Church Tradition," in *Evangelicalism and Dissent in Modern England and Wales*, ed. David W. Bebbington and David Ceri Jones (Abingdon, Oxfordshire: Routledge, 2020), 139–57.

56 Deborah Valenze, *Prophetic Sons and Daughters: Female Preaching and Popular Religion in Industrial England* (Princeton, NJ: Princeton University Press, 1985); Janice Holmes, *Religious Revivals in Britain and Ireland, 1859–1905* (Dublin: Irish Academic Press, 2000), chap. 4; Jennifer M. Lloyd, *Women and the Shaping of British Methodism: Persistent Preachers, 1807–1907* (Manchester: Manchester University Press, 2009).

57 Linda Wilson, *Constrained by Zeal: Female Spirituality among Nonconformists, 1825–1875* (Carlisle: Paternoster Press, 2000).

58 Jane Jordan, *Josephine Butler* (London: Hambledon Continuum, 2001); Timothy Larsen, *Feminism and Fundamentalism in Coalition: Christabel Pankhurst* (Woodbridge, Suffolk: Boydell Press, 2002).

59 Callum G. Brown, *The Death of Christian Britain: Understanding Secularisation, 1800–2000* (London: Routledge, 2001).

60 David W. Bebbington, "Evangelicals and the Role of Women, 1800–1930," *Christian Arena* 37:4 (1984), 19–23.

1:11) and touched on their increasing public prominence in the movement by the late twentieth century (1:15 and 1:16). Far more, however, remains to be said about the role of women in the Evangelical movement over the centuries.

Developments

Since the appearance of *Evangelicalism in Modern Britain* several fields of research on matters within its ambit have made striking advances. Some have now entered into mainstream studies of British religion and society, with many nineteenth-century topics, for example, being lucidly delineated in Stewart J. Brown's *Providence and Empire* (2008).[61] One subject where there has been marked progress is spirituality, the subject of 1:10, 2:3 and 2:4 in this collection. James Gordon made a major contribution with his sweeping survey of *Evangelical Spirituality* (1991), broken up into cameo chapters comparing two rough contemporaries each.[62] A volume emerging from the Dr Williams's Centre for Dissenting Studies on *Heart Religion* (2016) brought together essays on aspects of Evangelical devotional life, especially during the eighteenth century.[63] Study of that century yielded monographs on individual authors such as Anne Steele, the daughter of a Hampshire Baptist minister, whose poetry was much read and whose hymns were widely sung.[64] For the nineteenth century, apart from Linda Wilson's important book on female spirituality mentioned in the last paragraph, Pat Jalland explored the Evangelical Anglican experience of death in the family and Mary Riso examined the obituaries of Evangelical Nonconformists in order to discover their attitudes to the approach to death, so greatly expanding the scope of the chapter on the subject here (1:11).[65] The present author contributed *Holiness in Nineteenth-Century England* (2000), three-quarters of which concerned Evangelicals.[66] And for the twentieth century Ian Randall wrote a comprehensive analysis of the range of spirituality across the denominations during the interwar years in his *Evangelical*

---

61 Stewart J. Brown, *Providence and Empire: Religion, Politics and Society in the United Kingdom, 1815–1914* (London: Pearson/Longmans, 2008).
62 James M. Gordon, *Evangelical Spirituality* (London: SPCK, 1991).
63 *Heart Religion: Evangelical Piety in England and Ireland, 1690–1850*, ed. John Coffey (Oxford: Oxford University Press, 2016).
64 Cynthia Y. Aalders, *To Express the Ineffable: The Hymns and Spirituality of Anne Steele* (Milton Keynes: Paternoster Press, 2008).
65 Pat Jalland, *Death in the Victorian Family* (Oxford: Oxford University Press, 1996); Mary Riso, *The Narrative of the Good Death: The Evangelical Deathbed in Victorian England* (Farnham, Surrey: Ashgate, 2015).
66 David W. Bebbington, *Holiness in Nineteenth-Century England* (Carlisle: Paternoster Press, 2000).

Experiences (1999), showing the strong polarization into liberal and conservative schools.[67] The corporate dimension of spiritual expression was supremely, as the instance of Anne Steele illustrates, in hymnody, which is discussed in another collective volume emanating from the Dr Williams's Centre, *Dissenting Praise* (2011).[68] The practical side of spirituality, however, was shown in the caring activities of congregations, whether for church members or for those beyond their bounds. This topic, less well covered in the literature, has nevertheless been explored for nineteenth-century Presbyterians and Congregationalists in Scotland, England and the United States in Charles Cashdollar's extremely illuminating book *A Spiritual Home* (2000).[69] The result of this output is that a much clearer picture of the experienced religion of the Evangelicals has emerged. In addition, because changing attitudes to the Bible, the cross and conversion inevitably found expression in devotional writing, modifications to the core of Evangelical faith were often clearly displayed in the record of spiritual practices.

One particular dimension of Evangelical spirituality where there has been a historiographical leap forward is in views on eschatology. The subject of events at the end of the world has been set in a long perspective, covering from the Reformation to the year 2000, by Crawford Gribben in his *Evangelical Millennialism in the Transatlantic World* (2010).[70] He has also coedited *Prisoners of Hope?* (2004), a collection that illuminates the thought of Edward Irving and John Nelson Darby, the two colossi that bestrode the subject in the early nineteenth century.[71] Irving has been accorded a biography by Timothy Grass and Darby an extensive study by Donald Akenson.[72] The Christian Zionism, a desire for the Jews to return to the Holy Land, that emerged from

---

67 Ian M. Randall, *Evangelical Experiences: A Study in the Spirituality of English Evangelicalism, 1918–1939* (Carlisle: Paternoster Press, 1999).
68 *Dissenting Praise: Religious Dissent and the Hymn in England and Wales*, ed. Isabel Rivers and David L. Wykes (Oxford: Oxford University Press, 2011).
69 Charles D. Cashdollar, *A Spiritual Home: Life in British and American Reformed Congregations, 1830–1915* (University Park, PA: Pennsylvania State University Press, 2000), chaps. 7 and 9.
70 Crawford Gribben, *Evangelical Millennialism in the Transatlantic World* (Basingstoke: Palgrave Macmillan, 2010).
71 *Prisoners of Hope? Aspects of Evangelical Millennialism in Britain and Ireland, 1800–1880*, ed. Crawford Gribben and Timothy C. F. Stunt (Carlisle: Paternoster Press, 2004).
72 Timothy Grass, *Edward Irving: The Lord's Watchman* (Milton Keynes: Paternoster Press, 2011); Donald H. Akenson, *Exporting the Rapture: John Nelson Darby and the Victorian Conquest of North-American Evangelicalism* (New York: Oxford University Press, 2018).

the adventist expectations of these circles and was to have a long subsequent career, has been expounded by Donald Lewis.[73] But the most significant change of perspective in millennial studies, and probably in Evangelical history, since the publication of *Evangelicalism in Modern Britain* has been the result of the appearance of Martin Spence's monograph *Heaven on Earth* (2015). Spence shows that historicist premillennialism, the prevailing scheme of prophecy in the mid-nineteenth century, differed much more sharply from Darby's dispensationalism than had been supposed, not least in my book. According to Darby's futurist school, most scriptural prophecies awaited fulfillment in the future and until then the world was dissolving in chaos. According to the historicists, however, the book of Revelation revealed the gradual outworking of the prophecies in history down to the present day. The adherents of this school were not backward-looking world-rejectors but progressive optimists who believed that the world should be put to rights before the second advent. They numbered Lord Shaftesbury, the most dedicated social reformer of the century, in their ranks and were aligned with others who labored for secular improvement.[74] This advance in our understanding modifies the chapter on the advent hope in the present volume (1:8), while confirming its point that premillennial teaching appealed to the Victorian elite. It means that premillennialism must be treated seriously as a significant component of mainstream intellectual life.

Matters of the mind among Evangelicals have not been ignored by historians. The worldview of the eighteenth-century movement has been expounded by Bruce Hindmarsh in his *John Newton and the English Evangelical Tradition* (1996) and subsequently in his book on *The Spirit of Early Evangelicalism* (2018) that has previously been taken into consideration.[75] Isabel Rivers' *Vanity Fair and the Celestial City* (2018) has scrutinized all the dimensions of Evangelical literary culture, alongside that of Dissent, during the eighteenth century, discovering much about networks, publishers and booksellers as well as about the content of every genre of religious publication.[76] Joseph Stubenrauch has provided a perceptive analysis of the

---

73 Donald M. Lewis, *The Origins of Christian Zionism: Lord Shaftesbury and Evangelical Support for a Jewish Homeland* (Cambridge: Cambridge University Press, 2010).
74 Martin Spence, *Heaven on Earth: Reimagining Time and Eternity in Nineteenth-Century British Evangelicalism* (Eugene, OR: Wipf and Stock, 2015).
75 D. Bruce Hindmarsh, *John Newton and the English Evangelical Tradition: Between the Conversions of Wesley and Wilberforce* (Oxford: Clarendon Press, 1996); *Spirit of Early Evangelicalism*.
76 Isabel Rivers, *Vanity Fair and the Celestial City: Dissenting, Methodist and Evangelical Literary Culture in England, 1720–1800* (Oxford: Oxford University Press, 2018).

next epoch of the Evangelical intellectual world, showing the centrality of the doctrine of "means," that is human methods for attaining divine goals, during the early nineteenth century.[77] Boyd Hilton's book on *The Age of Atonement* (1988), again already mentioned, discusses the contrast between the predominant and the minority Evangelical ways of understanding the world in the same period.[78] The attempt of the Evangelical theologians of the Church of England to come to terms with the trends of the times later in the century and into the twentieth is the theme of Martin Wellings' *Evangelicals Embattled* (2003).[79] There is a study of parallel Evangelical Nonconformist developments over a longer period by Dale A. Johnson, but the fullest exposition of Nonconformist views was in a series of weighty essays by Alan Sell covering from the eighteenth century to the end of the twentieth.[80] A collection of articles on a specific discipline, church history, over an equally long period of time has been published as *Making Evangelical History* (2019).[81] The overall effect of this body of secondary literature, though filling in many gaps, has not been to change the fundamentals of the case made out in *Evangelicalism in Modern Britain*. The doctrine of means in Stubenrauch's book, for example, brings to the fore the enduring importance of pragmatism in the legacy of the Enlightenment; and the predominant and minority worldviews discussed by Hilton correspond closely to Enlightenment and Romantic stances.[82] If anything, the fresh literature has buttressed the analysis in terms of the stages of cultural influence on the Evangelical mind.

A subsidiary aspect of the life of the mind is the relationship between religion and science. The essays here forming 1:14 and 2:14 illustrate the tight bond between the two forged by natural theology—a merger of natural science and orthodox doctrine—and their subsequent estrangement. Bruce Hindmarsh has worked out in more detail than before the attitude of the earliest Evangelicals to the natural world, stressing their eagerness to see God

---

77 Joseph Stubenrauch, *The Evangelical Age of Ingenuity in Industrial Britain* (Oxford: Oxford University Press, 2016).
78 Hilton, *Age of Atonement*.
79 Martin Wellings, *Evangelicals Embattled: Reponses of Evangelicals in the Church of England to Ritualism, Darwinism and Theological Liberalism, 1890-1930* (Carlisle: Paternoster Press, 2003).
80 Dale A. Johnson, *The Changing Shape of English Nonconformity, 1825-1925* (New York: Oxford University Press, 1999); Alan P. F. Sell, *Dissenting Thought and the Life of the Churches: Studies in an English Tradition* (San Francisco: Mellen Research University Press, 1990) and many subsequent titles.
81 *Making Evangelical History*, ed. Atherstone and Jones.
82 Stubenrauch, *Evangelical Age of Ingenuity*, spec. 29-40; Hilton, *Age of Atonement*.

in everything and their use of nature as a cause for devotion.[83] John Hedley Brooke authoritatively expounded and situated natural theology in his widely used textbook *Science and Religion: Some Historical Perspectives* (1991).[84] The dissemination of natural theology to the masses by the Religious Tract Society is the theme of Aileen Fyfe's *Science and Salvation* (2004) and one of its classic exponents, John Pye Smith, the subject of an essay by Richard Helmstadter in a collection of articles on *Science and Dissent* (2004).[85] The problems caused for Evangelicals by the collapse of natural theology under the assault of popular Darwinism are addressed by Martin Wellings in his book on Anglican Evangelicals.[86] Stuart Mathieson stresses the breadth of the encounter with science in his study of the Evangelical apologetic organization, the Victoria Institute.[87] The reconciliation of faith with evolutionary theory was one of the aims of liberal Evangelicalism in the early twentieth century, its leading exponent, Charles Raven, occupying a prominent position in the story told by Peter Bowler in *Reconciling Science and Religion* (2001).[88] Meanwhile conservative Evangelicals commonly rejected Darwin, and so the research scientists who shared their convictions in theology but not their inhibitions about evolution had a difficult task to vindicate their case. The successful efforts of the Research Scientists' Christian Fellowship to achieve that goal are compared with the less successful attempts on the other side of the Atlantic in Christopher Rios' *After the Monkey Trial* (2014).[89] Once more, though *Evangelicalism in Modern Britain* does not give pride of place to the engagement with science, the new evidence adduced by this literature gives little cause to modify what is said either there or in the essays in this collection.

Revivals have attracted more attention over the past thirty years. John Coffey made a penetrating critique of John Kent's earlier interpretation of Dwight

---

83   Hindmarsh, *Spirit of Early Evangelicalism*, chaps. 4 and 5.
84   John Hedley Brooke, *Science and Religion: Some Historical Perspectives* (Cambridge: Cambridge University Press, 1991), chap. 6.
85   Aileen Fyfe, *Science and Salvation: Evangelical Popular Science Publishing in Victorian Britain* (Chicago: University of Chicago Press, 2004); Richard Helmstadter, "Condescending Harmony: John Pye Smith's Condescending Harmony," in *Science and Dissent in England, 1688–1945*, ed. Paul Wood (Aldershot, Hampshire: Ashgate, 2004).
86   Wellings, *Evangelicals Embattled*, chap. 5.
87   Stuart Mathieson, *Evangelicals and the Philosophy of Science: The Victoria Institute, 1865–1939* (Abingdon, Oxfordshire: Routledge, 2020).
88   Peter J. Bowler, *Reconciling Science and Religion: The Debate in Early Twentieth-Century Britain* (Chicago: University of Chicago Press, 2001), 277–86.
89   Christopher M. Rios, *After the Monkey Trial: Evangelical Scientists and a New Creationism* (New York: Fordham University Press, 2014).

L. Moody's revivals as exercises in social control.[90] In an unprecedented way, in *The Expansion of Evangelicalism* (2006) John Wolffe offered revivals as the chief explanation for Evangelical growth in early nineteenth-century Britain as well as in the United States.[91] The campaigns of the American revivalists who descended on Britain during the nineteenth century were recounted by Nigel Scotland.[92] In *Religious Revivals in Britain and Ireland* (2000) Janice Holmes showed the importance of other Victorian revivalists as well as investigating the great Ulster awakening of 1859 and its impact in England.[93] Historians were attracted to study the nations outside England that played a large part in the history of revival. There was a critical edition of the detailed testimonies from the Cambuslang Revival in Scotland of 1742.[94] The long sequence of revivals in Scotland from before Cambuslang down to 1940 was chronicled by Tom Lennie in three substantial volumes showing the strength of the revival tradition there and Kenneth Jeffrey analyzed a specific revival of 1858–62 in the north-east of Scotland.[95] Robert Tudur Jones made the Welsh Revival of 1904–5 a major feature of his portrayal of religion in *Faith and the Crisis of a Nation: Wales, 1890–1914* (1981–82).[96] The centenary of the Welsh Revival gave rise to several publications, notably Noel Gibbard's *Fire on the Altar* (2005) and *Revival, Renewal and the Holy Spirit* (2009), a collection of papers

90 John Coffey, "Democracy and Popular Religion: Moody and Sankey's Mission to Britain, 1873–1875," in *Citizenship and Community: Liberals, Radicals and Collective Identities in the British Isles, 1865–1931*, ed. Eugenio F. Biagini (Cambridge: Cambridge University Press, 1996), 93–119.
91 John Wolffe, *The Expansion of Evangelicalism: The Age of Wilberforce, More, Chalmers and Finney*, A History of Evangelicalism (Nottingham: InterVarsity Press, 2006).
92 Nigel Scotland, *Apostles of the Spirit and Fire: American Revivalists and Victorian Britain* (Milton Keynes: Paternoster Press, 2009).
93 Holmes, *Religious Revivals in Britain and Ireland*.
94 *The McCulloch "Examinations" of the Cambuslang Revival (1742)*, ed. Keith Edward Beebe, 2 vols. (Woodbridge, Suffolk: Boydell Press for the Scottish History Society, 2011).
95 Tom Lennie, *Land of Many Revivals: Scotland's Extraordinary Legacy of Christian Revivals over Four Centuries, 1527–1857* (Fearn, Ross-shire: Christian Focus, 2015); *Scotland Ablaze: The Twenty-Year Fire of Revival That Swept Scotland, 1858–79* (Fearn, Ross-shire: Christian Focus, 2018); *Glory in the Glen: A History of Evangelical Revivals in Scotland, 1880–1940* (Fearn, Ross-shire: Christian Focus, 2009); Kenneth S. Jeffrey, *When the Lord Walked the Land: The 1858–62 Revival in the North East of Scotland* (Carlisle: Paternoster Press, 2002).
96 Robert Tudur Jones, *Faith and the Crisis of a Nation: Wales, 1890–1914* (originally *Ffydd ac argyfwng cenedl: Cristionogaeth a diwylliant yng Nghymru 1890–1914*, 2 vols., Abertawe: Tŷ John Penry, 1981–82), ed. Robert Pope (Cardiff: University of Wales Press, 2004).

from a centenary conference.⁹⁷ The annual conferences of the Ecclesiastical History Society were devoted in 2006-7 to "Revival and Resurgence in Christian History," gathering together several papers on classic revivals and concern for revival in Britain.⁹⁸ My own book on *Victorian Religious Revivals* (2012) contained accounts of local awakenings in several parts of the world, two of them English Methodist and one Scottish Presbyterian.⁹⁹ The study of revival entered a new phase, with critical yet sympathetic historical accounts coming to the fore. The subject deserves fuller treatment in future discussion of the history of Evangelicalism in Britain.

Another dimension of Evangelical history that has attracted more extensive study is the phenomenon of Fundamentalism, the militant assertion of certain doctrines held to be basic to the faith, together with the repudiation that the Fundamentalist tendency provoked. The account of a Fundamentalist controversy in Wesleyan Methodism in 2:7 of this collection relates to an episode before the First World War, but the crisis in the United States immediately after the war when the term "Fundamentalist" was coined had its echoes in Britain. Another essay of mine explored the self-image of the few who were willing to avow Fundamentalism during the inter-war years as martyrs for the truth.¹⁰⁰ In 2008 and 2009 a publicly funded research project examined systematically the nature and extent of Christian Fundamentalism in Britain. In due course it produced a volume on *Evangelicalism and Fundamentalism in the United Kingdom during the Twentieth Century* (2013). The book concluded that beyond the small number of individuals and groups that were prepared to affirm a Fundamentalist stance there were many Evangelicals who showed sympathies of a Fundamentalist kind. There was a surprising number of Anglicans who could properly be called Fundamentalists, but a much smaller proportion of Baptists than might have been expected from the contemporary American scene. Other conservative Evangelicals also resisted identification as Fundamentalists. Free Methodists in the North-West of England, for example, who

---

97 Noel Gibbard, *Fire on the Altar: A History and Evaluation of the 1904–5 Revival in Wales* (Bridgend: Bryntirion Press, 2005). The same author had published *On the Wings of the Dove* (Bridgend: Bryntirion Press, 2002) on the international effects of the Welsh Revival.
98 *Revival and Resurgence in Christian History*, ed. Kate Cooper and Jeremy Gregory, Studies in Church History, vol. 44 (Woodbridge, Suffolk: Boydell Press, 2008).
99 David W. Bebbington, *Victorian Religious Revivals: Culture and Piety in Local and Global Contexts* (Oxford: Oxford University Press, 2012).
100 David W. Bebbington, "Martyrs for the Truth: Fundamentalists in Britain," in *Martyrs and Martyrologies*, ed. Diana Wood, Studies in Church History, vol. 30 (Oxford: Basil Blackwell, 1993), 417–51.

had been prepared to secede from the Methodist Church because it seemed to be moving too far in a liberal theological direction, were nevertheless stoutly averse to being seen as Fundamentalists.[101] This reluctance to proclaim oneself a Fundamentalist was also evident in the two leading figures in the British Evangelical movement during the later twentieth century, Martyn Lloyd-Jones and John Stott. Studies of both showed that, although they displayed some Fundamentalist traits, they were insistent on putting space between their position and full-blown Fundamentalism.[102] Further research has vindicated the refusal in the conclusion of *Evangelicalism in Modern Britain* to permit any equation of the movement with Fundamentalism.[103]

This Collection

The essays assembled in these two volumes represent work that amplifies—rather than modifying—the work on the Evangelical quadrilateral set out in the book of 1989. The quadrilateral is sometimes called a definition, a word I have occasionally used, but a preferable term would be "characterization." The fourfold formula attempts to summarize the leading characteristics of Evangelicalism. The characterization is not theological, as it is sometimes called, but phenomenological, reflecting the movement's most salient features. Although three of its components—Bible, conversion, cross—relate to doctrines, the fourth component—activism—barely does at all. Furthermore, the Bible was read, conversion was experienced and even the cross was inspirational, all dimensions of life rather than theology. The quadrilateral certainly does not claim to say what the Evangelical movement ought to be, but pinpoints what the evidence shows to have been its leading features over time. The essays in this volume try to fill out the picture in various ways and so to supplement *Evangelicalism in Modern Britain*. Many of them began as papers delivered to audiences of different types, which helps account for

---

101 Andrew Atherstone, "Evangelicalism and Fundamentalism in the Inter-War Church of England," David Bebbington, "Baptists and Fundamentalism in Inter-War Britain," and Derek Tidball, "'Secession is an Ugly Thing:' The Emergence and Development of Free Methodism in Late Twentieth-Century England," in *Evangelicalism and Fundamentalism in the United Kingdom during the Twentieth Century*, ed. David Bebbington and David Ceri Jones (Oxford: Oxford University Press, 2013), 55–75, 95–114 and 209–29.
102 Robert Pope, "Lloyd-Jones and Fundamentalism," in *Engaging with Martyn Lloyd-Jones: The Life and Legacy of "the Doctor"*, ed. Andrew Atherstone and David Ceri Jones (Nottingham: InterVarsity Press, 2011), 197–219; Alister Chapman, *Godly Ambition: John Stott and the Evangelical Movement* (New York: Oxford University Press, 2012), 40–48.
103 Bebbington, *Evangelicalism in Modern Britain*, 275–76.

the variation in approach. Some are more popular, summative and heavily dependent on existing secondary literature while others are more detailed, original and largely based on evidence drawn from primary research. That difference accounts in the main for the contrasting proportions of footnotes. For the purposes of these volumes the essays have been reproduced largely as they originally appeared in print in the places indicated in the list of credits, but alterations have been made to avoid overlap, to correct errors and to standardize usage. Cross-references to where a topic is discussed elsewhere in the two books have been added, but no attempt has been made to bring the text or references up-to-date. The discussions in this introduction and its companion in volume 2 are intended to suggest ways in which scholarship has moved on, though (almost always) without invalidating the points made in the chapters. The story is brought into the twenty-first century by chapters 1:15 and 1:16, but they still attempt to be historical rather than normative. All the chapters are designed to exhibit the parameters of Evangelical Christianity in Britain. They help explain why William Gaskell considered that Evangelicalism constituted "the popular theology." Perhaps its tendencies were not as evil as he supposed.

I

The Character and Culture of Evangelicals

1

The Nature of Evangelical Identity

In 1850 John Sirgood, a bootmaker originally from Gloucestershire, moved from South London to the village of Loxwood on the northern edge of Sussex and set up a religious community called the Dependent Brethren, or Cokelers. In London Sirgood had learned from William Bridges, the founder of the Plumstead Peculiars, the doctrine of the new birth. Sirgood proceeded to spread it in the rural area around Loxwood until, at his death in 1885, his followers numbered about two thousand. Their hymns were unaccompanied and, before each verse was sung, it was read out in the traditional manner designed for the illiterate. Spontaneous testimonies peppered their worship services. Like other holiness groups, the Cokelers believed that the power of God could preserve them from committing sins. They were teetotalers, pacifists and favored traditional clothing. The men wore historic Sussex smocks long into the twentieth century. They strongly believed in mutual assistance, taking this principle to the length of running the village stores on a cooperative basis. One of their hymns ran:

> Christ's combination stores for me
> Where I can be so well supplied
> Where I can one with brethren be
> Where competition is defied.

For a while their commercial activities brought them a modest measure of prosperity. Another distinctive belief, however, undermined their very existence. Although Sirgood himself was married, the movement officially encouraged celibacy. In the light of 1 Corinthians chapter 7 it was thought better to avoid marriage if at all possible. Despite Sirgood's enthusiastic evangelism, the numbers in the community soon went into rapid decline, reaching a mere two hundred by 1940. It retained only two congregations in the 1990s. The Cokelers formed an unusual and highly localized body.¹

In January 1883, by contrast, there assembled the Islington Conference of Evangelicals in the Church of England. The meeting had been an annual event ever since 1827, when Daniel Wilson, soon to be bishop of Calcutta, had invited a few like-minded clergymen to consultations in his parish vestry at Islington. Numbers had grown, papers had been formalized and the occasion had turned into the best gauge of Evangelical opinion in the established church. Attenders, proud to call themselves "Evangelical Churchmen," were conscious of debating issues of public importance. How far, they asked in 1883, was it advisable to invoke the Public Worship Regulation Act of 1874 against ritualist clergy who imitated Roman Catholic practices? Such advanced High Churchmen were breaking with the principles of the Reformation that many Evangelicals saw as the bedrock of the Church of England. It was right, argued the more bellicose Protestants at Islington, to press the bishops to prosecute the ritualists and so harry them out of the national church. Canon Lefroy, one of the leaders of the militants, offered prayer that the eyes of one of the bishops should be opened to the evils he was permitting in his diocese. His petition, however, shocked those present who, under the spreading influence of the Oxford Movement, had themselves been swayed in a High Church direction. One of this group, P. F. Eliot, vicar of Holy Trinity, Bournemouth, and later dean of Windsor, contended that Evangelicals must be more sparing in their criticism, more positive in their teaching and more insistent on the value of the sacraments. They must certainly not play down the authority of the Church of England for the sake of joint action with other Evangelicals outside its bounds. "I would not move one single inch from church principles," declared Eliot, "for the sake of conciliating or co-operating with Dissent." Here was a robust assertion of loyalty to the established church as the divinely commissioned instructor of the whole English people.²

There is clearly a marked difference between the Cokelers of Sussex and the Evangelical Churchmen in conference at Islington. What was there in common between allegiance to "Christ's combination stores" and to "church principles"? On the one hand, there were humble folk, chiefly agricultural laborers and their families, who looked to their patriarchal leader

1   Roger Homan, "The Society of Dependents: A Case Study in the Rise and Fall of Rural Peculiars," *Sussex Archaeological Collections* 119 (Lewes: Sussex Archeology Society, 1981), 195–204.
2   *Record*, 19 January 1883, 56. On the Islington Conference, see 2:1: "The Islington Conference: The Seat of Authority in Anglican Evangelicalism."

for guidance on details of everyday behavior. On the other, there were cultivated men, rising to the top of their profession, who were willing to disagree with each other over issues of policy in church and state. One body consisted of Dissenters; a speaker at the other expressed profound distaste for all Dissent. An intensely sectarian ideal contrasted with a vision of catholicity. Yet the two groups shared far more than simply being contemporaries in Victorian England. Islington Anglicans, like Sussex Cokelers, were Christians committed to proclaiming the gospel. Members of each party wished to turn their lukewarm neighbors, whether gentry or yokels, into zealous servants of Jesus Christ. They believed in evangelism. It seems plausible to call both groups Evangelicals. The attenders of the Islington meetings were explicitly so: they represented the self-conscious Evangelical party in the Church of England. The nineteenth-century Cokelers might not have avowed the label, but their remaining descendants in the faith were in the later twentieth century to form a bond with the Union of Evangelical Churches, an Essex grouping also established by a former follower of William Bridges and previously known as the Peculiar People.[3] Cokeler celibates as much as Islington sacramentarians were part of the diverse Evangelical family.

A Single Movement?

The question arises whether the diversity has been so great as to render the description "Evangelical" meaningless. Donald Dayton has argued, in an American context, that the use of the word obscures reality. Apart from identifying different groups to different people, he suggests, the term is applied to bodies of such bewildering heterogeneity as to make the category useless. Dayton despairs of discovering any set of characteristics that separate off all Evangelicals on the one hand from all non-Evangelicals on the other. Since there is no cluster of qualities to constitute a "family resemblance," the word should be dropped in favor of more useful terms of analysis.[4] It might be thought that the problem would be greater, not less, in a British setting. Gilbert Kirby, when as an Englishman becoming international secretary of the World Evangelical Fellowship in 1962, gathered (as he told readers in the United States) "that the line between the evangelical and the non-evangelical is much more clearly

---

3 Mark Sorrell, *The Peculiar People* (Exeter: Paternoster Press, 1979), 112.
4 Donald W. Dayton, "Some Doubts about the Usefulness of the Category 'Evangelical,'" in *The Variety of American Evangelicalism*, ed. Donald W. Dayton and Robert K. Johnston (Knoxville: Wipf and Stock, 1991), 245–51.

drawn there than here."[5] If the demarcation of Evangelical boundaries in Britain has indeed been less sharp, then the task of defining the essential elements of Evangelicalism becomes even harder. The theologian, concerned to specify what religion ought to be in principle, might be able to isolate the desirable features of Evangelical faith, but the historian, content to analyze what religion has been in practice, might be excused for abandoning the effort to establish the common features of the Evangelical movement. In that case Cokelers and Islingtonians would be assigned to different departments of the religious world. Evangelical identity would be dissolved.

Two considerations make that conclusion premature. One is that Evangelicalism forms, on any account, one of three leading tendencies in modern British religion. In the period since the eighteenth century, Evangelicalism together with liberalism and Catholicism may have ebbed as well as flowed but has always been present in the ecclesiastical scene. Liberals (the Anglicans among them often being called Broad Churchmen) such as Thomas Arnold in the early nineteenth century have wanted to bring Christianity into line with modern knowledge. Catholics (both Anglican and Roman) such as John Henry Newman have insisted on the authority of the church, its ministry and sacraments. Alongside them Evangelicals such as Charles Simeon have wanted to propagate the gospel. It is true that the streams have sometimes flowed together. There have been Evangelicals with High Church tendencies, such as P. F. Eliot; between the 1920s and the 1950s there was a powerful liberal Evangelical movement. Yet the Evangelical tradition has not been broken, ever contributing its dynamic to the churches and beyond them to society at large. It must surely be possible to establish what characteristics, apart from transient incidentals, were transmitted from generation to generation. Together the characteristics would constitute Evangelical identity.

The second consideration, pointing in the same direction, is that a significant proportion of the Christian world has been willing, over the same period, to accept the designation "Evangelical." In the eighteenth century, admittedly, the word was rarely used in a party sense, yet that is a period in which it is fairly easy to identify who gave their allegiance to the revival movement led by John Wesley, George Whitefield and their contemporaries. From the beginning of the nineteenth century the description was gladly adopted by an increasing number inside and outside the established churches. It was common, especially in the twentieth century,

---

5   Gilbert W. Kirby, "A Britisher Writes a Letter to Americans," *United Evangelical Action*, September 1962, 12–13, quoted in David M. Howard, *The Dream That Would Not Die: The Birth and Growth of the World Evangelical Fellowship, 1846–1986* (Exeter: Paternoster Press, 1986), 61.

to refuse the honor to others who claimed it. Thus those of a more conservative theological inclination often denied that liberal Evangelicals were properly Evangelicals at all. Yet the name retained its appeal as a self-description. At the 1989 English Church Census, when nationwide churchmanship was investigated for the first time, 28 percent of all worshipers attended a congregation reported by its leader to be Evangelical. More ticks were given to the category "Evangelical" than to any other label.[6] Christians have been ready, even eager, to avow their Evangelical faith. They must have meant something, and it must surely be possible to give an account of what they meant. It seems reasonable to explore whether self-proclaimed Evangelicals have displayed common characteristics over time.

Mistaken Identities

It is sometimes suggested that "Evangelical" should be equated with "Low Church." In 1888, for instance, W. H. B. Proby published *Annals of the Low Church Party in England* as a study of the Evangelical movement. He was suggesting that, by contrast with his own High Church position, Evangelicals had consistently neglected Catholic doctrines and dignified worship. It is true that Evangelicals have commonly criticized Roman Catholicism and its admirers among Anglo-Catholics. Thus in 1850 Hugh Miller, the editor of the newspaper identified with the Free Church of Scotland, denounced popery as "Christianity's counterfeit," and as late as 1959 Evangelicals petitioned that the use of vestments should cease in the Church of England because of their association with the Roman mass.[7] Anti-Catholicism has been a potent factor in modern British history, and Evangelicalism has been a driving force behind it.[8] Yet an unreflecting hostility to Rome has not been a constant feature of Evangelical history. Thomas Chalmers, later the founder of the Free Church of Scotland, was one of many Evangelicals who supported Roman Catholic emancipation from legal restrictions in 1829; and several of those who signed the 1959 petition subsequently welcomed the creation of an organization of Evangelical Catholics loyal to the Roman communion but subscribing to the

---

6 Peter Brierley, *Prospects for the Nineties: Trends and Tables from the English Church Census: All England: Denominations and Churchmanship* (London: MARC Europe, 1991), 50, 13.
7 *Witness*, 9 January 1850, 3; "A Memorial Addressed to Leaders of the Church of England in a Time of Crisis and Opportunity," November 1959.
8 John Wolffe, *The Protestant Crusade in Great Britain, 1828–1860* (Oxford: Clarendon Press, 1991).

statement of Evangelical beliefs in the Lausanne Covenant.[9] There have been many symptoms of Catholic taste and principle among Evangelicals. Congregational chanting in the Church of England, for example, which has usually been attributed to the Oxford Movement, was in fact an innovation introduced by the Evangelicals in York.[10] During its first decade in 1838 the Baptist Union of Great Britain and Ireland proclaimed its constituents a part of "the Catholic Church."[11] The truth is that, although wariness of Rome has often driven Evangelicals towards a Low Church stance, it has not been an essential element of Evangelicalism. More of the returns to the English Church Census of 1989 from Low Church congregations declined the title "Evangelical" than claimed it.[12] Evangelicalism cannot be identified with Low Churchmanship.

Again, the idea has been put forward that Evangelicals are Christians with elaborate prophetic views. It is supposed that Evangelicals are bound to the vista of world history known as dispensationalism. Under this scheme, it is held that the Almighty has dealings with humanity on different terms in each age, or "dispensation." The age of the church is nearly over; the second coming of Jesus Christ may be expected at any moment; true believers will be "raptured" to join him in the skies before a period of Great Tribulation; then he will return again to inaugurate a millennium of peace and plenty on the earth. Although this view is admittedly widespread in the United States, it has been shown that even there it does not unify Evangelicals.[13] Dispensationalism has been much less prevalent in Britain. It was sufficiently strong during the Second World War for Ernest Kevan, the principal of London Bible College, to seek assurances before he assumed office that he could state his own rejection of the notion of a millennium when the need arose.[14] That juncture, however, probably represented the peak of dispensationalism's influence and, along with other schemes of prophetic interpretation, it has subsequently gone into decline. In the mid-nineteenth century, by contrast, it was the entirely different postmillennialism, according to which the second coming of Christ was to be expected after the

---

9 Stewart J. Brown, *Thomas Chalmers and the Godly Commonwealth in Scotland* (Oxford: Oxford University Press, 1982), 183–89; "What Is an Evangelical Catholic?" (Dublin: Evangelical Catholics, 1992).
10 Nicholas Temperley, *Jonathan Gray and Church Music in York* (York: St Anthony's Press, 1977).
11 *Baptist Magazine*, June 1838, 256.
12 Brierley, *Prospects for the Nineties*, 13.
13 Dayton, "Some Doubts," 249–50.
14 Gilbert W. Kirby, *Ernest Kevan: Pastor and Principal* (London: Eastbourne Victory, 1968), 29, 55.

millennium, that held the ascendancy among Evangelicals. There has been no unanimity on this subject.[15] Beliefs contributing to Evangelical identity have to be sought elsewhere.

Are Evangelicals, then, to be equated with Fundamentalists? It is often assumed that they are. During 1986–87 a vigorous correspondence in *Life and Work*, the magazine of the Church of Scotland, began with a denunciation by a former moderator of the General Assembly of "Fundamentalists." Replies protested that conservative Evangelicals were misrepresented by the label.[16] In Britain, again by contrast with America, self-professed Fundamentalism, though emerging in the 1920s, never developed into a major force.[17] Fundamentalism commonly has three prominent connotations: belief in biblical inerrancy, a pugnacious manner and a repudiation of the intellect. Although the idea of inerrancy has circulated among Evangelicals, it was widely accepted by their nineteenth-century teachers that the Bible contains mistakes about inessentials. The belief that the scriptures must necessarily be immune to error was rare even during the first half of the twentieth century.[18] The vitriolic denunciations of opponents, so common in the United States during the 1920s, were paralleled in Britain but only on a small scale. Temperate Christian leaders such as F. B. Meyer deliberately set their faces against militancy.[19] And British Evangelicalism has embraced many different attitudes to the mind. It is true that early General Baptist preachers in the East Midlands could be described by their own historian as "generally very illiterate,"[20] but the counterexample of John Wesley, an Oxford scholar who was constantly reading, writing and educating, is sufficient to disprove the suggestion that Evangelicalism has been intrinsically anti-intellectual. In truth, the Evangelicals, though including people with Fundamentalist traits in their ranks, have never been uniformly marked by Fundamentalist attitudes. The two terms are far from synonymous.

15 See 1:8: "The Advent Hope in British Evangelicalism since 1800."
16 Especially N. M. de S. Cameron to editor, *Life and Work*, January 1987, 38.
17 David W. Bebbington, "Martyrs for the Truth: Fundamentalists in Britain," in *Martyrs and Martyrologies*, ed. Diana Wood, *Studies in Church History*, vol. 30 (Oxford: Blackwell, 1993), 417–51.
18 David F. Wright, "Soundings in the Doctrine of Scripture in British Evangelicalism in the First Half of the Twentieth Century," *Tyndale Bulletin* 31 (1980), 87–106.
19 Ian Randall, "A Christian Cosmopolitan: F. B. Meyer in Britain and America," in *Amazing Grace: Evangelicalism in Australia, Britain, Canada and the United States*, ed. George A. Rawlyk and Mark A. Noll (Montreal: McGill-Queen's University Press, 1994), 180–81.
20 Adam Taylor, *The History of the English General Baptists*, 2 vols. (London: T. Bore, 1818), 2:56.

Evangelical Characteristics

If Evangelicals have not been consistently Low Church, dispensationalist or Fundamentalist, what features has their tradition consistently displayed? Although the principle of biblical inerrancy has not been uniform, love and respect for the scriptures have been deeply ingrained in the movement. In every room of the home of T. B. Smithies, a Victorian Wesleyan who was prolific in issuing Christian periodicals, it was said that the visitor could see that the place of honor was given to the Bible.[21] Likewise, Samuel Pollard, a minister in the Bible Christian denomination of the same period, was devoted to the scriptures: "How he loved the Word of God his Bibles with their annotations plainly reveal. No duty, however important, was allowed to keep him long from his daily practice of reading the Word, which he usually did on his knees."[22] The Bible was at the heart of the devotional life. Some Primitive Methodists of a remote village stuck pins in the family Bible to mark the promises of God until there were two or three thousand pins in the volume.[23] Ordinary people were passionately eager to grasp the message of the scriptures. A millhand at Middleton in Lancashire who belonged to the Wesleyan Methodist Association scraped together the enormous sum of £16 to purchase Adam Clarke's commentary so that he could understand his Bible better.[24] The curriculum of Evangelical theological colleges was built around the Bible. The one aim of James Acworth, president of Rawdon Baptist College between 1835 and 1863, was that his pupils should read and understand what he loved to call "the Words of God."[25] Of a self-taught Welsh Baptist minister it was said that, though he did not know the meaning of verbal inspiration, he believed in practice that the scriptures were infallible. "His Bible," commented his son, "was everything to him."[26] Delight in the scriptures has been a thread running through the whole Evangelical movement from John Wesley, who called himself a man of one book, to John Stott, who specialized in close exposition of the biblical text. Evangelicalism has been nothing if not biblicist.

---

21   George Rowe, *T. B. Smithies (Editor of "The British Workman"): A Memoir* (London: T. Woolmer, 1884), 72.
22   William J. Mitchell, *Brief Biographical Sketches* of Bible Christian Ministers and Laymen, 2 vols. (Jersey: Beresford Press, 1906), 2:43.
23   James Stephenson, *The Man of Faith and Fire: Or the Life and Work of the Rev. G. Warner* (London: Robert Bryant, 1902), 184.
24   *Wesleyan Methodist Association Magazine*, October 1853, 487.
25   William Medley, *Rawdon Baptist College: Centenary Memorial* (London: Kingsgate Press, 1904), 26.
26   Edward Davies and Rhys Davies, *The Life of the Late Rev. David Davies* (Brecon: Brecon and Radnor Express Offices, 1914), 174, 85.

Equally pronounced has been a preoccupation with the cross of Christ. In "the system of evangelical truth," according to Dan Taylor, the leader of the eighteenth-century New Connexion of General Baptists, the atonement made for us by the sufferings of Christ as our surety was the remedy for the ruined condition of sinful humanity. "By reading the New Testament," he went on, "you will easily see that it is not only the very fundamental doctrine of Christianity, and the only ground of hope to a sinner; but it is the chief stimulus to every part of holiness."[27] Evangelicalism has been centrally concerned with the good news of salvation, and it was the cross that was the means of salvation. Pardon and purity "through the blood of Jesus" was the burden of the Bible Christian Samuel Pollard's preaching.[28] Ministers, exhorted the Baptist Union in 1837, should "keep the cross of Christ ever in view."[29] "Preach the doctrines of the cross," echoed John Rattenbury in his 1872 ordination charge to new Wesleyan ministers.[30] It was normal in theological reflection on the atonement to stress the way in which Christ acted as a substitute for guilty human beings in suffering the penalty of their sin.[31] Liberal views diverging from Evangelical orthodoxy were commonly detected primarily by their downgrading of the sacrifice of Christ on the cross. Thus, the theology of the American Congregationalist Horace Bushnell was condemned by a reviewer in the *Baptist Magazine* of 1866 for making the death of Christ merely incidental to his incarnation. "But in the sacred scriptures," the reviewer pointed out, "the death or blood of Christ is everywhere prominent."[32] The cross became the kernel of popular piety. When a Primitive Methodist class leader, seized with inflammation of the bowels, was told in 1849 that the doctor could do no more, his reply was to quote to his wife a Charles Wesley hymn recounting that "Jesus died for me." "Yes," said she, "the atonement." He then fixed his eyes upon her, responding emphatically, "Yes, he died, he died for me."[33] For Christopher Chavasse, later a bishop, the Evangelical message was still in the 1930s what it had been in the eighteenth century—the cross.[34] The theology of the movement constantly emphasized the work of Christ on Calvary.

---

27 *Minutes of an Association of General Baptists, 1789* (London: Henry Fry, 1789), 5.
28 Mitchell, *Brief Biographical Sketches*, 1:42.
29 *Account of the Twenty-Fifth Annual Session* of the Baptist Union (London, 1837), 30.
30 *The Rev John Rattenbury: Memorials*, ed. Henry Owen Rattenbury (London: T. Woolmer, 1884), 109.
31 E. G. C. Williams in *Baptist Magazine*, March 1862, 161–64.
32 *Baptist Magazine*, June 1866, 365.
33 *Primitive Methodist Magazine*, January 1850, 61.
34 *Record*, 13 April 1933, 208.

Another distinguishing characteristic of Evangelicalism has been conversion. People were not automatically Christians, preachers insisted, either by nature or by virtue of their baptism. A decisive reorientation was needed before a person could properly be called a Christian. The process could often make deep emotional demands. "His experience prior to the spiritual change effected in his life," it was said of a Devon Bible Christian converted in 1859, "is not unlike that of many others who 'know their sins forgiven.' Conviction, contrition, wrestling in prayer, and mighty struggling, these were the prelude to the happy day when the peace of God first became his blest possession."[35] For this man the transaction culminated in an event that could be fixed at a point in time, but for others it was so gradual as to prevent any precise dating. A 1992 report showed that in Evangelical churches only 37 percent of people had undergone a sudden conversion. Although this proportion was much higher than the figure of 20 percent for congregations of all churchmanships, it represents a definite minority.[36] The lack of a dateable experience often seemed a spiritual disadvantage. Thus a Manchester Methodist of the early nineteenth century who, though active in church work, could not fix the time or place of his conversion, was sometimes plagued with doubts about its reality.[37] Whether sudden or gradual, however, conversion was usually considered, as stated by an Evangelical clergyman speaking at the Islington Conference in 1860, a virtual synonym for regeneration.[38] Jesus himself had said that to be born again, to enjoy the new birth by the power of the Holy Spirit, was essential. Thus, it created a great stir when George Whitefield denied that John Tillotson, an earlier archbishop of Canterbury, had ever gone through the new birth.[39] The experience was what revivalists such as Whitefield aimed to multiply. Over five weeks during 1859 it was reported that two hundred souls had professed conversion at special services in Bethesda Chapel, Gateshead, run by William Booth, later the founder of the Salvation Army.[40] The postwar crusades of Billy Graham, which did so much to bring Evangelicals together, stood in the same tradition. The movement has been conversionist throughout its history.

Consequently, it has also been activist. The quest for souls has constantly driven its adherents into fresh evangelistic initiatives. The urgent need to

---

35 Mitchell, *Brief Biographical Sketches*, 1:79.
36 John Finney, *Finding Faith Today: How Does It Happen?* (Swindon: British and Foreign Bible Society, 1992), 24.
37 *Wesleyan Methodist Association Magazine*, February 1854, 85.
38 *Record*, 13 April 1933, 208.
39 Harry S. Stout, *The Divine Dramatist: George Whitefield and the Rise of Modern Evangelicalism* (Grand Rapids, MI: Eerdmans, 1991), 101.
40 *Methodist New Connexion Magazine*, April 1859, 224.

spread the gospel was a frequent theme of the great Baptist preacher C. H. Spurgeon. "Brethren," he told his students, "do something; do something; do something."[41] He was echoed in the twentieth century by Ernest Kevan. "Man was made for work," he used to say. "He is never happier than when he is doing it."[42] The sheer energy of prominent Evangelicals can be amazing. The Wesleyan John Rattenbury, for example, used to preach between four hundred and five hundred sermons a year.[43] Their dynamism has spilled out in many directions—into the overseas missionary movement, into organized philanthropy, into social reform. Victorian Britain teemed with Evangelical activity. Thomas Penrose, a Primitive Methodist minister, may be taken as representative:

> Penrose was above everything else a man of action, whose hands were ever willing and whose feet were ever ready, to do the great Master's bidding . . . He was filled with a burning zeal for the glory of his Saviour and weal of his fellow-men, which was manifested in his indomitable perseverance in building chapels and schools, collecting large sums of money for his work; in promoting the cause of education; in sympathy and help for the poor, obtaining suitable situations for promising young men and women, and relief for suffering tradesmen; in his able advocacy for the temperance cause; and in the active interest he took in all local movements for the welfare of those amongst whom he lived.[44]

To be busy, to be useful, always ranked higher in the Evangelical scale of things than more passive virtues such as the cultivation of the contemplative life. Evangelicals down the centuries have typically thrown themselves into work for God.

Devotion to the Bible, proclamation of the cross, zeal for conversions and unbounded activism have been the regular hallmarks of the Evangelical movement. They have created a shared ethos that has transcended denominational boundaries. That is not to deny the fierce rivalries that have sometimes existed. Debates within Evangelicalism between Calvinist and Arminian or between Baptist and paedobaptist often formed the stuff of village life in nineteenth-century Wales.[45] Methodists could be dismissive of what they rook to be Baptist

---

41 Charles H. Spurgeon, *Lectures to My Students* (London: Marshall, Morgan and Scott, 1954), 217.
42 Kirby, *Ernest Kevan*, 42.
43 *John Rattenbury*, ed. Rattenbury, 50.
44 William J. Brownson, *Heroic Men: The Death Roll of the Primitive Methodist Ministry* (London: Joseph Toulson, 1889), 305.
45 David Davies, *Reminiscences of My Country and People* (Cardiff: William Lewis, 1925), 19–20.

formalism, as in the obituary of a Hull New Connexion woman. "Her parents," ran the narrative, "attended the Baptist chapel, but, like too many, they rested in outward ceremonies; for while honesty and integrity were in their moral character, there was no evidence of scriptural and saving piety."[46] Baptists were entirely capable of responding with similarly critical sentiments. Yet from the eighteenth to the twentieth centuries there was often an overriding awareness of common ground among Evangelicals. It was particularly strong around the beginning of the nineteenth century in the era that gave birth to the interdenominational London Missionary Society, Religious Tract Society and British and Foreign Bible Society.[47] Even the barrier between the established Church of England and Dissent was broken down. In 1799 for instance, Union Chapel, Islington, was set up as a joint Anglican-Congregational cause with a Prayer Book service in the morning and extemporary prayer in the evening.[48] Although the high degree of cooperation, especially between Church and Dissent, subsequently diminished, it became permanently embodied in the Evangelical Alliance from 1846 and continued to find expression in a multitude of local ventures such as the Mildmay conference for Christian workers and its associated institutions.[49] Mildmay's founder, the clergyman William Pennefather, voiced the spirit of Evangelical unity in 1865. "If the standard of the Cross be uplifted in Africa," he wrote, "and its banner unfurled in Asia, God is in each case glorified; though Episcopalians may have raised it in Sierra Leone, and Baptists have displayed its glories in Serampore."[50] The Church Missionary Society and the Baptist Missionary Society were not so much competitive as complementary. Because Evangelicals shared a common allegiance to the cross, they could rejoice in each other's missionary triumphs.

Conclusion

Evangelicals such as Pennefather, who have recognized the substantial unity of the movement, have existed in every generation. But even when there has been negligible desire for joint action and little awareness of common ground, there have been certain attributes that have given the movement a distinct character.

46 *Methodist New Connexion Magazine*, December 1850, 614 (Sarah Carlton).
47 Roger H. Martin, *Evangelicals United: Ecumenical Stirrings in Pre-Victorian Britain, 1795–1830* (Metuchen, NJ: Scarecrow Press, 1983).
48 William Hardy Harwood, *Henry Allon, D.D.: Pastor and Teacher* (London: Cassell and Co., 1894), 16–18.
49 Harriette J. Cooke, *Mildmay: Or the Story of the First Deaconess Institution* (London: E. Stock, 1893).
50 William Pennefather, *The Church of the First-Born: A Few Thoughts on Christian Unity* (London: John F. Shaw, 1865), 10.

It would have been inconceivable in the late nineteenth century for P. F. Eliot, the vicar of Bournemouth, to cooperate with John Sirgood, the leader of the Cokelers. Yet, for all their differences, the establishmentarian and the sectarian were united in the gospel emphases of the Bible, cross, conversion and activism. Although the balance between the elements in this quadrilateral has changed over time, each has always been prominent in the Evangelical tradition. Wherever all four were stressed, whether or not contemporaries were aware of their affinities, Evangelicalism existed. The boundaries of the movement could be sharp, as they were between Sirgood's body and the rest of the Christian world, or blurred, as they were between Eliot's brand of High Church Evangelicalism and full-blown Anglo-Catholicism. Yet the four criteria provide a way of specifying what sections of the Christian world fell within the Evangelical community at any particular time. By the end of the twentieth century this community embraced, alongside members of the established churches and the historic branches of Nonconformity, a range of twentieth-century denominations: the Pentecostals, the black majority churches and many varieties of independents, charismatic and noncharismatic. The Evangelicals across these denominations were all united in the bonds of the gospel. As many of them discovered through joint expressions of their activism such as Spring Harvest or local Evangelical councils, they all tried to be obedient to the Bible, faithful to the cross and eager for conversions. They professed a common Evangelical identity.

2

Revival and Enlightenment in Eighteenth-Century England

The Evangelical Revival of the eighteenth century is the paradigm of all revivals. It was a movement that bound together converts, whether Anglican, Dissenting or Methodist, in a united front for the propagation of the gospel. It was not an isolated local phenomenon, but a national, even international, endeavor that gathered force from the 1730s down to the end of the century. Although this chapter concentrates on England, the salient characteristics of the eighteenth-century revival were to mark Evangelicalism throughout the world deep into the nineteenth century and beyond. So it is important to locate its relationship to the cultural trends of the time. The English revival has often been seen as hostile to the Enlightenment, the movement of thought associated with the *philosophes* of France who cast doubt on the message of the scriptures, and those in the churches who were tinctured by this way of thinking. Thus the revival has been described as "a reaction against certain features of the orthodox theology and religious outlook of the early Enlightenment."[1] According to this analysis, contemporary churchmen appealed only to the head. The attraction of the revival for the heart was a response to the deficiencies of the cerebral approach. Piety challenged reason. The movement was an emotional protest against the intellectual hegemony of the age.

This plausible thesis rests on two premises. First, there is the supposition that the Enlightenment was intrinsically antagonistic to spiritual religion. The grand sweep of eighteenth-century thought is normally depicted as irreligious in tendency.[2] Voltaire, Hume and Gibbon are treated as representative

---

1 Geoffrey Best, "Evangelicalism and the Victorians," in *The Victorian Crisis of Faith*, ed. Anthony Symondson (London: SPCK, 1970), 38.
2 Paul Hazard, *European Thought in the Eighteenth Century* (Harmondsworth, Middlesex: Penguin, 1965); Peter Gay, *The Enlightenment: An Interpretation* (London: Weidenfeld and Nicolson, 1967).

figures. The elimination of religion, at least in its revealed and institutional forms, is presented as the ultimate goal of their endeavors. The Deists of the early eighteenth century were certainly part of such a secularizing trend. Its influence was also felt within the churches. The dominant latitudinarianism in the Church of England and the Arians who proliferated among the Dissenters were alike in wishing to make the Christian religion more palatable to educated opinion. Accordingly, it is held, traditional orthodoxy was cast to the winds. "Reason," wrote an Evangelical critic of Gibbon in 1781, "has impertinently meddled with the Gospel."[3] It seems natural to cast the Enlightenment in the role of a liberalizing body of thought at odds with the revival's firm grasp of biblical teachings.[4]

The second premise is that the revival was conspicuously unenlightened. The "emotional transports" of its Methodist dimension have been censured as deluding the common people about their true interests.[5] And there is a great deal of evidence suggesting that Evangelicalism was a matter of heat rather than light. "The dales are flaming," reported one Methodist to another in 1798 about a spate of conversions. "The fire hath caught, and runs from one dale to another."[6] Young converts would open the Bible at random for guidance; an ex-corporal on the fringe of Methodism claimed to be more perfect than the unfallen Adam; and the leading evangelist George Whitefield, who rarely preached without weeping, had his first sermon complained of to the bishop for driving fifteen people mad.[7] A catalogue of apparent irrationalism, what the century decried as "enthusiasm," could be charged against the movement. The ethos of the Evangelical Revival seems at variance with the Age of Reason.

Both premises, however, are open to question. Enlightenment thought may have been as good a medium for vital Christianity as it was for more secularizing tendencies; and the Evangelical Revival may have shared the characteristic worldview of progressive eighteenth-century thinkers to a far greater extent than

---

3   Roland N. Stromberg, *Religious Liberalism in Eighteenth-Century England* (London: Oxford University Press, 1954), 168.

4   Brian W. Young, *Religion and Enlightenment in Eighteenth-Century England* (Oxford: Clarendon Press, 1998), 1.

5   Edward P. Thompson, *The Making of the English Working Class* (Harmondsworth, Middlesex: Penguin, 1968), 402.

6   Leslie F. Church, *The Early Methodist People* (London: Epworth Press, 1948), 122.

7   James Lackington, *Memoirs of the First Forty-Five Years of the Life of James Lackington* (London: For the Author, 1795), 62; Stanley Ayling, *John Wesley* (London: Collins, 1979), 211–12; John Gillies, *Memoirs of the Life of the Reverend George Whitefield* (London: Dilly, 1772), 10.

has normally been supposed. Some of the more recent literature has suggested that there were in reality affinities between the revival and the Enlightenment.[8] After all, the metaphor of light was regularly used by Evangelicals to describe the central experience of conversion. Revival in England, as in America, was perceived as the spread of "New Light." It is worth exploring how far revival and Enlightenment were bound up in the same cultural nexus.

Common Characteristics

The rise of the Evangelical movement in the eighteenth century was associated with a shift in the doctrine of assurance. The Puritans of the previous century had held that certainty of being in a state of grace, though desirable, is normally late in the experience of believers and attained only after struggle. Evangelicals, by contrast, commonly asserted that the norm is for assurance to be given to believers at conversion. Some, including John Wesley and the Anglican William Romaine, believed that certainty of acceptance by God necessarily accompanies saving faith; others, especially John Newton, believed that such certainty is not essential to faith. Yet all insisted that assurance was to be expected early in the Christian life and by all. They were claiming the reliability of knowledge in the field of religion. That was to share the confidence of the age in the validity of experience. The philosopher John Locke, by denying the existence of innate ideas, had cleared the ground for greater trust in the powers of the mind to grasp the world through the five senses. Wesley, like many others in the revival, saw awareness of God as a new sense, analogous to hearing or sight. Faith, he explained, "is with regard to the spiritual world what sense is to the natural."[9] The rank and file of the revival formulated their experience in the same way. The realization that the Almighty allows human beings to be certain that they are numbered among the saved was a strengthening of the status of knowledge typical of the thinkers of the century. Here was a fundamental affinity between the revival and the Enlightenment.

There were many other characteristics in common. Both were dedicated to empirical method. The prestige of John Locke in philosophy and, even more, of Isaac Newton in natural science, set a premium on the technique

---

8   David W. Bebbington, *Evangelicalism in Modern Britain: A History from the 1730s to the 1980s* (London: Unwin Hyman, 1989); Bruce Hindmarsh, *John Newton and the English Evangelical Tradition: Between the Conversions of Wesley and Wilberforce* (Oxford: Clarendon Press, 1996); Grayson M. Ditchfield, *The Evangelical Revival* (London: UCL Press, 1998).

9   John Wesley, "An Earnest Appeal to Men of Reason and Religion" [1743], in *The Works of John Wesley*, vol. 11: *The Appeals to Men of Reason and Religion and Certain Related Open Letters*, ed. Gerald R. Cragg (Oxford: Clarendon Press, 1975), 46.

of investigation. It was high praise to call preaching "experimental," that is, "explaining every part of the work of God upon the soul."[10] In argumentation Evangelical leaders such as Henry Venn, vicar of Huddersfield, habitually appealed for authority not to scripture alone but to "observation and scripture."[11] The rational evidences of Christianity were valued as much by Evangelicals as by divines of broader schools. Wesley encouraged Methodists to use medical remedies he had himself investigated and approached spiritual experience in exactly the same scientific spirit. A corollary of respect for empiricism was contempt for more traditional modes of analysis. Disputation was considered an unproductive exercise. Wesley dismissed ancient ecclesiastical debates as "subtle, metaphysical controversies."[12] Likewise fine Puritan distinctions were criticized by John Newton since they were "not scriptural modes of expression, nor do they appear to me to throw light upon the subject."[13] Metaphysics, scholasticism, systematization—these belonged to the darkness of the past. The spirit of inquiry was illuminating religion as much as other fields of knowledge.

The optimism of the Enlightenment was also shared by Evangelicals. Happiness was treated as the proper goal of individuals and of society.[14] Wesley went further than the Calvinists in his estimate of the attainability of happiness on earth. According to his *Plain Account of Christian Perfection* (1766), believers may progress to a state where they are free from all voluntary transgressions of known laws. They are then in a state of "perfect love."[15] All Evangelicals, however, believed that the ultimate welfare of believers, together with that of society at large, is guaranteed by divine providence. "If we be sincere in intention," avowed John Newton, "we cannot make a mistake of any great importance."[16] For many, hope of a future millennium of truth, peace and plenty reinforced their optimism. Millennialism was a widespread intellectual concern in the

10   *Wesley's Veterans*, ed. John Telford, 7 vols. (London: Robert Culley, 1912), 2:147.
11   Henry Venn, *The Complete Duty of Man*, 3rd ed. (London: For S. Crowder and G. Robinson, 1779), 2. On the Evangelicals' attitude towards science, see 1:14: "Science and Evangelical Theology in Britain from Wesley to Orr."
12   John Wesley to Charles Wesley, 8 June 1780, in *The Letters of the Rev. John Wesley*, ed. John Telford, 8 vols. (London: Epworth Press, 1931), 7:21.
13   John Newton, *The Works of the Rev. John Newton* (London: For the Author's Nephew, 1880), 586.
14   Roger Anstey, *The Atlantic Slave Trade and British Abolition, 1760–1810* (London: Macmillan, 1975), 163.
15   Harald Lindström, *Wesley and Sanctification* (London: Epworth Press, 1946). On this doctrine, see 2:3: "Entire Sanctification in Methodism during the Nineteenth Century."
16   *The Thought of the Evangelical Leaders*, ed. John H. Pratt (Edinburgh: Banner of Truth Trust, 1978), 77.

eighteenth century that merged with the beginnings of the idea of progress. Not all Evangelicals embraced millennial expectations: George Whitefield, for example, professed to have no interest in the subject.[17] Others, however, especially as the century advanced, were animated by high hopes. The progress of the gospel was certain. "Slavery and war shall cease!" announced the Baptist John Ryland. *"In fine, the whole earth shall be full of the knowledge of Jehovah, as the waters that cover the depths of the seas!!!"*[18] A sanguine temper undergirded the Evangelical movement as it developed.

Doctrinal moderation, a feature of the latitudinarianism that prevailed in the eighteenth-century Church of England, was also evident in the theology of the Evangelicals. The Arminianism of John Wesley has been seen as a revolutionary creed because it propagated belief in human freewill.[19] What has been less widely appreciated is that the Calvinism of non-Methodist Evangelicals was of a similar stamp. The clergyman Thomas Haweis wrote a biblical commentary as a Calvinist, but hoped that "there is not a line I have written at which a spiritually minded Arminian need stumble."[20] "That a man is a free agent," wrote the Baptist Robert Hall Sr, "cannot be denied, consistently with his being accountable for his own actions."[21] The statement was possible from a Calvinist because Hall, like many other Evangelicals in the Reformed tradition, embraced the distinction made by the great American theologian Jonathan Edwards between natural and moral inability. Naturally human beings are free, but morally they are unable to obey God. Hence they are culpable and condemn themselves to divine judgment. Since nobody is predestined to reprobation, all have a duty to believe and the gospel should be preached to all. This theological position, often called "moderate Calvinism" in the secondary literature, was normal among Anglican Evangelicals. Its wide embrace, its benevolent tone, were symptomatic of the age.

An ethical emphasis was a further feature of the revival that linked it to the Enlightenment. It is true that Evangelicals themselves commonly denounced clergymen for preaching mere morality. They were censuring the idea that salvation can be by works: "it was *faith* alone that did everything without a grain of morality."[22] Yet their own insistence that salvation is by faith alone did not

17 *The Works of the Reverend George Whitefield*, ed. John Gillies (London: Dilly, 1771), 1.
18 John Ryland, *Salvation Finished, as to Its Impenetration at the Death of Christ and with Respect to Its Application to the Death of the Christian* (n.p., 1791), 21. On this postmillennialism, see 1:3: "Gospel and Culture in British Evangelicalism."
19 Bernard Semmel, *The Methodist Revolution* (London: Heinemann Educational, 1974).
20 Arthur S. Wood, *Thomas Haweis, 1734–1820* (London: SPCK, 1957), 116.
21 Robert Hall, *Help to Zion's Travellers* (Bristol: William Pine, 1781), 236.
22 Lackington, *Memoirs of the First Forty-Five Years*, 48.

preclude moral instruction. Haweis' *Evangelical Principles and Practice* (1762) gives far more space to practice than to principles. The idea of sanctification dominates Wesley's theology. Whitefield used to define true religion as "a universal morality founded upon love of God, and faith in the Lord Jesus Christ."[23] Evangelicals repeatedly repudiated the slander that they denied the duty of the believer to observe the moral law. A few higher Calvinists in both the Church of England and Dissent made remarks that veered towards antinomianism, but only a handful on the fringe of the movement, such as Robert Hawker of Plymouth and the eccentric William Huntington, actually taught it. Faith, according to Henry Venn, "is not understood, much less possessed, if it produce not more holiness, than could possibly be by any other way attained."[24] Evangelicals, like their contemporaries, were eager to enforce the duties of morality.

While they did not apply utilitarian principles to ethics, leaders of the revival adopted the criterion of utility in many areas of policy. That was another bond with the theory and practice of the Enlightenment. Field preaching, the grand strategy of the Evangelical movement, was justified on pragmatic grounds: it led to the salvation of souls. To be "useful" was the highest ambition of a preacher. In a similar spirit Martin Madan, a London Evangelical clergyman, actually recommended polygamy as a remedy for prostitution, though others hastened to disavow his views.[25] This was not the only question of expediency where there was division of opinion. There were some clergymen, notably Samuel Walker of Truro, whose respect for church order prevented them from endorsing Wesley's employment of laymen as preachers. Even Walker, however, rejoiced that there were "good men of all persuasions, who are content to leave each other the liberty of private judgment in lesser things, and are heartily disposed to unite their efforts for the maintaining and enlarging Christ's kingdom."[26] Wesley was prepared to go much further. "What is the end of all ecclesiastical order?" he asked. "Is it not to bring souls from the power of Satan to God, and to build them up in His fear and love? Order, then, is so far valuable as it answers these ends; and if it answers them not, it is nothing worth."[27] Hence Wesley was prepared to undertake ordinations of clergy for America even though that responsibility was restricted to bishops by the Church of England. Hence, too, he was willing to turn a blind eye to female preaching. The climax of the pragmatic spirit came with the foundation, in 1795, of "The Missionary Society," later the London Missionary Society, designed to unite Evangelicals of all types in the furtherance

23 Gillies, *Memoirs of the Life of the Reverend George Whitefield*, 287.
24 Venn, *Complete Duty of Man*, xi.
25 Wood, *Thomas Haweis*, 159–60.
26 George Davies, *The Early Cornish Evangelicals, 1735–60* (London: SPCK, 1951), 71.
27 *Letters of the Rev. John Wesley*, ed. Telford, 2:77–78.

of the gospel. "*Expediency*," declared Charles Simeon, the leading Evangelical Anglican by the turn of the century, "is too much decried."[28] It was another attitude of the enlightened world that Evangelicals upheld.

Their taste was similarly adjusted to the spirit of the age. "The commencement of this century," wrote Haweis in 1800, "has been called the *Augustan age*, when purity of stile [sic] added the most perfect polish to deep erudition, as well as the *belles lettres*. A Newton, an Addison, need only be mentioned, out of a thousand others, whose works will be admired to the latest posterity; and afford the noblest specimens in the English language." What Haweis most approved about the Augustans was their union of "conciseness with precision."[29] Wesley shared the same ideal in his "Thoughts on Taste" (1780) and the exemplar was again Joseph Addison.[30] Although Newton was representative of other Evangelicals in moving on in the later eighteenth century to show symptoms of the age of sensibility, he never wholly abandoned Augustan values.[31] The classical principles of order, balance and harmony appealed to the early Evangelicals as much as to the Augustan *littérateurs*. They formed even Wesley's eye for the natural world, so that he attributed to the Creator an earth before the flood that was "without high or abrupt mountains, and without sea, being one uniform crust."[32] Dissenters adopted the same criteria. Cornelius Winter, a disciple of Whitefield, quoted with approval William Cowper's identification of elegance with simplicity.[33] The greatest monument to Evangelical taste, however, is the hymnody of John Wesley's brother, Charles. Disciplined emotion, didactic purpose, clarity and succinctness are qualities for which he is preeminent among hymn-writers. A single line serves to exhibit all his traits: "Impassive he suffers, immortal he dies."[34] Charles Wesley turned contemporary literary idiom into a powerful vehicle for revival.

---

28 Abner W. Brown, *Recollections of the Conversation Parties of the Rev. Charles Simeon* (London: Hamilton, Adams, 1863), 93.
29 Thomas Haweis, *An Impartial and Succinct History of the Rise, Declension and Revival of the Church of Christ* (London: For J. Mawman, 1800), 221.
30 James L. Golden, "John Wesley on Rhetoric and Belles Lettres," *Speech Monographs* 28 (1961), 252–53.
31 Hindmarsh, *John Newton and the English Evangelical Tradition*, 284–88.
32 *The Works of John Wesley*, vol. 22: *Journals and Diaries V (1765–75)*, ed. William Reginald Ward and Richard P. Heitzenrater (Nashville, TN: Abingdon Press, 1993), 213 (17 January 1770).
33 William Jay, *Memoirs of the Life and Character of the Late Rev. Cornelius Winter*, 2nd ed. (London: For William Baynes, 1812), 279.
34 Charles Wesley, "Invitation to Sinners," in *The Poetical Works of John and Charles Wesley*, ed. George Osborn, 11 vols. (London: Wesleyan Methodist Conference Office, 1868–72), 4:371.

Evangelical Contributions to the Enlightenment

It is evident, therefore, that Evangelical religion was firmly embedded in the progressive cultural milieu of the eighteenth century. It shared assumptions with the mainstream of educated opinion. Its substantial appeal to the elite is often disguised by its numerically larger impact on the common people. Yet the upper classes of England were sometimes attracted. At least three Lincolnshire gentry became staunch supporters of Wesley's Methodism.[35] There were eight "gentlemen" and twenty-one "gentlewomen" among the 790 Bristol Methodists in 1783.[36] Whitefield, perhaps because of his elaborate histrionic skills, drew a significant number of the nobility to hear him and the Countess of Huntingdon became the patroness of a whole denomination. Evangelicals could also find their way into the highest circles of literature and art. Hannah More, an Evangelical blue-stocking, moved easily among Sir Joshua Reynolds, Samuel Johnson and Edmund Burke. "I made such a figure lately," she playfully reported to her family in 1777, "in explaining Arianism, Socinianism, and all the isms, to Mr. Garrick."[37] Although most of the fashionable world shunned revivalism as a species of enthusiasm, there were points of intersection with those fired by vital Christianity. The Evangelical leaders were not divorced from elite culture.

It was typical of Enlightenment thinkers to wish to bring knowledge from the elite to the masses. The English Enlightenment in particular produced not eminent philosophical systematizers but popularizers in many fields.[38] The Evangelicals should be numbered in their ranks. Their primary aim was to fit their hearers for heaven, but they also wished to bring the barbarous within the pale of civilization. Whitefield, dismayed by the absence of cultivation among the colliers of Kingswood, Bristol, gave priority to "the civilizing of these people" as well as to their evangelization.[39] The darkness of rude ways had to be dispelled. Wesley, like other arbiters of taste, supposed laughter to be a sign of ill breeding. Accordingly, with his usual briskness, he directed that

---

35 Church, *The Early Methodist People*, 164; Leslie F. Church, *More About the Early Methodist People* (London: Epworth Press, 1949), 44, 117–25.
36 John Kent, "Wesleyan Membership in Bristol, 1783," in *An Ecclesiastical Miscellany* (Bristol: Bristol and Gloucestershire Archaeological Society, 1976), 111.
37 William Roberts, *Memoirs of the Life and Correspondence of Mrs. Hannah More*, 2nd ed. (London: R. B. Seeley and W. Burnside, 1834), 104.
38 Roy Porter, "The Enlightenment in England," *The Enlightenment in National Context*, ed. Roy Porter and Mikuláš Teich (Cambridge: Cambridge University Press, 1981), 3, 5.
39 Gillies, *Memoirs of the Life of the Reverend George Whitefield*, 37.

his preachers must avoid laughing.[40] He expressed satisfaction with the effects of his civilizing mission at Nottingham:

> although most of our society are of the lower class, chiefly employed in the stocking manufacture, yet there is generally an uncommon gentleness and sweetness in their temper, and something of elegance in their behaviour, which, when added to solid, vital religion, make them an ornament to their profession.[41]

Manners had been successfully softened. Similarly, the missionary enterprise that took its rise at the end of the eighteenth century aspired to carry civilization as well as the gospel to the ends of the earth. Although there was much variety of opinion about the best strategy for confronting barbarism, there was unanimity that missions should aim for its elimination.[42] Evangelicals were promoting an Enlightenment program for the improvement of the people at home and abroad.

Its chief dimension, other than the imparting of vital faith, was education. The revival was often charged with deprecating scholarship since it flourished among the illiterate and uncritical, and it is true that books were sometimes suspect as sources of error. Whitefield and Wesley concurred that Latin, the foundation of polite culture, was "of little or no use" to the preacher.[43] Yet this comment was part of the Enlightenment preference for the vernacular and is no evidence for a low estimate of learning. On the contrary, Wesley created a publication industry for his followers. He issued grammars of English, French, Latin and Greek, short histories of England and of the Christian church, an outline of Roman history, a compendium of natural philosophy in five volumes and a "Christian Library" of practical divinity in fifty.[44] The first lay connexional officials were appointed to run the Book Room, and when, in 1778, Wesley launched the *Arminian Magazine* he acquired his own printing presses.[45] By 1791 seven thousand monthly copies of the magazine were circulating, in

---

40 Beverly S. Allen, *Tides in English Taste, 1619–1800* (Cambridge, MA: Harvard University Press, 1937), 94–95.
41 *Works of John Wesley*, vol. 23: *Journals and Diaries VI (1776–86)*, ed. Ward and Heitzenrater (Nashville, TN: Abingdon Press, 1995), 56 (18 June 1777).
42 Brian Stanley, "Christianity and Civilization in English Evangelical Mission Thought, 1792–1857," in *Christian Missions and the Enlightenment*, ed. Brian Stanley (Grand Rapids, MI: Eerdmans, 2001), 167–97.
43 Jay, *Cornelius Winter*, 70.
44 Church, *More About the Early Methodist People*, 47.
45 Horace F. Mathews, *Methodism and the Education of the People, 1791–1851* (London: Epworth Press, 1949), 171.

comparison, for example, with 4,550 of the *Gentleman's Magazine* six years later.[46] Wesley prepared a "Female Course of Study, intended for Those who have a Good Understanding and Much Leisure" entailing five or six hours' work a day for three to five years, but he concentrated his educational efforts on his traveling preachers, since they were expected to transmit what they learned.[47] "I trust," wrote Wesley of the preachers, "there is not one of them who is not able to go through such an examination, in substantial, practical, experimental divinity, as few of our candidates for holy orders, even in the university . . . are able to do."[48] Every preacher, in turn, was to be a book agent. Wesley was undertaking a campaign of systematic enlightenment.

His efforts were duly rewarded. Methodism produced prodigies of learning. A Lowestoft class leader knew Latin, Greek and Hebrew; a child of Methodist parents read the greater part of the Bible before she was four; and an older girl composed her journal in faultless French. Humbler Methodists would meet on weekday evenings to instruct their unlettered friends in how to sing the Sunday hymns, and by such means literacy spread.[49] Other Evangelicals, though in less dragooned fashion than the Methodists, were equally dedicated to fostering elementary education, since literacy was a condition for reading the Bible. Hence they gave their powerful support to the Sunday school movement as it gathered momentum from the 1780s. The instruction was frequently undenominational, in part a corollary of the policy of pragmatic cooperation in furtherance of the gospel. In the early days, in fact, Unitarians and others often participated alongside the various types of Evangelical, a sign that in educational work the Enlightenment ideal of propagating useful knowledge took precedence over the preservation of gospel purity.[50] It has been estimated that by 1801 there were over two hundred thousand regular attenders at the Sunday schools, chiefly drawn from the poor.[51] Literary societies and libraries in churches and chapels helped carry education to a higher level. Evangelicalism generated at least its fair proportion of scholars at the turn of the nineteenth

---

46 Richard E. Brantley, *Locke, Wesley and the Method of English Romanticism* (Gainesville, FL: University of Florida Press, 1984), 118.
47 Earl K. Brown, *Women of Mr. Wesley's Methodism* (New York: Edwin Mellen Press, 1983), 51.
48 *Works of John Wesley*, vol. 11, ed. Cragg, 296.
49 Church, *Early Methodist People*, 12, 243; Church, *More About the Early Methodist People*, 46, 49.
50 William Reginald Ward, *Religion and Society in England, 1790–1850* (London: B. T. Batsford, 1972), 12–20.
51 Thomas W. Laqueur, *Religion and Respectability: Sunday Schools and Working-Class Culture, 1780–1850* (New Haven, CT: Yale University Press, 1976), 44.

century. Isaac Milner, subsequently president of Queens' College, Cambridge, for instance, had his degree results starred "incomparabilis."[52] The revival did not turn its adherents into ignorant bigots. On the contrary, it proved effective in spreading a thirst for knowledge.

The revival challenged popular culture in the name of reason and religion. The customary ways of the eighteenth century added color to humdrum lives, but they were shot through with roughness, cruelty and paganism. Traditional holidays gave scope for drunkenness, torturing animals or indulging in relics of nature worship like the Abbots Bromley horn dance. Evangelicalism, as is often stressed, opposed such patterns of behavior. Thus William Grimshaw, the rugged incumbent of Haworth in the West Riding of Yorkshire, attended local feasts to preach the gospel and protested to his parishioners against the annual races. But his normal demeanor was not that of a religious professional, let alone an obsessional fanatic. "A stranger might be in company with him from morning to night," commented John Newton, "without observing anything that might lead him to suppose he was a minister; he would only think that he saw and heard a pious, plain intelligent man."[53] Reason dictated Grimshaw's attitudes. William Romaine, a scholarly but angular clergyman, would have claimed the same for his response to the custom of conversing after church. "He not only spoke against such conversations from the pulpit," according to his biographer, "but frequently interrupted them, when he came out, by tapping the shoulders of those who were engaged in them; and once, if not oftener, by knocking their heads together, when he found them particularly close."[54] Those associated with the revival were taking the offensive against the improprieties of popular habits. It is hardly surprising that there was a bitter response, whether (at a higher social level) by means of vituperative satire or (at a lower level) by mob violence. Much of the persecution suffered by gospel preachers must be seen as retaliation against the threat that their civilizing mission posed to custom.

Those aroused to serious concern for the welfare of their souls formed a counterculture shunning worldliness. Wesley formed "awakened sinners" into classes, admission being regulated by quarterly ticket. The classes were not designed for converts only: indeed, their purpose was to encourage conversions in their ranks. Yet their members were subject to strict discipline, having to avoid evils such as taking God's name in vain, sabbath-breaking

---

52 Doreen M. Rosman, *Evangelicals and Culture* (London: Croom Helm, 1984), 217.
53 George G. Cragg, *Grimshaw of Haworth* (London: Canterbury Press, 1947), 98.
54 William B. Cadogan, "The Life of the Rev. William Romaine, A. M.," in *Works of the Late Reverend William Romaine, A. M.*, 8 vols. (London: For T. Chapman, 1796), 7:80.

and drunkenness, to do good by charity, through visiting the sick and similar means, and to attend the divine ordinances.[55] Even higher standards were expected of members of bands, which consisted of those professing conversion. Anglican Evangelicals established similar groups, with Grimshaw of Haworth, for instance, holding a parish class. The group was sharply demarcated from the ways of the world. Before conversion John Iredale, a grocer in a village near Halifax, used to fill the baskets of customers while they attended church on Sunday; after conversion under the ministry of Henry Venn he refused to desecrate the sabbath and so lost business.[56] Elizabeth Evans, the prototype of the Methodist preacher Dinah Morris in George Eliot's *Adam Bede*, was converted in about 1797. "I had entirely done with the pleasures of the world," she wrote, "and with all my old companions. I saw it my duty to leave off all my superfluities in dress; hence I pulled off all my bunches—cut off my curls—left off my lace—and in this I found an unspeakable pleasure. I saw I could make a better use of my time and money, than to follow the fashions of the vain world."[57] Early Methodists, driven together for mutual support, generated a strong community spirit. Ten soldiers in a regiment, for example, were "joined in such love for one another that we had in effect all things in common."[58] The result was a new cultural ambience, the religion of the cottage, where there was particular scope for women to act as counselors and exhorters.[59] If the revival confronted traditional folkways, it created fresh and (it may be suggested) more enlightened patterns of life.

Conclusion

The relationship between revival and Enlightenment was therefore remarkably close. John Fletcher, long Wesley's lieutenant, argued "not only that feeling and rational Christianity are not incompatible, . . . but also that such feelings, so far from deserving to be called madness and enthusiasm, are nothing short of the actings of spiritual life."[60] Emotion, fervor, even irrationality are inseparable from the human condition, but progressive opinion in the eighteenth century

---

55 John Lawson, "The People Called Methodists: Our Discipline," in *A History of the Methodist Church in Great Britain*, ed. Rupert Davies, A. Raymond George and Gordon Rupp, 4 vols. (London: Epworth Press, 1965–88), 1:192–94.
56 Church, *Early Methodist People*, 157.
57 Church, *More About the Early Methodist People*, 160.
58 *Wesley's Veterans*, ed. Telford, 1:73.
59 Deborah M. Valenze, *Prophetic Sons and Daughters: Female Preaching and Popular Religion in Industrial England* (Princeton, NJ: Princeton University Press, 1985).
60 Patrick P. Streiff, *Jean Guillaume de la Fléchère, John William Fletcher, 1729–1785, ein Beitrag zur Geschichte des Methodismus* (Frankfurt am Main: Peter Lang, 1984), 241.

kept them bridled. So did Evangelicals, investigating them in a dispassionate spirit of scientific enquiry. Such analysts were adopting the method of the Enlightenment. It follows that the age of reason was by no means necessarily heading in an irreligious direction. England could throw up a Matthew Tindal, the Deist writer, but equally it produced John Wesley, a zealous propagator of scriptural Christianity. The situation elsewhere in Britain was little different. In Wales a literary efflorescence was largely stimulated by a Great Awakening that was intimately allied with the English revival.[61] In Scotland alongside the skeptical David Hume there was a group of cultivated ministers of religion who stood at the pinnacle of intellectual achievement, some of whom were latitudinarian in their beliefs but some of whom, like John Erskine, were promoters of revival.[62] There was a desire throughout Western civilization during the eighteenth century for religion to be at once purer and more rational.[63] Sometimes this aspiration took the form of a suspicion of revelation that tended to strip away the supernatural; but equally it could lead to a confidence in scripture that rejoiced in God's power to save. There was nothing intrinsically hostile to spiritual religion about the Enlightenment.

Nor was the revival a reaction against the Age of Reason. It is simply wrong to suppose that Wesley intended to debunk the Enlightenment or that the "burgeoning Evangelical revival anathematized rational religion."[64] On the contrary, the stronger doctrine of assurance fostered by the revival was associated with the rising confidence of the age in knowledge gained from sense experience. The characteristics of the eighteenth-century Evangelicals—empiricism, optimism, moderation, moralism, utilitarianism and Augustanism—were equally features of the rising cultural mood. And Evangelicals, as much as *philosophes* across the English Channel, wished to propagate their brand of elite culture to the masses, but achieved their aim far more effectively. There was born a popular Christian counterculture that by the mid-nineteenth century had grown to dominate England. The revival was responsible for spreading enlightened values across the country. Conversely, the Enlightenment provided a vehicle for the gospel to penetrate minds shaped by the assumptions of the times. It has been suggested that to see the Age of Reason as responsible, at least in part, for the success of the eighteenth-century revival is to set up an alternative

---

61 Derec Ll. Morgan, *The Great Awakening in Wales* (London: Epworth Press, 1988).
62 John R. McIntosh, *Church and Theology in Enlightenment Scotland: The Popular Party, 1740–1800* (East Linton, East Lothian: Tuckwell Press, 1998).
63 Sheridan Gilley, "Christianity and Enlightenment: An Historical Survey," *History of European Ideas* 1:2 (1981), 103–21.
64 Porter, "The Enlightenment in England," 16–17.

explanation to the work of God.[65] To posit an antithesis, however, between the human agency of a movement of secular thought and the divine agency of a renewal of spiritual vitality would be mistaken. The Enlightenment was not a reason for the rise of Evangelicalism that excludes the Almighty, but can rather be considered an instrument in the hands of God for fulfilling his purposes. Just as the early church could see in the Roman Empire, despite its phases of overt hostility to the gospel, a *preparatio evangelica*, so the intellectual climate of the eighteenth century, despite points of incompatibility, made possible the diffusion of revival. The Spirit of God worked through the spirit of the age. The faith John Wesley favored, he once remarked, was "a religion founded on reason, and every way agreeable thereto."[66] The Evangelical Revival was closely bonded with the Enlightenment.

---

[65] Michael Haykin, "Evangelicalism and the Enlightenment," in *Loving the God of Truth: Preparing the Church for the Twenty-First Century*, ed. Andrew M. Fountain (Toronto: Toronto Baptist Seminary and Bible College, 1996), 103–21.

[66] Wesley, "An Earnest Appeal," 55.

3

Gospel and Culture in British Evangelicalism

"To say," declared W. H. Groser, secretary of the Sunday School Union, in 1900, "that the Church has remained unaffected by influences permeating our national life would be to assert that we are independent of our social environment."[1] That supposition, he assumed, was absurd. People are molded by their circumstances and consequently the Christian community is swayed by its setting. That process takes place in many ways. Political factors can impinge on churches, absorbing their time and energy in exercising power or else in avoiding its exercise. Perhaps the impact of the state is greatest when it is hostile, but during the era since the eighteenth century, with a few notable exceptions, the public authorities in Britain have been generally benign, or at least neutral, towards religion. Likewise economic conditions can shape church life, with abundant or restricted resources drastically affecting the conduct of congregational affairs. Wealth and poverty have certainly altered church methods in Britain, but usually the chief effect has been on the scale of operations rather than their substance. The concern of this chapter is with a more fundamental aspect of the condition of human beings, their cultural formation. The subject is the basic assumptions that have colored the way Evangelical Christians have looked at the world and ordered their affairs—what we might call the spectacles behind their eyes. How have cultural attitudes shaped the expression of the Christian gospel in Britain?

---

1 *Sunday School Chronicle* (1900), 729, quoted in Philip B. Cliff, *The Rise and Development of the Sunday School Movement in England, 1780–1980* (Redhill, Surrey: National Christian Education Council, 1986), 197.

Popular Culture

One aspect of culture that undoubtedly affected Evangelicals was its popular dimension. There were deep-seated patterns of inherited custom among the common people that necessarily interacted with the gospel. This was the plebeian culture celebrated by E. P. Thompson, with a respect for fairness, a strain of neighborliness and a variety of rough but vibrant ways.[2] It was remolded by the process of industrialization and the growth of literacy but nevertheless retained much of its resilience into the twentieth century before it was transformed once more by the mass media. It included a great deal of superstition, with traditional events such as bonfires and well dressings marking the cycle of the seasons and consultations with wise women as in the novels of Thomas Hardy. Popular beliefs of this kind were by no means confined to the countryside but still flourished in London in the early twentieth century. Charms, amulets and a powerful sense of luck remained deeply rooted among cockneys.[3] This dimension of popular culture, open to the supernatural, seems to have formed an initial advantage for evangelists on entering an area. Thus, in west Cornwall, belief in a shadowy spirit called "Bucca" who had to be propitiated if fisherman were to expect success helped prepare the way for the huge impact of Methodism on the region.[4] Although there were tensions between superstition and orthodoxy, the locals at least had a lively awareness of a spiritual dimension to life. As Evangelical faith put down roots in an area, furthermore, its sacred worldview often meshed into folk religion. At Staithes on the North Yorkshire coast, for example, a Methodist harvest festival of the late twentieth century was plausibly explained by a visiting sociologist as having as much to do with the potency of nature as with distinctively Christian faith.[5] There seems to have been, for good or ill, a great deal of common ground between Evangelicalism and popular culture.

Nevertheless the relationship between the two was more often one of antagonism. Many of the earliest Methodist preachers of the eighteenth century were greeted with fierce opposition, often encouraged by local clergy or gentry but generated chiefly by a sense that the community was under attack by outsiders.

---

2 Edward P. Thompson, *The Making of the English Working Class* (Harmondsworth, Middlesex: Penguin, 1968), chap. 3.
3 Sarah C. Williams, *Religious Belief and Popular Culture in Southwark, c. 1880–1939* (Oxford: Oxford University Press, 1999).
4 William Bottrell, *Traditions and Hearthside Stories of West Cornwall*, 2nd series (Penzance: For the Author by Beare and Son, 1873), 246.
5 David Clark, *Between Pew and Pulpit: Folk Religion in a North Yorkshire Fishing Village* (Cambridge: Cambridge University Press, 1982), 104–5.

Thus in Pendle Forest in Lancashire in 1748, John Bennet's singing band of Methodists was resisted by a rabble with drums, music and guns.[6] For much of the nineteenth century respectable Evangelicals were sharply marked off from the rough elements in the parish who never darkened the doors of a place of worship. Their entertainments, which seemed an alternative to true religion and a source of perennial temptation, came under severe Evangelical censure. At Derby, for instance, the annual races, which had long been a haunt of betting touts and their cronies, were eventually suppressed by the magistrates in 1835 as a result of Evangelical pressure.[7] The sharpest encounters often took place over drink. The center of male sociability among the poor was the alehouse and the number of drink outlets was immense. In Lambeth in 1905 there were 172 churches, chapels and mission halls but as many as 430 public houses and beerhouses.[8] Drunkenness was always a target of church censure, but down to the middle years of the nineteenth century total abstinence was rare except in Primitive Methodism. Increasingly, however, drink seemed the supreme obstacle to conversion. From the 1870s Nonconformity and much of Scottish Presbyterianism turned decisively against alcohol. Even the Church of England launched a strong temperance society, supported chiefly by Evangelical clergy. There were annual temperance sermons; Bands of Hope encouraged the young to take the pledge; and the temperance campaign turned into a political cause. Plebeian culture, on the other hand, remained wedded to the public house. A gulf was created between the poor who liked a drink and the churchgoers who on principle shunned alcohol. Consequently gospel and culture in its popular dimension were in perpetual collision for much of the twentieth century.

Enlightenment Values

Other features of culture, however, became indigenized within the Evangelical movement and the bulk of this paper will take them as its theme. High culture is usually contrasted with the popular variety, but in reality tendencies that began in the elevated circles of cultural innovators gradually spread to a much wider public over time. The rank and file of Evangelicals were therefore affected by the

---

6   David Hempton, *Methodism: Empire of the Spirit* (New Haven, CT: Yale University Press, 2005), 90.
7   Anthony Delves, "Popular Recreation and Social Conflict in Derby, 1800–1850," in *Popular Culture and Class Conflict, 1590–1914*, ed. Eileen and Stephen Yeo (Brighton: Harvester, 1981), 107.
8   Jeffrey Cox, *The English Churches in a Secular Society: Lambeth, 1870–1930* (New York: Oxford University Press, 1982), 24.

steady dissemination of the main currents in Western civilization over the last three centuries. The first major wave of influence that percolated down to them was the Enlightenment, emphasizing the ability of reason to discover truth and improve the human lot. John Locke and Sir Isaac Newton, the chief progenitors of Enlightenment in the English-speaking world, both contended that received knowledge was not to be taken on trust. That stance is often supposed to have made the Enlightenment intrinsically anti-religious, with human reason pitted against divine revelation. It is true that Voltaire, one of its greatest luminaries, set the tone of the French Enlightenment with his cry of *écrasez l'infâme*, a rallying call against the institutional embodiment of revealed religion. It is also true that many of the British religious thinkers of the eighteenth century who were most affected by the spirit of the age, whether latitudinarians in the Church of England, moderates in the Church of Scotland or Socinians in Dissent, became in varying degree detached from traditional Christian convictions. Scholarship, however, has shown that the Enlightenment was immensely varied in its expressions, so that, in north Germany for example, it was closely bound up with Pietism.[9] Similarly in England and Scotland, although there were outright opponents of Christian teaching such as the Deists and David Hume, there was a great deal of overlap between Enlightenment thinking and orthodox theology. There was no automatic antagonism between the intellectual temper of the age and the rising Evangelical movement.

On the contrary, Evangelicalism was permeated with Enlightenment values from the inception of the movement and on into the nineteenth century.[10] Both, in the first place, were dedicated to empirical method. Locke and Newton equally favored investigation as the method for discovering truth. Each man was deeply respected by Evangelicals, even though they came to be most devoted to the common-sense philosophy of Thomas Reid, a product of the Scottish Enlightenment, as a foundation for their thinking. Although the Scottish school held that first principles have to be assumed, its methods were essentially empirical, not deductive. Its texts were standard in the curriculum of nineteenth-century theological colleges. Respect for empirical method led to sympathy for science. Natural theology, the prevailing British tradition of apologetics, formed a bridge between science and religion. Evangelicals heartily

---

9   *The Enlightenment in National Context*, ed. Roy Porter and Mikulas Teich (Cambridge: Cambridge University Press, 1982).
10 Further evidence of the bonding between Evangelical and Enlightenment values will be found in 1:2 and 1:7: "Revival and Enlightenment in Eighteenth-Century England" and "Global Evangelicalism in the Nineteenth Century."

approved when, in 1802, William Paley published his *Natural Theology*.[11] They frequently followed Paley in appealing to the evidences of a designing purpose in the world that confirmed the existence of a Designer. The most popular work by Thomas Chalmers, the leader of the Evangelical party in the Church of Scotland, was a series of *Astronomical Discourses* (1817) on the wonders of the heavens and the glories of their Maker.[12] Natural theology remained the framework within which Evangelical theologians came to terms with Darwin after 1859. Purpose, they argued, could still be discerned in an evolutionary world so long as it was not assumed to be absent. An Enlightenment framework continued to ensure that there was little or no gulf between science and religion in Evangelical thought for most of the nineteenth century.[13]

A second bond between Evangelicalism and the Enlightenment was optimism. A leading characteristic of the later Enlightenment of the second half of the eighteenth century was the idea of progress, the notion that humanity is advancing morally towards a better future. A similar optimistic temper marked Evangelicals. "More will in the end be saved than will perish," declared Thomas Scott, the leading Anglican Evangelical commentator on the Bible. "Diseases, wars, passions," he went on, "will all be subdued."[14] Scott's confidence in the elimination of the scourges of humanity was a result of postmillennial teaching, the belief that the second coming of Jesus will not take place until after a millennium of peace and prosperity. On this reading of biblical prophecy, the millennium will dawn as a result of the gradual extension of the gospel and the consequent spread of Christian values throughout the world. In this vein the *General Baptist Magazine* carried an article in 1854 on the millennium envisaging not only the disappearance of moral evils but also such secular benefits as the end of "the oppressive weight of taxes that grind nations to the dust." "Governments will still probably exist," the writer remarked, "but theirs will then be an easy office; for all will be a law unto themselves." This happy state of affairs

---

11   William Paley, *Natural Theology: Or Evidences for the Existence and Attributes of the Deity Collected from the Appearances of Nature* (London: For R. Faulder by Wilks and Taylor, 1802).
12   Thomas Chalmers, *A Series of Discourses on the Christian Revelation: Viewed in Connection with the Modern Astronomy* [1817] (Cambridge: Cambridge University Press, 2009).
13   See 1:14: "Science and Evangelical Theology in Britain from Wesley to Orr."
14   John H. Pratt, *The Thought of the Evangelical Leaders: Notes of the Discussions of the Eclectic Society, London, during the Years 1798–1814* (London: Banner of Truth Trust, 1978), 257 (7 June 1802).

might take some time, but could be expected to arrive around the year 2016.[15] The postmillennial view was not unanimous among eighteenth-century Evangelicals, but, in the wake of the upheavals of the French Revolution, it became their general opinion. The launching of the missionary movement at the same juncture seemed to vindicate the expectation of the universal triumph of the gospel. The vigor of Evangelical postmillennialism goes a long way towards explaining the strength of the Victorian idea of progress. They were mutually reinforcing and, as the century wore on, virtually indistinguishable.

Perhaps the most characteristic feature of the Enlightenment was its pragmatism. Traditional institutions, it was insisted, must be reformed so as to make them efficient. This was the stance of Jeremy Bentham and the current of utilitarian thought with which he was associated. Equally it was to be found among Evangelicals. They were far less committed than earlier generations of Protestants, whether Churchmen or Dissenters, to precise forms of church order. Instead they were willing to experiment. Because their grand goal was the rapid propagation of the gospel, they were impatient with any obstacles posed by traditional ways in the churches. Lay agency was one of the most significant expressions of their pragmatic temper. Christian initiatives were not left to the professional clergy but were taken up by laypeople, female as well as male. Thus Methodism was run by society stewards and the great majority of its sermons delivered by lay preachers. Likewise in the Church of Scotland Chalmers revived the office of deacon in 1819 so that businessmen could deploy their talents in the service of the church.[16] There were many other instances of a new flexibility in the area of ecclesiology. Thus early Anglican Evangelical clergy, eager to preach wherever there were needy sinners, often entirely ignored the parochial system of the church. Likewise during the early nineteenth century the Baptists, despite their existence as a denomination being predicated on their practice of believer's baptism, largely abandoned their insistence on the rite as a condition of participation in communion.[17] Matters of lesser importance than the proclamation of the gospel could be adapted for the sake of greater effectiveness. Societies rather than churchly agencies were likely to be better managed, and so the British and Foreign Bible

---

15 *General Baptist Magazine*, July 1854, 308–9. See also 1:8: "The Advent Hope in British Evangelicalism since 1800."
16 Stewart J. Brown, *Thomas Chalmers and the Godly Commonwealth in Scotland* (Oxford: Oxford University Press, 1982), 132–33.
17 Michael J. Walker, *Baptists at the Table: The Theology of the Lord's Supper amongst English Baptists in the Nineteenth Century* (Didcot, Oxfordshire: Baptist Historical Society, 1992), chap. 2.

Society and similar organizations were typical expressions of the Evangelical temper. If secular Enlightenment thinkers aimed to promote utility, Evangelical biographers frequently praised the usefulness of their subjects. The assimilation of the spirit of the age by Evangelicals meant that there was a close affinity between the two approaches.

Romantic Affinities

Another high cultural force, however, impinged on religion in the early nineteenth century. The new mood, Romanticism, developed in pioneering literary circles, especially in Germany, from the last years of the eighteenth century. In Britain its most celebrated exponents were the Lake Poets, William Wordsworth and Samuel Taylor Coleridge, and the historical novelist Sir Walter Scott. The term "Romantic," however, is used here not in a sense restricted to that generation of authors, but rather encompasses the whole cultural wave that spread out from them, enveloping first some of the highly educated and then a slowly increasing proportion of the population as the century wore on. The preferences of the era of Enlightenment were gradually—but by no means entirely—supplanted over the decades. Instead of the Enlightenment exaltation of reason there was an emphasis on will, emotion and intuition. Simplicity was replaced by mystery, the artificial by the natural and the novel by the traditional. The new taste underlay the appeal to history of the Oxford Movement in the Church of England and the ornate display of Ultramontane ritual in the Roman Catholic Church. Coleridge was a major inspiration for other Anglicans such as Thomas Arnold who shaped subsequent Broad Church theology. So Romanticism exerted a powerful influence over the direction of Christian thought in the Victorian age.

Evangelicalism was far from immune.[18] Edward Irving, a minister of the Church of Scotland in London, acknowledged Coleridge as his mentor. It was Irving who, more than any other, transposed Evangelical doctrine into a Romantic key. In a memorable sermon lasting over six hours delivered before the London Missionary Society in 1824, he denounced unsparingly the methods of his host organization. The society, he claimed, had capitulated to modern business methods in a spirit of expediency. Missionaries should instead go out without resources other than a total reliance on the Almighty for their support. The rational calculation of the Enlightenment must be abandoned in favor of radical faith. Again, Irving was ready with Romantic eyes to recognize dramatic events as bearing the authentic hallmarks of the supernatural.

---

18   Further evidence of the bonding between Evangelical and Romantic values will be found in 1:7: "Global Evangelicalism in the Nineteenth Century."

Accordingly when, in 1831, speaking in tongues broke out in his congregation, he readily accepted its miraculous credentials. The legitimacy of speaking in tongues was to be an article of faith in the Catholic Apostolic Church that institutionalized Irving's convictions. Most significantly of all, Irving came to believe that Jesus would return soon and in person. In 1827 he published *The Coming of Messiah in Glory and Majesty*, a translation from Spanish of a work by a Chilean Jesuit, contending for Jesus' imminent dramatic advent.[19] In the book he dropped the postmillennial expectation of the gradual advance of the gospel in order to embrace the premillennial hope that the second coming would precede the millennium. That was to abandon the characteristic eschatology of the Enlightenment for that typical of Romanticism. Irving was the person who did most to inject Romantic presuppositions into the Evangelical bloodstream.

Another man who seconded Irving's efforts was John Nelson Darby. The outlook of Darby was colored by Romantic taste. Poetry, for Darby, was an attempt "to create, by imagination, a sphere beyond materialism, which faith gives in realities."[20] These are the hallmarks of the new sensibility: imagination, the supersession of the material and faith itself. At first, as an Irish clergyman, he held views of apostolic succession comparable to those of the Oxford Movement. Then, as he moved into Brethren circles, he developed as strong an insistence on the supremacy of faith over reason as Irving. His species of premillennial teaching, dispensationalism, bore the mark of a characteristic feature of Romantic thought, cultural relativism. There were no permanent standards by which to evaluate every part of human history, but rather the dispensations were separate stages when God's dealings with humanity were distinct—a principle that enabled him to repudiate Irving's acceptance of the revival of the gift of tongues as something alien to the present age. Other men who left a substantial legacy to Brethren also drank deeply from the Romantic well. Anthony Norris Groves was the epitome of the wandering missionary depending wholly on the Almighty that Irving had envisaged, and George Müller was an immensely influential exemplar of living by faith rather than by rational planning. Brethren as a whole embraced an ecclesiology that bore the Romantic impress. Christian assemblies were formed not by human act but by "gathering to the Lord." They had no defined membership but consisted of

---

19 Juan Josafat Ben-Ezra, *The Coming of Messiah in Glory and Majesty*, trans. Edward Irving (London: L. B. Seeley, 1827), vi.
20 Heyman Wreford, *Memories of the Life and Last Days of William Kelly* (London: F. E. Race, n.d.), 81, quoted in Max S. Weremchuk, *John Nelson Darby* (Neptune, NJ: Loizeaux Brothers, 1992), 167.

those who were "in fellowship," vital elements in an organic community. Their leadership was not constituted by formal procedures but by the emergence of men with appropriate gifts. All was natural and spiritual. The Brethren movement can be seen as adopting a Romantic version of Evangelical faith.[21]

The main effect of the Romantic mood in the Evangelical movement as a whole, however, was to push many of its adherents in a more theologically liberal direction. The central shift was in the doctrine of God. The theologians who had written under the sway of Enlightenment thinking had understood the Almighty primarily as the just governor of the universe. A younger generation falling under Romantic influences, by contrast, saw him primarily as Father. The pacesetters of the new view were the Scots John McLeod Campbell and Thomas Erskine, who complained that earlier writers had depicted God in legal imagery rather than in terms of the family.[22] The Almighty was now seen, however, essentially as father of all, so that no distinction was drawn between those who were adopted into his family and those who were not. The effect of this doctrine of the fatherhood of God was therefore to blur the line between the converted and the unconverted. There were other Romantic innovations. They included a shift in emphasis away from the atonement to the incarnation, the premier doctrine in the estimate of High Churchmen and Broad Churchmen alike. Theologians influenced by F. D. Maurice, such as the Wesleyan John Scott Lidgett, commonly took this path. The problem here was that the centrality of the cross was being eclipsed. Again, the biblical higher criticism that impinged on Evangelical scholarship in the later Victorian years was founded on German Romantic premises. The development of doctrine in ancient Israel, it was believed, must have conformed to an evolutionary pattern. After much debate, William Robertson Smith was dismissed from the Free Church College at Aberdeen in 1881 in part for embracing this point of view. So Romantic currents of thought were beginning to erode the accepted understandings of conversion, the cross and the Bible, three of the Evangelical fundamentals.

Yet aspects of the Romantic vision could also point in a theologically conservative direction. The faith principle became in the later years of the nineteenth century the animating idea behind a wave of new missionary bodies beginning in 1865 with Hudson Taylor's China Inland Mission. Premillennialism stiffened the backbone of Evangelicals in the Church of England, though not spreading to many people outside its ranks other than Brethren. And the

---

21 See 2:13: "The Brethren in International Evangelicalism."
22 David W. Bebbington, *The Dominance of Evangelicalism: The Age of Spurgeon and Moody* (Leicester: InterVarsity Press, 2005), 156–57.

Keswick movement, beginning in 1875, taught a Romantic prescription for holy living. The Lake District, where its annual convention gathered, had once been the home of Wordsworth and Coleridge. Those associated with Keswick, such as Frances Ridley Havergal, often possessed poetic taste or talent. The substance of the teaching, that holiness was attainable by faith rather than by effort, bore witness to the twin Romantic emphases on moments of crisis and personal trust. The mode in which sin was dealt with, according to Keswick teachers, was not by removing it ("eradication") but by repressing it ("victory"), an enduring process that was typical of Romantic categories. The whole enterprise can be recognized as a recasting of spirituality in a Romantic style. By 1900, despite dogged resistance by J. C. Ryle, it had come to dominate Anglican Evangelicalism.[23] Before the end of the nineteenth century parts of the Romantic inheritance had strengthened theological conservatism within the Evangelical movement.

Twentieth-Century Romanticism

It was in the twentieth century, however, that a Romantic way of looking at the world became most widespread among the British public. In the Garden City movement at the start of the century, for example, the advocacy of rural features in new cities such as front gardens and open spaces can be seen as an expression of the wistful quest for the purer influences of the countryside that was near the heart of Romantic sensibility. Again, when the Labour Members of Parliament of 1906 were asked who had molded them most intellectually, the reply was not Karl Marx but John Ruskin, the prophet of fostering the beautiful in the world of work and one of the greatest Romantic prose writers. The Roman Catholic Church exercised a fascination over sensitive minds in the earlier twentieth century because of its insistence on the value of tradition inherited from the past and the capacity of faith to respond to symbols. The continuing Ultramontane ethos of the mass had what Ronald Knox, the son of an Anglican Evangelical bishop but himself a Catholic convert, called a "dramatic and appealing character."[24] The first half of the twentieth century was an era when the cultural legacy of Romanticism reached its apogee.

The effects were felt in all the strands of Evangelical life. From the first decade of the twentieth century, "Liberal Evangelicals" started to emerge in the

---

23 David W. Bebbington, *Holiness in Nineteenth-Century England* (Carlisle: Paternoster Press, 2000), chap. 4. For Ryle, see 2:2: "Bishop J. C. Ryle: Holiness, Mission and Churchmanship."

24 Horton Davies, *Worship and Theology in England*, 5 vols. (Princeton, NJ: Princeton University Press, 1961–75), 5:61.

Church of England. At first the phrase was used of Evangelicals who leant not in a Broad Church direction, towards a more liberal theology, but in a High Church direction, towards a more Catholic form of churchmanship. Typically it described those clergy who wished to adopt liturgical practices once thought alien to Evangelicalism, such as vestments, a choir and flowers on the communion table. In 1904 one self-professed "Liberal Evangelical" explained that his standpoint meant that he was able to introduce flowers to his church without "noxious teaching."[25] The reason often given was that young people, because of their improved aesthetic preferences, could be retained only by a higher churchmanship. Liberal Evangelicals organized themselves from 1906 in a body which from 1923 took the title the Anglican Evangelical Group Movement. By the 1920s it had become more committed to a broader theology, especially in wholeheartedly welcoming biblical criticism. Its ethos was most fully expressed in the Cromer Convention, an annual devotional gathering on the lines of Keswick. It was exclusively Anglican, highly clerical and tolerant of addresses that verged on pantheism. Edward Woods, later bishop of Lichfield, would go out on the cliffs carrying a copy of Wordsworth in his pocket.[26] The convention was a carrier of the Romantic spirit.

The Methodists possessed a parallel body in the Fellowship of the Kingdom, which emerged at the end of the First World War. It recast traditional Methodist teaching in terms of three watchwords, Quest, Crusade and Fellowship. The Quest sought spiritual experience; the Crusade meant outreach; and the Fellowship was for members meeting in fortnightly groups. The very terminology was redolent of knightly enterprise at the court of King Arthur. Its publications illustrate the same Romantic ethos. J. Arundel Chapman, for instance, described biblical inspiration in these terms:

> A poem such as Wordsworth's *Michael*, the picture of the Austrian Tyrol in June, a piece of music such as Bach's Mass in B Minor, the view of the Langdale Pikes, differ markedly, but they are all alike in this—that they get us.[27]

Inevitably many Methodists gravitated in a High Church direction, a Methodist Sacramental Fellowship being launched in 1935. According to K. Harley Boyns, a minister who wrote a pamphlet called *Our Catholic Heritage*, "The past, with its conquests, its fragrance, its saints, its immortal splendour, is

---

25 *Record*, 23 September 1904, 954 (A. H. Hope-Smith).
26 Ian M. Randall, *Evangelical Experiences: A Study in the Spirituality of English Evangelicalism, 1918–1939* (Carlisle: Paternoster Press, 1999), 56.
27 John Arundel Chapman, *The Bible and Its Inspiration* (London: Epworth Press, 1928), 5.

ours."²⁸ The echoes of the Oxford Movement's discovery of an idealized Christian tradition nearly a century before are unmistakable.

A similar pattern is evident among churches possessing a Reformed inheritance. Many congregations of the Church of Scotland, largely reunited from 1929, introduced more frequent communion, service books with fixed liturgies and the observance of the Christian year. So close did the Church of Scotland move to the Church of England that by the 1950s there was nearly a merger of the two established churches. Although a campaign by the *Scottish Daily Express* ensured the scheme's rejection because it entailed the acceptance of bishops, the Presbyterian leaders themselves were willing to embrace episcopacy.²⁹ In Wales the trend was less marked, but greater dignity of worship did appear among the Calvinistic Methodists, from 1930 called the Presbyterian Church of Wales. A book about the home missionary work of the Welsh Presbyterians published in the late 1940s captured in its title the same spirit as the Methodist Fellowship of the Kingdom: *The Romance of the Forward Movement*.³⁰ Among the English Congregationalists there were two tendencies shaped by Romantic influences, pointing in different directions. On the one hand there was an advance of theological liberalism, which proceeded far beyond the bounds of Evangelicalism. Thus T. Rhondda Williams, one of its leading exponents and chairman of the Congregational Union in 1929, regretted that Wesley and Whitefield had been burdened by "the incubus of a traditional theology."³¹ On the other hand there was the so-called Genevan movement that gathered around Nathaniel Micklem of Mansfield College, Oxford, from the 1930s. Micklem stressed the place of Calvinists within any fully developed understanding of Catholic tradition. His friend Bernard Lord Manning of Jesus College, Cambridge, shared his vision, extending it to the other Free Churches. For him the early Methodists of Lincolnshire singing the hymns of Charles Wesley about the cross were the modern equivalents of

---

28 K. Harley Boyns, *Our Catholic Heritage* (London: Epworth Press. 1919), 8. On the Fellowship of the Kingdom, see also 2:4: "The Dimensions of Methodist Spirituality, c.1800–1950."

29 Tom Gallagher, "The Press and Popular Protestant Culture: A Case-Study of the *Scottish Daily Express*," in *Sermons and Battle Hymns: Protestant Popular Culture in Scotland*, ed. Graham Walker and Tom Gallagher (Edinburgh: Edinburgh University Press, 1990), 193–212.

30 Howell Williams, *The Romance of the Forward Movement of the Presbyterian Church in Wales* (Denbigh: Gee and Son, 1949).

31 Thomas Rhondda Williams, *The Working Faith of a Liberal Theologian* (London: Williams & Norgate, 1914), 40, quoted in Alan. P. F. Sell, *Nonconformist Theology in the Twentieth Century* (Milton Keynes: Paternoster Press, 2006), 15.

mediaeval penitents wending their way across the same wolds chanting of the five wounds of Christ.[32] The evocation of the past once more provided a sanction for the exaltation of the church and the sacraments. The supreme instance was W. E. Orchard, the minister who conducted high mass at the Congregational King's Weigh House Chapel in London before seceding to Rome.[33] The High Church remodeling of the Reformed tradition could hardly go further.

Baptists had a rather different blend of currents flowing among them. Many of the denominational leaders, such as the Cambridge classicist T. R. Glover, fitted into much the same liberal Evangelical mold as the Anglican Evangelical Group Movement. Among the rank and file, however, there were sympathies for the more conservative expressions of the Romantic legacy. Queensberry Street Baptist Church, Old Basford, Nottingham, is an instructive case study. In 1929 an energetic member still in his twenties, a children's dress manufacturer named Douglas Stocken, stayed in the Aberystwyth holiday home run by the Young Life Campaign, a dynamic evangelistic organization. There Stocken was quickened by its version of Keswick spirituality centering on "full surrender." Returning to Nottingham, he threw himself into Young Life Campaign activities and became church secretary three years later. The church was renewed by the Keswick message, becoming the most vigorous Baptist cause in the area. There was a range of striking changes. The church began to concentrate on "soul winning." Bazaars were abandoned as worldly entertainments. The church now raised money only by voluntary giving. Premillennial teaching became standard. Queensberry Street drew away from other Baptist churches but closer to Anglican Evangelicals and Brethren who also supported the Young Life Campaign and Keswick. There was, in short, a transformation of cultural atmosphere. The Romantic style had at last filtered down to a Nottingham suburb.[34] Baptists included in their ranks a good number professing similar higher life and adventist beliefs. That helps explain the alignment of more Baptists than of other Nonconformists with the conservative Evangelical coalition in the postwar era.

The pattern of Evangelical life in the early twentieth century was therefore molded by the cultural inheritance from the previous century. The Romantic legacy made it common to present the Christian faith in rather ethereal

---

32 Bernard L. Manning, *The Making of Modern English Religion* (London: Student Christian Movement, 1929), 141–42.
33 Elaine Kaye, *The History of the King's Weigh House Church* (London: George Allen and Unwin, 1968), chap. 8.
34 David W. Bebbington, *A History of Queensberry Street Baptist Church, Old Basford, Nottingham* (Nottingham: For the Church, 1977), 38–39.

form, blurring the sharp lines of doctrine and concentrating on the fatherly love of God. That generated the liberal tendency. At the same time certain doctrinal themes, especially those surrounding the church, sacraments and ministry, chimed in with Romantic preoccupations. The same trend that made the Roman Catholic Church specially attractive gave rise to a higher churchmanship among many Evangelicals. Yet Romantic influence had also generated beliefs with conservative implications. Keswick teaching and the advent hope, popular among Anglicans, Brethren and others such as the Baptists of Queensberry Street, stiffened resistance to liberalism. The cultural mood that had animated the avant-garde of the early nineteenth century had spread so as to become a diffuse but potent element in the church life of the twentieth century.

Later Developments

The first major challenge to these ecclesiastical styles arose in the 1930s. It came from the Oxford Group led by Frank Buchman, a Pennsylvania Lutheran minister. Teams of life-changers, often Oxford undergraduates, visited an area to urge personal surrender to God. Individuals were drawn into groups where they talked frankly about their efforts to achieve the four ethical absolutes: honesty, purity, unselfishness, love. Adherents were encouraged to spend daily quiet times jotting down thoughts in notebooks as a way of discovering the guidance of God. The Oxford Group aroused suspicion in many Evangelical quarters because its meetings often dispensed with prayers, hymns or scripture readings. "Such a movement," darkly observed the Brethren magazine the *Witness*, ". . . can only have one end (Rev. 3.16)."[35] The later history of the Oxford Group, which turned in 1938 into Moral Rearmament, might seem to have borne out this judgment, for it became less distinctively Christian. For a while, however, at the depth of the Great Depression, the movement attracted attention to the Christian message, won converts and in the eyes of some observers seemed to presage revival. For all its idiosyncrasies, it brought a fresh burst of evangelistic vitality into the land.

The impact of the Oxford Group can be traced to its cultural role. Buchman wanted to remove every obstacle to the transmission of the gospel and so deliberately adopted the latest fashions. His movement therefore reflected the new cultural mood that had been created by the literary and artistic avant-garde in the years before and after 1900. This was the phenomenon variously called "Modernism" or "Expressionism." It bore little relation to the contemporary movement of theological modernism, which was an advanced form of liberalism, but took its name because it embraced the modern as an alternative

---

35 *Witness*, January 1937, 17.

to Romantic nostalgia for the past. It could equally be called "Expressionist" because of a characteristic commitment to free self-expression. Cultural Modernism was as original a phase in the history of Western civilization as the Enlightenment or Romanticism, and can best be understood as a cultural wave succeeding them. Its origins can be traced particularly to Friedrich Nietzsche in the 1870s and Sigmund Freud in the 1890s. From Nietzsche came the belief that there is no intrinsic order in the universe. Hence, it came to be held, there is no correspondence between words and things, so that language cannot represent reality. From Freud, Jung and their circle came the perceptions of depth psychology. There was exploration of the recesses of the subconscious, leading to the view that thought cannot be distinguished from feeling. The novelists such as James Joyce who explored the stream-of-consciousness technique and the artists such as the Surrealists who turned the world of dreams into their subject matter were typical exponents of this fresh cultural manner. The Oxford Group was its leading embodiment in religion.

The Buchmanites therefore displayed many of the most typical characteristics of the period's cultural pioneers. They believed in self-expression, telling each other in their groups how they really felt. Accepting the basics of depth psychology, they pursued mutual counseling. Personal relations had to be authentic, and so the Groupers went in for first names. They would even, according to a critical representation, have called Saint Peter "Pete."[36] Like Modernist artists, they rejected any notion of boundaries, not distinguishing the sacred from the secular and so, to the scandal of most Evangelicals of their day, going for rambles on a Sunday. Their doctrine was unspecific, for, like the mood they represented, they refused to pin down words to a single meaning. In the spirit of the Bohemian creators of Modernist art, they disliked institutions and so normally sat loose to the churches. Yet, because they were so anti-institutional, they relied on authority to hold them together and gave a degree of control to Buchman that some contemporaries likened to that of Hitler. For a while during the 1930s these techniques had an enormous appeal for the young, the prosperous and the educated, the sector of the population most swayed by recent cultural innovations. As war supervened and Moral Rearmament turned in fresh directions, the permeation of the churches and of society largely came to a halt. The lasting penetration of Evangelicalism by the new cultural mode in this period was therefore very limited.[37]

---

36 John Moore, *Brensham Village* (London: Collins, 1946), 171.
37 On the Oxford Group, see 2:15: "The Oxford Group," and David W. Bebbington, *Evangelicalism in Modern Britain: A History from the 1730s to the 1980s* (London: Unwin Hyman, 1989), 235–40.

The major impact of Modernism/Expressionism was therefore deferred until the 1960s, the decade of the expressive revolution in society at large. By then the cultural movement had evolved as it spread to a wider public, but it had not been superseded. The phenomenon that has come to be called "Postmodernism," which many would date from the 1960s, did not replace Modernism. Postmodernism is so called because it rejects Modernity, the legacy of the Enlightenment, not Modernism. In reality the two formed one stream of cultural influence. Thus in the field of architecture the Bauhaus school of the 1920s constituted the cutting edge of the "Modern Movement." Its central principle was giving precedence to the functional over questions of traditional design. A major Postmodernist monument, Richard Rodgers' Pompidou Centre in Paris, by placing its service ducts on the outside, bears witness to the same priority. For all the differences of appearance, there is an underlying continuity between the two. The essence of both is authenticity, the hallmark of Expressionism. Late twentieth-century Postmodernism was an increasingly diffused version of the cultural forces that sprang into being around the opening of the same century.

The chief way in which this cultural phenomenon impinged on Evangelicals was through charismatic renewal. Charismatics baptized the rising cultural mood into a Christian guise. Its characteristics therefore echo those of the Oxford Group in the 1930s. There are exceptions: the Group had none of the exuberant worship that was so salient in the renewal movement, but in the earlier period there was no question of altering the existing style of church services. Nevertheless the similarities are marked. The worship style of the charismatic movement was itself about self-expression, showing by gestures such as hand raising how people felt inside. The prayer counseling therapy that became a feature of renewal drew extensively on depth psychology. An insistence on authentic personal relations led to a rejection of individualistic churchgoing and sometimes to the creation of Christian communities. The sacred and the secular were not held apart so that, for example, there was an unprecedented surge of creativity in such matters as the making of banners and the inclusion of dance in worship. There was a tendency to downgrade fixed theological formulas and even, in some charismatic house churches, to insist that theology must be expected to change over time. A dislike of the institutionalism of existing denominations provided much of the spur to form new house churches. And at certain points, especially in the 1970s, there were authoritarian tendencies within the movement. The so-called "heavy shepherding" of that juncture, sometimes extending to the choosing of life partners for adherents, was subsequently largely repudiated, but the attributes of leadership became a much more common theme at conferences. The charismatic movement represented the rising temper of the age.[38]

The growth of charismatic renewal is one of the most striking features of late twentieth-century Christian history. It revitalized many existing congregations and gave rise to substantial networks of new churches. Even where it did not come to dominate, it commonly affected the style of church life, especially in worship. Seconded by technological improvements, a multiplicity of instruments was introduced and the visual came to rival the verbal. One symbolic change was the legitimation of applause. Noise in church had been frowned on in the period when Romantic norms prevailed since it was conceived to be a profane intrusion on the sacred. The expressive revolution in worship, however, encouraged clapping both to keep time with the rhythm of the music and to show appreciation of particular contributions to services.[39] All this was specially welcome to the young, the educated and the successful. The young appreciated worship that approximated to pop music; the educated were aware of the latest cultural trends; and the successful could pay for their taste to be gratified. Holy Trinity, Brompton, the leading bellwether congregation among Evangelicals by the end of the twentieth century, was full of the young, the educated and the successful. The appeal of Holy Trinity was partly a consequence of the clear exposition of the gospel that the church set out in its Alpha evangelistic programme, but it was also partly the result of its close adaptation to the cultural currents of the time. Just as the gospel in its Enlightenment form had exerted a strong appeal in the early decades of the Evangelical movement and in its Romantic style in the century or so from the 1830s, so its embodiment in a Modernist/Expressionist idiom proved to be powerful in the years around 2000.

Conclusions

A number of conclusions flow from this analysis. In the first place, it is evident that Evangelicals have been deeply embedded in their cultural settings. W. H. Groser was right to claim that churches are molded by their environments. It is impossible to understand the patterns of theological and ecclesiastical change without attention to the cultural context. Secondly, popular culture did not shape the trends in the expression of the gospel as much as developments in high culture. It is true that local customs impinged on how Evangelicals spread and lived the faith, but the deferred impact of intellectual innovations was far

---

38   On charismatic renewal, see 2:16: "The Rise of Charismatic Renewal in Britain."
39   See 1:16: "Evangelicals and Public Worship, 1965–2005."

greater because they soon meshed with major theological concerns. Popular culture in the sense of secular ways of life probably exerted its greatest influence by repulsion, creating a gulf between the churches and the mass of the people. The high cultural movement of the Enlightenment, in the third place, provided the intellectual framework within which early Evangelicals operated. Empiricism, optimism and pragmatism all constituted common ground between Evangelicals and their progressive contemporaries, so giving them a powerful apologetic advantage. The growth of the movement owes a great deal to this extensive intellectual affinity. Fourthly, the succeeding cultural wave of Romanticism immersed many Evangelicals. Its consequences were manifold, fostering liberal developments in theology and more elaborate liturgical practice, but also giving rise to distinctly conservative doctrinal trends, especially through the faith principle, premillennial teaching and the Keswick Convention. And finally the emergence of a novel Modernist/Expressionist mood exercised a comparable effect on the Evangelical movement in the twentieth century. After a stunted initial impact in the 1930s, it exerted a transforming influence over Evangelical life in the decades after the 1960s. Overall it is clear not only that the host culture has helped shape the articulation of the gospel but also that it has contributed in no small measure to its degree of success.

4

Evangelicalism and Cultural Diffusion

The relationship between gospel and culture has been much studied by missiologists in recent years. Andrew Walls and other experts on the history of world missions have shown that Christianity, especially in its Evangelical form, has proved remarkably adaptable to a wide range of diverse societies, taking up aspects of their ways of life and merging them with the distinctive features of the faith. The gospel, like the Bible, is eminently translatable.[1] That does not mean that theology is merely a function of culture, for it has proved an immensely creative force in its own right in the world of ideas. But the research of missiologists has brought to light something of the closeness of the integration of religion with its human setting, the potential for changes in the relationship over time and the resulting complexity of the interaction between gospel and culture. The same insights can be applied to Britain much more fully than they have been. Evangelical ideas have been part of the surrounding intellectual ambience, have been modified under its influence and have acted and reacted on British society in many and various ways. The object of this chapter is to examine one aspect of the way in which Evangelicalism and its host culture in Britain have been related, the process of diffusion. Its subject is therefore the pattern whereby attitudes and opinions have flowed within the movement. Because the processes have taken place over time, they fall within the province of the historian, but because the purpose here is to generalize rather than to particularize they could equally be regarded as the concern of the sociologist, the anthropologist or even, in some respects, the

---

1   Andrew Walls, *The Missionary Movement in Christian History: Studies in the Transmission of Faith* (Edinburgh: T&T Clark, 1996); *The Cross-Cultural Process in Christian History: Studies in the Transmission and Appropriation of Faith* (Edinburgh: T&T Clark, 2002).

geographer. So the scope of the coverage is broad: how ideas have typically been transmitted within the Evangelical movement over the last two and a half centuries or so.

The subject of culture initially calls for definition. The word, as Raymond Williams showed in his *Culture and Society*, has altered its meaning significantly over time and remains rather elusive.[2] Three contemporary usages may be distinguished. First there is the notion of high culture, the expression of civilization in literature, art and music. The novels of Jane Austen, the canvases of Poussin or the fugues of Bach are quintessential forms of high culture. The word "culture" is most commonly used in this way in Britain. When we speak of a cultured person, we mean somebody who appreciates Mozart or enjoys reading Homer. Secondly, there is the concept of popular culture, whether revealing itself in peasant customs of the past or in contemporary soap operas. This usage has traditionally been more common in the United States, where the *Journal of Cultural Studies*, published from Bowling Green University, Tennessee, concentrates on topics such as the worldview of Hollywood and the techniques of advertising. But the notion has also become firmly embedded in academic life in Britain, generating its own discipline of "Cultural Studies." The third way in which the term is employed is much broader than either of the other two, concentrating not on civilization, whether high or low, but on the whole web of attitudes prevailing in a society. This is the manner in which the word has normally been used in anthropology, which has even extended it beyond the sphere of ideas to "material culture," that is the sum of social artifacts. The third meaning of the concept was once confined to specific academic circles in Britain, but subsequently it became familiar in such phrases as the "enterprise culture" and is now in widespread use. In its broadest sense, the word can apply to virtually any feature of a society: a society's culture is how it is.

The usage here is an amalgam of all three of these ways of applying the word "culture." Evangelicalism has contained expressions of each of them. In the field of worship, for example, organ playing is a technique that can display the characteristics of high culture; flower arrangement in church can sometimes form a part of popular culture; and the raising of hands by charismatic worshipers falls within culture in its broadest definition. The usage that blends all three has advantages because of its all-encompassing quality. It recognizes the importance of ideas, and so allows the theology that has been central to Evangelicalism to assume a prominent place in the analysis. Equally, because it

---

2   Raymond Williams, *Culture and Society, 1780–1950* (London: Chatto & Windus, 1959).

embraces material culture, it gives weight to such matters as the architectural style of buildings or the physical shape of tracts. The word "culture" is therefore being deployed in this paper in a comprehensive sense.

The theme of diffusion also deserves comment. The concept signifies the ways in which ideas or practices have spread over time. It has two chief dimensions, which, though related, must be distinguished. One is the social. What is upheld by one social group at a particular point can be transmitted to another group either suddenly or gradually, so that an obscure notion can become general. The different groups can be explored to discover which was first to maintain a point of view, which received it from the first and how rapid the process was. Equally, however, diffusion may be a spatial development. The study of how attitudes have passed from one area to another has yielded significant findings. In particular, geographers have examined not just patterns of distribution at a single juncture but also the taking up of innovations first in one place and then in another. It will be valuable to look at both the social and the spatial dimensions of diffusion.

There are various aspects of the relationship between Evangelicalism and diffusion that could be explored. One is the spread of Evangelical religion itself. This is a major theme in Mark Noll's *The Rise of Evangelicalism* (2004). Taking the Evangelical Revival in the United Kingdom and Great Awakening in America jointly as his subject, he shows much of how and why the movement spread during the eighteenth century.[3] A classic account of the same process, though in a fictional microstudy, is George Eliot's "Janet's Repentance." In the early nineteenth century an Evangelical clergyman brings the gospel to the town of Milby, meeting a wall of hostility but eventually surmounting it by his diligence.[4] Although there is great scope for study of the introduction of the Evangelical movement into fresh places, however, that is not the theme of this chapter.

Another issue that could be scrutinized is how secular influences were transmitted through Evangelicalism. This topic has become familiar to historians as a dimension of the social control thesis that reached the peak of its popularity in the 1970s. The ruling classes, it was argued by historians sympathetic to a Marxian position, used religion as one of the devices for keeping down the proletariat, especially in the age of industrialization. A full-blooded instance of this viewpoint can be found in Allan MacLaren's study

---

3   Mark A. Noll, *The Rise of Evangelicalism: The Age of Edwards, Whitefield and the Wesleys* (Leicester: InterVarsity Press, 2004).

4   George Eliot, "Janet's Repentance," *Scenes of Clerical Life* (Edinburgh: William Blackwood and Sons, 1858).

of Aberdeen in the 1840s, which contends that the Evangelical faith that gave rise to the Free Church of Scotland was in part a vehicle for disciplining the lower orders.[5] A powerful counterblast was issued in the study of nineteenth-century Sunday schools by Thomas Laqueur, who showed that these alleged agencies of social control did not merely peddle ideas of deference but were authentic expressions of working-class culture. Laqueur's project entailed careful analysis, as far as possible, of the teaching actually transmitted in these largely Evangelical bodies.[6] The results of this kind of study can be illuminating, especially in resisting misrepresentations of Evangelical religion; but again that is not the topic here.

Instead the subject for discussion in this chapter is the diffusion of ideas and practices within Evangelicalism. It is about the transmission of what had been indigenized within the movement. How did innovations pass from group to group and area to area? Premillennial teaching about prophecy, for example, became newly popular within the period: what were the processes involved in its dissemination? Again, whereas the gown had traditionally been worn by Anglican clergymen when preaching, Evangelicals influenced by the legacy of the Oxford Movement began to adopt the surplice in the pulpit during the later years of the nineteenth century: who did so and where was it done? The schemes of diffusion within the Evangelical movement are worthy of study in their own right.

It might be thought that the task of identifying any significant pattern would be impossible. When people embraced premillennialism, they did so freely, as a matter of conviction, so that the distribution of those who had adopted it by any given point, it might be expected, would be random. To suggest any group trends might be interpreted as an unjustified assumption of social determinism, a slight on personal responsibility. Free, individual decisions, however, do commonly reveal significant consistencies. The sociological pioneer Emile Durkheim found that even Paris suicides, which might be expected to be among the ultimate expressions of individual autonomy, fell into discernible patterns.[7] That was because those who did away with themselves were subject to the same social pressures as other people and responded accordingly, though in more dramatic fashion than others. Likewise Evangelicals, though

---

5   A. Allan MacLaren, *Religion and Social Class: The Disruption Years in Aberdeen* (London: Routledge & Kegan Paul, 1974).

6   Thomas W. Laqueur, *Religion and Respectability: Sunday Schools and Working-Class Culture, 1780–1850* (New Haven, CT: Yale University Press, 1976).

7   Emile Durkheim, *Suicide: A Study in Sociology*, trans. John A. Spaulding and George Simpson, ed. George Simpson (London: Routledge & Kegan Paul, 1952).

enjoying the degree of liberty normally assigned to human beings, were also molded by the influences that are the common lot of humanity. As members of their communities, as readers and in a host of other ways they were affected by a variety of social factors. To generalize about responses is not to deny responsibility for choices.

Social Diffusion

What, then, has been the pattern of cultural diffusion among Evangelicals? Initially, we can focus on the social rather than the spatial trends, the way in which different groups adopted beliefs and manners rather than the places where they did so. The predominant overall schema, we may say at the outset, was for novelties to spread from above to below, from an elite to the masses. The great Evangelical Member of Parliament and antislavery activist William Wilberforce wrote in 1797 of "the general diffusion of the sentiments of the higher orders."[8] Ideas, he was claiming, would trickle down from the top of society to its lower reaches. His view might be discounted as the normal opinion of one of the well-to-do of the time, naturally expecting that the higher orders would automatically be imitated by the rank and file of a deferential population. Again, Wilberforce's conviction might be thought to reflect the presumption of the Enlightenment that the more refined could spread the light of knowledge to the lower orders who had previously been benighted in darkness. It is true that the next age, when Romantic ideas were in currency, stressed the countervailing capacity of the ordinary people, the folk, to retain the admirable qualities of former generations and to transmit them upwards to their superiors. So it should not be assumed that Wilberforce was correct in declaring that the flow of influence was chiefly downwards. Yet on investigation that is exactly what does turn out to be the case with Evangelicals. Normally ideas and practices spread downwards from groups with greater advantages to a wider constituency.

More particularly, three characteristics normally marked those who were affected earlier rather than later by innovations in the Evangelical world. In the first place, they were highly educated. Those with more experience of learning tended to read more extensively and so to be more exposed to fresh ideas. In particular university graduates, who for most of the period could claim to enjoy a form of elite status, were more likely to experiment with new notions. Hence charismatic renewal, far from being the mindless extravagance that was

---

8   William Wilberforce, *A Practical View of the Prevailing Religious System of Professed Christians in the Higher and Middle Classes in This Country Contrasted with Real Christianity*, 4th ed. (London: T. Cadell and W. Davies, 1797), 10.

sometimes depicted in the press, initially attracted a disproportionate number of graduates. The church led by Bryn Jones at Bradford, the fulcrum of the largest network of restorationist congregations in the 1980s, for example, included many elders boasting degrees and four holders of doctorates when they were less common than they have since become.[9] Innovations in the Evangelical world normally struck the more educated before the less qualified.

A second variable normally affecting who was likely to embrace novelty was class. In a secular context, a study of Derby in the 1950s showed that the middle classes usually accepted new ideas more readily than the working classes.[10] The phenomenon was explained as primarily the result of the greater amount of reading done by the middle classes. Just as more education was associated with innovation, so was a higher position on the class scale, and that was because the two were closely related. In the days before free university places, those who could afford a better education were those with higher incomes. A similar pattern has been evident in Evangelicalism. Denominations with a higher social profile have been notably more receptive to new ideas. During the later years of the nineteenth century, Congregationalists were significantly more inclined to liberalize their theology than their near denominational neighbors the Baptists.[11] Their respectability made many of the Congregationalists want, as it were, to smooth off the rough edges of their faith, to domesticate their religion. They showed a greater willingness to accept newer notions of, for example, the universal Fatherhood of God. At the same time, however, Anglican Evangelicals, whose social standing was on average even higher, also embraced novelty in the shape of Keswick holiness teaching, which tended to stiffen theological conservatism.[12] It was not necessarily liberal views that attracted people of superior status; rather, it was novelty. So sections of the Evangelical movement with a higher class position were disproportionately drawn to fresh convictions.

The third most striking factor affecting willingness to take up something new was age. Teenagers and young adults were usually more malleable than their elders. Hence there was standardly a generational difference between Evangelicals upholding traditional ways and those wanting to move on. The most innovative body associated with the Evangelical movement in the earlier

9   Andrew Walker, *Restoring the Kingdom* (London: Hodder and Stoughton, 1985), 188.
10 Theodore Cauter and J. S. Downham, *The Communication of Ideas: A Study of Contemporary Influences on Urban Life* (London: Chatto & Windus, 1954).
11 Mark Hopkins, *Nonconformity's Romantic Generation: Evangelical and Liberal Theologies in Victorian England* (Milton Keynes: Paternoster Press, 2004).
12 David W. Bebbington, *Evangelicalism in Modern Britain: A History from the 1730s to the 1980s* (London: Routledge, 1993), chap. 5.

twentieth century, for example, was the Oxford Group, a network of young people led by the American evangelist Frank Buchman. They would arrive enthusiastically in an area urging the inhabitants to change their lives by an act of surrender, shunning inherited theological terminology in favor of language that offered the fewest barriers to the gospel.[13] They were often Oxford students, as the title of the body suggests, and so they were frequently privileged in terms of academic opportunities and social standing as well. As in many other cases, such as the ready reception of Romantic notions in the 1830s by the early Brethren or the appeal of radical charismatic renewal in the 1980s, the three factors of learning, class and age intertwined.[14] Those who were eager to adopt new ways within the Evangelical movement were primarily the educated, the well-to-do and the young.

Means of Diffusion

What were the means by which Evangelical innovations spread? The most obvious agency among Protestants was the pulpit. Ministers provided teaching for their flocks, usually (until fairly recently) twice each Sunday and often during the week as well. Hence the instruction that the ministers themselves had received was crucial. For many, the colleges where they trained were the chief sources of their distinctive ideas. Fundamentalists in the interwar years spoke darkly of the wells of learning being poisoned by Modernism, in some cases founding new institutions such as the Bible Churchmen's College in Bristol and the School of Evangelism at Barry in South Wales to replace the older tainted bodies.[15] Although by that time most of the theological colleges were in university cities so that it was impossible to isolate candidates for the ministry from wider influences, the colleges did transmit a particular style. Thus at Zion Baptist Church, Cambridge, in the 1950s, a deacon claimed to be able to identify the college background of any visiting preacher within five minutes of the opening of the sermon. Men from Spurgeon's College, for example, were noted for their breezy anecdotes.[16] Ideas flowed from those responsible for training through the ministers to the pews.

---

13   See 2:15: "The Oxford Group."
14   See 2:13: "The Brethren in International Evangelicalism"; Walker, *Restoring the Kingdom*, 188.
15   Walter S. Hooton and John S. Wright, *The First Twenty-Five Years of the Bible Churchmen's Missionary Society (1922–47)* (London: Bible Churchmen's Missionary Society, 1947), chap. 4; Noel Gibbard, *Taught to Serve: The History of Barry and Bryntirion Colleges* (Bridgend, Glamorgan: Evangelical Press of Wales, 1996).
16   George Hayden was the deacon. I am grateful to his son, the late Dr Roger Hayden, for the point.

A second agency of diffusion was the mass gathering. These were by no means a novelty of the late twentieth century. Dissenting bodies held district association meetings from the later eighteenth century, acting as media for the dissemination of the latest views of doctrine and practice. The Northamptonshire Baptist Association, for instance, was where many of its ministers first heard of the theology of Jonathan Edwards and its sanction for the proclamation of the gospel uninhibited by worries over whether their hearers had been predestined to salvation. The result was a series of discussions that culminated in the foundation of the Baptist Missionary Society in 1792.[17] Likewise the annual meetings of Anglican Evangelicals at Islington from 1827 to 1982 attracted around a thousand attenders by the start of the twentieth century to listen to addresses by leading clergy on questions of contemporary policy. The Islington conferences functioned as the magisterium of the movement, usually trying to steady the rank and file in their existing opinions but sometimes urging new courses of action. In 1908, for example, the conference discussed "The Church and Social Problems," recommending in a year when the rise of the Labour Party was in the public eye that the clergy should take up questions of politics, municipal life, housing, the treatment of children, the sweated trades and temperance. The theme of social issues was not to be repeated at Islington until 1968. Already, however, sixty years previously, the gathering had given Evangelical clergy the green light for involvement in combating the ills of Edwardian England.[18] Mass meetings could be powerful agents of innovation.

Literature, thirdly, was an extraordinarily important means by which fresh ideas spread. Evangelicals were masters of the art of using publications to disseminate their convictions, founding the prolific Religious Tract Society in 1799 and the mighty British and Foreign Bible Society five years later. Although Bibles were published without note or comment, the tracts engaged with many topics, including even science. Around the middle of the nineteenth century the Religious Tract Society published a monthly series of sixpenny booklets arguing that all spheres of life were providentially ordered and so illustrated the analogies between the scientific and the spiritual worlds. Even a New Zealand caterpillar infected with fungus was deployed to illustrate Christian teaching.[19] Although the chief

17   See 1:5: "The Legacy of Jonathan Edwards in Britain."
18   *Record*, 17 January 1908, 57–68. See 2:1: "The Islington Conference: The Seat of Authority in Anglican Evangelicalism."
19   Aileen Fyfe, *Science and Salvation: Evangelical Popular Science Publishing in Victorian Britain* (Chicago: University of Chicago Press, 2004), 116.

effect was to reinforce existing beliefs, the exploration of fresh intellectual areas by readers was undoubtedly the result. Denominational periodicals, which contained very diverse material, exercised an even more widespread effect. In the early nineteenth century the *Evangelical Magazine* and the *Methodist Magazine* both sold about twenty thousand copies a month.[20] Such periodicals could be the means of disseminating novelties, as when John Campbell recommended the Gothic style for chapel building in the *Congregational Year Book*.[21] And separate titles were pervasive. George Warner, a Primitive Methodist minister, was said to have published during his lifetime between thirty and forty thousand books and pamphlets commending his brand of teaching about entire sanctification.[22] Although its relative influence declined with the rise of other media during the twentieth century, Christian literature continued to play a large part in stimulating Evangelicals to take up new causes.

It is also true, in the fourth place, that organizations have been major agencies of diffusion. The Methodist device of the class meeting, a weekly gathering of about a dozen people for fellowship and uplift, was extremely influential in encouraging members to go on to meet fresh spiritual challenges. Small-scale prayer meetings and fellowship groups have been characteristic of the Evangelical movement over the centuries, providing a forum for the dissemination of practices new as well as old. Thus it was in cottage meetings, away from the formalities of chapel services, that female leadership of worship advanced among Methodists in the early nineteenth century.[23] A plethora of youth organizations has marked Evangelical history, but the chief among them has undoubtedly been the Sunday school. Over 75 percent of children in Britain aged five to fourteen were enrolled in a Sunday school during the Edwardian years.[24] These bodies may have declined during the subsequent century, but Sunday school still retained a major hold on the children of the unchurched population right down until the arrival, around 1960, of the television in the working-class sitting room and of the car in the street outside. Here were

---

20 Fyfe, *Science and Salvation*, 49.
21 John Blackburn, "Remarks on Ecclesiastical Architecture as Applied to Nonconformist Chapels," in the *Congregational Year Book* (London: Jackson and Walford, 1847), 161.
22 John Stephenson, *The Man of Faith and Fire: Or the Life and Work of the Rev. G. Warner* (London: Robert Bryant, 1902), 276.
23 Deborah Valenze, *Prophetic Sons and Daughters: Female Preaching and Popular Religion in Industrial England* (Princeton, NJ: Princeton University Press, 1985), 41–49.
24 Callum G. Brown, *The Death of Christian Britain* (London: Routledge, 2001), 168.

institutions that conveyed Evangelical ideas, with their enduring substance and their passing variations, to a very high proportion of the population.

Individuals, fifthly, must not be forgotten. Major figures could exercise an exceptional influence through their personal role, reinforced in print. Edward Irving, the flamboyant minister of the Church of Scotland in London during the 1820s, for example, made an enormous impact on contemporary Evangelicals. Cultivating a friendship with the poet Samuel Taylor Coleridge, Irving imbibed many of his distinctive notions together with his entire Romantic style of thinking. The Scottish minister applied the new approach to traditional doctrine and came up with a whole string of fresh readings: the principle of living by faith as a missionary, the expectation of an imminent and personal second advent, the possibility of speaking in tongues and much else were implanted in the Evangelical world by his agency.[25] Other individuals have been hardly less significant. During the twentieth century the influence of Martyn Lloyd-Jones, especially on his native Wales, was immense, leading to the setting up of the Evangelical Movement of Wales to consolidate the forces of the movement in the principality.[26] Equally the pervasive influence of John Stott within and beyond the Anglican world can hardly be underestimated. It was Stott, for example, who did the most to persuade conservative Evangelicals to return to a policy of social engagement from which they had previously withdrawn.[27] So individuals could play a decisive part in changes of direction.

By such means as these, therefore, ideas and practices spread through the Evangelical community. The general social pattern of diffusion, as we have seen, was from more elite groups downwards to the rank and file. The predominant flow is clear, reflecting the processes that sociologists have discovered in other fields. Yet, as might be expected, the particular circumstances of Evangelicalism have made the reality of the process far more complex. A sequence of qualifications needs to be made to the overall principle.

Variations in the Pattern

Firstly, the nature of the elite within Evangelicalism deserves attention. Secular societies usually contain more than one type of elite, and so it has

---

25 Bebbington, *Evangelicalism in Modern Britain*, chap. 3. See also 1:3: "Gospel and Culture in British Evangelicalism."
26 Noel Gibbard, *The First Fifty Years: The History of the Evangelical Movement of Wales, 1948–1998* (Bridgend, Glamorgan: Evangelical Press of Wales, 2002).
27 David W. Bebbington, "The Decline and Resurgence of Evangelical Social Reform," in *Evangelical Faith and Public Zeal: Evangelicals and Society in Britain, 1780–1980*, ed. John Wolffe (London: SPCK, 1995), 185, 192.

been in the Evangelical movement. There have been two types of leader, the intellectual and the social. The intellectual group largely consisted of theologians, but also included thinkers in other fields such as Hannah More, the late eighteenth-century friend of Samuel Johnson who wrote novels, improving literature and government propaganda in the wake of the French Revolution.[28] The individuals in this group might be socially superior, as were many of Hannah More's circle such as William Wilberforce, but that was by no means always the case. Writers who exerted considerable sway over the Evangelical world could be people of lowly social standing. One such was T. B. Smithies, the Methodist editor of innumerable journals in the high Victorian years. From 1851 onward he was responsible for the *Band of Hope Review*, the *British Workman*, the *Children's Friend*, the *Infant's Magazine*, the *Friendly Visitor*, the *Family Friend*, the *Weekly Welcome*, the *Band of Mercy Magazine* and the Earlham series of tracts. Smithies, who selected ideas that met the eyes of millions, was originally a humble insurance clerk.[29] Opinion formers need not be figures of fame or fortune.

Yet many were individuals of high social standing. Evangelicalism in its heyday was well staffed by the aristocracy and gentry. Nearly every Victorian subscription list boasted a number of peers at its head. Landowners could exert themselves to ensure the spread of new ideas, especially among their own tenants and in the vicinity of their own estates. Thus in 1853 William Macdonald Macdonald, a laird in the parish of Craig on the east coast of Scotland who belonged to the small but stoutly Evangelical English Episcopal denomination, ensured that good literature circulated in the fishing village of Ferryden by opening a reading room at his own expense. Because the reading room was also a coffee room, Macdonald helped to identify Evangelical religion with the temperance movement, a link that became deep-seated in the community.[30] In the twentieth century J. Arthur Rank, enjoying the income from his flour milling empire, could direct resources to causes of which he approved in Methodism. Believing that films could do good as well as harm, he donated projectors to the churches and took up film-making himself, a decision that led him to help create the British cinema industry and eventually to receive a

---

28 Anne Stott, *Hannah More: The First Victorian* (Oxford: Oxford University Press, 2003).
29 George S. Rowe, *T. B. Smithies (Editor of "The British Workman"): A Memoir* (London: Partridge, 1884), 52–55.
30 Andrew Douglas, *History of the Village of Ferryden*, 2nd ed. (Montrose: The Author, 1857), 55.

peerage.[31] So the social elite of the country at large could be a powerful factor in the spread of new practices. The Evangelical groupings from which novelties proceeded were primarily intellectual circles, but in the second place included people of high social station.

Nor was the popular culture that evolved within Evangelicalism a unitary phenomenon. In reality—and this is the second qualification of the generalization—the attitudes of Evangelicals in the pews were remarkably diverse. It is true that the evidence would suggest that there was little significant division between the sexes in terms of the grasp and observance of Evangelical faith. Female spirituality among Evangelical Nonconformists around the middle of the nineteenth century was virtually indistinguishable from that of their menfolk.[32] Yet there were other lines of demarcation that were sharper. Even within the British Isles, Evangelicals were diverse in nationality. Wales, unlike England, was dominated for much of the period by Nonconformity and Scotland had its own overwhelmingly Presbyterian tone. Evangelical currents flowing powerfully among Anglicans in England were likely to make less impact elsewhere in Britain. Language differences could reinforce barriers to the reception of new ideas. Thus it was believed that the first book to teach premillenialism in the Welsh language was not published until 1919, nearly a century after its equivalent in English.[33] Similarly in the Scottish Highlands the Gaelic language functioned as a preservative of orthodox Calvinism.[34] Theology itself, furthermore, erected obstacles to the spread of novelties. Calvinism in particular could be resistant to fresh ways of thinking, so that, for instance, the Strict and Particular Baptists arose in the early nineteenth century through refusing to accept the doctrinal innovations of the age.[35] Consequently the believers in the pew were often protected from change by national, linguistic and theological defenses. The rank and file remained notably diverse, for by no means all the novel ideas and practices eventually filtered down to everybody.

A third point to be made is that dissemination was not always intentional. Sometimes it was indeed deliberate, with a section of opinion eager to spread some "new teaching." That was true, for example, among Welsh Independents

---

31   David J. Jeremy, *Capitalists and Christians: Business Leaders and the Churches in Britain, 1900-1960* (Oxford: Oxford University Press, 1990), 350-51.

32   Linda Wilson, *Constrained by Zeal: Female Spirituality amongst Nonconformists, 1825-1875* (Carlisle: Paternoster Press, 2000).

33   *Christian*, 6 March 1919, 19.

34   Donald E. Meek, *The Scottish Highlands: The Churches and Gaelic Culture* (Geneva: WCC Publications, 1996), 41.

35   Kenneth Dix, *Strict and Particular: English Strict and Particular Baptists in the Nineteenth Century* (Didcot, Oxfordshire: Baptist Historical Society, 2001).

in the early nineteenth century, who posited a middle way between traditional Calvinism and the Arminianism of the Wesleyan Methodists. Taking up what they called the "New System" from the writings of the theologian Edward Williams, they successfully commended their convictions as well calculated to bring about church growth.[36] In other instances, however, the process of diffusion was unconscious. Because deference was such a potent force in British society, there was much aping of higher social groups by lower ones. Hence in the later nineteenth century, one of the chief factors molding the style of Nonconformist worship in prosperous urban congregations was the imitation of the decency and order of the Church of England, which was perceived as altogether more respectable. By 1869 one Congregational chapel had a communion table emblazoned with the sacred monogram "IHS," two reading desks, a gowned minister, repetition of the Lord's Prayer and the *Te Deum*, and even two "crimson velvet bags" for the offering.[37] The innovations had not been urged on them by the Anglicans; they were simply copied. The process of change could be a matter of the assimilation of attractive options that were in the air.

The general thesis about the flow of influence also needs qualification, fourthly, in respect to its direction. It may normally have been a question of ideas and practices percolating down the social scale, but in some cases the reverse was true. What was at one point confined to the popular level could subsequently be taken up and recommended by leaders of opinion. Thus the distinctive Methodist belief in entire sanctification was in the early nineteenth century a plebeian preoccupation, but from the 1870s it was taken up and propagated by a group of prominent ministers and laymen.[38] The leaders could even find themselves displaced by the led. This was preeminently true in the Welsh Revival of 1904–5, when an obscure candidate for the Calvinistic Methodist ministry, Evan Roberts, became a national hero in the principality. Ministers of great experience deferred to Roberts as he spoke at informal services where dozens were converted. He was, said a contemporary, "like a particle of radium in our midst."[39] It was certainly possible, especially at times of great stirring, for people of powerful influence to emerge from the grassroots of the movement.

A fifth consideration is that, if the downward cultural flow could sometimes be reversed, it could also be modified by the direction becoming predominantly,

---

36 See 1:5: "The Legacy of Jonathan Edwards in Britain."
37 *Freeman*, 16 April 1869, 302.
38 See 2:3: "Entire Sanctification in Methodism during the Nineteenth Century."
39 Eifion Evans, *The Welsh Revival of 1904* (London: Evangelical Press, 1969), 72.

as it were, horizontal rather than vertical, that is at the same social level. Thus the temperance movement, a great enthusiasm of Nonconformist Evangelicals by the opening of the twentieth century, began as a nonreligious movement. It was originally, around the 1830s, a cause beloved by secular-minded artisans wanting to improve themselves, and was frowned on by most Evangelicals as another gospel that threatened the true one. But temperance was steadily adopted by Christians of similar social groups, especially by Primitive Methodists, and eventually total abstinence became de rigueur for chapel membership.[40] This profound change of manners was primarily due to rubbing shoulders with equals. Again, various influences swept into the British Isles from across the Atlantic. Individual communion cups were first adopted instead of a single chalice as a health precaution in 1894 in the United States. Four years later they were introduced at Thorne Congregational Church near Doncaster and from there spread rapidly throughout the chapel world.[41] The sacred solos of Ira D. Sankey, the singing assistant of the evangelist Dwight L. Moody, form a more celebrated example of the reception of American innovations.[42] Thus novelty could be assimilated from abroad. There was therefore a transverse pattern of influence operating on British Evangelicalism, both from outside Evangelicalism and from outside Britain.

Each of these qualifications acts as a caveat against seeing too much uniformity in the process of assimilating fresh influences. The social pattern of the dissemination of innovations within Evangelicalism was therefore predominantly from the elite to the masses, but there were many exceptions to the rule. So long as similar reservations are kept in mind, it is also possible, however, to outline the general geographical dimensions of the process. This is the way in which ideas and practices have spread over space. Although it is closely connected with the analysis in terms of social groups, the topic deserves some consideration in its own right.

Spatial Diffusion

Geographers who have studied the take-up of innovations have decided that a possible explanation is what they call contagion. On this understanding a preference for some novelty is spread, like a disease, as the result of personal

---

40   Brian Harrison, *Drink and the Victorians: The Temperance Question in England, 1815–1872* (London: Faber and Faber, 1971); David W. Bebbington, *The Nonconformist Conscience: Chapel and Politics, 1870–1914* (London: George Allen & Unwin, 1982), 46–51.
41   *Christian World*, 22 November 1894, 871; 9 August 1900, 12; 16 August 1900, 9.
42   John Kent, *Holding the Fort: Studies in Victorian Revivalism* (London: Epworth, 1978), chap. 6. On Moody, see 1:6: "Dwight L. Moody and Transatlantic Evangelicalism."

contact. In a classic account of the diffusion of car ownership in Sweden after the First World War, Torsten Hägerstrand showed that at successive dates the fashion for buying vehicles moved from west to east, from the side of the country facing Denmark to the side facing Finland. The possession of motor cars advanced as fresh Swedes admired the gleaming new vehicles owned by their neighbors.[43] Evangelical processes of diffusion in Britain seem to have followed a comparable pattern. Some areas have usually been early to adopt change, and other areas have normally lagged behind. The place where fresh ideas have normally been most highly favored is London, which, as the capital and the largest city, has been the most likely place for novelties to be broached. From there, they have extended to the South-East of England and then steadily advanced outwards. The resulting pattern approximates to that of center and periphery, a familiar one in historical geography. The spread of charismatic renewal in the earliest period, down to 1963, reflects something of this schema. By that date the new movement had a significant presence in London, the home counties and the South-West, had slightly touched the Midlands and Yorkshire but was virtually unknown in the North-East, the North-West and Wales.[44] Renewal had put down roots near the center, was beginning to affect the inner periphery but had not yet influenced the outer periphery. Contagion would appear to have been at work.

Other geographers, however, have pointed to another spatial process affecting the adoption of novelty. This is the principle of hierarchy, according to which the popularity of innovations is directly related to the size of urban areas. On this interpretation, fresh ways and attitudes would spread from London to the big cities first rather than to immediately adjacent areas, then to rather smaller places and eventually, much later, to rural nooks and crannies. Again, there is some evidence for this pattern appearing in Evangelicalism. To take the same instance as before, renewal was already known in Scottish cities by 1963 when it had not yet reached the northernmost parts of England.[45] Larger places, that is to say, were affected before some of the intermediate territory. Networks of friends, families and former college contacts were at work, linking similar people in different places. Consequently there was a tendency for an urban/rural split to emerge, with cities taking up novelties before the surrounding countryside. This, of course, had been the pattern in the late

---

43   Torsten Hägerstrand, *Innovation Diffusion as a Spatial Process*, trans. Allan Pred (Chicago: University of Chicago Press, 1967).
44   Peter Hocken, *Streams of Renewal: The Origins and Early Development of the Charismatic Movement in Great Britain* (Exeter: Paternoster Press, 1986), 112.
45   Hocken, *Streams of Renewal*, 112.

Roman Empire, when cities were evangelized before their hinterlands, so that the word for countryfolk, *pagani*, became the label for unbelievers, "pagans." Equally, however, it was true of the employment of denominational hymn books among Cambridgeshire Baptists in the early 1970s. The city churches sang from the 1962 edition, the larger village chapels by and large used the 1933 edition and the smaller chapels retained the 1900 edition.[46] The larger the place, the more popular were innovations.

A persuasive case has been made out by the geographer Brian Robson for the reality of spatial diffusion normally being a combination of the two processes that have just been outlined. He shows, for example, that the early take-up of telephones in the late nineteenth century was chiefly round London, the result of contagion, and also in large cities, a symptom of hierarchy.[47] An equivalent pattern is evident at the same time in the foundation of local Councils of the Evangelical Free Churches, a movement that grew largely spontaneously during the 1890s to coordinate the work of the chapels. Most of the earliest Free Church Councils were established in big cities, but then smaller councils were set up in adjacent villages as well as in smaller towns further away. The last parts of the country to be covered by the councils were rural counties without major centers of population, such as Dorset and Westmorland.[48] Evangelical phenomena therefore broadly fit the geographers' models for the spread of innovations over space.

Conclusion

For a full picture of the process of diffusion among Evangelicals, the spatial dimension must be added to the social. Normally, we may conclude, ideas and practices have first been adopted by an intellectual elite, and to a lesser extent a social elite, especially in London. From there they have spread to the educated, the well-to-do and the young, particularly in the cities. In the twentieth century, as urban segregation by status grew, there are signs that the more prosperous suburbs may have been more liable to change than the city centers, for it was there that the most responsive social groups were chiefly to be found. The role of Holy Trinity, Brompton, during the 1990s, as the creator of the Alpha program of evangelism, however, showed that churches in favored parts of inner cities could still have a remarkable capacity for innovation. By contrast, rural areas such as Radnorshire, with congregations that are by and large less well educated, less prosperous and less youthful, have not been notable for

---

46   Personal observation.
47   Brian T. Robson, *Urban Growth: An Approach* (London: Methuen, 1973).
48   Bebbington, *Nonconformist Conscience*, 68.

pathbreaking change. In 2003 the highpoint of the anniversary services of one Baptist chapel in the county was a (very capable) rendition of Sankey solos composed before 1900.[49] The process of diffusion has been neither uniform nor automatic, but it has tended to follow particular lines.

The findings have an application to broader scholarship. Evangelicalism has been a major force in British society, achieving nothing short of cultural dominance in the mid-nineteenth century. Since then it has shrunk to a much smaller element, by 1998 constituting only 2.8 percent of the English population.[50] Nevertheless it is a far from negligible grouping. What academic study of the movement, in its present as well as its past dimensions, needs to take into account is its huge internal variety. When considered at all, Evangelicalism is often treated as monochrome and unchanging. What study of the process of cultural diffusion illustrates is that, since it has been in constant flux, it has proved a remarkably heterogeneous phenomenon. Lifestyle, organization, worship and even theology have regularly been molded and remolded. Emphases have varied over time and space. Some sense of how Evangelicalism has altered is essential if the place of the churches in modern Britain is to be appreciated. It is also essential to the understanding of modern British culture.

---

49 Sarn Baptist Church, from personal observation.
50 *UK Christian Handbook Religious Trends No. 2*, ed. Peter Brierley (London: Harper-Collins, 1999), 123.

II

Evangelicals, Americans and the Wider World

5

The Legacy of Jonathan Edwards in Britain

The name of Jonathan Edwards does not loom large in histories of theology in Britain. The American is usually ignored, as in Bernard Reardon's study of *Religious Thought in the Victorian Age*, or relegated to a single allusion, as in Tudur Jones' *Congregationalism in England, 1662-1962*.[1] By contrast, accounts of parallel developments in the United States give Edwards pride of place. That is true of general overviews such as Mark A. Noll's *America's God* and E. Brooks Holifield's *Theology in America* as well as more specialist works such as Allen C. Guelzo's *Edwards on the Will: A Century of American Theological Debate* and Joseph A. Conforti's *Jonathan Edwards, Religious Tradition & American Culture*, both of which examine the subsequent reputation of the theologian.[2] It is not surprising that American authors should lay stress on a homegrown product, but it is more lamentable that writers about Britain should neglect him. The lacuna may be laid at the door of multiple presuppositions. One is a certain insularity, the silent assumption that Britain was self-contained in its doctrinal concerns, or, if affected at all, then swayed almost exclusively by influences emanating from Germany. Another is that the Church of England led the way in Christian intellectual affairs to

---

1 Bernard M. G. Reardon, *Religious Thought in the Victorian Age: A Survey from Coleridge to Gore* (London: Longman, 1980); Robert Tudur Jones, *Congregationalism in England, 1662-1962* (London: Independent Press, 1962), 170.
2 Mark A. Noll, *America's God: From Jonathan Edwards to Abraham Lincoln* (New York: Oxford University Press, 2002); E. Brooks Holifield, *Theology in America: Christian Thought from the Age of the Puritans to the Civil War* (New Haven, CT: Yale University Press, 2003); Allen C. Guelzo, *Edwards on the Will: A Century of American Theological Debate* (Middletown, CT: Wesleyan University Press, 1989); Joseph A. Conforti, *Jonathan Edwards, Religious Tradition and American Culture* (Chapel Hill, NC: University of North Carolina Press, 1995).

the extent that patterns of thinking in other denominations were of little or no importance. And a third is that what mattered in Anglican thought in the nineteenth century was the emergence of the Oxford Movement and of liberal theology because they shaped the developments of the twentieth century, a belief that has discouraged the scrutiny of Evangelical thought at the time. All these notions may be detected in Reardon's lucid book on Victorian theology, the standard work of a previous generation. Yet in reality British readers frequently absorbed American texts, which after all were written in their own language. Many of these readers were outside the Church of England, for at mid-century nearly half the population at worship in England and Wales was Nonconformist and Scotland was overwhelmingly Presbyterian. And Evangelicalism, though it was to be eclipsed during the twentieth century, was in the ascendant in British society at large during much of the nineteenth century. Hence at that period an American who was a non-Anglican Evangelical was likely to enjoy a wide influence. Despite the general neglect of Jonathan Edwards in the literature, his legacy to subsequent generations in Britain is amply worth exploring.

The near silence about Edwards in nineteenth-century Britain contrasts starkly with contemporary opinion. The two Congregationalists who edited the first collection of Edwards' works, which appeared in 1806-11 in Britain rather than in America, could assert that the theologian "ranks with the brightest luminaries of the Christian church, not excluding any country, or any age since the apostolic."[3] If that bold claim might be considered the partisan appraisal of coreligionists, we can point to the judgment of Henry Rogers, the editor of a more popular selection from Edwards' works issued in 1834, that the American was "held in profound veneration by thinking men of all parties."[4] This selection reached a twelfth edition by 1879, demonstrating the wide circulation of the texts composed by Edwards. Rogers' verdict is further confirmed by the publications of the Religious Tract Society (RTS), a pan-Evangelical agency that printed much of the popular Christian literature of the time. The society put into print a range of titles by Jonathan Edwards. It published *Sinners in the Hands of an Angry God* by 1831; *The History of Redemption* appeared that year, followed two years later by *Select Sermons of President Edwards*; the *Exchange of Christ* and the *Life of David Brainerd*

---

3   *The Works of President Edwards*, ed. Edward Williams and Edward Parsons, 8 vols. (London: For James Black and Son, 1817), 1:iv.

4   Henry Rogers, "An Essay on the Genius and Writings of Jonathan Edwards," in *The Works of Jonathan Edwards, A. M.*, 12th ed. (London: William Tegg & Co., 1879), i. Again, however, Rogers was a Congregationalist.

came out around the same time; and at about mid-century the society went so far as to publish the *Treatise Concerning Religious Affections* in five hundred pages, an exceptionally long book for it to put on its list.[5] As late as the 1880s the society issued *Pardon for the Greatest Sinners* and a life of Edwards in its "New Biographical Series."[6] There was clearly a demand for the writings of the theologian and even an interest in his own story down to around 1890. By comparison the American Tract Society, the equivalent of the RTS in the United States, removed Edwards from its publication lists in 1892.[7] We can therefore conclude that British attention to the American lasted virtually as long as in his own country.

Edwards appealed to the British public not just because he was a profound explorer of Christian doctrine. As the titles printed by the RTS suggest, he was valued as a stirring preacher who could challenge unbelievers. His life of Brainerd, the pioneer evangelist among the Native Americans, exercised a fascination over a missionary-minded public. And his warm encouragement of spiritual experience, as in the *Treatise Concerning Religious Affections*, acted as an aid to devotion. This book was, according to Rogers, "one of the most valuable works on practical and experimental piety ever published."[8] Yet it was as an authority shaping theological discourse that his influence was greatest. The Edwardsean paradigm was the framework within which a great deal of nineteenth-century theology was conceived. The doctrinal inheritance of Calvinist teaching remained powerful within most of the non-Anglican denominations, whether in England, Scotland or Wales. For the ministers in the Calvinist traditions of the Baptists, Independents and Presbyterians, the great task was to adapt their received body of doctrine to the currents of thought associated with the Enlightenment. The fresh ideas associated with light, liberty and progress needed to be accommodated if the message of the gospel was to receive a hearing. Edwards taught that new light dawned in revival, that liberty was compatible with necessity and that the Almighty willed the progress of the gospel for the welfare of humanity. So Edwards defended Calvinism in a way intellectually acceptable to the age. British preachers appreciated the writings of others associated with Edwards

---

5   Thomas H. Johnson, *The Printed Works of Jonathan Edwards, 1703–1758: A Bibliography* (Princeton, NJ: Princeton University Press, 1940), xi, 26, 91, 106, 96, 59, 43.
6   Jonathan Edwards, *Pardon for the Greatest Sinners* (London: Religious Tract Society, 1882); John Radford Thomson, *Jonathan Edwards* (London: Religious Tract Society, 1889).
7   Conforti, *Edwards, Religious Tradition and American Culture*, 143.
8   Rogers, "Essay," xlvii.

for the same reason. In particular Joseph Bellamy's *True Religion Delineated* (1750), with its teaching of a governmental theory of the atonement, gained widespread endorsement. "Were I forced to part with all mere human compositions but three," wrote John Ryland, later president of Bristol Baptist Academy, in 1790, "Edwards' 'Life of Brainerd,' his 'Treatise on Religious Affections,' and Bellamy's 'True Religion Delineated,' ... would be the last I should let go."[9] So it might be more accurate to speak of an Edwardsean legacy rather than simply the legacy of Edwards. But it is plain that this mode of thinking provided the way in which Evangelical Calvinists in Britain conceptualized their ideas.

The Reception of Edwards

The British reception of Edwards began during the eighteenth century. He first came to notice as a spokesman of revival. His *Faithful Narrative* (1737) was initially published in London, not America, and by 1750 ran to as many as seven British editions. John Wesley, though a stern foe of Calvinism, enthusiastically abridged Edwards' books relating to religious revival, including several of them in the Christian Library he commended to his Methodist followers. A circle of Scottish Presbyterian ministers identified with revival became Edwards' enthusiastic correspondents and one of them, John Erskine, minister of Old Greyfriars, Edinburgh, turned into his chief promoter globally, sending his writings to the Netherlands and Germany as well as England. It was Erskine who worked up a set of Edwards' sermons into the *History of the Work of Redemption*, first published in Edinburgh in 1774.[10] Erskine also drew the attention of the Particular Baptists of the English East Midlands to Edwards' writings. John Ryland was at the heart of a group of ministers in the Northamptonshire Baptist Association who were fired by the American's vision. In 1784 they issued an English edition of Edwards' *Humble Attempt* and, in accordance with its principles, recommended monthly prayer meetings for the advance of the gospel throughout the world. It was from this circle that William Carey emerged to found in 1792 the Baptist Missionary Society, the first of the Anglo-American missions.[11] Through this British initiative, the modern missionary movement can claim Jonathan Edwards as its spiritual progenitor.

---

9   John Ryland to Joseph Kinghorn, 1790, in Martin H. Wilkin, *Joseph Kinghorn of Norwich* (Norwich: Fletcher and Alexander, 1855), 183.
10 Jonathan Yeager, *Enlightened Evangelicalism: The Life and Thought of John Erskine* (New York: Oxford University Press, 2011), 171–72.
11 Brian Stanley, *The History of the Baptist Missionary Society, 1792–1992* (Edinburgh: T&T Clark, 1992), 4–6.

Edwards' theological influence, however, was much more widespread. A survey of its dimensions from the later eighteenth century onwards can usefully begin with the Baptists. During their early years in the seventeenth century, the Particular Baptists had found no difficulty in reconciling their Reformed beliefs with evangelistic practice, but in the following century many of their ministers, especially in London, adopted a higher form of Calvinism. The sovereignty of God, they believed, entailed the belief that the Almighty would unquestionably bring about his purpose of gathering the elect into his church. Human intervention seemed unnecessary, even impious. Free offers of the gospel from the pulpit seemed subversive of their confidence in divine providence. Yet preachers wanted to lead their hearers to salvation. How could they proclaim the need for repentance and faith without infringing their Calvinist convictions? Jonathan Edwards provided a solution to their dilemma through the distinction between natural and moral inability in his *Freedom of the Will*. Human beings, according to Edwards, possessed the natural ability to believe the gospel. If they had suffered from natural inability, they would have been made by an arbitrary Creator with no opportunity for salvation, a charge often mounted by opponents of Calvinism. Instead, Edwards argued, some people showed a moral inability to embrace the gospel. Their refusal to repent and embrace the salvation offered them was the result of their own persistence in sin and so their eventual perdition was their own responsibility. Everybody was summoned to believe and so preachers could call on their hearers to respond. The message was one of "duty faith." Ministers therefore need have no inhibitions about making every effort to spread the gospel. Not only could they make free offers from the pulpit; they could also undertake fresh measures like the missionary society. The Reformed faith was rendered consistent with vigorous evangelism.

Baptists

The most significant disseminator of the resulting Evangelical Calvinism among the Baptists was Andrew Fuller. As a leading member of the Northamptonshire Baptist Association, Fuller participated in the excitement of discovering Edwards' ideas during the 1770s. In 1785 he published *The Gospel Worthy of All Acceptation*, which was built on the contrast between natural and moral inability. The distinction, Fuller explained, was "calculated to disburden the Calvinistic system of a number of calumnies with which its opponents have loaded it."[12] He argued that all hearers of the gospel were under an obligation

---

12 Andrew Fuller, *The Gospel Worthy of All Acceptation*, preface, in H. Leon McBeth, *A Sourcebook for Baptist Heritage* (Nashville, TN: Broadman Press, 1990), 133.

to believe and so all preachers should make free offers of salvation. This was the theology of the Baptist Missionary Society, of which Fuller became secretary. He went further than Edwards in modifying his Calvinist inheritance. In debate after the publication of *The Gospel Worthy*, Fuller went on to accept that in one sense the atonement was universal in scope. The work of Christ, he held, was sufficient for all. Yet he did not move from the traditional Calvinist belief that only the elect would be saved, for the application of the atonement depended on "the sovereign pleasure of God."[13] Thus, although Fuller's position was not identical with Edwards', he was still defending a form of Calvinism. Moreover he retained his admiration for the American until the end of his life. In his last letter to John Ryland before his own death in 1815, Fuller wrote that if critics of Edwards' theology "preached Christ half as much as Jonathan Edwards did . . . their usefulness would be double what it is."[14] Although exercising freedom as a theologian, Fuller was loyal to the Edwardsean paradigm.

Other men played a similar part to Fuller. During the eighteenth-century tendency towards a higher type of Calvinism, Bristol Baptist Academy, the only denominational seminary in the country, had preserved a more moderate form that did nothing to discourage evangelism. Already in 1772 its president, Caleb Evans, was teaching the difference between natural and moral inability on the basis of Edwards' *Freedom of the Will*.[15] Evans' successor as president, John Ryland, was a particularly zealous advocate of the Edwardsean standpoint. In 1780 he published the theologian's sermon on "The Excellency of Christ" at the low price of fourpence each or "3 shillings per Dozen to those who give them away."[16] He even called his sons "David Brainerd Ryland" and "Jonathan Edwards Ryland."[17] The students who passed through the academy in preparation for Baptist ministry, roughly two hundred in the period of Ryland's presidency from 1793 to 1825, were imbued with the theology of Edwards. Ryland's assistant in his last seven years and subsequently his successor, Thomas Crisp, adopted exactly the same point of view. So did two of the products of the academy who went on to be founding presidents of the next two Baptist academies to be established. William Steadman built up Horton Academy near Bradford

---

13 Andrew Fuller, "Three Conversations," in *The Complete Works of the Rev. Andrew Fuller*, ed. Andrew G. Fuller, 5 vols. (London: Holdsworth and Ball, 1832), 2:520.
14 Andrew Fuller to John Ryland, 28 April 1815, in John Ryland, *Life and Death of the Rev. Andrew Fuller* (Charlestown, MA: Samuel Etheridge, 1818), 332–33.
15 Roger Hayden, *Continuity and Change: Evangelical Calvinism among Eighteenth-Century Baptist Ministers Trained at Bristol Baptist Academy, 1690–1791* (Milton under Wychwood, Oxfordshire: Nigel Lynn, 2006), 125.
16 Johnson, *Printed Works*, 95.
17 Conforti, *Edwards, Religious Tradition and American Culture*, 69.

to be a powerhouse of evangelism in the North of England between 1805 and 1835; and William Newman did the same for Stepney Academy between 1810 and 1826, making it a center for the diffusion of moderate Calvinism in London and its vicinity. These men did not offer varied theological standpoints, wanting students to evaluate their relative merits with a critical eye. On the contrary, they taught dogmatically and required acquiescence. Crisp, for example, according to the memories of one of his students, when conducting examinations "looked rather for an exact repetition of what he had said than for our own impressions."[18] College-trained Baptist ministers of the early nineteenth century were uniformly shaped in an Edwardsean mold.

The transition from a high Calvinism to the moderate version represented by Edwards was sharply contested in Wales. The first Baptist academy to be set up in Wales, at Abergavenny in 1807, had another Bristol graduate trained by John Ryland, Micah Thomas, as its president. Thomas was a keen advocate of the Edwardsean approach to theology as embodied in Fuller's writings. As a result he was charged by the high Calvinists of south Wales as veering towards Arminianism. In 1811 he published a sermon called *Salvation of Sovereign Grace* in order, as he put it, to "refute groundless insinuations."[19] The rumors of his defection from sound doctrine, however, continued to circulate and in 1834 critics were given ammunition by five disaffected students. They complained that at worship he used John Wesley's notes on scripture, claiming that they were superior to the comments of John Gill, the doughty eighteenth-century champion of high Calvinist orthodoxy among the Baptists. The affair was complicated by petty attacks on Thomas for refusing permission for students to attend the local Welsh society and requiring residents to be in their rooms by 8 p.m. The resulting controversy brought down the academy. The local Baptist association refused further financial support, a rival institution was planned, Thomas resigned, the academy closed and a new institution had to be created elsewhere, at Pontypool. There, under a president trained at Stepney and a tutor from Bristol Academy, the position of Edwards, Fuller and the newer Calvinism was reinstated.[20] This episode reveals clearly that contemporaries recognized the sharp difference between the model of theology propounded by Gill and the type associated with Edwards. Micah Thomas contrasted the two. The point of view embodied in Gill's thought was "that

---

18 Frederick Trestrail, *Reminiscences of College Life in Bristol* (London: E. Marlboro and Co., 1879), 22.
19 D. Mervyn Himbury, *The South Wales Baptist College (1807–1957)* (Cardiff: South Wales Baptist College, 1957), 22.
20 Himbury, *South Wales Baptist College*, 31–43.

stringent and exclusive system" which was designed "to guarantee the orthodoxy of the preacher," differing from "the universally benign atmosphere of that blessed economy, which is . . . 'good tidings of great joy to all people.'"[21] In the end this warm-hearted Edwardseanism triumphed.

The newer pattern was enduring among the Baptists. It is true that the older style of Calvinism remained strong in areas other than Wales. In East Anglia, for example, a body of Strict and Particular Baptists separated from the associations that endorsed Fullerism, denouncing duty faith unsparingly.[22] It is also true that a newer form of anti-confessional teaching began to outflank Edwards' moderate brand of Calvinism. Some began to propose that the Bible only was a sufficient grounding for a preachable theology. At Regent's Park College, the new president inducted in 1844, Benjamin Davies, a biblical scholar, refused to teach systematic theology, preferring to approach doctrine only through biblical exegesis.[23] At Horton Academy, James Acworth, president from 1836 to 1863, who was described as "impatient of system and formulas," urged his students to make "your own system" based on study of the word of God.[24] Yet the prevailing mode of theological instruction remained indebted to Edwards. Joseph Angus, president of Regent's Park from 1849, reverted to having first- and second-year students read two of Fuller's works.[25] Angus was still endorsing the views of Edwards and Bellamy on the tests of regeneration as late as 1895.[26] When Charles Spurgeon, the great preacher at what from 1861 became the Metropolitan Tabernacle, took up the task of ministerial training six years earlier, he insisted that Calvinistic teaching should be given in his college. Despite Spurgeon's love of seventeenth-century Puritan writings, the type of Calvinism inculcated was that of Edwards. The principal of Spurgeon's institution from 1881 to 1893, David Gracey, recommended Edwards rather than Charles Hodge, the American Presbyterian exponent of a higher Calvinism, on the subject of the imputation of sin. Gracey quoted

---

21 Himbury, *South Wales Baptist College*, 36.
22 Tim Grass, *"There My Friends and Kindred Dwell": The Strict Baptist Chapels of Suffolk and Norfolk* (Ramsey, Isle of Man: Thornhill Media, 2012).
23 Robert E. Cooper, *From Stepney to St Giles': The Story of Regent's Park College, 1810–1960* (London: Carey Kingsgate Press, 1960), 52; *Report of the Committee of the Baptist College at Stepney for MDCCCXLIV* (London: H. Teape and Son, 1844), 8.
24 William Medley, *Centenary Memorial of Rawdon Baptist College* (London: Kingsgate Press, 1904), 26.
25 *Report of the Committee of the Baptist College at Stepney for MDCCCLIV* (London: H. Teape and Son, 1854), 9.
26 Joseph Angus, *Six Lectures on Regeneration* (London: Alexander and Shepheard, 1897), 68.

Edwards with approval and praised the American's theological method.[27] Many of the Baptists remained attached to the outlook of Edwards down to the end of the nineteenth century and beyond.

Congregationalists

The same is true of the Congregationalists. The figure among them equivalent to Andrew Fuller among the Baptists was Edward Williams, president of Oswestry Academy from 1781 to 1791 and of Rotherham Academy from 1795 down to his death in 1813. It was Williams who, with Edward Parsons, produced the first collected edition of Jonathan Edwards' works. The notes, signed "W," were from Williams' pen, recasting Edwards' often ungainly prose into a more assimilable form. "There is," Williams remarks at one point in a note to a sentence by Edwards, "a little intricacy in this mode of expression," before going on to give a concrete illustration of the point.[28] Readers were undoubtedly helped in their understanding. "I esteem EDWARDS'S works," wrote a correspondent from Wales, "a far more valuable possession, on account of your notes."[29] Williams concentrated particularly on passages in *Freedom of the Will* explaining the nub issue of the relationship between liberty and necessity. Arminians, he points out at one point, wrongly supposed that "to allow *any* kind of necessity, is the same as to allow an infallible *decree*."[30] Edwards showed, however, that events need not be decreed even though they are caused. Human beings could be at once necessitated by causes and free in their actions. This principle, Williams explained in his *Essay on the Equity of the Divine Government* (1809), was the kernel of the defense of Calvinism against its detractors. He was faithfully reproducing Edwards' central contention. The point is repeated in his other weighty book, *A Defence of Modern Calvinism* (1812). Reading Williams was said to have reclaimed whole churches in England from a higher Calvinism.[31] Just as Fuller persuaded many Baptists to adopt Edwards' version of the faith, so Williams convinced a large number of Congregationalists.

Because Williams was Welsh, his writings made a particular impact in the principality. One of Williams' former students, John Roberts of Llanbrynmair,

---

27 David Gracey, *Sin and the Unfolding of Salvation* (London: Passmore and Alabaster, 1894), 109, 118, 28.
28 *Works of President Edwards*, ed. Williams and Parsons, 1:187.
29 John Roberts to Edward Williams, 20 July 1808, in Joseph Gilbert, *Memoir of the Life and Writings of the Late Edward Williams, D.D.* (London: For Francis Westley, 1825), 440.
30 *Works of President Edwards*, ed. Williams and Parsons, 1:241.
31 Gilbert, *Edward Williams*, 467.

Montgomeryshire, spread his tutor's views in the Welsh language. In 1807 Roberts published a *Friendly Address* to Arminians arguing that they mistook the claims of Calvinists such as himself. They did not contend that the Almighty was the author of perdition, but that human beings were themselves responsible for their everlasting loss.[32] The principle reflected Edwards' teaching on natural and moral inability. Two years later Roberts showed the source of his views by issuing extracts from Edwards' *Religious Affections*.[33] His next publication, called a *Humble Attempt*, again drew, even in its title, from Edwards. His central case this time, in the manner of Fuller, was that the benefits of the atonement are universal.[34] Roberts was advocating a moderate Calvinist body of theology, differing both from the Arminianism of the Wesleyan Methodists and the high Calvinism that prevailed in Wales. He identified it as identical with Edward Williams' position, reporting to his former tutor that hundreds of "our poor Welsh pious people" approved his views.[35] This "New System," as it was called, grew rapidly in favor and gave the impetus to the rapid expansion of the Congregationalists in North Wales. In the south of the principality David Davies, tutor at the college in Carmarthen from 1835 to 1855, did much to propagate the views of Williams.[36] The high standing of Edwards in the estimation of the school of Edward Williams gave rise to a demand for the publication of Edwards' works in Welsh. A succession of titles appeared: the *History of Redemption* in 1829, the *Religious Affections* in 1833, the *Freedom of the Will* in 1865, the *Two Dissertations* at about the same time and *Original Sin* in 1870.[37] Each of them was translated by a Congregational minister. Virtually the whole Welsh denomination became committed to the standpoint of Jonathan Edwards.

The most distinguished student of Edward Williams was John Pye Smith, tutor at the Congregationalists' Homerton Academy in London from 1800 onwards and its president from 1806 to 1850. Pye Smith was most celebrated for his book *The Scripture Testimony to the Messiah* (1818–21), a powerful refutation of Unitarian belief, but he was a remarkable polymath, publishing on geology and the Bible in 1839 and mounting a reasoned defense of pacifism

---

32   William Evans, *An Outline of the History of Welsh Theology* (London: James Nisbet and Co., 1900), 126.
33   John Roberts, *Cyfarwyddiadau ac Anogaethau i Gredinwyr . . . a Gasglwyd yn Benauf Allan o Waith Jonathan Edwards* (Bala: R. Sanderson, 1809). I am grateful to Professor Densil Morgan for this reference.
34   Evans, *Welsh Theology*, 131–32.
35   Gilbert, *Edward Williams*, 442.
36   *The Dictionary of Welsh Biography down to 1940* (Oxford: B. H. Blackwell, 1959), 114.
37   Johnson, *Printed Works*, 90, 43, 71, 82, 76.

before it became respectable.[38] He thought nothing of delivering a lecture at the opening of a series on the divine decrees in 1832 with an elaborate statement about the gradual communication of revelation. His diary records that on that occasion he gave an "account of the theory of Spinoza, Simon, Beck, De Wette, Vater, Gesenius, Gramberg, & Hartman, concerning the O. T."[39] Pye Smith continued Williams' enterprise of propagating Edwards' views. The London tutor's regular lectures on systematic theology made frequent reference to Edwards' collected works but also to other writings, the *Miscellaneous Observations* (1793) and the *Remarks on Important Theological Controversies* (1796). Pye Smith endeavored to explain Edwards' terminology in language more comprehensible to his students, for example by turning the American's definition of virtue as "love for being in general" into "voluntary obedience to the known will of God." In his zeal to communicate the substance of Edwards' teaching, he went so far as to criticize Edward Williams' notes. His admiration for Edwards shines through the lectures. On natural depravity he comments that "President Edwards has so established and elucidated the subject as, in my humble opinion, to leave no just ground for doubt." Since Pye Smith also valued the piety of the New Englander, he also recommended his students to read Edwards' resolutions for life "*frequently*, and with *self-application*."[40] Because of his role in teaching students for half a century, the influence of Pye Smith was pervasive in his denomination. Two of the first three tutors at the Lancashire Independent College, founded in 1843 to strengthen Congregational witness in the North-West of England, were Pye Smith's trainees.[41] In the next decade Pye Smith's bust was placed in the new library of Spring Hill College, Birmingham.[42] When one of his former students went out with the London Missionary Society to India, a portrait of Pye Smith was the most conspicuous object in the drawing room of the missionary's home in Bangalore.[43] This highly influential figure cast his weight behind the intellectual synthesis provided by Edwards.

---

38 Geoffrey F. Nuttall, *New College, London, and Its Library* (London: Dr Williams' Trust, 1977), 10.
39 Diary of John Pye Smith, Congregational Library, London, L/18/23, 26 March 1832.
40 John Pye Smith, *First Principles of Christian Theology*, ed. William Farrer (London: Jackson and Walford, 1854), 354, 155, 389, 5.
41 Frederick J. Powicke, *David Worthington Simon* (London: Hodder & Stoughton, 1912), 77.
42 Elaine Kaye, *Mansfield College, Oxford: Its Origin, History and Significance* (Oxford: Oxford University Press, 1995), 20.
43 Edward P. Rice, *Benjamin Rice or Fifty Years in the Master's Service* (London: Religious Tract Society, 1888), 20.

It is true that the sway of Edwards was not uniform across Congregationalism. Thus when F. J. Falding was inaugurated as president of its Rotherham College in 1853, he declared "his decided preference for the older English theology."[44] By that he meant Owen and Howe, Bunyan and Baxter, the Puritan divines of the age before Edwards. Others, such as the prominent publicist John Campbell, shared a taste for the Puritans.[45] Again, in the 1860s candidates for Airedale College were expected to show some knowledge of A. A. Hodge's *Outlines of Theology*, which inculcated a much sterner form of Calvinism than that of the New England school stemming from Edwards.[46] Yet the predominant debt of Congregational theologians for much of the century was to the Edwardsean approach. David Bogue, president of Gosport Academy in Hampshire, referred to Edwards more than to any other author in his lectures and, as the chief trainer of candidates for the London Missionary Society in the first quarter of the century, laid stress on the life of Brainerd as an exemplar.[47] George Payne, tutor of the Western Academy in Exeter and then Plymouth from 1829 to 1848, was deeply swayed by Edward Williams, with whom he corresponded before 1812, and owed much directly to Edwards. Payne's *Lectures on Divine Sovereignty, Election, the Atonement, Justification and Regeneration*, published in 1836, the year he held the chair of the Congregational Union, transmitted the same outlook to others.[48] Ralph Wardlaw, who taught at the Glasgow Congregational Academy from 1811, produced the nearest approximation to an Edwardsean body of divinity for Congregationalism in his *Systematic Theology* (1856–57), and his three-volume treatise was used at both Airedale and Lancashire Independent Colleges shortly after publication.[49] But perhaps the greatest Congregational advocate of Edwards was Henry Rogers, an erudite man with an attractive personality who briefly in the 1830s held the chair of English Language and Literature at the new University College, London, before going on to the Congregational Spring

---

44 *British Banner*, 21 September 1853, 681.
45 Robert Ferguson and A. Morton Brown, *Life and Labours of John Campbell* (London: Richard Bentley, 1867), 404.
46 Lucy A. Fraser, *Memoirs of Daniel Fraser, M.A., LL.D. (Glasgow)* (London: Percy Lund, Humphries & Co., 1905), 71.
47 David Bogue, Lectures on Theology, Congregational Library, London, L14/3. I am grateful to Dr Cullen Clark for this reference.
48 Kaye, *Mansfield College*, 17.
49 Ralph Wardlaw, *Systematic Theology*, 3 vols. (Edinburgh: A. and C. Black, 1856–57); Kaye, *Mansfield College*, 108; *Lancashire Independent College ... Report ... 1859* (Manchester: Septimus Fletcher, 1860), 10.

Hill College, Birmingham, (1840) and Lancashire Independent College (1858), where he served as president. Unusually for a Dissenter, Rogers was accepted as a man of letters in society at large.[50] Consequently his edition of Edwards' works, the standard Victorian version, containing a discriminating introductory essay, was a respected monument to the American theologian. It confirmed the importance of Edwards to the British branches of the denomination to which he had belonged.

Presbyterians and Anglicans

In Scottish Presbyterianism the reputation of Edwards had been established by John Erskine during the eighteenth century, but it was Thomas Chalmers, the leader of the Evangelical party within the Church of Scotland in the early nineteenth century, who did most to disseminate the perspective of the American. As a student at St Andrews University Chalmers grappled with the *Freedom of the Will*, a text valued by his professor of divinity, George Hill, who, though not an Evangelical, saw Edwards as a capable champion of Reformed doctrine, especially on original sin.[51] After Chalmers' subsequent embracing of Evangelical faith, Edwards came alive for him. "The American divine," Chalmers wrote in 1821, "affords, perhaps, the most wondrous example, in modern times, of one who stood richly gifted both in natural and in spiritual discernment." Edwards combined "deep philosophy" with a "humble and child-like piety," showing that Evangelicals could deploy an acute intelligence in the service of the gospel.[52] Like so many of his contemporaries, Chalmers found in Edwards the solution to the resolution of the debate between freedom and necessity and so a vindication of moderate Calvinism.[53] There was no book he recommended more strenuously, he avowed, than Edwards' *Freedom of the Will*.[54] As professor of divinity at Edinburgh from 1828 to 1843 and afterwards as the undisputed leader of the Free Church of Scotland, Chalmers set the doctrinal tone of Scottish Presbyterianism. His influence extended more widely, too. Chalmers' *Prelections*, in which he argued for Edwards against his own former professor Hill, was used in 1854 at the Congregationalists' New College

---

50   *Congregationalist* 6 (1877), 654–64.
51   George Hill, *Lectures in Divinity*, 3 vols. (Edinburgh: For Waugh and Innes, 1821), 2:372, 3:101.
52   Thomas Chalmers, *The Christian and Civic Economy of Large Towns*, 3 vols. in 1 (Glasgow: For William Collins, n.d.), 1:318.
53   Thomas Chalmers, "Edwards' Inquiry, with Introductory Essay," *Presbyterian Review* 2 (1831), 252–53.
54   Conforti, *Edwards, Religious Tradition and American Culture*, 52.

in London.⁵⁵ Joseph Angus, who was to lead Regent's Park College for the Baptists and take a favorable view of Edwards, attended Chalmers' lectures in Edinburgh.⁵⁶ Lewis Edwards, a theologian who came to exercise unparalleled sway over the Calvinistic Methodists of Wales, also studied at Edinburgh and made Chalmers his hero.⁵⁷ Chalmers reinforced the sway of Jonathan Edwards over theological minds throughout Britain.

The Presbyterians of Scotland showed an enduring appreciation of Edwards. Two extra volumes of the theologian's works were published in Edinburgh to add to the Edward Williams edition in 1847 and they were reissued in 1875.⁵⁸ The practical and devotional works also appeared in fresh editions from the Scottish press. The *Life of Brainerd*, which stimulated the Scottish minister Robert Murray McCheyne to throw himself into missionary work, was republished in five new Scottish editions between 1824 and 1851.⁵⁹ Edwards' *Religious Affections* was widely valued by the Presbyterians of the middle years of the century.⁶⁰ The Evangelical Calvinism of Edwards, as transmitted through Chalmers, continued to exercise its sway. William Cunningham, Chalmers' successor as principal of New College, the Free Church institution in Edinburgh, praised Edwards' "great work on Original Sin."⁶¹ In resisting the critique of Calvinism by Sir William Hamilton, the leading Scottish philosopher of his day, Cunningham denied on Edwardsean grounds that necessity implied fatalism. Yet, he surmised, the doctrine of necessity did seem likely, because the argument of Edwards against the self-determining power of the will had not been answered.⁶² Cunningham's colleague in New College, John Duncan, expressed his admiration that "Jonathan Edwards and the New-Englanders" managed to combine the elements of law and ethics that other theologians prized apart. Edwards, he believed, contained elements of pantheism, a view that, because of early sympathies

---

55 Thomas Chalmers, *Prelections on Butler's Analogy, Paley's Evidences of Christianity and Hill's Lectures in Divinity* (Edinburgh: Sutherland and Knox, 1849), 131; *New College, London . . . Report . . . 1854* (n.p.: no pub., 1854), 8.
56 Ian Randall, *"Conscientious Conviction:" Joseph Angus (1816–1902) and Nineteenth-Century Baptist Life* (Oxford: Regent's Park College, 2010), 2.
57 *Dictionary of Welsh Biography*, 191.
58 Johnson, *Printed Works*, 112.
59 Andrew A. Bonar, *Memoir and Remains of the Rev. Robert Murray M'Cheyne* (Dundee: William Middleton, 1844), 19; Johnson, *Printed Works*, 54–58.
60 *Congregationalist and Christian World*, 3 October 1903, 467.
61 William Cunningham, *Historical Theology*, 2 vols. (Edinburgh: T and T Clark, 1870), 1:339.
62 William Cunningham, *The Reformers and the Theology of the Reformation* (Edinburgh: T and T Clark, 1862), 471, 512.

for that position, Duncan appreciated.⁶³ Nineteenth-century Presbyterians respected Edwards for a variety of reasons, but there is no doubt that he continued to occupy a firm place in their affections.

The Church of England had a less vigorous tradition of Reformed theology. Despite the firm attachment of its Reformers and many subsequent seventeenth-century divines to Calvinist doctrine, in the eighteenth century the principles of Calvin were associated with the Puritans who had killed King Charles I. Consequently the early Evangelicals who adopted a Calvinist position commonly played down their allegiance, preferring to stress their loyalty to Bible teaching. Jonathan Edwards also seemed too much of a metaphysician for many of them. John Newton, the former slave ship captain who became one of the most influential Evangelical clergy, at first enthused over Edwards, but subsequently regretted recommending his *Freedom of the Will* because the American school was too addicted to "Scheme, System, & Notion."⁶⁴ Thomas Scott, known as a biblical commentator but also a writer on doctrine, explained the distinction between natural and moral inability in a way clearly indebted to Edwards, and yet avoided mentioning the American.⁶⁵ One of the Evangelical Anglicans most attached to Edwards was Isaac Taylor, a *littérateur* of interdenominational sympathies, who in 1831 issued an edition of the *Freedom of the Will* which compared the American's "athletic force of intellect" to that of Aristotle. He went further. "We claim Edwards as an *Englishman*," he wrote: "he was such in every respect but the accident of birth in a distant province of the empire."⁶⁶ Taylor praised Edwards for redeeming Calvinistic doctrines from scorn, yet was wary of the abstract metaphysics so prominent in the New Englander's pages. The controversy over free will, Taylor claimed, did not affect common life. Nor had Edwards settled the debate with the Arminians. Instead pious Calvinists and pious Arminians, Taylor predicted, would meet on the common ground of the Bible.⁶⁷ Taylor held similar views to those of Charles Simeon, the Cambridge don who set the course of mainstream Anglican Evangelicals in the first half of the nineteenth century. Simeon repudiated the theoretical structure of Calvinism for the sake of insisting on the teaching

---

63 David Brown, *Life of the Late John Duncan, LL.D.* (Edinburgh: Edmonston and Douglas, 1872), 69.
64 Bruce Hindmarsh, *John Newton and the English Evangelical Tradition: Between the Conversions of Wesley and Wilberforce* (Oxford: Clarendon Press, 1996), 167, 154.
65 Thomas Scott, *Remarks on the Doctrines of Original Sin, Grace, Free-Will, Justification by Faith, Election and Reprobation, and the Final Perseverance of the Saints*, 2nd ed. (London: A. Macintosh, 1817), 94.
66 Isaac Taylor, "Introductory Essay," in Jonathan Edwards, *An Inquiry into the Modern Prevailing Notions Respecting the Freedom of the Will* (London: James Duncan, 1831), xx, xxi n.
67 Taylor, "Introductory Essay," xxv, xxvi, xlii, lii.

of scripture alone. "Be Bible Christians," he urged, "not system Christians."[68] For most Evangelicals in the Church of England, Edwards did not erect the theological framework of their thinking that was so powerful among non-Anglicans.

Yet the relative weakness of Edwards' doctrinal influence does not mean that Anglicans failed to value him. The *Life of Brainerd* was the inspiration for the quixotic journey of Henry Martyn as a pioneer missionary to Iran.[69] Through Martyn's example, Brainerd became the model for many another Anglican missionary of the nineteenth century. Josiah Pratt, secretary of the Church Missionary Society from 1802 to 1824, abridged Edwards' *Life of Brainerd* for publication and his successor as secretary, Edward Bickersteth, issued a fresh edition in 1834.[70] The other text by Edwards to achieve wide popularity among Anglicans was the *Religious Affections*. In 1802 William Wilberforce found it an "excellent book." It used "simple and clear" reasoning to make "close scrutiny of the heart, and accurate observations of its workings."[71] Charles Bradley, shortly to become incumbent at St John's, Clapham, through Wilberforce's patronage, published an edition of *Religious Affections* in 1827, claiming it as the most valuable of Edwards' works. "Indeed," he wrote, "there is not a work in the English language, in which a greater knowledge of the human heart is manifested."[72] Nor did esteem for the *Religious Affections* fade away in the second half of the century. J. C. Ryle, bishop of Liverpool from 1880 to 1900, also highly estimated its worth.[73] Thus Edwards was respected among Anglican Evangelicals more for his encouragement of Christian activism and devotion than for his divinity. They aligned with the Methodists, who, as Arminians, maintained a principled objection to Edwards' doctrinal position while appreciating his practical works. The standard nineteenth-century edition of the *Life of Brainerd* was an adaptation of John Wesley's drastic abridgement.[74] Edwards formed the piety of Evangelicals even when he did not mold their theology.

68 Abner W. Brown, *Recollections of the Conversation Parties of the Rev. Charles Simeon, M.A.* (London: Hamilton, Adams & Co., 1863), 269.
69 Conforti, *Edwards, Religious Tradition and American Culture*, 69.
70 Josiah Pratt, *The Life of the Rev. David Brainerd* (London: R. B. Seeley and W. Burnside, 1834), vii.
71 Robert I. and Samuel Wilberforce, *The Life of William Wilberforce*, 5 vols. (London: John Murray, 1839), 3:66.
72 Jonathan Edwards, *A Treatise Concerning the Religious Affections in Three Parts*, ed. Charles Bradley (London: for L. B. Seeley and Son, 1827), vii.
73 John C. Ryle, *Holiness*, 3rd ed. (London: William Hunt and Co., 1887), vi. For Ryle, see 2:2: "Bishop J. C. Ryle: Holiness, Mission and Churchmanship."
74 Conforti, *Edwards, Religious Tradition and American Culture*, 69.

Opposition and Decay

Edwards, however, did not go unscathed by criticism. Because of his wide influence, opponents of Calvinism sometimes singled him out for censure. In 1827 Edward Grinfield, a traditional High Churchman associated with the Society for the Propagation of the Gospel, condemned Edwards' *History of Redemption*, which he described as "one of the most popular manuals of Calvinistic Theology," for showing narrowness in restricting salvation to the elect.[75] Later in the century the eminent theologian F. D. Maurice, the most significant inspirer of the Broad Church tradition in the Church of England, offered strong praise for the *Freedom of the Will*. This philosophical formulation of Old Calvinism, Maurice wrote in 1862, "still remains its most original and in some respects its most important product." Yet Maurice went on to offer trenchant criticism of its capitulation to eighteenth-century modes of thought by depicting the Almighty as a "happy Being" with no participation in the miseries of his creatures. The incarnation of the "Man of sorrows," the express image of his Father, revealed on the contrary, according to Maurice, that God feels intense sympathy for suffering humanity.[76] Maurice heralded a revolution in theology, a shift from a cross-centered perspective associated with Evangelicals to a more liberal way of thinking focused on the incarnation. Two of the other leading figures in the transformation, both Scots, developed their ideas by critiquing Edwards. Thomas Erskine, who wrote *The Doctrine of Election* (1837) as a lay Episcopalian, praised Edwards as "a good and holy man" but argued that *Freedom of the Will* mistakenly appealed to logic rather than conscience. It therefore limited the love of God to a few, whereas the coming of Jesus to earth showed that his Father was "the common Father of men, prodigals and all." Hence Edwards' book was "directly opposed to the gospel of Jesus Christ."[77] Erskine's friend John McLeod Campbell, deposed from the ministry of the Church of Scotland and subsequently a Congregationalist, undertook a sophisticated analysis of Calvinist teaching in his book *The Nature of the Atonement* (1856). McLeod Campbell found Edwards more satisfactory than later writers of the same school such as Pye Smith and Chalmers, but ultimately condemned him for describing the work of Christ in the language of

---

75 Edward W. Grinfield, *The Nature and Extent of the Christian Dispensation with Reference to the Salvability of the Heathen* (London: For C. & J. Rivington, 1827), 427–28.
76 Frederick D. Maurice, *Modern Philosophy* (London: Griffin, Bohn and Co., 1862), 469, 470–71.
77 Thomas Erskine, *The Doctrine of Election*, 2nd ed. (Edinburgh: David Douglas, 1878), 347–48.

the law rather than the family.[78] Both critics were attacking the whole Calvinist tradition, but recognized that Edwards was among its most powerful advocates. Edwards remained a representative figure even for those who broke from the school that he defended.

The Edwardsean paradigm was gradually supplanted on both sides of the Atlantic in the later years of the nineteenth century. In his classic study of the process in America, Frank H. Foster dated the crucial shift to the years 1880-95. At the start of that period the New England theology stemming from Edwards reigned in the seminaries of the Congregationalists; by the end, it had vanished.[79] The last vigorous exponent of the New England scheme, Edwards A. Park, retired as president of Andover seminary in 1868 and as professor of theology there in 1881, and within five years it was rocked by a controversy over the liberal position upheld by those in command of the institution.[80] In Britain there was a parallel process. Thomas Crisp retired as president of Bristol Baptist Academy in 1868 and Henry Rogers as president of Lancashire Independent College in 1869. Both were exponents of Edwards' general standpoint. The Leicester Conference controversy of 1877-78 over the possibility of defining the bounds of Christian fellowship by religious experience rather than doctrine, a position inimical to Edwards' point of view, showed the emergence of a significant school of theological liberals within Congregationalism by that date. In 1880 R. W. Dale, emerging as the denomination's leading theologian, pronounced Calvinism dead.[81] Nevertheless what requires stress is the enduring influence of the moderate Calvinism stemming from Edwards. At some of the colleges it was still dominant until late in the century. It was being taught by Robert Thomas at the Congregationalists' Bala College down to his retirement in 1880 and by Joseph Angus at the Baptists' Regent's Park College down to 1892.[82] Those trained at these and similar institutions would have ministries that extended long afterwards. Although a number of them would no doubt modify the views they had imbibed at college, others would not. Some would certainly have preached essentially Edwardsean theology until well into the twentieth century.

78 John McLeod Campbell, *The Nature of the Atonement*, introd. Edgar P. Dickie (London: James Clarke and Co., 1959), 50-51, 72, 101.
79 Frank H. Foster, *A Genetic History of the New England Theology* (Chicago: Chicago University Press, 1907).
80 Daniel D. Williams, *Andover Liberals: A Study in American Theology* (New York: King's Crown Press, 1941).
81 Mark Hopkins, *Nonconformity's Romantic Generation: Evangelical and Liberal Theologies in Victorian England* (Carlisle: Paternoster Press, 2004), 53.
82 *Dictionary of Welsh Biography*, 963; Cooper, *From Stepney to St Giles'*, 71.

Conclusion

The virtual silence of the secondary literature about the legacy of Jonathan Edwards in Britain is unjustified. Commentators during the nineteenth century were well aware of the stature of the American theologian, and his works were in wide demand. Edwards and his successors in the tradition of New England theology enabled ministers to adapt their inherited Calvinism to the enlightened spirit of the age. In the eighteenth century Edwards was warmly received by several groups, including the Baptists who launched the modern missionary movement. In particular, his distinction between natural and moral inability provided a way of reconciling the divine sovereignty of Calvinism with the imperative to preach the gospel. Andrew Fuller and the tutors of the Baptist colleges adopted his moderate Calvinist standpoint, though there was resistance, especially in South Wales. The Congregationalists were led in the same direction by Edward Williams, whose views scored a notable triumph in Wales. John Pye Smith propagated Edwards' position, as did other tutors within the Congregational denomination. Thomas Chalmers was primarily responsible for a vogue for Edwards in Scotland, where his writings were widely appreciated. In the Church of England there was less enthusiasm for the theological core of Edwards' teaching, but Anglican Evangelicals, like Methodists, valued his missionary and devotional texts. Critics of Calvinism naturally turned their fire on Edwards because he was seen as its champion. As a more liberal theology came into fashion, Edwardseanism faded in Britain, just as it did in the United States, but some trained in that moderate Calvinist tradition will have retained their principles into the twentieth century. Later in that century there was to be a revival of interest in Jonathan Edwards through the work of Martyn Lloyd-Jones and the Banner of Truth Trust. Edwards once more became a favored theologian.[83] At an earlier period, however, and over a long time, Edwards provided the foundations for the normative scheme of Evangelical Calvinist theology. Jonathan Edwards exerted a profound effect on Britain.

---

83 *Engaging with Martyn Lloyd-Jones: The Life and Legacy of "the Doctor,"* ed. Andrew Atherstone and David Ceri Jones (Nottingham: Apollos, 2011).

6

Dwight L. Moody and Transatlantic Evangelicalism

Dwight Lyman Moody, always known as D. L. Moody, died on 22 December 1899. His name is inseparably linked with that of his fellow American Ira David Sankey, so that Moody and Sankey are like Bryant and May matches or Marks and Spencer stores. Both were evangelists, the one a preacher, the other a singer. As an evangelist, Moody urged conversion on his hearers. It was not necessary, he taught, for people to know where or when their lives had been changed, but they did need to be converted to Christ if they were to go to heaven. Sudden conversion was the norm.[1] Moody preached from the Bible, alluding to many different passages in any single address. He was a man of one book. The evangelist's study, it was noticed, contained nothing but literature designed to help his understanding of the Bible.[2] He emphasized the doctrine of the cross, the atoning work of Christ. According to Moody's sermon on "The Blood," one of the most celebrated, "People say we ought to preach up Christ's life and moral character ... But Christ died for our sins. He didn't say we were to preach His life to save men. Christ's death is what gives us liberty."[3] And Moody exhorted converts to be activists, seeking out others to bring to the cross. He used to quote John Wesley as saying, "All at it, and always at it," adding, "Every Christian ought to be a worker."[4] These were the salient features of Moody's ministry: conversion, Bible, cross and activism. They are also the hallmarks of Evangelicalism. Moody was an archetypal Evangelical.

---

1 Stanley N. Gundry, *Love Them In: The Life and Theology of D. L. Moody* (Chicago: Moody Press, 1999), 131–32. I am grateful to Stan Gundry for sending me a copy of his study of Moody's theology.
2 T. J. Shanks, *D. L. Moody at Home* (London: Morgan and Scott, n.d.), 12.
3 W. H. Daniels, *D. L. Moody and His Work* (London: Hodder and Stoughton, 1875), 426.
4 Gundry, *Love Them In*, 170.

Furthermore he was a transatlantic figure. Himself an American who seemed very much an enterprising man of the New World, he visited Britain no fewer than six times, always for several months and on two occasions for years at a time. He had the greatest respect for Charles Haddon Spurgeon, the famous Baptist preacher of Victorian London, reading his sermons regularly. On Moody's earliest trip to England, in 1867, the first place he made for was the Metropolitan Tabernacle, Spurgeon's vast church at the Elephant and Castle.[5] The American forged strong links with other British leaders of the Evangelical movement. Moody was so prominent in the life of Britain that he qualified, though a foreigner, for an entry in the *Oxford Dictionary of National Biography*. Evangelicalism in the Victorian era was very much an international phenomenon, tying together the English-speaking world. Moody was one of those whose universal celebrity bound it into a unity. Indeed, with Spurgeon, Moody was probably the most influential Evangelical of the later nineteenth century. Why was he such a significant figure? It will be helpful, in order to tease out the answer, to examine aspects of his career in turn.

Formative Influences

The formative factors in Moody's life must begin with his hometown of Northfield, Massachusetts. There he was born on 5 February 1837.[6] Northfield was a small township of attractive white clapboard homesteads on the Connecticut River near the state line with New Hampshire and Vermont. It lay in the heart of rural New England. This was the region to which the Puritans of the seventeenth century had traveled, though the spot that later became Northfield was then deep in Indian territory. By the early eighteenth century it was well settled. In 1733 the town was affected by the revival at the nearby Northampton, Massachusetts, under Jonathan Edwards. But by the early nineteenth century Congregationalism, until 1833 the established religion of the state, had become unorthodox. By the time of Moody's birth the village church was Unitarian, though the family's connection with the church was tenuous. The young Dwight did not receive infant baptism until he was five. By then his father, a bricklayer, was dead. He was therefore brought up by his mother, born Betsey Holton, a forceful woman. Even in

---

5   Robert Shindler, *From the Usher's Desk to the Tabernacle Pulpit: The Life and Labours of Pastor C. H. Spurgeon* (London: Passmore and Alabaster, 1892), 208.

6   James F. Findlay, Jr, *Dwight L. Moody: American Evangelist, 1837–1899* (Chicago: University of Chicago Press, 1969), 35. Basic biographical information is taken from this standard life of Moody.

her eighties she insisted on doing the housework herself.[7] Her son took after her in strength of character. He left home at seventeen, moving to Boston to work in an uncle's shoe shop. There, in the metropolis of New England, he was converted. While still in his thirties, however, he returned to settle in Northfield, buying a house in 1875 and taking up agriculture in the township. To visitors to his home he seemed in later life a shrewd, laconic New England farmer.[8] In his career as an evangelist he gave a similar impression, appealing to British audiences partly because of his Yankee yarns. His speech always betrayed his origins, allowing Cambridge undergraduates to make fun of his pronunciation of "Daniel" as a single syllable, "Dan'l."[9] Here was a man thoroughly molded by his Massachusetts background.

After only a couple of years in Boston, Moody moved on to Chicago, where the second main phase of his formation took place. The capital of the Midwest was already flourishing when the young man, not yet twenty, reached there in 1856. It was the railhead for beef supplies from the prairies to the cities of the east. Chicago was a vigorous, expanding city throughout Moody's lifetime. Only a year after his arrival, in 1857, the great revival that began in New York City struck Chicago. Moody threw himself into its noon prayer meetings and was fired with enthusiasm for Sunday school work with children.[10] That effort eventually led, in 1864, to the creation of the Illinois Street Church with Moody as pastor. Home, church and other Christian agencies, however, were all destroyed in the huge Chicago fire of 1871. The experience seems to have loosened Moody's bonds with the city, for soon he set off for a long stay across the Atlantic. Yet he did not abandon his connections with Chicago later in his career. In 1887 he founded the Chicago Evangelization Society to sustain and develop the activities in which he had engaged thirty years before; and six years later he held an evangelistic campaign in the city during the Chicago World's Fair. Moody ever remained the go-ahead Chicagoan.

A third shaping factor was the Mildmay Conference in England. In 1867 Moody traveled to London to explore the Evangelical scene in Britain. With typical energy, he took the initiative in starting a London noon prayer meeting on the Chicago model. Soon, however, he was drawn into the circle of the Mildmay Conference, an annual gathering for Christian

7   Shanks, *Moody at Home*, 11.
8   Henry Drummond, *Dwight L. Moody: Impressions and Facts* (New York: McClure, Phillips and Co., 1900), 40.
9   George E. Morgan, *"A Veteran in Revival:" R. C. Morgan: His Life and Times* (London: Morgan and Scott, 1909), 209.
10 Kathryn T. Long, *The Revival of 1857–58* (New York: Oxford University Press, 1998), 127.

workers organized by William Pennefather, the minister of St Jude's, Mildmay Park. Its attenders, among the keenest Evangelicals of their day, heard messages on themes relating to holiness and mission. Although Mildmay was predominantly Anglican, it also included members of the Brethren (the so-called "Plymouth Brethren") such as George Müller, the famous founder of a Bristol children's home and protagonist of living by faith. Moody became close to R. C. Morgan, a publisher of Christian literature and the most open of the open school of Brethren. Morgan's weekly periodical the *Christian* was to be crucial in publicizing Moody's later evangelistic campaigns in Britain, a copy being sent to every minister in the United Kingdom.[11]

Through these contacts Moody made the acquaintance of Henry Moorhouse, a Brethren evangelist originally from Manchester. Moorhouse traveled across the Atlantic in the reverse direction later in the same year. He was a self-assured young man, confiding to his diary on arriving in New York, "Christians seem all dead," and immediately setting about correcting their "erroneous doctrines."[12] He was similarly didactic on reaching Chicago, where he instructed Moody on how to give "Bible readings," that is talks based on going through scripture to discover the main passages relating to particular themes.[13] This method Moody made his own, becoming his characteristic expository device. In 1872 the American was back in England, this time speaking from the platform of the Mildmay Conference. Pennefather, its organizer, was one of the two men who issued an invitation to Moody to return to lead an evangelistic mission in Britain. Moody therefore owed a major debt to the Mildmay circle. He acknowledged the conference as the model for his own annual gatherings for Christian workers begun at Northfield in 1880.

In 1873–75 Moody responded to Pennefather's invitation by coming to the British Isles to conduct an evangelistic campaign. Accompanied for the first time by Sankey, he held a series of meetings in York and the North-East of England, building up to a longer mission in Edinburgh. But the climax was in Glasgow from February to April 1874. In Scotland, the Free Church and the United Presbyterians had been deeply affected by the revival fires that spread from the United States after 1857, and so were receptive to a man whose methods had been cast in that furnace. Furthermore, the two churches had experienced a crisis in 1873: proposals for union between them were turned

11 Findlay, *Moody*, 164.
12 John Macpherson, *Henry Moorhouse: The English Evangelist* (London: Morgan and Scott, 1913), 51.
13 Macpherson, *Henry Moorhouse*, 66, 90.

down in a heated controversy that threatened schism.[14] Consequently Moody and Sankey suited the moment. They were agents of revival and offered an alternative to institutional wrangling.

They made a huge impact on Glasgow, where there were perhaps three thousand converts. A Glasgow United Evangelistic Association was begun to continue the work and a Tent Hall was erected on Glasgow Green near the city center as its focus. Moody stayed in Glasgow with Andrew Bonar, minister of Finnieston Free Church, the brother of Horatius the hymn-writer and the biographer of the saintly Robert Murray McCheyne. Bonar's union of scholarship, zeal and devotion made a profound impression on Moody. The Scotsman traveled to speak at the 1881 conference at Northfield, where Moody named a new building Bonar Hall and there was even a Bonar Glen.[15] Clearly Bonar was influential over Moody; so was the Glasgow experience as a whole. It showed that the evangelist was capable of stirring a large population. His first breakthrough to fame came not in the United States but in Glasgow. He returned to the city for a six months' mission in 1882 and treated it as the British equivalent of Chicago, a place where modern evangelistic methods could be implemented for imitation elsewhere. Moody was molded by Britain as well as by America.

Evangelistic Method

Moody's distinctive evangelistic style deserves analysis. In the first place it was notably urban. The modern city was the creation of the nineteenth century. By the early 1870s, nearly a quarter of the American population, together with over half the British population, was urbanized. Moody brought the gospel to this new world. After Glasgow in 1874 he moved on to Belfast, Dublin, Manchester, Sheffield, Birmingham and Liverpool—all great cities. The itinerary culminated in London from March to June 1875. Moody preached in four centers on a rota, the Agricultural Hall, Islington, drawing an audience of twelve thousand from the first evening. In all the evangelist was said to have addressed over two and a half million people in the capital. He returned to London in 1883–84, this time preaching on eleven separate sites. He was targeting the largest city in the world, devising strategies for making its evangelization manageable. In the United States he similarly concentrated on cities, starting with Brooklyn in 1875. He divided it into sections for preaching in each area on the London model. Already in 1874 he had urged the need to train others specifically as

---

14 Ian Hamilton, *The Erosion of Calvinist Orthodoxy* (Edinburgh: Rutherford House Books, 1990), chap. 3.
15 Shanks, *Moody at Home*, 14, 17.

urban evangelists.[16] It is symbolic that the collapse just before his death in 1899 occurred during a campaign in Kansas City. Before Moody's time, revivalism had been predominantly rural. It was associated most with remote fishing villages and mining communities, and, in America, with the backwoods of the frontier. Although the 1857–60 revival had started to shift the balance towards an urban environment, it was Moody who did most to relate revivalism to the conditions of the modern city. He began the tradition of big meetings in major population centers that continued down to the time of Billy Graham.

Moody also injected into the revival tradition the methods of business. He was himself a shoe salesman when he moved to Chicago, and a very successful one. "He would never sit down in the store," a fellow clerk remembered, "to chat or read the paper, as the other clerks did when there were no customers; but as soon as he had served one buyer he was on the lookout for another." He would stand outside, hovering for any potential customer in the street. "There is the spider again," his friends would say, "watching for a fly."[17] Accordingly he prospered. In 1859, as a salesman on commission, he earned $5,000 more than his salary.[18] He did not lose his business gifts in later life. At Northfield in the 1870s, for instance, he was considering buying land for a school. One day he spoke to a friend about his wish to obtain a plot of sixteen acres near his home, and the friend agreed that it was a good idea. Immediately Moody went to the owner, fixed the price, made out the papers and completed the purchase the same day.[19] He invested in R. C. Morgan's publishing firm, Morgan and Scott, which issued his sermons.[20] He also owned the copyright of Sankey's hymn book, first published by Morgan and Scott in 1873 and immensely profitable. But Moody did not keep the income from the hymn book himself, instead directing it through trustees to charities and later to the schools he founded.[21] Moody had a genius for extracting money for good causes. He was, according to his Scottish friend Henry Drummond, "the most magnificent beggar Great Britain has ever known."[22] He was also an excellent manager, ever looking out for people with the right skills for particular jobs. The 1857–58 revival in the United States was called the "Businessman's Revival" because so many participated. Moody maintained this ethos, bringing business acumen to revivalism.

16 Findlay, *Moody*, 313; Gundry, *Love Them In*, 35.
17 Drummond, *Moody*, 56.
18 Gundry, *Love Them In*, 35.
19 Drummond, *Moody*, 87.
20 Findlay, *Moody*, 364.
21 Drummond, *Moody*, 91–93.
22 Drummond, *Moody*, 112.

His approach to revivals was lay rather than clerical. Moody himself was not ordained. On his first visit to London at a meeting in the Exeter Hall, the powerhouse of Evangelical enterprise, he was introduced as "The Reverend." He created a flutter by saying that the chairman had made a mistake because he was not "The Reverend" at all, but only a sabbath school worker.[23] Moody created an unecclesiastical atmosphere in his missions, using halls, temporary iron buildings, even the Royal Opera House, Haymarket. His chief supporters were laymen such as John Wanamaker of Philadelphia. Moody bought an old railroad station there for evangelistic meetings, and when he had finished with it Wanamaker took over the building, turning it into a hardware and fancy goods store.[24] Late in life, Moody urged the laity to take part in the debates of ministers and theologians in order to speak out against destructive biblical criticism.[25] And he wanted to train lay evangelists, what he called "gapmen" between the clergy and the ordinary laity, "men who will go out and do work that the educated ministers can't do: get in among the people, and identify themselves with the people."[26]

Moody was eager, however, that not only laymen should be mobilized but also laywomen. He believed that women made better city missionaries. One reason was that during the day housewives were at home and so a female missionary could speak more easily to them; the other, according to Moody, was that "the women have got more tact."[27] It has been suggested that Moody's preaching, like Sankey's singing, catered specifically for women.[28] There was a great deal of sentiment about lost boys and weeping mothers. Certainly Moody often spoke of a domestic setting in an age when women were supposed to be tenders of the home while men were out in the public sphere. At a time of sharp gender differentiation, Moody made sure that there was a place for women as well as men in his mission plans, both as agents and constituency.

In the past revivalism had been most powerful when spontaneous. All the members of a small community could be ignited with concern for their souls. Now, however, in targeting large cities, using business methods and gathering lay support, Moody adopted careful organization. It was claimed by

23 J. C. Pollock, *Moody without Sankey: A New Biographical Portrait* (London: Hodder and Stoughton, 1963), 67–68.
24 Alfred W. W. Dale, *The Life of R. W. Dale of Birmingham* (London: Hodder and Stoughton, 1898), 334.
25 Gundry, *Love Them In*, 215.
26 Gundry, *Love Them In*, 153.
27 Shanks, *Moody at Home*, 113.
28 Long, *Revival of 1857–58*, 91.

a contemporary defender of Moody's work in Scotland that there was nothing new about his methods except the singing.[29] It is true that the greatest innovation was the music. From half an hour before the start of a mission service there was congregational singing; and during the proceedings there were Sankey's plaintive solos—though Moody failed to appreciate them because he was tone deaf. But the music was itself a sign of planning. The attractive melodies were designed to cater for the taste of the young, and so to aim for a particular market.[30] The missions were a form of commercial entertainment, the religious equivalent of the music hall that was developing rapidly at the same period.[31] There were also other features of careful planning. There was house-to-house visitation; the mission meeting doors were closed at a specified time so as to ensure a punctual start; and advertisements were placed in mass-circulation dailies. Perhaps the greatest innovation was the inquiry room. At the end of an evangelistic meeting, those who were burdened about their sins were invited to stay behind—or rather those who had to go were invited to leave, allowing personal discussion between the inquirers who remained and individual counselors. It was estimated that four-fifths of the results came from these one-to-one encounters.[32] The method was to be copied throughout the twentieth century. Moody was remarkable for adapting mass evangelism to a new age.

Theological Message

The evangelist's theological style, to which we should turn next, was the subject of much debate at the time. In Britain he was criticized by John Kennedy, the conservative Free Church of Scotland minister at Dingwall, and by J. K. Popham, a prominent Strict Baptist in England. Both came forward as champions of Calvinism, claiming that Moody was preaching the Arminian message that all could be saved. How valid was this criticism? It was true that he stressed human agency in securing conversions, which could appear Arminian, and his colleague Sankey was a Methodist. On the other hand, however, Moody's hero Spurgeon was a doughty defender of the Reformed tradition. The evangelist did not reject the doctrine of election, as some Calvinist critics alleged. Moody merely believed that the doctrine was not to be preached to

---

29 Horatius Bonar in the *Christian*, 8 January 1874, 7.
30 Moody in the *Christian*, 22 January 1874, 5.
31 Peter Bailey, *Leisure and Class in Victorian England: Rational Recreation and the Contest for Control, 1830–1885* (London: Routledge & Kegan Paul, 1978), chap. 7.
32 Dale, *R. W. Dale*, 319.

unbelievers, only to believers.[33] He actually held certain distinctive Calvinist positions. In his *Notes from My Bible*, for example, he distinguishes between the *position* of believers, which is eternally secure, and their *condition*, which might lapse into sin.[34] The implication was that he upheld the doctrine of the perseverance of the saints. Furthermore, he was attacked by Methodists as well as by Calvinists. It seems clear that he had forged an uncomplicated soteriology designed to cater for both parties. "I don't try," he once remarked, "to reconcile God's sovereignty and man's free agency."[35] He framed a generalized Evangelicalism that tried to be the highest common factor of the Calvinist and Arminian systems.

Part of the reason for the criticism mounted by Kennedy was the mildness of Moody's message. Traditional Evangelical theology had stressed God as judge; the more liberal thinkers of the day were describing God as father. Moody stood with the latter. He emphasized love as central to the gospel, perhaps under the influence of Henry Moorhouse. That does not mean, as James Findlay's biography suggests, that Moody held the moral influence theory of the atonement.[36] Stan Gundry shows that, on the contrary, he maintained the doctrine of penal substitution. Hell was mentioned, but not frequently, and it was never dwelt on. Rather Moody tended to speak of death as the end to be feared. He found the commentaries of Joseph Parker, the Congregational minister of the City Temple, particularly helpful.[37] Parker was an Evangelical, but strongly touched by modern influences and so mild in expression.

Moody was never trained in theology and was ill-equipped to read widely. Rather he picked up ideas from the experts, holding brainstorming sessions to draw them out. The Northfield Conferences were organized partly for his own benefit, so that he could absorb the teaching of eminent preachers of the day.[38] He was therefore shaped by contemporary currents of opinion, not by long-standing traditions. The thinking of the period was being molded by the dissemination of the ideas of the Romantic age focusing, not on reason, but on will and emotion. Accordingly Moody enlarged the place of human volition in his system so that a person could will to be saved; and the emotion of sentimentalism was his stock in trade. The supremely contemporary packaging of the gospel goes a long way towards explaining Moody's impact.

33 Gundry, *Love Them In*, 141.
34 D. L. Moody, *Notes from My Bible* (London: Morgan and Scott, 1896), 121.
35 Gundry, *Love Them In*, 141.
36 Findlay, *Moody*, 232.
37 Gundry, *Love Them In*, 45, 97–102, 43.
38 Shanks, *Moody at Home*, 31.

One doctrine particularly attractive to the Romantic temper was that of the premillennial second advent. On this understanding the second coming would take place before the millennium of peace, plenty and gospel triumph. The return of Christ was to be expected soon. Such prophetic teaching revived during the nineteenth century. Unlike most other aspects of Romantic influence, it tended to stiffen theology and so to bolster a conservative position. Moody often preached on the second coming as imminent. In his writing he urged that his readers should have "the promise of the Lord's coming bright in our hearts."[39] Association with the Brethren encouraged this conviction. He was deeply swayed by John Nelson Darby's codified version of premillennialism, dispensationalism, according to which history is divided into periods, or dispensations, in which the divine dealings with humanity are distinctive. Moody's own Northfield Congregational Church had as its minister from 1895 C. I. Scofield, whose dispensationalist notes on the Bible were to spread Darbyite views to a large proportion of the Evangelical world in the twentieth century.[40] Moody himself used the term "dispensations," but he was not a strict dispensationalist, referring to only three dispensations rather than the seven espoused by Darbyites.[41] Nevertheless his premillennialism was firm. He expected the world to end very soon and preachers of that persuasion predominated at the Northfield Conferences. The conferences formed, in fact, probably the chief agency in late nineteenth-century America for the diffusion of such views in the United States. Carried along by the current of contemporary thinking, Moody was in effect a theological innovator.

At the same time as Moody's great campaign in the British Isles of the 1870s, there emerged a fresh movement within Evangelicalism. Centered on Keswick, the town in the Lake District where annual conventions were held from 1875, the new teaching was that believers could attain sanctification by faith. By contrast with the received Calvinist belief that holiness could be reached only by a sustained struggle to do right, Keswick held that it came through a moment-by-moment dependence on the Almighty. The message was similar to the teaching of John Wesley that it is possible to arrive at a stage of Christian perfection on earth, but it did not follow the Wesleyan tradition in celebrating the eradication of the old sinful nature. For Keswick the old nature was still present, but was repressed. Moody

---

39 Moody, *Notes from My Bible*, 30. On premillennialism, see 1:8: "The Advent Hope in British Evangelicalism since 1800."
40 Findlay, *Moody*, 406–7.
41 Moody, *Notes from My Bible*, 43.

stood close to Keswick. In 1871 he underwent a special experience of the Holy Spirit in which he received what he called power for service.[42] One of the two sponsors of his British campaign in 1873 was Cuthbert Bainbridge, the Methodist owner of a Newcastle department store, who upheld Wesleyan holiness doctrine.[43] Leading figures from the Keswick Convention spoke at the Northfield Conferences in the 1890s: H. W. Webb-Peploe, F. B. Meyer, Andrew Murray.[44]

Moody himself appeared on the Keswick platform in 1892. Yet he did not wholly identify with the movement, holding to the broader view taught at Mildmay which accepted that effort might be needed for sanctification. His parting message to young converts at Liverpool in 1875 was to remind them that they would always have two natures, flesh as well as spirit, to the end of their pilgrimage on earth.[45] Although that was formally a caution against the Wesleyan rather than the Keswick view, its intention was to dampen down expectations of special spiritual attainments by faith. Nevertheless Moody did insist on practical holiness, denouncing the opera, dancing and cards.[46] In a sense he was a fellow traveler of Keswick, participating in the rising tide of interest in holiness that marked many Evangelicals of the late nineteenth century. It was one of the ways in which Moody was of real theological importance. A stress on avoiding worldliness, together with a gospel neutral between Calvinism and Arminianism, a mild tone and premillennial teaching, was to become the orthodoxy of conservative Evangelicalism in the earlier twentieth century. Moody, as much as any individual, was its creator.

Social Approach

Moody's social style is as worthy of examination as his theological style. The late nineteenth century was an era of the rise of respectability. Anyone, even among the working people, could aspire to that goal, which entailed independence and a certain dignity, but it helped if a person's status could be confirmed by the great and the wealthy. Moody's friend the hymn-writer Daniel W. Whittle once remarked that the evangelist's greatest danger was his "Ambition to lead and influence Rich Men."[47] Moody had to court his American business

---

42 Findlay, *Moody*, 132. On Keswick teaching, see 1:10: "Holiness in the Evangelical Tradition."
43 Thomas H. Bainbridge, *Reminiscences*, ed. Gerald France (London: C. H. Kelly, 1913), 55, 67.
44 Findlay, *Moody*, 407.
45 *Christian*, 19 August 1875, 9.
46 *Christian*, 22 January 1874, 5; 7 May 1874, 7.
47 Pollock, *Moody without Sankey*, 211.

donors, such as Hiram Camp, president of the New Haven Clock Company, who gave a munificent $25,000 for the purchase of land near Northfield.[48] On the other side of the Atlantic there were similar patrons such as Quintin Hogg, a West Indies sugar merchant, but in Britain there was less respect for new wealth than for old status. Moody mingled with aristocrats, especially Lord Cairns, a Conservative Lord Chancellor, and with Arthur, Lord Kinnaird. He was remembered at the home of Lady Ashburton for playing "energetic croquet."[49] Yet Moody was by no means universally popular in the higher reaches of society. Queen Victoria commented tartly that his London mission was "not the *sort* of religious performance that I like."[50] In reality Moody should not be classed as a social climber. He was willing on occasion to resist his patrons. When the redoubtable Lord Shaftesbury asked him to alter the balance of his London preaching places, he refused.[51] He wanted the support of the elite for his missions, but deference was not Moody's lodestar.

The evangelist should be identified, in fact, not with the social elite but with the mass of the people. There have been a number of different interpretations of the phenomenon of Moody's revivalism. According to John Kent, it was an exercise in social control. The possessors of wealth and status were using religion as a tool to keep the lower orders submissive.[52] John Findlay's biography gives some credence to this viewpoint,[53] and there is certainly some evidence in its favor. In 1887, for instance, it was said that Chicago businessmen thought Moody's evangelistic training school "the best, most direct, and most economical means of counteracting . . . rabid socialism."[54] Nevertheless it is clear that in Britain, at least, Moody was seen as more of a threat to the social order than as its bulwark. John Coffey has shown that Moody appeared to represent the values of American democracy by contrast with the existing aristocratic social order of the United Kingdom. He was a common man, standing for popular principles. Moody, according to Kent, made little or no impact on the working classes because they were averse to being controlled. That estimate, however, seems to be mistaken. Although Moody disliked counting converts, it appears that he did reach the working people. At Liverpool, for example, a report of

48 Shanks, *Moody at Home*, 21.
49 Clyde Binfield, *George Williams and the Y.M.C.A.: A Study in Victorian Social Attitudes* (London: Heinemann, 1973), 225.
50 Pollock, *Moody without Sankey*, 145.
51 Pollock, *Moody without Sankey*, 142.
52 John Kent, *Holding the Fort: Studies in Victorian Revivalism* (London: Epworth Press, 1978), chaps. 4–6, 9.
53 Findlay, *Moody*, 71, 73, 326–27.
54 Gundry, *Love Them In*, 163.

his mission was explicit that "[r]ough, ill clad working men were there."[55] Other contemporary accounts confirm this observation. Working people were attracted, if only by the music hall atmosphere of the rallies.

The social significance of Moody emerges most clearly from an episode when he proposed to hold a special meeting for the boys of Eton College, the most prestigious of the public schools of England. There was a horrified reaction from spokesmen of the upper classes; a debate took place on the subject in the House of Lords; and the event was transferred from a large tent to a private garden.[56] *The Times* opined that a revivalist service at Eton would be "something to boast of in the lower ranks of the religious world."[57] Moody stood not with the aristocracy against the poor but with the masses against the elite. He was an unashamed populist.

Moody showed a corresponding concern for the welfare of the people. His missions gave rise to major efforts in philanthropy. The Glasgow Tent Hall became famous for its free Sunday morning breakfasts for down-and-outs and its free Sunday dinners for destitute children. There were also refuges for homeless children and an orphanage by the sea at Saltcoats. A group of men associated with the Glasgow campaign threw themselves into politics to achieve Christian objectives.[58] While very much Evangelicals, they were expressing an early version of the social gospel. The chief cause taken up was temperance. Moody was himself a total abstainer who endorsed the growing temperance movement, though without urging the pledge to abstain from strong drink. At Edinburgh in 1874, when asked about the problem of intemperance, he gave a dramatic reply: "it would be a happy day for Scotland if every minister hurled the intoxicating cup from his table."[59] Moody was the moving force behind the British Workmen's Public House Company in Liverpool, which, despite its name, was designed to set up cheap restaurants without alcohol for working people.[60]

Moody is usually represented in the secondary literature on the United States as retreating from social issues in his later years towards an exclusively

---

55 John Coffey, "Democracy and Popular Religion: Moody and Sankey's Mission to Britain, 1873–1875," in *Citizenship and Community: Liberals, Radicals and Collective Identities in the British Isles, 1865–1931*, ed. Eugenio F. Biagini (Cambridge: Cambridge University Press, 1996), 97.
56 Pollock, *Moody without Sankey*, 147–49.
57 Coffey, "Democracy and Popular Religion," 107.
58 Iain G. C. Hutchison, *A Political History of Scotland, 1832–1924: Parties, Elections and Issues* (Edinburgh: John Donald, 1986), 136–38.
59 *Christian*, 22 January 1874, 6.
60 Morgan, "A Veteran in Revival," 52.

conversionist policy.[61] It is true that in 1898 he declared that he was sick and tired of hearing of reform: the need of human beings, he insisted, was not to be patched up but to be regenerated.[62] What he was taking exception to, however, was reform as an alternative to the gospel. He never objected to reform as a partner of the gospel. Thus in 1884 he urged the improvement of the housing of the working classes in London, an issue only just coming to prominence.[63] He was prepared to criticize capitalists sharply, denouncing in 1897 the payment by American employers of "starvation wages."[64] There can be no doubt that in his day Moody was broadly aligned with progressive forces in favor of social reform. The evangelist wanted to help the mass of the people, not to rise above them or control them.

Impact

The impact of the man, which also calls for assessment, had several dimensions. First and foremost was his preaching. Because Moody aimed for a mass audience, his sermons were marked by simplicity. In fact his style was shaped by his early talks to children in Chicago, where he discovered his power of storytelling. In his subsequent preaching, Bible stories came strikingly alive. His delivery was extempore and very rapid, the word "Jerusalem" sounding on his lips as though it had only two syllables. There was wit and pungency in his observations. "There is no better man in the world than a Scotchman," he remarked (admittedly not in a sermon), "if he is headed right, but he is very troublesome if he is headed wrong."[65]

Moody objected to what he called "text-preaching," that is, taking a single verse and hanging an essay round it. Instead he called for expository preaching, which he believed to be rare in the United States.[66] Moody's manner of preparation for exposition was idiosyncratic. He carried with him on his travels a series of large linen envelopes, each on a different topic. He filled them with anything relevant that he encountered, whether slips of paper, cuttings or extracts. Before an address he would bring out the appropriate envelope, look through the whole of the contents, select a few of the items, put them in order and jot down a few thoughts. Hence no

---

61   Long, *Revival of 1857–58*, 125.
62   Gundry, *Love Them In*, 97.
63   Findlay, *Moody*, 361.
64   Gundry, *Love Them In*, 155.
65   Shanks, *Moody at Home*, 112.
66   Shanks, *Moody at Home*, 183.

two sermons were ever the same.[67] Sermons on particular themes, however, were repeated very frequently. During the years 1881 to 1899, for example, he preached on "The New Birth" no fewer than 184 times.[68] All was undergirded by an earnest manner, since he never forgot his primary purpose of persuading his hearers to decide for Christ. His preaching therefore possessed great immediacy.

Another aspect of Moody's impact came through education. The evangelist himself had received only a basic education in the township school, where he had not been very attentive. His letters in maturity were mis-spelt and showed a homely disregard for grammar. Possibly as a result, Moody held learning in high esteem. In 1882 he felt honored to be invited to conduct missions at the universities of Cambridge and Oxford. When he was settled in Northfield in the late 1870s he began a series of major educational ventures. He started by adding an extension to his own house, with accommodation for only eight girls. It developed, in 1879, into the Northfield Seminary for Young Ladies. Two years later he established an equivalent institution for young men, the Mount Hermon School. Both were designed to produce evangelists, but alongside the more practical stream there was a classical stream and the schools sent their pupils forward to elite colleges. Other institutions were more specifically intended to train soul-winners. In 1889 Moody set up a training center for lay missionaries, significantly in Chicago. After the evangelist's death, it became a memorial to him, taking the title Moody Bible Institute from 1910. In 1890 Moody launched an equivalent institution for women at Northfield. It taught the Bible, dressmaking, cooking, drawing, music, hygiene and health because it was to train women who could visit and care for the poor.[69] Two years later Moody was responsible for stimulating the foundation of a similar Bible Training Institute in Glasgow. The idea had already been maturing in the mind of J. Campbell White, a Free Church chemical manufacturer, but it was Moody who stirred the Glaswegians into action, suggesting the name of the first principal.[70] The evangelist inspired a remarkable range of educational institutions. Although they were meant primarily to produce more evangelists, they showed a definite respect for education in its own right. Through these

---

67 Drummond, *Moody*, 70.
68 Gundry, *Love Them In*, 126.
69 Findlay, *Moody*, 397 n. 16.
70 F. V. Waddleton, "The Bible Training Institute, Glasgow" (Unpublished typescript, [1979]), 11–12.

agencies, furthermore, Moody exerted an influence over thousands in his own day and in subsequent generations.

The impact of the evangelist was particularly felt in the field of Christian unity. Moody was an irenic character who was notably friendly to people of other persuasions, even Roman Catholics. This quality was particularly useful on his missions to Ireland with its large Catholic presence, but it was also in evidence at home. He gave a handsome sum for the erection of a Roman Catholic church in Northfield and in return the Catholics brought stone for the building of Moody's own church there. All his work was interdenominational. While he was a Congregationalist, his wife was a Baptist. He had been shaped by the Young Men's Christian Association, attending lectures in its Boston building in 1854 even before he was converted. In Chicago he rose to become the Y.M.C.A. president from 1866 to 1870; his first London contacts were through the Y.M.C.A.; and he attained the United States national presidency of the organization in 1879. Its ethos was undenominational, believing in aggressive work among the young without any restraints by particular church bodies. It appealed to Moody, who once dismissed the "miserable sectarian spirit."[71] Cooperation between Christians of different traditions was essential for Moody's missions, but the sense of unity that he fostered had longer lasting effects. At the Northfield Conference of 1886, young attenders fired with zeal started the Student Volunteer Missionary Union which led on in Britain to the Student Christian Movement.[72] With other similar ventures in interdenominational cooperation, the S.C.M. formed the institutional base for the ecumenical movement that was to prove so significant in the twentieth century.

Moody's concern with unity, furthermore, was also important within the Evangelical movement. He tried to keep together the diverging theological wings of Evangelicalism of his day, the conservative and the liberal. He himself belonged himself to the conservative strand, his prophetic views locating him firmly there. He deplored the biblical criticism that by the 1890s was dampening the message of young ministers. Yet equally he regretted the "bad temper and personal recriminations" of some of those who denounced biblical criticism publicly and unsparingly.[73] He defended his Scottish friend Henry Drummond when others wanted him excluded

---

71   Gundry, *Love Them In*, 174.
72   Tissington Tatlow, *The Story of the Student Christian Movement of Great Britain and Ireland* (London: Student Christian Movement Press, 1933), 17–19.
73   George Adam Smith in Drummond, *Moody*, 25, 28.

from Northfield for inadequate theological views.[74] Moody tried to bring the two sides together, aiming for a combination of doctrinal orthodoxy and Christian charity. He was actively reining in the polarizing tendency that was to lead to the Fundamentalist/Modernist controversies which tore apart American Protestantism after the First World War. Part of his influence was as a force for unity.

The personality of the man was of the essence of his impact. Moody looked a powerful character: stout, square-shouldered, sporting a long, black beard. He had a tendency to be outspoken, sometimes causing offence, but he was restrained by his wife Emma, whom he married in 1862. She traveled as her husband's secretary, exuding calmness and self-control, but she did not quench his youthful high spirits. He loved practical jokes. He would, for example, meet fresh visitors to Northfield at the station driving a horse and buggy, and because he did not reveal his identity they would assume that he was merely a servant.[75] "You will find," Henry Drummond used to say, "a great deal of the boy in Moody."[76] Yet he accumulated stores of sound experience. His recommendation that prayer meeting rooms should have plenty of fresh air so that people did not fall asleep is a good instance of the practical common sense for which he was noted.[77]

Despite his fame, Moody retained an uncontrived humility. He concluded a private communion service in London in 1874, for example, with a prayer that he should himself be kept from falling.[78] Out of aversion to the development of any personality cult, he tried to avoid having his photograph displayed. In 1897 the American *Ladies' Home Journal* had to whiten the hair of an old photograph of the evangelist because he refused to permit the publication of a recent picture.[79] The genuine lowliness helps to explain the verdict of Drummond on Moody: "the biggest human he ever met."[80] Much of the impact of Moody derived from the complementing of his sustained dynamism by thoroughly attractive character traits.

---

74 On Drummond, see 2:14: "Henry Drummond: A Presbyterian, Evangelicalism and Science."
75 Drummond, *Moody*, 40.
76 Smith in Drummond, *Moody*, 15.
77 Shanks, *Moody at Home*, 108
78 *Andrew A. Bonar, D. D.: Life and Letters*, ed. Marjorie Bonar (London: Hodder and Stoughton, 1893), 245.
79 Findlay, *Moody*, 369.
80 Smith in Drummond, *Moody*, 4.

Conclusion

What then did Moody bequeath to the twentieth century? There was a modern evangelistic style adapted to urban society. It was not just that Moody held missions in cities, for he also inspired and trained others for urban evangelism. The founder of the Church Army that often gave edge to the witness of the Church of England in the twentieth century, Wilson Carlile, first came to prominence in Christian work during Moody's London campaign of 1875.[81] Again, Moody's theological style established the norms of conservative Evangelical orthodoxy in the twentieth century. The Moody Bible Institute, dedicated to his memory, was as near the center of the American Evangelical world in the first half of the twentieth century as any organization. Moody's views also spread far and wide through his writings, his lieutenants and his other institutions. And his social style encouraged an appeal to the mass of the people. One of the converts from his Glasgow mission of 1874, James Mathers, eventually emigrated to Australia in 1897, becoming a city missionary in Sydney. In 1901 a Mrs Jones, a woman in the most deprived district of the city, broke Mathers' jaw with a bottle in a drunken outburst. Two years later, however, to Mathers' great surprise, Mrs Jones and her husband were converted.[82] There is a cameo of the long-term results of Moody's achievement. That this set of events took place in the southern hemisphere illustrates the pervasive influence of the evangelist. Moody made a great impact on his own day through preaching, education, a concern for unity and sheer personality, but he also did as much as any man to shape the international Evangelical movement of the twentieth century. His brand of transatlantic Evangelicalism spread over the whole globe.

---

81 Morgan, "A Veteran in Revival," 184–85.
82 Malcolm Prentis, "City of God, City of Man: Images of the Slum, 1897–1911," in *Gritty Cities: Images of the Urban*, ed. Lynette Finch and Chris McConville (Annandale, NSW: Pluto Press, 1999), 104–7.

7

Global Evangelicalism in the Nineteenth Century

In 1851 there was published in Boston, Massachusetts, a book entitled *Evangelism in the Middle of the Nineteenth Century* by Charles Adams of Lowell. Its introduction contended that it was the will of God that all nations should hear the gospel proclaimed by the Christian church. Every true believer, without regard for "sect or denomination," was responsible for cooperating with the Almighty in spreading the glad tidings of salvation. The appeal was not to all Protestants, for Adams discounted the Unitarians whom he saw around him in New England. His concern was with what he called "evangelical christendom," the body of those who had been brought to "believe in Christ with a heart unto righteousness." This community had undertaken astonishing efforts during the previous half century. "A greater missionary work has transpired," Adams declared as he warmed to his theme, ". . . than what was wrought during the fifty years subsequent to the ascension of the Lord Jesus." There had been a mighty stirring of the church. "Every denomination of Christians termed Orthodox," he went on, "have arisen, with one accord, for the spread of the gospel among all nations." What was more, there were signs that providence was on their side. Missionaries were in the field, the Bible societies were at work and nearly the whole world was open to evangelization. The press wielded more power than in the past and there were better facilities for traveling by land and sea. It was clear that God was preparing for the further progress of Christianity over the remainder of the century. Accordingly, Adams presented his readers with a survey of the forces in the divine army mobilized for the conquest of the world. Beginning with America, he listed the Christian bodies operating in each land, ranging through Europe, Asia, Africa and what he called Oceanica. Romanism, the Greek Church and the Armenian Church are relegated to an appendix alongside Judaism, Mohammedanism and Paganism. Adams, confident that only his coreligionists possessed the truth, was commending the interests of Evangelicalism alone.[1] He was depicting a vigorous global movement.

Adams and his contemporaries were very conscious of the existence of a single Evangelical cause. Only five years before Adams' book appeared, there had assembled in London a gathering of representatives from many lands to create an Evangelical Alliance. Naturally the great majority of the roughly eight hundred attenders were British, but as high a proportion as 10 percent were from the United States and 6 percent were from continental Europe. There were said to be members of some fifty different denominations at the conference. Although the meeting was fraught with difficulties, especially over whether slaveholders should be admissible to the new organization, the enterprise was an indication that believers from many Protestant traditions possessed a strong sense of solidarity. The venerable Scottish Congregational theologian Ralph Wardlaw expressed the common spirit in proposing the first resolution, which affirmed:

> that the church of the living God, while it admits of growth, is one church, never having lost, and being incapable of losing its essential unity. Not, therefore, to create that unity, but to confess it, is the design of their assembling together. One in reality, they desire also, as far as they may be able to attain it, to be visibly one: and thus, both to realize in themselves, and to exhibit to others, that a living and everlasting union binds all true believers together in one fellowship of the Church of Christ.[2]

The repeated insistence on unity is a sign that the framers of the resolution were aware that outsiders, seeing the motley diversity of the religious regiments marshaled for the occasion, would dismiss the new organization as fated to splinter into fragments. But the initiators of the venture wanted to give institutional expression to their common Evangelical identity. The reality of the nineteenth century was that Evangelicals formed a self-aware international force.

Yet the phenomenon of global Evangelicalism is neglected in much of the historical literature. The very success of the movement in so many countries has led historians to concentrate on its individual national slices to the exclusion of the grander whole. Evangelicalism made a significant impact in at least

---

1 Charles Adams, *Evangelism in the Middle of the Nineteenth Century* (Boston: Gould and Lincoln, 1851), quoted at 21, 24, 30.
2 *Proceedings of the Conference Held at Freemasons' Hall, London, 1846* (London, 1847), 44, quoted in J. B. A. Kessler, *A Study of the Evangelical Alliance in Great Britain* (Goes, Netherlands: Oosterbaan & Le Cointre N. V., 1968), 37.

five sectors of the world. It flourished in the British Isles, though much less in Catholic southern Ireland than elsewhere in the islands. Evangelicals molded the United States, as much on its advancing western frontier as on its populated eastern seaboard. Other lands of extensive British settlement—Canada, Australia, New Zealand and the Cape being the chief—were home to sizeable Evangelical communities. Although Evangelicalism found the European continent much less congenial soil, there was some penetration into many lands, with an enduring legacy in, for example, Sweden. And there was the missionary enterprise that carried the gospel to other parts of the world, enjoying astonishing success in places such as the Polynesian islands and reaching unexpected regions such as the borders of Siberia and Mongolia. There is a natural tendency for historians, who cannot achieve omniscience, to concentrate on only one of these five dimensions of the Evangelical world, and often on only a single national unit within it. Thus a recently translated book by R. Tudur Jones, in many ways a profoundly illuminating analysis of Welsh Christianity at the end of the century, suffers from treating the nation's "Evangelical Accord" in an exclusively Welsh context. Most of the features of the Welsh experience could be paralleled in other lands, but Tudur Jones commonly attributes developments in the principality to unique features of national life rather than to factors that were also impinging on Evangelicals elsewhere.[3] The religious history of England, America and other countries has often suffered from a similar failure to locate Evangelical bodies within the broader international perspective in which they saw themselves. By concentrating on particular territories for investigation, the historiography has done a disservice to the common features of the global Evangelical movement.

An equally distorting effect has been produced by the tendency of historians to write about individual denominations. Institutional histories inevitably concentrate on particular confessional groups; and personal allegiance leads many church historians to research only their own ecclesiastical body. The nineteenth-century Evangelical mosaic contained a bewildering variety of denominational families. Again they may be divided into a number of main categories. First there was an Evangelical presence within the Anglican communion, which, though it was also home to High and Broad Churchmen, contained many whose loyalty was to the preaching of the gospel that they shared with other denominations. Then there were the Reformed Churches, most of them Presbyterian, which dominated Scotland and had strong representation in other parts of the world. The Congregationalists were like the

---

3   Robert Tudur Jones, *Faith and the Crisis of a Nation: Wales, 1890–1914*, trans. Sylvia Prys Jones and ed. Robert Pope (Cardiff: University of Wales Press, 2004), 16.

Presbyterians in inheriting Calvinist teachings but unlike them in asserting the independence of the local church from any external authority. Baptists were similar to Congregationalists, though often more populist and practicing believer's baptism by immersion. Methodists, Arminian in theology like their founder John Wesley, were the most enterprising of nineteenth-century Evangelical groupings, growing immensely during its hundred years. There were also Moravians, Quakers with an Evangelical standpoint, Brethren and many others on the sectarian fringe of Evangelicalism. Faced with this immense diversity, historians may be excused for preferring to write about a single confessional grouping. Again, however, there can be detrimental consequences for our understanding of the past. Much of the writing on Scotland, for example, has dwelt on the Presbyterian experience to the exclusion of other denominations. Since over 80 percent of churchgoers held some Presbyterian allegiance, the concentration is understandable, but it has had the effect of artificially insulating Scottish Christianity from its Evangelical context. Interactions with thought and practice from other sectors of the Evangelical world have been neglected.[4] The denominational differences, real and fascinating though they are, must not blind us to the centrality in nineteenth-century experience of Evangelical identity.

Common Characteristics

This chapter seeks to redress the balance by drawing attention to the common features of Evangelical religion that transcended the internal fissures within the global movement, whether national or denominational. It may begin with the characteristics that together formed the characteristic marks of Evangelicalism, the first being devotion to the Bible. Elizabeth Rose, the wife of an American Methodist minister of the Troy Conference, who died in 1862 at the age of thirty-one in Lebanon, New York, showed this quality while in the last stages of pulmonary consumption. "She was a great lover of the Bible," according to her obituarist, "making it her constant companion and reading it in family worship, either sitting or lying in bed, even when unable to speak above a whisper."[5] Another Methodist woman, though this time writing in England eleven years later, explained her conviction that "it cannot be amiss to refer to

---

4   E.g. Alexander C. Cheyne, *Transforming the Kirk: Victorian Scotland's Religious Revolution* (Edinburgh: Saint Andrew Press, 1983), 72. Cheyne points to liberalizing influences from elsewhere but among external Evangelical influences only Moody and Sankey receive attention.
5   *Christian Advocate and Journal* (New York), 4 September 1862, 286. Places of publication are indicated for periodicals in this chapter in order to avoid confusion.

the Bible as the highest authority on all subjects on which it professes to speak authoritatively, to seek its thoughts as the basis of our own, and to endeavour to appropriate its teaching for the guidance of our lives."[6] The same sense that the Bible was the decisive authority in matters of faith and practice became widespread even among the Quakers, who had traditionally downplayed the role of the scriptures relative to the inward light, when they were affected by the rise of Evangelicalism in their ranks. "We reverently lay our hand on the Testaments, Old and New," ran a leading article in the *Friend*, the British journal of Evangelical Quakerism in 1852, "and by them we stand."[7] When, towards the end of the century, the Evangelical Alliance organized a series of meetings in and around London to bear witness to the "cardinal truths of the Gospel," the first was on scripture, covering its inspiration, authority, and sufficiency.[8] The family Bible on the parlor table was the most obvious outward symbol of Christian allegiance in Evangelical homes on every continent. The scriptures formed one of the bonds that held the global Evangelical movement together.

The doctrine of the cross was another. For an agent of the American Missionary Association, an abolitionist Congregational body, who was working in Illinois in 1858, the "great vital points" of the faith included "that Christ has made an all-sufficient atonement."[9] The emphasis on the death of Christ as the source of salvation was universal in the Evangelical movement. The reputed words on his deathbed of an English Wesleyan, William Johnston, in the previous year showed a comparable doctrinal stress, clearly appropriated as the basis of a personal faith. "I look to the Crucified," he declared, "I rest in the atonement—Glory be to Jesus!"[10] Phrases associated with the death of Christ became Evangelical shibboleths. Thus a soldier who was on guard at Gibraltar, when challenged by an officer for the watchword, came out with the phrase most prominent in his mind, "The precious blood of Christ." What the officer thought is not recorded, but a fellow soldier is said to have found the Savior as a result of overhearing the words.[11] In an editorial on "The Cleansing Blood," the leading American Methodist newspaper the *Christian Advocate* pointed out in 1872 that the cross was central to behavior as well as to teaching. "As the sacrifice of Christ lies at the foundation of all Christian doctrine,"

6   M.A.Y., "Bible Thoughts about Women," *Wesleyan Sunday School Magazine*, 1873-74, 121, quoted in Linda Wilson, *Constrained by Zeal: Female Spirituality amongst Nonconformists, 1825-1875* (Carlisle: Paternoster Press, 2000), 52.
7   *Friend* (London), February 1852, 29.
8   *Freeman* (London), 6 January 1888, 13.
9   *American Missionary* (New York), July 1858, 59.
10 *Wesleyan Methodist Magazine* (London), March 1860, 283.
11 *Christian Advocate and Journal*, 4 March 1858, 33.

it contended, "so is its application essential to all Christian purity and life."[12] The atonement brought peace to the saved and challenge to the sinner. First and foremost, the great English Baptist preacher Charles Haddon Spurgeon told his students, they should preach "Christ and him crucified."[13] It was a priority every Evangelical shared.

A further common feature of Evangelicalism was belief in conversion. It was a fundamental premise of Evangelicals that many who went by the name of Christian were not true believers. Thus William Oakley, who long served with the Anglican Evangelical Church Missionary Society in Sri Lanka, found many English families on the island who showed no regard for religion. They needed to have a change of direction that set them for the first time on the highroad of salvation. Oakley therefore "sought the conversion of nominal Christians."[14] A commonly used synonym for conversion was being born again or regenerated. Thus a correspondent of the *Friend* insisted that the right of children of Quakers to membership in the Society of Friends must not be allowed to obscure their personal need of grace. "May we, then, individually be willing to examine," it urged, ". . . whether we know for ourselves, what it is to be regenerated."[15] Another theological term associated with the experience was justification, often limited to the divine forgiveness of sinners on their first trusting Jesus for salvation. For William Taylor, a globe-trotting American Methodist evangelist who was eventually appointed bishop of Africa, when God sees individuals surrender, he acquits them. "That part of the transaction," according to Taylor, "is called justification by faith."[16] The nature of conversion, however, might be formulated in different ways. For many, especially the more respectable worshipers, it might be understood as a gradual process of which the subject might be unconscious until it was complete; but for others, especially the more red-hot evangelists, it was necessarily experienced as a sudden event. Thus Reginald Radcliffe, a leading English revivalist, insisted in 1860 "that conversion is an instantaneous work."[17] Yet what the movement did agree on was that conversion, whether slow or fast, conscious or unconscious, was the essential opening of the spiritual life. Without it, a person was not a Christian at all.

12   *Christian Advocate* (New York), 3 October 1872, 316.
13   Charles H. Spurgeon, *Lectures to My Students* (London: Marshall, Morgan & Scott, 1954), 337.
14   "The Rev. William Oakley," in *Brief Sketches: C.M.S. Workers*, vol. 2 (n.p., n.d.), 7.
15   *Friend*, July 1852, 129.
16   William Taylor, *William Taylor of California, Bishop of Africa: An Autobiography*, rev. C. G. Moore (London: Hodder & Stoughton, 1897), 204.
17   *Christian* (London), 21 January 1860, 21.

A final characteristic of all Evangelicals was activism. Those who had read in their Bibles about the urgency of salvation, who felt gratitude for the work of Christ on the cross and who believed that they themselves had been converted were highly motivated for the task of conveying the gospel to others. The result was a whirl of evangelistic efforts. "Piety in these days," announced the *Presbyterian Home Missionary* of New York in 1884, "shows itself more in work than in reflection and meditation."[18] Ministers were particularly devoted to activity: "work, work, work," said William Morley Punshon, a prominent Wesleyan minister who served in Canada as well as Britain, "is the *lex vitae* of a Methodist preacher in either hemisphere."[19] Even retirement did not put an end to the pertinacity of ministers in proclaiming the good news. Samuel Howe, an American Methodist who was superannuated from the ministry in 1830, nevertheless continued to preach, turning railroad cars into his pulpit: "He would arise and occupy the two or three minutes of stopping, so as often to move the passengers to tears on the subject of their souls' salvation."[20] Local evangelism spilled over into both world mission and social concern, with the same impetus to incessant endeavor driving a William Carey in India and a Lord Shaftesbury in England. Friedrich Tholuck, perhaps the leading scholar identified with the German *Erweckungsbewegung*, or awakening, was a passionate supporter of missions. In 1847, on returning from the Evangelical Alliance in England, he commended the example of what he had witnessed to his German coreligionists, urging them "to give to their Christianity a more practical form, a more vigorous impulse, and to enter on a course of more active usefulness."[21] It was a recognition that Evangelicalism had no time for idleness. Bible, cross, conversion and activism—these were the key features of the movement, whatever the religious body, whatever the national allegiance.

The common Evangelical ethos, however, was also apparent in many other aspects of the movement. The trajectory of its theology, for example, illustrates the way in which Evangelicalism, though internally diverse, was being forged into a single entity. At the start of the period there was a considerable gulf between the Arminianism of the Methodists, together with a few others, and the Calvinism of most Evangelical groupings. Arminians believed that all might be saved by exercising their freewill; Calvinists held that God chose a particular number for salvation. The type of moderate Calvinism held by

---

18 *Presbyterian Home Missionary* (New York), March 1884, 51.
19 Frederic W. Macdonald and A. H. Reynar, *The Life of William Morley Punshon, LL.D.* (London: Hodder and Stoughton, 1881), 316.
20 *Christian Advocate and Journal*, 18 March 1858, 44.
21 *Evangelical Christendom* (London), August 1847, 241.

those who had been influenced by the Evangelical awakening, however, had abandoned "double predestination," the high Calvinist view that the Almighty condemned individuals to perdition. Theologians such as the Congregationalists of the New England school and the English Baptist Andrew Fuller taught, on the contrary, that sinners were responsible for the loss of their own souls. The tendency to a lowered version of the Reformed tradition went further, with the revivalist Charles Finney, for example, according a much larger role to human ability in conversion. The distance between Calvinists and Arminians steadily narrowed until, in the last third of the century, there were signs that it had virtually disappeared. Dwight L. Moody was able to frame his evangelistic messages so that they were acceptable to both parties.[22] In 1890 a commentator in southern Africa, noting that "Christian Churches are now converging in doctrine," saw no difference of substance between the teachings of Wesleyans and Presbyterians.[23] Nine years later the National Council of the Evangelical Free Churches in England and Wales issued a catechism that was equally endorsed by theologians from Methodism and from the denominations with a Reformed inheritance.[24] The most obvious theological division in the ranks of the movement had been largely healed.

There was a similar convergence in the area of spirituality, which was molded by the same doctrinal traditions. The American Methodist *Christian Advocate* set out in 1858 what it saw as a main contrast between the denominations. The Methodists, it claimed, taught feeling first, and thinking afterwards. "*Methodism addresses the heart*" and so differed from "the more ratiocinative Congregationalism or Presbyterianism."[25] Methodists, furthermore, looked for entire sanctification, a sudden leap into holiness after conversion, whereas those with a Reformed background expected advances in the Christian life to be gradual, the result of sustained struggle. There was therefore a definite difference between denominational forms of spirituality that did not entirely disappear. As the century wore on, however, there was more interaction between them. In national organizations, leaders of the various bodies cooperated with each other; in remote places, union churches brought people upholding different approaches together in single congregations. Methodists started singing the hymns of the Congregationalist Isaac Watts and everybody else started singing the hymns of Charles Wesley. So the area of common ground

---

22 See 1:6: "Dwight L. Moody and Transatlantic Evangelicalism."
23 *Christian Express* (Lovedale, South Africa), 1 November 1890, 163–64.
24 *An Evangelical Free Church Catechism for Use in Home and School* (London: National Council of the Evangelical Free Churches, 1899).
25 *Christian Advocate and Journal*, 18 March 1858, 41.

in spirituality increased. Many Methodists became more reflective in matters of faith, so that they insisted more on thinking; and their distinctive quest for entire sanctification gradually faded, so that they emphasized the need for steady effort instead.[26] There was in any case a great deal of shared devotional practice. Prayer was a priority for all, whether in private or in public. The weekly prayer meeting, remarked an American handbook on the subject published in 1878, had been ceasing to be a "spiritual refrigerator" as it steadily grew in importance "in the estimation of Christians of all denominations."[27] Likewise anticipation of heaven was a remarkably prominent theme across the confessional boundaries. Especially as death approached, there was, at least down to the 1870s, an eagerness to talk openly about the glory land that was in prospect for the believer.[28] By the end of the century there was a high degree of union of soul among Evangelicals.

Association with Modernity

The unity extended beyond the soul to the mind. The intellectual orientation of most Evangelicals during the nineteenth century was molded by the legacy of the Enlightenment. Reason, to a striking extent, was their lodestar. This characteristic has been obscured in some of the older literature by a stress on the undoubted repudiation by nineteenth-century Evangelicals of rationalist thinking. Thus a leading article in the *Record*, the Anglican Evangelical newspaper, at the opening of 1863 roundly condemned "the vagaries of Prussian or German rationalism." But what it was rejecting was the abuse of reason, not reason itself. It commended "the good sense of LOCKE," so appealing to the mastermind of the English Enlightenment, and also "the 'Common Sense' of REID," the leading Christian philosopher of the Scottish Enlightenment.[29] Thomas Reid's principle that there are matters, such as the existence of God, which, because they are beyond doubt, are the common property of all human minds was almost universally endorsed by nineteenth-century Evangelicals.[30] They also embraced other values derived from the Enlightenment. Happiness loomed large in their vocabulary, at least in the earlier part of the century.

---

26 David W. Bebbington, *Holiness in Nineteenth-Century England* (Carlisle: Paternoster Press, 2000), chaps. 2, 3.
27 Lewis O. Thompson, *The Prayer-Meeting and Its Improvement*, 5th ed. (Chicago: F. H. Revell, 1881), x.
28 Wilson, *Constrained by Zeal*, 59–63. See also 1:11: "The Deathbed Piety of Evangelical Nonconformists in the Nineteenth Century."
29 *Record* (London), 2 January 1863.
30 Mark A. Noll, "Common Sense Traditions and American Evangelical Thought," *American Quarterly* 37:2 (1985), 216–38, at 220–25.

Thus in 1828 Adam Clarke, an able and urbane Wesleyan minister, published a whole sermon urging the view that happiness was the natural possession of Christians, once more citing Locke, among others.[31] Again, there was a fundamental conviction that the gospel was on the side of the civilization that the Enlightenment aspired to diffuse throughout society. John Mackenzie, a prominent Congregational missionary in Botswana, declared at his ordination in 1858 that preachers of the gospel must teach "the arts of civilized life."[32] Reason, happiness, civilization—these Enlightenment principles were the secure property of Evangelicals.

Hence there were several ways in which Evangelicals were aligned with modernizing facets of Enlightenment thought. They echoed the typical optimism of the later years of the Age of Reason in their version of the Christian hope. They confidently expected that, as a result of the advance of the missions of their day, the whole world would turn to Christ. The church, according to John Angell James, the Congregational minister at Carr's Lane, Birmingham, was "assured of increase, triumph, and universal dominion."[33] This was the postmillennial understanding of the future, so called because it postulated that the second advent of Christ would not take place until after ("post"-) the arrival of the millennium predicted in the book of Revelation. In that coming era, Satan would be bound and so his malignant influence would be prevented from damaging the progress of the gospel and its values. "When Christ shall reign spiritually on earth," rhapsodized an American coreligionist, W. H. Johnstone, in 1857, "then covetousness shall cease, the wealth, and influence, and power, and glory of the Universe will be given to Zion, millions will be saved . . . and the kingdoms of this world [will] become the kingdoms of our Lord and His Christ."[34] This postmillennialism was the general stance of nineteenth-century Evangelicals, though over time the theological content of their beliefs about the future tended to become vaguer. Already in 1850 the idea of the coming millennium was being subordinated to a more this-worldly ideal in a book called *The Theory of Human Progression*.[35] As the century went on, most Evangelicals continued to suppose that the world was getting better, but

---

31 Adam Clarke, *Discourses on Various Subjects Relative to the Being and Attributes of God and His Works in Creation, Providence and Grace*, 3 vols. (London: J. and T. Clarke, 1828–30), 1, sermon 11.
32 *Papers of John Mackenzie*, ed. Anthony J. Dachs (Johannesburg: Witwatersrand University Press, 1975), 72.
33 John A. James, *The Church in Earnest* (London: Hamilton, Adams, 1861), 356.
34 *American Missionary*, December 1857, 282–83.
35 *Baptist Magazine* (London), October 1850, 614–22.

did not know very clearly why. As heirs of the Enlightenment, they were as much advocates of the idea of progress as their secular-minded contemporaries.

Equally, for much of the century, Evangelicals were as forward as any other school of thought in endorsing science. Their belief in reason underlay a devotion to what they called the "Baconian rules of inductive reasoning," the principles of empirical investigation attributed to Francis Bacon whereby the natural world could be made to yield up its secrets.[36] Likewise postmillennialism encouraged Evangelicals to see the "unimagined ways in which science has become auxiliary to the social improvement of mankind" as signs of the advance towards the glorious times to come.[37] Scientific notes regularly appeared in religious magazines, for there was a conviction that there was a harmony between God's revelation in his word and in his work. "It is truly," declared the Scottish theologian Thomas Chalmers in 1816, "a most Christian exercise to extract a sentiment of piety from the works and appearances of nature."[38] Chalmers, like many others, deployed scientific discoveries to defend the Christian religion, defining the field as natural theology. In particular, the adaptation of living things to their purpose seemed firm evidence of an intelligent Creator. Popular lecturers such as Thomas Cooper, once an infidel champion, dwelt on the theme of design in the universe.[39] Charles Darwin's case that evolution rather than design explained the adaptation did not end the discussion, for Evangelical apologists began to take broader ground, arguing that the Almighty used natural processes to achieve his ends.[40] After Darwin there was an awareness that science was not automatically an ally in the battle of belief, but as yet there were only the beginnings of the twentieth-century sense that science was likely to be ranged in the ranks of the enemy. The predominant attitude among nineteenth-century Evangelicals was that the records of scientific endeavor served as an invaluable apologetic armory.

There was also an alliance between Evangelical religion and commercial enterprise. The rule-governed universe seemed to be one where the Almighty

---

36 *Christian Observer* (London), September 1854, 625.
37 *Evangelical Christendom*, January 1847, 2.
38 Thomas Chalmers, *Discourses on the Christian Revelation Viewed in Connexion with the Modern Astronomy with Others of a Kindred Character* (Edinburgh: Sutherland and Knox, 1848), 21.
39 Timothy Larsen, *Contested Christianity: The Political and Social Contexts of Victorian Theology* (Waco, TX: Baylor University Press, 2004), 118–19.
40 James R. Moore, *The Post-Darwinian Controversies: A Study of the Protestant Struggle to Come to Terms with Darwin in Great Britain and America, 1870–1900* (Cambridge: Cambridge University Press, 1979). On science, see further 1:14: "Science and Evangelical Theology in Britain from Wesley to Orr."

had arranged that trade would generate prosperity. The development of systems of exchange was another symptom of progress towards the millennium. Hence it was natural for spokesmen for missions to argue that they should go hand in hand not only with civilization but also with trade. In the peroration of a celebrated speech at Cambridge in 1857, the Scottish explorer-missionary David Livingstone announced that he was returning to Africa to "make an open path for commerce and Christianity."[41] There was an undoubted congruence between the teaching of Evangelicals and the qualities needed in the burgeoning market economy—integrity, diligence, self-reliance. It should not, however, be supposed that Evangelical religion closed its eyes to a ruthless pursuit of profit. On the contrary, it developed elaborate bodies of thinking about commercial ethics, condemning, as did the American New School Presbyterian Albert Barnes in 1841, "the insatiable love of gain."[42] When any of its adherents failed in business, it was a matter of shame and, in the case of gathered churches, of ecclesiastical discipline. Thus Sir Samuel Morton Peto, the immensely rich railway entrepreneur and founder of Bloomsbury Baptist Chapel in central London, was censured by his own church when, in 1867, he became bankrupt even though it was a result of a bank failure entirely beyond his control.[43] Nevertheless Evangelicals did not see economic affairs as a worldly intrusion into the spiritual sphere. Large churches increasingly operated as commercial ventures, organizing systematic giving, listing donations and using proper bookkeeping methods. The deacons at the King's Weigh House, a Congregational church in London, discussed in 1860 the introduction of a regular "statement of the Income and Expenditures of the various Societies in connexion with the Church."[44] Prosperity founded on efficiency seemed as natural a goal in the church as in business. Evangelical congregations of all lands and every denomination, at least in the big cities, seemed wholly identified with modernity in its economic dimension.

---

41 Andrew C. Ross, *David Livingstone: Mission and Empire* (London: Hambledon and London, 2002), 121.

42 Albert Barnes, "Vindication of Revivals and Their Influence on This Country," *American National Preacher*, 15 (January 1841), 23, quoted in R. W. Pointer, "Philadelphia Presbyterians, Capitalism and the Morality of Economic Success," in *God and Mammon: Protestants, Money and the Market, 1790–1860*, ed. Mark A. Noll (New York: Oxford University Press, 2001), 171–91, at 182.

43 Faith and Brian Bowers, "Bloomsbury Chapel and Mercantile Morality," *Baptist Quarterly* 30 (1984), 210–20.

44 Charles D. Cashdollar, *A Spiritual Home: Life in British and American Reformed Congregations, 1830–1915* (University Park, PA: Pennsylvania State University Press, 2000), 157.

Enemies of the Evangelicals

If Evangelicals were generally in favor of the cluster of forces usually associated with the modernizing inheritance of the Enlightenment—reason, optimism, science and commerce—they also knew what they were against. The Bible taught them that their grand enemy was sin, conversion was away from sin and it was sin that had brought about the need for the atonement. So hostility to sin was rooted in their key characteristics. Accordingly they not only denounced wrongdoing from the pulpit but also took action against it in public. The typical way in which Evangelicals engaged with the ills of society was to organize campaigns against whatever they regarded as wickedness. The best method of rousing Evangelical audiences against British colonial slavery, the leading agitator in the cause discovered in the early 1830s, was to denounce it as "criminal before God."[45] Already at the beginning of the century William Wilberforce had led efforts to reform manners by enforcing laws against blasphemy and sabbath-breaking and to induce parliament to prohibit the slave trade, a measure achieved in 1807. Subsequently other issues were taken up when the Evangelical public decided a wrong could be put down. The temperance movement was transformed into a Christian campaign when it was concluded that strong drink was the cause of personal ruin for thousands. Because alcohol was so dangerous, some Evangelicals decided that its sale was an outright sin. Thus Amzi C. Dixon, an energetic Baptist minister, was horrified to discover on moving to Baltimore, New Jersey, in 1882, that liquor dealers were listed on the membership roll.[46] Broader campaigning against public evils that was to issue in the social gospel movement towards the end of the century was at first less a diversion from Evangelical priorities than an addition to them. The social gospel, too, should be understood primarily as an effort to combat what sensitive Christian consciences had diagnosed as the sinful features of the urban-industrial society that was spreading around the world. At a Methodist ordination service in Melbourne in 1891, for instance, the ex-president of the denominational Conference charged the candidates that the work of the ministry should include not only preaching, pastoral work and administration, but also social philanthropy. "You will . . . take a leading part," he told the young men before him, "in movements for checking intemperance, gambling and impurity."[47] Such mass mobilizations against sin were another standard feature that united nineteenth-century Evangelicals.

45 George Stephen, *Anti-Slavery Recollections in a Series of Letters Addressed to Mrs Beecher Stowe* [1854] (London: Cass, 1971), 248.
46 Helen C. A. Dixon, *A. C. Dixon: A Romance of Preaching* (New York: G. P. Putnam's Sons, 1931), 88.
47 *Spectator and Methodist Chronicle* (Melbourne), 20 March 1891, 280.

They also agreed, however, that there was another enemy to be resisted. The Roman Catholic Church was a redoubtable rival for the souls of the world, with Irish folk carrying their faith to the uttermost parts of the earth. A young Free Church of Scotland minister named Robert Taylor sent from Edinburgh to Sydney in 1845 was dismayed to find himself on board the outward vessel with a party of priests. Having unsuccessfully tried to start a disputation with them in Latin, he noticed with a critical eye that they were devoting a very large proportion of the Lord's Day to playing chess. "The Pope," he concluded, "has evidently marked Australia as his own."[48] Rome appeared to grow sterner as the century wore on. The Syllabus of Errors of 1864, anathematizing modern trends, alarmed Protestants because it seemed to assert even higher papal claims over the temporal allegiance of Catholics than in the past. In the following year the leading Baptist newspaper in the United States commented that "the moral pestilence of Romanism" was "directly at variance with the spirit of our political institutions."[49] What was more, Catholic teaching appeared to have infiltrated into the Anglican communion. The Oxford Movement of the 1830s was perceived by Evangelicals as an attempt to reverse the Reformation and so to "unprotestantize" the Church of England. The ritualists who were inspired by the ideals of the Tractarians to introduce elaborate ceremonial into their services constituted a Trojan horse. "Ritualism," declared one of their most eloquent opponents, J. C. Ryle, "is nothing but Romanism in the bud, and Romanism is Ritualism in flower."[50] The efforts of like-minded Anglicans, enjoying the sympathy of the whole range of Evangelical opinion, to resist the rising tide of ritualism occupied a great deal of their energies during the later nineteenth century. Evangelicals throughout the world were resolute opponents of the Roman Catholic Church and of those who imitated its practice.

Unifying Mechanisms

How did such a high degree of consensus emerge about what Evangelicals endorsed and what they rejected? There were chiefly three mechanisms at work. First, there was the printed word. Evangelicals used the press, in the words of the report of the Church Missionary Society in 1801, "as a most

---

48 *Home and Foreign Missionary Record of the Free Church of Scotland* (Edinburgh), January 1846, 277.
49 *Examiner and Chronicle* (New York), 11 May 1865.
50 John C. Ryle, *Bishops and Clergy of Other Days* (London: William Hunt and Co., 1868), 2. On Ryle, see 2:2: "Bishop J. C. Ryle: Holiness, Mission and Churchmanship."

powerful auxiliary in their grand design."⁵¹ The Bible itself was naturally the book most printed. The interdenominational British and Foreign Bible Society, founded in 1804, calculated that already, only thirteen years later, it had issued 1,808,261 Bibles, Testaments and scripture portions. In that period the society had printed copies in as many as nineteen languages.⁵² The cause was immensely popular, with humble folk devising imaginative money-raising schemes. Thus at Witchampton, Dorset, £2 came in 1867 from "the parrot of a worthy woman, who had taught it to ask for Contributions with a tin Collecting-box attached to its cage."⁵³ The society had many imitators abroad. A book called *Bible Stories*, originally published in 1832 for educational use by the German and Foreign School Society of Calw, Würtemburg, was translated from German into English, Danish, Bohemian, Hungarian, Wendish, Polish, Canarese, Tamil, Bengali, Hindustani and Chinese.⁵⁴ Small tracts circulated in enormous numbers. The Religious Tract Society, established in 1799, even before the British and Foreign Bible Society, and equally representative of Evangelicalism as a whole, specialized in issuing these telling leaflets. By the middle of the century it was publishing in 110 languages and 4,363 titles appeared on its list.⁵⁵ By that time, however, the Religious Tract Society had ventured beyond tracts themselves to publish books, many of them reissued by the American Sunday School Union, that related faith to every sphere of knowledge. Geography, agriculture, political economy, natural science and many other subjects were covered in its "monthly series" of volumes, which always touched on the atonement. Here was a publishing venture that aimed to create a Christian mind among a mass audience. The Religious Tract Society was also responsible for publishing weekly periodicals, *Leisure Hour* and *Sunday at Home*, and later the *Boys' Own Paper* and the *Girls' Own Paper*, which reached a huge readership.⁵⁶ Its transatlantic sister organization, the American Tract Society, proudly claimed in the year 1849–50 that its publications, which, in order to maximize the statistical impact, it calculated in pages, amounted

---

51 *Proceedings of the Church Missionary Society for Africa and the East* 1 (1801–5), 80.
52 William Canton, *A History of the British and Foreign Bible Society*, 5 vols. (London: John Murray, 1904–10), 1:318.
53 Leslie Howsam, *Cheap Bibles: Nineteenth-Century Publishing and the British and Foreign Bible Society* (Cambridge: Cambridge University Press, 1991), 183.
54 *Evangelical Christendom*, May 1847, 147.
55 Roger H. Martin, *Evangelicals United: Ecumenical Stirrings in Pre-Victorian Britain, 1795–1830* (Metuchen, NJ: Scarecrow Press, 1983), 156.
56 Aileen Fyfe, *Science and Salvation: Evangelical Popular Science Publishing in Victorian Britain* (Chicago: University of Chicago Press, 2004), 76, 108, 177–81.

to 280,697,500.⁵⁷ Similar publishing ventures were set up in other lands, with China, for example, having thirty Christian presses by the early years of the twentieth century.⁵⁸ The resulting vast body of literature helped ensure that Evangelicals thought alike across national and denominational boundaries.

Institutions were a second agency by which Evangelical solidarity was fostered. The nineteenth century was the age of the rise of benevolent associations. In America the chief bodies existing by mid-century, apart from the publishing societies, were the missionary organizations, of which the American Board of Commissioners for Foreign Missions, founded in 1810, was the chief, the home missions, the Sunday School Union, the Education Society and the Seaman's Friend Society.⁵⁹ The British equivalents had their headquarters in the Exeter Hall in London's Strand, where each year the May Meetings, the annual rallies of each organization, were held. Many of them, including all the leading missionary societies, belonged to particular denominations, but the coordination of their annual meetings and the regular exchange of speakers between them were signs that they were a part of a unitary Evangelical venture. Furthermore, they were aware of being integrated into an international network that bound them together. Seamen's missions, for example, regularly exchanged news, copied methods and lent personnel.⁶⁰ In Wellington, New Zealand, it was agreed in 1848 to establish a Bible society, a tract and book society and a monthly periodical on British models.⁶¹ A handbook on Sunday school techniques published in London in 1871 recommended an American plan for issuing library books, even urging readers to "Use *Geist's* adhesive *tags* for backs of books."⁶² An eagerness to meet the needs of young people was responsible for a large number of international ventures. The Young Men's Christian Association, launched in London in 1844, soon became a flourishing body on other shores. When a visiting Canadian Maritimer attended its annual meeting in the Exeter Hall in 1850, he was impressed that it aimed "to carry the religion of the Bible into the counting house." "An Institution of this kind," he remarked, "is wanted in Halifax and St. John exceedingly."⁶³ In the following year a

57   Adams, *Evangelism*, 299.
58   John H. Ritson, *Christian Literature in the Mission Field* (Edinburgh: Continuation Committee of the World Missionary Conference, 1910, 1915), 44–48.
59   Evans, *Evangelism*, 287–303.
60   Roald Kverndal, *Seaman's Missions: Their Origin and Early Growth* (Pasadena, CA: William Carey Library, 1986).
61   *Evangelical Christendom*, September 1848, 293.
62   James C. Gray, *The Sunday-School World* (London: Elliot Stock, 1871), 306.
63   *Christian Messenger* (Halifax, NS), 22 March 1850, 94.

Y.M.C.A. was founded in Montreal and another in Boston. Likewise the Christian Endeavor Society, founded in Portland, Maine, in 1881, and the Boys' Brigade, established in Glasgow two years later, rapidly turned into global movements. Parachurch agencies of various kinds transmitted ideas and enthusiasms from one side of the world to another, welding the movement they served into a single entity.

The third form of linkage between the branches of the Evangelical movement, and the most important one, was through personnel. The nineteenth century was an age of migration, when large numbers moved from the British Isles to other parts of the world. The chief destination was always the United States, with more than half the emigrants from England and Wales choosing America as their promised land in nearly every decade down to the end of the century.[64] Others, however, traveled to the various settler territories within the British Empire, whether Canada, the Cape, Australia or New Zealand. In 1846 the periodical of the Free Church of Scotland found their behavior perverse. It noted that it had heard from "the vast colony of New South Wales, where so many of our dear countrymen have been led to resort, in search of the bread that perisheth, leaving behind them the rich stores of Gospel privileges that they enjoyed in their native land."[65] Since they had gone out, however, it must send ministers after them. Of the roughly 320 Presbyterian ministers in Australasia in 1871, the Free Church claimed to be "intimately connected" with at least 300.[66] These links maintained a sense of common purpose across the globe. Furthermore, the correspondence of emigrants with relations and friends, often kept up for many years, passed on religious news as well as more secular information. Much of it found its way into Christian periodicals, with journals such as the *Baptist Magazine* peppering its pages with news from abroad. Every issue from September to December 1850, for example, carried the latest information from America.[67] Christian leaders found their way to other parts of the world, whether on evangelistic tours, official business or rest cures. Thus the extraordinary career of James Thomson, a Scottish promoter of popular education and agent of the British and Foreign Bible Society in Latin America from 1818 to 1830, led to the creation of pockets of Protestant

---

64 Dudley Baines, *Migration in a Mature Economy: Emigration and Internal Migration in England and Wales, 1861-1900* (Cambridge: Cambridge University Press, 1985), 62-63.
65 *Home and Foreign Missionary Record of the Free Church of Scotland*, January 1846, 276.
66 *Home and Foreign Missionary Record*, April 1871, 75.
67 *Baptist Magazine*, September 1850, 555; October 1850, 625; November 1850, 686; December 1846, 786.

presence in several Hispanic countries.[68] Later in the century the American Methodist William Taylor crisscrossed the globe from California to the Cape in a sustained preaching ministry.[69] Missionaries to particular regions, who were able to return home for advocacy work more frequently as the century wore on, formed another bond between various parts of the world. The Evangelical movement was united by people as well as by literature and institutions.

Tendencies to Fragmentation

The picture of the solidarity of the movement, however, needs to be qualified in a significant way. Towards the end of the century there was a growing theological tension between the more liberal and the more conservative wings. The predominant trend in Evangelical thought from around the middle of the century was in the direction of greater liberalism. Partly this development was a consequence of the legacy of the Enlightenment, with its stress on freedom of inquiry. Many Evangelical bodies were increasingly reluctant to impose tests of orthodoxy on their members. Thus subscription to the Westminster Confession, the traditional standard of Presbyterian belief, was relaxed by the United Presbyterians in 1879 and by the other main Scottish denominations in subsequent years.[70] A larger part of the change, however, derived from an alteration of assumptions. A Romantic idiom increasingly supplanted the inheritance of the Enlightenment. The transformation is evident in altering conceptions of God. There was a shift from the ideal of the Almighty as a ruler presiding over a justly administered government endorsed by enlightened thought to that of him as a Father at the head of a kindly managed family favored by Romantic taste. Many Congregationalists, who were most affected by this development, began to entertain wider hopes about human destiny and, as an American Baptist newspaper complained in 1878, to "discard the recognized evangelical idea of the atonement."[71] At the same time there was a growing acceptance, at least in intellectual circles, of the biblical criticism emerging from Germany and so commonly bound up with the Romantic worldview entrenched in the psyche of that land. The *cause célèbre* was the controversy in the Free Church of Scotland between 1876 and 1881 over the acceptability of German critical methods in the writings of the young scholar William Robertson Smith.[72]

---

68 *The Blackwell Dictionary of Evangelical Biography, 1730–1860*, ed. Donald M. Lewis, 2 vols. (Oxford: Blackwell, 1995), 2:1100–101.
69 *Taylor of California*, rev. Moore.
70 Cheyne, *Transforming of the Kirk*, chap. 3.
71 *Religious Herald* (Richmond, VA), 21 February 1878.
72 Cheyne, *Transforming of the Kirk*, chap. 2.

Although the protracted proceedings were eventually resolved by Robertson Smith's dismissal, his views gained ground because of their identification with solid scholarship. The tendency of the times was towards broader views in accordance with the canons of Romantic feeling and German thought.

There was nevertheless a countervailing trend, equally associated with Romantic opinion, in a theologically conservative direction. A close friend of Samuel Taylor Coleridge, the chief fount of the Romantic philosophy of religion in English-speaking lands, was Edward Irving, minister of the Church of Scotland serving in London during the 1820s. Drawing inspiration from Coleridge, Irving struck out on new theological paths. He condemned the mechanistic and commercial methods of the benevolent societies as savoring of the Enlightenment, urged a more spiritual approach to spreading the gospel and recommended that missionaries should go out, like the first apostles, "destitute of all visible sustenance, and of all human help."[73] They would then be compelled to rely on the Almighty for all their needs. This was the faith principle, soon taken up by George Müller, who ran a great orphanage in Bristol on the basis that the Lord would provide for all its needs in answer to prayer, and eventually by Hudson Taylor, the founder of the China Inland Mission in 1865. The ideal became the inspiration of a whole set of undenominational faith missions that imitated it. Another of Edward Irving's innovations, however, was to prove equally fraught with consequences. Disgusted with what he saw as the groundless optimism of the postmillennial school, Irving worked out the elements of a premillennial scheme, holding that the personal second coming of Christ was imminent. His longer-lived contemporary John Nelson Darby, the leader of the exclusive branch of the Brethren movement, elaborated the same teaching in the form of dispensationalism.[74] Although dispensational doctrine was to make far greater headway in later years, it was already being propagated at Moody's Northfield conferences before the end of the nineteenth century. A third novel body of thought that similarly invoked the heightened supernaturalism typical of Romanticism was the holiness revival. Originating in the Methodist doctrine of entire sanctification, the new holiness teaching, as expounded by Phoebe Palmer of New York, differed by stressing the immediate availability of a higher life. Taken up from 1875 by the Keswick Convention, the message was embraced by many Evangelicals around the world, especially within the Anglican communion. Each of these nineteenth-century novelties helped lay the foundations for the

---

73   Edward Irving, *For Missionaries after the Apostolical School: A Series of Orations* (London: Hamilton, Adams and Co., 1825), 18.
74   See 1:8: "The Advent Hope in British Evangelicalism since 1800."

Fundamentalism that was to emerge in the following century. Because they stiffened the conservative resistance to the general liberal drift, they contributed to a growing theological polarization within Evangelicalism. These developments heralded the breakup of the earlier solidarity of the movement.

Conclusion

Down to 1900, however, it was the unity of the movement rather than its divisions that was most striking. Its typical characteristics of Bible, cross, conversion and activism bound it together in every land. Its theology and spirituality showed a bridging of the earlier divide between Calvinist and Arminian. The close identification of Evangelicalism as a whole with the temper of the Enlightenment was evident in its appeal to reason, its postmillennial hope and its engagement with science. The association of the movement with commerce confirmed that it was, in its day, the epitome of modernity. Evangelicals were agreed, too, in what they opposed, seeing sin in society and Romanism in the church as their grand foes. Their common platform across the world was reinforced by a shared literature, linked institutions and an exchange of personnel. Although there was a tendency at the end of the century for a new kind of theological division to emerge along conservative/liberal lines, fragmentation was deferred until later years. It is true that national variations were part of the reality of Evangelical world, for divergent circumstances still ensured differences. Yet, as the Australasian Wesleyans reported to the British Conference in 1858, the differences between them were merely in "minor details."[75] Denominational dissimilarities were probably greater than national contrasts, but in this age it was the coordinated efforts and common mind of Evangelicals that were most striking. A Congregational missionary to southern Illinois reported in 1857 that he was working in concert with three Old School Presbyterian churches, as many Cumberland Presbyterian churches, a few Methodists and a Freewill Baptist church. "These," he commented, "are all the evangelical denominations now attempting to make inroads on the great host of the common enemy."[76] It was the unity of the nineteenth-century global Evangelical movement that was of world historical significance.

---

75 *Minutes of the Methodist Conferences*, 14 (London: John Mason, 1862), 148.
76 *American Missionary*, July 1857, 160.

III

Evangelicals, Doctrine and Experience

8

The Advent Hope in British Evangelicalism since 1800

There has existed within the Protestant churches of Great Britain since the 1820s a powerful millenarian movement.[1] Churches that had been created or renewed by the Evangelical Revival of the eighteenth century, with its consuming conversionist zeal, included from that decade groups of self-styled "students of prophecy." In the manner of millenarians down the centuries, they expected the imminent and total transformation of this world into a sublime state of harmony and justice. But their eyes were fixed less on the blessings of the millennium to come than on the second advent of Jesus Christ that would precede it—what Edward Irving, the foremost champion of the new teaching in the 1820s, called Christ's "own personal appearance in flaming fire."[2] The advocates of adventism laid great stress on the point that the return would be personal. The reason is that previously belief in a visible return by Christ in the flesh had been no part of accepted doctrine.[3] Many Protestants, according to Irving, were startled by statements "that Christ will appear again

---

1 Many of the features of its earlier years are analyzed in Ernest R. Sandeen, *The Roots of Fundamentalism: British and American Millenarianism, 1800–1930* (Chicago: University of Chicago Press, 1970), chaps. 1, 3, and 4. See also William H. Oliver, *Prophets and Millennialists: The Uses of Biblical Prophecy in England from the 1790s to the 1840s* (Auckland, NZ: Auckland University Press, 1978).
2 Edward Irving, "Preliminary Discourse," in Juan Josafat Ben-Ezra, *The Coming of Messiah in Glory and Majesty*, trans. Edward Irving (London: L. B. Seeley, 1827), vi. This strange work, purporting to be written by a Jew but in fact composed by an exiled Chilean Jesuit, was translated by Irving, a prominent minister of the Church of Scotland serving in London, and was influential in the early propagation of adventism.
3 Although noting a source mentioning the personal return (p. 12), Sandeen in *Roots of Fundamentalism* does not recognize the significance of this point.

in personal and bodily presence upon the earth."[4] The most respected Evangelicals did not believe it. Thomas Scott declared in 1802 that there would be "no visible appearance of Christ;"[5] and in 1830 Charles Simeon told a correspondent that it was a matter with which he had not the slightest concern.[6] Consequently the new school was marked out by its conviction of the personal return.[7] It was more than a bare doctrine. Since the content of the expectation was Jesus Christ himself, the advent hope became an object of devotion. For students of prophecy, the second coming was promoted to a rank of primary importance normally reserved by other Evangelicals for the cross of Christ.[8] Adventism was passionately felt.

Support for Adventism

The beginning of the movement can in part be explained in terms of the analysis of social scientists who have examined the origins of popular millenarianism. There was an existing religious way of thinking about the world, indeed an earlier, more moderate, millenarian tradition within Evangelicalism, waiting to be remodeled; there was a sense of distress in which a fundamental problem, seemingly insoluble by ordinary methods, could be remedied only by some miraculous happening; and in Irving there was a charismatic leader to launch the movement.[9] The established millenarian tradition, quickened by the crisis of the French Revolution and nurtured by the rising Protestant world missions, was the hope that vital Christianity would soon spread over

---

4   Irving in Ben Ezra, *Coming of Messiah*, xlix.
5   *The Thought of the Evangelical Leaders: Notes of the Discussions of the Eclectic Society, London, during the Years 1798–1814*, ed. John H. Pratt (Edinburgh: Banner of Truth Trust, 1978), 256.
6   Simeon to Miss E. Elliott, 19 February 1830, in *Memoirs of the Life of the Rev. Charles Simeon, M.A.*, ed. William Carus, 2nd ed. (London: J. Hatchard and Son, 1847), 658–59.
7   E.g., Hugh McNeile, *A Sermon Preached at the Parish Church of St Paul, Covent Garden, on Thursday Evening May 5, 1826, before the London Society for Promoting Christianity Amongst the Jews* (London: J. Duncan, 1826), 8, 23, 25; Gerard T. Noel, *A Brief Enquiry into the Prospects of the Church of Christ, in Connexion with the Second Advent of Our Lord Jesus Christ* (London: J. Hatchard and Son, 1828), 28, 37.
8   A critic observed of belief in an imminent personal advent that "when suffered to work its unimpeded way, it stops not till it has pervaded with its own genius the entire system of one's theology, and the whole tone of his spiritual character, constructing, I had almost said, a world of its own." David Brown, *Christ's Second Coming: Will It Be Premillennial?* 3rd ed. (Edinburgh: T&T Clark, 1853), 8.
9   The three conditions are found in Guenter Lewy, *Religion and Revolution* (New York: Oxford University Press, 1974), 246.

the whole earth and so, without any visible supernatural intervention, usher in a millennial age of spiritual blessing. Such a view, which in this form readily betrays its kinship with the Enlightenment idea of progress, is often labeled postmillennial since the appearance of Christ was expected only after the millennium.[10] The distress in the 1820s was caused by the relative failure of the organizations set up for the universal spread of the gospel. High hopes had been dashed.[11] Where ordinary means had failed, Irving and his school concluded, only the divine intervention of the second advent could succeed.[12] But there was another crucial factor at work apart from those familiar to social scientists. A new wave of thinking was affecting the educated of Europe in precisely this generation: Romanticism. Belief that the second coming was at hand appealed to minds fed on literature that reveled in the strange, the awesome, the dramatic, the catastrophic. There was nothing anomalous, according to this new way of looking at the world, in expecting the supernatural to break into the natural.[13] On the contrary, what seemed odd was the received postmillennial view that the present age would merge imperceptibly into a glorious future.[14] The new conviction is usually called premillennial, since Christ was expected to return before the millennium. Premillennialism was a symptom of the spread of Romantic cultural influences into Evangelical religion.

For that reason, those attracted by the new views in the earlier years of their circulation up to about the 1870s tended to be drawn from the social elite that was familiar with the cultural trend. The students of prophecy, it was noted in 1864, "are not mere ignorant enthusiasts, but belong in considerable numbers to the respectable and educated classes of society."[15] Lord Ashley, later the famous Lord Shaftesbury, was only one of the peers to embrace premillennialism;[16] H. M. Villiers, bishop first of Carlisle and then of Durham, was only

10   Oliver, *Prophets and Millennialists*, chap. 3; James A. De Jong, *As the Waters Cover the Sea: Millennial Expectations in the Rise of Anglo-American Missions, 1640–1810* (Kampen: Kok Publishers, 1970).
11   James H. Stewart, *Thoughts on the Importance of Special Prayer for the General Outpouring of the Holy Spirit* (London: J. Nisbet, 1821), 8.
12   [Henry Drummond], *Dialogues on Prophecy* (London: Nisbet, 1827), 22–25.
13   See Meyer H. Abrams, *Natural Supernaturalism: Tradition and Revolution in Romantic Literature* (London: Norton and Co., 1971).
14   Edward Irving, *The Last Days: A Discourse on the Evil Character of These Our Times, Proving Them to be the "Perilous Times" of the "Last Days,"* 2nd ed. (London: R. B. Seeley and W. Burnside, 1850), vii.
15   Patrick Fairbairn, "Preface" (dated 1864), *The Interpretation of Prophecy* (London: Banner of Truth Trust, 1964), 33.
16   Geoffrey B. A. M. Finlayson, *The Seventh Earl of Shaftesbury, 1801–1885* (London: Eyre Methuen, 1981), 103–4. Another peer was George Montagu, duke of Manchester, the

one of the episcopal bench to do so.[17] The Catholic Apostolic Church, the small body that sustained Irving's views after his death in 1834, included the seventh duke of Northumberland, a viscount, four baronets, two generals, four colonels, two D.D.s, one D.C.L. and one LL.D.; it was also disproportionately supported by lawyers, ex-clergymen, bankers, businessmen and physicians.[18] Likewise the well-to-do were drawn into the so-called "Plymouth Brethren," another premillennialist sect launched in the 1830s.[19] Because adventism appealed more to the better educated, it gathered far more Anglicans than Nonconformists in its earlier years. By 1855 it was thought that more than half the Evangelical clergy favored premillennial views, and by 1901 it was assumed that they all did.[20] Among Methodists, by contrast, the newer attitude made such little headway that at the turn of the twentieth century postmillennialism was still treated as denominational orthodoxy.[21] It was only from the 1870s that premillennialism began to gain a widespread popular following. Prophetic conferences and lecture tours became common, especially proliferating in the 1890s.[22] The study of prophecy was in fact a fashion that was percolating down the social scale. By the 1920s it had become dis-

---

author of *The Finished Mystery* (London: J. Hatchard and Son, 1847), which, though distinctive in detail (he wished to modify the school's teaching in the light of the Nicene Creed), is fundamentally premillennial.

17 Henry M. Villiers, as rector of St George's, Bloomsbury in the 1840s and 1850s, promoted an influential series of published annual lectures that did much to disseminate premillennialism and edited one of the volumes, *The Titles of Christ Viewed Prophetically* (London: no pub., 1857). Another episcopal adventist was E. H. Bickersteth, bishop of Exeter from 1885 to 1900 (*Some Words of Counsel* [Exeter: H. Besley and Son, 1888], 152–53), whose views were imbibed before 1850 from his father, Edward, an early advocate of premillennialism.

18 Robert L. Lively, "The Catholic Apostolic Church and the Church of Jesus Christ of Latter-Day Saints: A Comparative Study of Two Minority Millenarian Groups in Nineteenth-Century England" (Unpublished D. Phil. dissertation, University of Oxford, 1978), 258. Although the sample includes some twentieth-century members, they are relatively few.

19 Harold H. Rowdon, *The Origins of the Brethren, 1825–1850* (London: Pickering & Inglis, 1967), 50–53, 207–9, 230–33. See also 2:13: "The Brethren in International Evangelicalism."

20 *British and Foreign Evangelical Review*, 4 (1855), 697–710, cited by Sandeen, *Roots of Fundamentalism*, 40; H. W. Webb-Peploe addressing Islington Clerical Meeting, reported in the *Record*, 18 January 1901, 99.

21 Joseph A. Beet, *The Last Things* (London: Hodder and Stoughton, 1897), part 2; *John Brash: Memorials and Correspondence*, ed. Isaac E. Page (London: C. H. Kelly, 1912), 175–88.

22 *Christian*, 5 January 1893, 9; 22 June 1893, 20; 29 June 1893, 19; 25 July 1895, 7, 9.

tinctly eccentric in the educated world, but in the world of popular religion it had taken a firm hold.

Influence on Nineteenth-Century Britain

Partly because of its social prestige, the millenarian movement made a significant impact in the nineteenth century. The prevailing form of premillennial opinion was that normally called "historicist." On this view the book of Revelation and the prophecies of Daniel were to be interpreted as narratives that could be decoded by pairing symbols such as the vials of wrath with remarkable historical events. This jigsaw-like enterprise became more exciting, though more controversial, the nearer the expositor came to the present. "Some have calculated," declared the leading Anglican Evangelical newspaper in its New Year message on 1 January 1868, "that we are just arriving at the end of the 1,335 years spoken of by DANIEL the Prophet; whilst others, more cautious or more accurate, have been led to suppose that we have only reached the close of the 1,260 Apocalyptic years, so that 75 years still separate us from the final termination of the prophetic times."[23] Students of prophecy eagerly scanned the newspapers for events that would vindicate one scheme or another. Their gaze was particularly directed towards the Vatican, since it was common ground among historicist expositors that the papacy was the Antichrist. Their interpretation, deriving from Reformation sources, was often called the Protestant view, "the strongest bulwark against the revived zeal of the Romish Church."[24] The growth of premillennialism helps explain the increase of anti-Catholicism in nineteenth-century Britain. The debate over Catholic emancipation, Irish unrest and the influx of poor Irish refugees from the famine in the 1840s revived traditional fears, but prophecy provided the ideological framework within which it seemed imperative to denounce "the apostate Church of Rome, the favour and honour which we bestow on this great Antichrist, the dishonour we thus do to God."[25] Premillennial

---

23 *Record*, 1 January 1868.
24 Thomas R. Birks, *First Elements of Sacred Prophecy* (London: Painter, 1843), 2. The Reformation origins of historicist exegesis, which was popularized in Foxe's *Book of Martyrs*, are dissected in Richard Bauckham, *Tudor Apocalypse* (Oxford: Sutton Courtenay Press, 1978).
25 *Record*, 3 January 1850. The importance of prophecy in relation to anti-Catholicism has been noted by David N. Hempton, "Evangelicals and Eschatology," *Journal of Ecclesiastical History* 31:2 (1980), 184–85; and by Desmond Bowen, *The Protestant Crusade in Ireland, 1800–70: A Study of Protestant-Catholic Relations between the Act of Union and Disestablishment* (Dublin: Gill and Macmillan, 1978), 64–65.

belief entrenched anti-Catholicism as the chief attitude to world affairs of many nineteenth-century Protestants.

A second feature of their outlook was pessimism. The divine program of history dictated that world affairs were ripening towards the judgments associated with the second coming. In human terms, therefore, the future was bleak. Symptoms of decay were all around. One writer on "The Last Days" declaimed against levity: "We must have comic annuals, and comic almanacks, and comic newspapers; and such publications as *Nicholas Nickleby*, abounding with the lowest vulgarity, and frequently interlarded with profaneness, are often to be found upon the drawing room table of females of refined education."[26] More weightily, there was the specter of "Liberalism" stalking the world. Liberalism to students of prophecy meant the assertive exercise of human intelligence, the rejection of constituted authority and rebellion against God[27]—ironically, very much what it meant to Pope Pius IX.[28] It expressed itself in moves to disestablish the Church of England, for an established church represented national homage to God.[29] And Liberalism expressed itself in constitutional reform. "Household franchise and lodgers' franchise are fulfilling prophecy," it was noted in 1880, "and causing us to hear the chariot-wheels of the coming King."[30] The natural inclination to conservatism of the well-to-do, especially in the Church of England, was reinforced by prophetic views. A bewildered Methodist, sharing the normal Nonconformist optimism about the possibilities of reform that drew them to the Liberal Party, found the outlook of the Evangelical clergy disturbing. "Looking for our Lord's speedy coming," he commented, "they expect things to go from bad to worse, and frankly tell me they have no hope of amelioration."[31] Among Nonconformists the reforming impulse, directed into the temperance crusade or the organized peace movement, often appealed to predictions of a coming millennium that they were helping to bring in.[32] But the Anglican Evangelical

---

26 Joshua W. Brooks, *Essays on the Advent and Kingdom of Christ and the Events Connected Therewith*, 4th ed. (London: Simpkin Marshall & Co., 1843), 340.
27 James E. Gordon, *Original Reflections and Conversational Remarks, Chiefly on Theological Subjects* (London: no pub., 1854), 71.
28 Gordon, *Original Reflections*, 95; *Record*, 2 January 1856.
29 Edward B. Elliott, *Horae Apocalypticae: Or a Commentary on the Apocalypse*, 2nd ed. (London: Seeley, 1846), 287; Samuel Garratt, *Signs of the Times: Showing That the Coming of the Lord Draweth Near*, 2nd ed. (London: no pub., 1869), v, xi.
30 *Christian*, 22 April 1880, 12.
31 *John Brash*, ed. Page, 68.
32 William R. Lambert, *Drink and Sobriety in Victorian Wales, c.1820-c.1895* (Cardiff: University of Wales Press, 1983), 123, 125; Alexander Tyrrell, "Making the Millennium: The Mid-Nineteenth-Century Peace Movement," *Historical Journal* 21:1 (1978), 75–95.

newspaper condemned Peace Societies for their mistaken postmillennial eschatology.[33] Different millennial expectations contributed to dividing nineteenth-century Evangelicals politically as well as religiously.

The third chief dimension of the impact of premillennial belief was on missions. Opponents of the new prophetic views contended that they bred passivity. If the world was not to be converted through the church because Christ was really about to return, there seemed little point in evangelistic activity.[34] It is true that to some belief in the second advent was a form of escapism. According to his biographer, William Cadman, rector of St George's, Southwark, in the 1850s, "found relief from the degrading sights of sin and misery into which he was brought through daily contact, by the contemplation of a brighter era about to dawn."[35] Premillennialism, however, could be a spur to effort. The "shortness of the time for labour" before the second coming was a powerful motive even in the early part of the century,[36] and in the last two decades, as adventism became more popular, it provided the drive behind an outburst of missionary enthusiasm. "The evangelisation of the world in this generation" became the motto of the Student Volunteer Movement for Foreign Missions, an international body launched in 1886.[37] It was contended that, although there was no time for the conversion of the world, it was necessary to preach the gospel to every nation. That done, Christ would return. Missionary work would bring back the king.[38] The revitalization of Protestant missions at the end of the nineteenth century owed much to the spreading prophetic teaching.

Twentieth-Century Developments

Premillennial convictions created much less of a stir in the twentieth century because fewer names of note embraced them. Perhaps the best known figure

---

33   *Record*, 24 January 1850.
34   John Harris, *The Great Commission: Or the Christian Church Constituted and Charged to Convey the Gospel to the World* (London: Boston, Gould, Kendall and Lincoln, 1842), chap. 3.
35   Leonard E. Shelford, *A Memorial of the Rev. William Cadman, M.A.* (London: Wells Gardner, Darton, 1899), 49.
36   Obituary of Edward Bickersteth, *Christian Observer*, April 1850, 284.
37   The phrase was coined by an American premillennialist, Arthur T. Pierson, who frequently occupied British pulpits. Arthur T. Pierson, *Forward Movements of the Last Half Century* (New York: Funk & Wagnalls, 1900), 159.
38   Andrew Porter, "Evangelical Enthusiasm, Missionary Motivation and West Africa in the Late Nineteenth Century: The Career of G. W. Brooke," *Journal of Imperial and Commonwealth History* 6:1 (1977), 23–46.

in the adventist camp was Christabel Pankhurst, whose fame in the women's movement guaranteed a wide sale to her books.[39] Yet the prophetic movement played a crucial role within the religious world by encouraging the split that emerged in the 1920s between conservative and liberal Evangelicals. "The testimony of the coming again of the Lord Jesus Christ," it was said, "is practically dividing Christendom."[40] It was the hallmark of the conservative camp to believe in a personal second advent. The great majority were premillennialists, many of whom had rallied to the Advent Testimony and Preparation Movement launched in 1917. Their confidence in their case, already enhanced by the apocalyptic atmosphere of wartime, was confirmed by the Balfour Declaration, the surrender of Jerusalem to General Allenby and the British mandate over Palestine. These events appeared to fulfill biblical predictions that the end of "the times of the Gentiles" was at hand. The Jews would return to their own land, a sure sign of the second coming.[41] In the United States identical expectations gave rise to Fundamentalism.[42] It is not surprising that in the circle of the Advent Testimony Movement the same tendency is evident. There was keen sympathy for American Fundamentalists.[43] Some of the British leaders were prepared to use the term of themselves.[44] They professed biblical literalism, claiming to be "firm on the authority and infallibility of the Scriptures as the actual Word of God."[45] They rejected social reform as something within the ambit of the church.[46] There was a vigorous assault on evolution.[47] And, as in America, obsessive conspiracy theories sprang up. "The most sinister

---

39 Notably *The Lord Cometh: The World Crisis Explained* (London: Morgan and Scott, 1923).
40 *Advent Witness*, December 1923, 136.
41 F. S. Webster, "The A.B.C. of Our Manifesto," *Monthly Bulletin of the Advent Preparation Prayer Union*, June 1919, 2.
42 Sandeen, *Roots of Fundamentalism*, 243; George M. Marsden, *Fundamentalism and American Culture: The Shaping of Twentieth-Century Evangelicalism, 1870–1925* (New York: Oxford University Press, 1980), chaps. 16 and 17.
43 *Monthly Bulletin of the Advent Preparation Prayer Union*, October 1919, 39; *Advent Witness*, December 1923, 136.
44 Earle L. Langston, *How God Is Working to a Plan* (London: Marshall, Morgan and Scott, [1933]), 95.
45 Walter Young at an Advent Testimony meeting: *Record*, 27 April 1922, 279. Cf. *Advent Witness*, April 1921, 187–88, an article by A. H. Burton asserting the inerrancy of the Bible.
46 Earle L. Langston criticized the C.O.P.E.C. movement for misidentifying the work of the church in the light of prophecy: *Record*, 18 September 1924, 591. Cf. *Monthly Bulletin*, January 1920, 63.
47 *Advent Witness*, January 1923, 3; Langston, *How God Is Working*, 76–82.

rumours," announced the editor of the *Advent Witness*, "are gaining currency of the activities of the Communistic party. Secret instructions are arriving in Great Britain from Moscow, urging a determined effort to capture the youth of this country . . . Boy Scouts . . . are specially to be captured."[48] At one point a conference was projected to launch a public defense of basic doctrines, "The Fundamentals," though it mysteriously failed to take place.[49] So in Britain, as in the United States, premillennialism fostered a fiercely conservative form of popular Protestantism in the interwar period.

Yet in Britain Fundamentalism assumed nothing like its American proportions. There are many explanatory factors.[50] Thanks to the rise of Anglo-Catholicism, Evangelicals had long grown accustomed to a more marginal position in church and society than in the United States, and so did not feel suddenly threatened by the postwar inrush of secular values. Again, biblical criticism had become more widely accepted in Britain than in America, so that it seemed less practicable to eradicate it as a dangerous innovation.[51] And the much stronger social conventions insisting on decorum in public life ensured that the tone of British conservative Evangelicalism rarely attained the stridency of the American Fundamentalists. F. B. Meyer, the gentle and venerable Baptist divine who led the Advent Preparation Movement, commended its handbooks as "characterised by sobriety in thought and expression."[52] But one significant factor differentiating Britain from the United State lay within premillennial doctrine itself. In America the predominant version was not historicist but futurist. On this view, championed in the nineteenth century by J. N. Darby, the fertile mind behind the Exclusive Brethren sect in Britain, the events depicted in the book of Revelation are still to take place in the future. They will all occur, however, after believers have been caught up to meet Christ in the air at the start of his coming, the so-called "rapture," which, the followers of Darby stressed, could take place at any time. The Antichrist is not the papacy, but an individual still to come. The effect of these beliefs was to excite a more intense spirit of apocalyptic expectation, anticipating imminent translation to the skies and the rise of a hitherto unidentified

48 *Advent Witness*, July 1922, 75.
49 *Monthly Bulletin*, June 1920, 97–98; August 1920, 120.
50 Some are considered in George Marsden, "Fundamentalism as an American Phenomenon: A Comparison with English Evangelicalism," *Church History* 46:2 (1977), 215–32.
51 See 2:7: "The Persecution of George Jackson: A British Fundamentalist Controversy."
52 Walter P. Hicks, *The Second Coming of Our Lord Jesus Christ in Relation to the Present World Crisis* (London: Advent Testimony and Preparation Movement, 1925), iii.

Antichrist. Futurist premillennialism, which had gained the ascendancy in America by the 1880s, readily generated the paranoia of Fundamentalism half a century later.[53] Futurism made headway in Britain, particularly through the influence of the Brethren, up to 1878,[54] but in that year Henry Grattan Guinness, an evangelist who founded the Regions Beyond Missionary Union, began a historicist counteroffensive with the publication of *The Approaching End of the Age*.[55] With a flow of succeeding volumes, several exploiting the value of historicism for the anti-popery cause, it persuaded many prophetic students that futurism was a delusion.[56] Despite the popularity of the Scofield Bible published in 1909 with footnotes expounding a Darbyite interpretation,[57] there was still a roughly even balance between the two bodies of opinion in the wake of the First World War. Only after the Second World War did the futurist view triumph in the Advent Testimony Movement.[58] In the crucial decade of the 1920s prophetic dogmatism was impossible. Meyer and his adventist organization regularly insisted on the acceptability of either futurism or historicism and even (rather less plausibly) on their compatibility.[59] The need to avoid causing offence to either of the camps was always a reason for caution in public pronouncements. In Britain premillennialists exercised considerable self-restraint.

Millenarianism in recent British history has not been primarily a plebeian affair. It is true that in the early nineteenth century there was a variety of colorful proletarian groups expecting the second coming, but they formed only the fringe of the millenarian world.[60] The advent hope was a concern of the wealthy and the sophisticated that shaped their understanding of public

---

53 Sandeen, *Roots of Fundamentalism*. Darby's futurism, or "dispensationalism," is usefully summarized in Marsden, *Fundamentalism and American Culture*, chap. 5.
54 Sandeen, *Roots of Fundamentalism*, 81–90.
55 LeRoy E. Froom, *The Prophetic Faith of Our Fathers*, 4 vols. (Washington, DC: Review and Herald, 1946–54), 4:1194–1203.
56 Stevenson A. Blackwood in *Christian*, 29 April 1880, 5–6.
57 By 1913 it was already described as "so largely used by students and Christian workers:" *Christian*, 26 June 1913, 14.
58 *Advent Witness*, September 1950, 164; October 1950, 183.
59 *Advent Witness*, February 1921, 161; January 1922, 1. On compatibility: Earle L. Langston, *Christ and the Apostate Church* (London: C. J. Thynne, 1915), 3.
60 Edward P. Thompson, *The Making of the English Working Class* (Harmondsworth, Middlesex: Penguin Books, 1968), 420–31, 878–83; John F. C. Harrison, *The Second Coming: Popular Millenarianism, 1780–1850* (London: Routledge, 1979); Oliver, *Prophets and Millennialists*, chaps. 7–10; James K. Hopkins, *A Woman to Deliver Her People* (Austin, TX: University of Texas Press, 1982).

affairs. In the early twentieth century it has been a tenet of several sects,[61] but their attention to adventist doctrine was a reflection of what preoccupied a wider constituency. With the fading of Romanticism and the secularization of national life, the second coming was no longer a subject for discussion in the educated world. Yet it remained a vital part of the convictions of the conservative Evangelicals in the churchgoing population. If premillennialism tended to draw them towards the assertiveness of Fundamentalism that in America gave rise to several sects, it also inhibited them from going as far along that road as their American cousins.

Conclusions

Two conclusions follow. First, recent British experience does not confirm the still widely held opinion that millenarianism is a form of psychological compensation for the deprived.[62] Millenarianism undoubtedly has fulfilled that function, especially when it has emphasized the future status reversal whereby its adherents would prosper in the millennium. The advent hope in Britain, however, has focused on the person of Christ rather than on the millennium itself, and so has been well adapted to play a part in the devotional life of those who would not welcome a reversal of status. Instead of contributing to a revolutionary impulse, premillennialism has encouraged social and political conservatism. So the case of modern Britain would tend to support the view that religious bodies can be understood only by putting their millenarianism in the context of all their leading motifs.[63] Millenarian movements may differ greatly from the ideal type of a sect for the poor and outcast. Secondly, the advent hope goes a long way towards explaining the division in late twentieth-century British Protestantism between liberals and conservatives, between churches seeking an accommodation with the secular world and those trying

---

61 Elim: Bryan R. Wilson, *Sects and Society: A Sociological Study of Three Religions Groups in Britain* (Westport, CT: Greenwood Press, 1978), 25–28; Assemblies of God: Donald Gee, *Wind and Flame* (Nottingham: Assemblies of God Publishing House, 1967), 2; Holiness churches: Jack Ford, *In the Steps of John Wesley: The Church of the Nazarene in Britain* (Kansas City, MO: Nazarene Publishing House, 1968), 188–89; Gordon Willis and Bryan Wilson, "The Churches of God: Pattern and Practice," and Bryan R. Wilson, "The Exclusive Brethren: A Case Study in the Evolution of a Sectarian Ideology," in *Patterns of Sectarianism: Organization and Ideology in Social and Religious Movements*, ed. Bryan R. Wilson (London: Heinemann, 1967), 244–86 at 273, 287–342 (at 320).
62 Norman Cohn, *The Pursuit of the Millennium* (London: Oxford University Press, 1970), 281; Wilson, *Sects and Society*, 107, 317.
63 As contended by Peter Smith, "Millenarianism in the Babi and Baha'i Religions," in *Millennialism and Charisma*, ed. Roy Wallis (Belfast: Queen's University, 1982), 271.

to challenge it.[64] Premillennialism has not been the orthodoxy of all the churches, even within the Evangelical sector. Methodists, Congregationalists and most Presbyterians never embraced it, and the more liberal Anglicans did not adhere to it in the interwar period. With no expectation of the imminent end of all things, they attempted to reform the world and sacrificed much of their vigor in the process. Conservative Evangelicals among the Anglicans and the Baptists, together with the Brethren, the Pentecostals and many independents, have concentrated on the religious activities, especially evangelism, that have evident value in the shadow of the second coming.[65] Their relative vitality in subsequent years was in some measure the fruit of the advent hope.[66]

64 Alan D. Gilbert, *The Making of Post-Christian Britain: A History of the Secularization of Modern Society* (London: Longman, 1980), part 3.
65 Annual rates of membership change in the 1970s showed the Methodists, United Reformed Church (a Presbyterian/Congregational merger) and Congregationalists to have lost most; the Anglicans and Baptists to have lost fewer; and the Pentecostals, independents and "Others" to have gained. *Prospects for the Eighties* (London: MARC Europe, 1980), 16.
66 I am glad to acknowledge the support from the British Academy and from the Carnegie Trust for the Universities of Scotland that made possible the research on which this paper was based.

9

Evangelical Conversion, *c.* 1740–*c.* 1850

At some point in the late eighteenth century a girl named Grace, then about eighteen years old, went to live in the village of Downton, about seven miles southeast of Salisbury.[1] She stayed with her uncle, a man called Budden, who served as the Baptist minister there. "Soon after," according to the narrative in the *Baptist Magazine*:

> thro' the ministry of the word, she was convinced of the evil nature, and fatal consequences of sin; and of the necessity of an interest in Christ for salvation. She had heard a sermon, by which it appeared to her that there was no hope of her own salvation, nor scarcely of any beside. But a considerable time after, she heard another sermon, by which all the obstacles to salvation were removed, and she was enabled to commit her soul into the hands of Christ, and rely on him as her all-sufficient Saviour.[2]

In many ways, though brief, this is a classic account of conversion. The subject is a teenager, the agency is preaching and there is more than one stage in the process. Supremely, conviction of sin is followed by the release of commitment to Christ. The instance of Grace who went on to marry a man named Poore and died in 1809, may stand as typical of the subject of this paper, Evangelical conversion. The aim is to examine the nature of "the great change" as it

---

1   This paper was first delivered in a seminar held at New College, Edinburgh, on 3 December 1996, under the auspices of the North Atlantic Missiology Project, coordinated by the University of Cambridge, and supported by a grant from the Pew Charitable Trusts. The opinions expressed in this paper are those of the author and do not necessarily reflect those of the Pew Charitable Trusts.
2   *Baptist Magazine* [hereafter *BM*], November 1809, 457.

was experienced in the Evangelical movement between the middle years of the eighteenth century and the middle of the nineteenth.

Sources for This Study

Much of the evidence will be drawn from a sample of reports of conversions. Three periodicals have been used as sources for the sample. One is the *Evangelical Magazine*, a Calvinist journal that filled the gap left by the *Gospel Magazine*, which had folded in 1784. Though rather less doctrinally rigid, the *Evangelical Magazine* was still definitely Reformed. In this periodical, according to the first preface in 1793:

> the fundamental doctrines of the Gospel are elucidated and confirmed, misrepresentations exposed, errors refuted, and the lives and experience of eminent Christians faithfully recorded.[3]

The descriptions of religious experience are what is chiefly useful. Nearly every month the magazine carried obituaries which standardly recorded the conversions of their subjects. Rather like the Missionary Society, later the London Missionary Society, founded two years later, the journal was interdenominational but dominated by Independents. It therefore provides evidence for many denominations, even including a few Wesleyans who, in the eyes of their obituarists, subsequently saw the error of their ways and embraced Reformed belief; but a large number of cases are drawn from the Independent body. The second periodical is the *Baptist Magazine*, the organ of the mainstream Particular Baptists who had been drawn into the Evangelical movement. Most of the obituaries commemorate members of that denomination, with its Calvinist piety, but there is also a smattering of individuals from other branches of the movement. The earliest volumes of both periodicals were selected for study, 1793 and 1794 in the case of the *Evangelical Magazine* and 1809 and 1810 in that of the *Baptist Magazine*, in order to obtain a sample of conversions going back to the earliest days of the Evangelical Revival around 1740. With the aim of including cases from later in the period, the 1850 volumes of both periodicals have also been scrutinized. Consequently some subjects died as late as 1850 itself. In order to give a fuller overview of the movement, the first volume of the *General Baptist Repository*, published in 1822, was also examined. The General Baptists of the New Connexion, whose official journal this was, were as strongly Arminian as the Wesleyan Methodists. The sample consists of all the obituaries in

---

3   *Evangelical Magazine* [hereafter *EM*], 1793, 2.

these issues of the journals, even brief ones, so long as they contain reference to conversion. A number of obituaries, including an entry for the Queen Dowager in the *Evangelical Magazine* for 1850, could more properly be described as death notices.[4] Others again—as many as forty-one in the issues of the magazines under scrutiny—incorporate fuller biographical detail but no information about conversion. But to the obituaries have been added all the memoirs and biographical accounts inserted in the same volumes if their subjects fall within the period and if the narratives include mention of their conversions. The resulting sample consists of 140 cases of conversion.

The group provides reasonable coverage of the period. Ninety-one of the narratives record conversions that can confidently be assigned to a twenty-five-year time band. Of these, 8 percent took place before 1750; 16 percent in the years 1750–75; 35 percent in 1776–1800; 33 percent in 1801–25 and 9 percent in 1826–50. Over two-thirds therefore fall in the half-century around 1800. The sample cannot, however, claim to give a fair representation of the Evangelical movement overall. Although two obituaries in the magazine issues explored deal with men originally identified with the Scottish Secessionists, neither mentions its subject's conversion, and so no recorded instance in the sample comes from Scotland. There is, however, a previously published article on the converts of the Cambuslang revival of 1742 to which occasional reference will be made.[5] Although many individuals had an Anglican background, only five cases are of those who were converted in the Church of England rather than away from it. Anglican conversion narratives are, in fact, difficult to obtain in bulk. The *Christian Observer*, the premier Anglican Evangelical magazine launched in 1802, does include obituaries, but its ambitions to be a national journal of record meant that its first issue recounted the deaths of those remarkable only for social rank, public distinction, suddenness of death or prolongation of life beyond a century.[6] The great majority of the sample analyzed here, furthermore, were Calvinists. Only 15 percent, in fact, concern individuals reaching mature faith within an Arminian body. This bias, however, has its uses. The two chief existing studies of Evangelical conversions in England during this period deal mainly with those professing an Arminian theology. Julia Werner considers one hundred Primitive Methodist converts of the first generation and Michael Watts analyzes 670 conversions in the

---

4 *EM*, January 1850, 29.
5 Thomas C. Smout, "Born Again at Cambuslang: New Evidence on Popular Religion and Literacy in Eighteenth-Century Scotland," *Past & Present* 97:1 (1982), 114–27.
6 *Christian Observer*, January 1802, 78–80.

Dissenting denominations during the years 1780–1850.[7] Watts' large sample might be expected to be representative of Evangelicals outside the Church of England, but in reality most cases are drawn from Methodist periodicals, a few from the *Baptist Magazine* and others from separately published biographies. Only 68 of his 670 individuals are Calvinists, and a mere 13 are Independents. Hence a fresh sample leaning heavily in the Calvinist direction may help to redress the balance. The two groups, the one examined by Watts and the one considered here, may be regarded as complementary.

The sources for this study suffer from serious disadvantages for our purpose. In the first place, there is the problem of distortion. The accounts of the deceased were written for edification, not for record. Some obituaries are even cast in homiletic form, with three practical applications enumerated at the end. The briefest of notices are deeply influenced by the expectations of the times. The descriptions concentrate on standard features, particularly signs of piety displayed in the last few days of life. Other elements of a modern obituary, especially employment, are commonly passed over in silence. Even the date of birth and age at death are frequently omitted. Narratives are often framed in terms of conventions going back to Puritan hagiography that literary scholars have studied in some detail.[8] Conformity to scriptural archetypes, for example, is one recurring motif. Our purpose, however, entails, in so far as it is possible, going beyond the narrative to what lay behind it in human experience. There is a series of other difficulties. Articles were commonly written by ministers whose knowledge did not encompass any detailed information about the start of their subjects' Christian pilgrimage. The sample is skewed by the factor of who troubled to send in narratives to the magazines. The assiduous John Giles, minister of Eythorne Baptist Church in Kent, for instance, contributed all five entries to the August 1810 issue of the *Baptist Magazine*.[9] Other accounts were sent in by relatives whose nearness to the deceased affects the perspective. A poignant description of the death of a fourteen-year-old girl from typhus in 1850, for example, was composed by her father, the Independent minister at Petworth in Sussex. Inevitably in his grief he dwelt on her "lovely temper,"

7   Julia S. Werner, *The Primitive Methodist Connexion: Its Background and Early History* (Madison, WI: Wisconsin University Press, 1984), 155–57; Michael R. Watts, *The Dissenters*, vol. 2: *The Expansion of Evangelical Nonconformity* (Oxford: Clarendon Press, 1995), 49–80.

8   E.g., Daniel B. Shea, Jr, *Spiritual Autobiography in Early America* (Princeton, NJ: Princeton University Press, 1968); Patricia Caldwell, *The Puritan Conversion Narrative: The Beginning of American Expression* (Cambridge: Cambridge University Press, 1983).

9   *BM*, August 1810, 430–34; Frank Buffard, *Kent and Sussex Baptist Associations* (Faversham, Kent: no pub., 1963), 72.

passing over any misdemeanors that may have marred her life.[10] Perhaps above all the people commemorated in the magazines were disproportionately individuals of standing in their denominations, often ministers, their relations, or those in whom ministers confided. Ordinary sitters in the pews were by no means excluded—recent converts were a favored category—but there was a tendency for the *Evangelical Magazine* and the *Baptist Magazine* to concentrate on more prominent figures. The *General Baptist Repository*, like its Methodist counterparts, was less selective in its coverage, but the overall effect is to make the sample contain a larger number of the core and a smaller number of the periphery of the congregations that made up the Evangelical movement. Allowance must be made for all these distortions. Yet in one sense the very features that cause such problems constitute an advantage for the historian. These obituaries, with all their conventional phrases and personal viewpoints, reflect the real world of Evangelical Dissent. In these accounts we peer through the window of the meeting house to witness its authentic life.

A further problem, however, lies in the sheer imprecision of the many accounts. Two adjacent obituaries from the *Baptist Magazine* illustrate the point. Of John Goffe, a deacon of the second Baptist church in Brighton who died in 1850, all we are told about his life before he was baptized and joined Shipston-on-Stour Baptist Church in 1810 is that he was called at an early age to know the Lord. What is the early age? How was he called? Why did it happen? Virtually the only thing we learn is that he did experience conversion. Again, of Hannah, the wife of Robert Ellis, Baptist minister at Sirhowy, Gwent, who died at thirty-five in 1850, the only information about her conversion is that she professed Christ when young. There is in this instance not even a baptismal date to provide guidance about chronology. With that very scanty knowledge we have perforce to be content.[11] The terminology can also suffer from vagueness. Sometimes it is unclear whether or not the writers intended to convey that their subjects had been converted by a particular stage in their experience. The difficulty is particularly apparent in the use of the phrase "religious impressions." At times it appears to mean only a sense of spiritual anxiety, and in some cases the reader is told that the phase was transient. Thus a girl who later became Mrs Elizabeth Tracey of Barrow-upon-Soar, Leicestershire, attended a Methodist Sunday School and there received "serious impressions," but thereafter took up the vanities of the world such as card playing before she was soundly converted.[12] In other cases, however, the phrase seems to imply

10   *EM*, October 1850, 535–37.
11   *BM*, August 1850, 501.
12   *General Baptist Repository* [hereafter *GBR*], April 1822, 139.

vital religion, especially when the word "permanent" is added. There is considerable scope for misinterpretation here when the context does not clearly point one way or the other. There is a further problem with the Baptists. Commonly the obituarist gives a date for the subject's baptism after the person's conversion. It would be helpful to be able to take the one as a surrogate for the other, but that would lead to serious misrepresentation since there was frequently a gap between conversion and baptism. George Osborn, for example, who was to become an itinerant preacher, was converted as a young man in about 1760, but was not baptized until the age of seventy-seven, nearly half a century later. Although Osborn's is an extreme case—a consequence of his having remained an Independent until his last years—other recorded instances of delay prevent the historian from treating conversion and baptism as being necessarily close in time. Lack of detailed information in each of these respects, however, does not prevent the set of obituaries in the periodicals from being a rich source for our understanding of spirituality in the period. They enable us to construct something approaching a prosopography of conversion.

Characteristics of Converts

What was conversion at this time? According to George Redford, Independent minister at Angel Street, Worcester, writing near the end of the period in a booklet issued by the Religious Tract Society, and therefore enjoying interdenominational endorsement, conversion

> is a change, or a turning about of our mind or heart, and signifies a reversing of our moral and religious state, a complete transformation of the character—from irreligion to piety, from sin to holiness, from unbelief to faith, from impenitence to contrition and confession, from the service of the world to the service of God, from uneasiness to peace, from fear to hope, from death to life.[13]

It is not surprising that so drastic a change often entailed a crisis. A typical illustration is found in the experience of Elizabeth, who later married William Nichols, pastor of North Collingham Baptist Church, Nottinghamshire. There was a prelude. Elizabeth's brother died of tuberculosis in 1808, when she was twenty-two years old, and "she discovered the depravity of her heart." She went to visit relatives living ten miles away and there meditated on the Bible and other devotional writings. Then came the turning point:

---

13   George Redford, *The Great Change: A Treatise on Conversion* (London: Religious Tract Society, 1844), 1.

one day walking alone in the fields ... she was favoured with such a discovery of the Love of God in the gift of his Son ... as filled her soul with joy unspeakable, mingled with godly sorrow for her past sins, so that for some time she was unable to leave this highly favoured spot, concerning which the words of Jacob might be adopted, *Surely God is in this place*.[14]

The time was distinct; so, clearly, was the place. Although Elizabeth did not dare speak of her enlightenment for some while, it was the decisive event of her short life. She, too, died of tuberculosis only two years later. A crisis similar to Elizabeth's can be attributed to a particular juncture in life for as large a proportion as 45 percent of the sample of individuals whose conversions are recorded, and must have been passed through by many others for whom insufficient details are supplied. In the late eighteenth and early nineteenth centuries sudden conversions were common. Yet a decisive turning point was not considered essential. Thomas Reader, for example, who subsequently became an Independent minister, was brought up in the second quarter of the eighteenth century, before the Evangelical Revival had made its impact on the Old Dissent, but the comment of his biographer, writing in 1794 when the revival was in full flood, is highly significant: "We do not recollect to have heard whether Mr. R. had dated his conversion to any particular time."[15] Such a remark demonstrates that a datable experience was by no means thought indispensable. Of the subjects of the case histories studied here, only 8 percent are actually stated to have undergone a gradual conversion rather than reaching a crisis. It is said of the unnamed future wife of another Baptist minister, John Stock, for example, that "so early and gradual was the work of grace upon her soul, that she could never refer to any particular period at which she was conscious of its commencement."[16] Frequently, as in this case, those who had received a religious upbringing fitted this mold. Thus the process was so indiscernible for William Stanger, of Tydd St Mary, Lincolnshire, who as the grandson of a General Baptist minister had been given careful Christian nurture, that he seems to have found it difficult to assess whether he was qualified for baptism and so to have deferred the event until late in life.[17] A religious education, this and other obituarists noted, made it natural for the spiritual life to evolve gradually. Nevertheless, that awareness did not mean conversion was supposed to be avoidable on a byroad to heaven. The observation of the biographer of Thomas Reader is revealing in this respect too: the implication of

14 *BM*, July 1810, 392.
15 *EM*, November 1794, 443.
16 *BM*, January 1850, 129.
17 *GBR*, November 1822, 422.

remarking that he was unaware whether his subject identified his conversion with any particular time was that, even if Reader did not give a date, he had been converted. Whether sudden or developmental, conversion was regarded as the obligatory entrance on the Christian life.

Before the great change, there had often been a period of profligacy. There is frequently an understandable lack of precision on this topic. A woman in Kent was said to have been "worldly," a London artist to have been marked by "folly and vanity."[18] More specifically a copper plate printer in the city was reported to have been "gay and thoughtless, excessively fond of Cards, the Theatre and gay Company."[19] On rare occasions more heinous sins were indicated. Before being converted at Norwich Tabernacle, one woman had been a London prostitute and subsequently contemplated murdering her husband.[20] However, it was not particular sins that constituted the kernel of the problem with which evangelists grappled. Rather it was conceived to be the innate fallenness of the human heart, the state of sinfulness rather than a series of individual sins. Hence many converts are described as having previously lived exemplary lives. Thus Catherine Anning, the daughter of a Devon farmer, was respected before her conversion "for her amiable, industrious and prudent conduct, and especially for her dutiful behaviour towards her aged parents."[21] Likewise William Johnson, the son of a General Baptist couple at Sawley Cliff in Derbyshire, was "very steady in his conduct, and obedient to his parents," but that was not the point: he was "destitute of real religion" and so still had to pass through the wicket gate of conversion.[22] Indeed, the great problem for many people was their virtue. Anne Prangnell, of Lockerly, Hampshire, for example, was "very vain of her goodness."[23] Evangelists had to knock away the "false props" upon which such people rested before they could be induced to put their reliance on Christ.[24] This type of legalism, the supposition by the subjects that they were capable themselves of fulfilling the obligations of the divine law, is mentioned as afflicting 9 percent of the sample. For them, as much as for flagrant sinners, conversion entailed a radical transformation of life.

What was the age of the subjects at conversion? Of the sixty-three who were reportedly converted at a particular age, 22 percent underwent the experience

18   *BM*, August 1810, 434; *EM*, October 1850, 532.
19   *BM*, June 1810, 320.
20   *EM*, December 1793, 265–66.
21   *BM*, February 1809, 65.
22   *GBR*, February 1822, 58.
23   *BM*, October 1810, 519.
24   *BM*, February 1809, 68.

at 15 or below; 46 percent between 16 and 20; 14 percent between 21 and 25; 5 percent between 26 and 35; 6 percent between 36 and 65; and 6 percent at 66 or above. There were instances of the very young. Thus Master G. A. F. Barss, who died in 1793 at the tender age of four years four months, is presented as a converted character. He used to pray in imitation of his father and to prattle about having a "good heart" and going to heaven.[25] Equally there were cases of the elderly. Christopher Hunter, who died in 1822 in Redburn, Lincolnshire, is a striking example. He lived as a stranger to godliness until his ninetieth year, but then a passing General Baptist evangelist exhorted a group of senior citizens about the way of salvation. Hunter found peace in believing and was immersed on Easter Tuesday 1820, at almost the end of his ninety-first year.[26] The very young and the very old, however, were the exceptions. The figures clearly demonstrate that adolescence was the peak time for conversions. Nearly half of them were between the ages of 16 and 20; and 82 percent of all conversions that can be assigned to a specific age took place at 25 years old or below. These proportions can be usefully compared with the results of other analyses. Werner's figures for Primitive Methodists are rather different: only 43 percent of their conversions took place under the age of 25, and nearly as many were aged between 25 and 34 as were between 16 and 24.[27] The discrepancy is explained by the fact that Werner is examining the first generation of Primitive Methodists. In the earliest wave of their expansion, a higher proportion of adults would be recruited. Again, in Smout's study of the Cambuslang converts of 1742 only 22 percent were 19 or under, probably because younger people were less free to travel to the communion season when the revival took place. Fully 75 percent, however, were 29 or under, a concentration of response in the early years of life very similar to the present findings.[28] In Watts' examination of Evangelical Nonconformists the results were even closer: half the conversions were between 14 and 20 years old and 74 percent at 25 or younger.[29] The tendency for the great change to take place early in life became even more marked as the nineteenth century wore on,[30] but it is evident that even before 1850 it was extremely likely to happen in a person's youth. Watts suggests that the explanation is in the rise of sexual fears, especially anxiety about masturbation, and cites one instance

---

25 *EM*, Supplement for 1794, 549–50.
26 *GBR*, November 1822, 455–56.
27 Werner, *Primitive Methodist Connexion*, 155.
28 Smout, "Born Again at Cambuslang," 116.
29 Watts, *Dissenters*, 2:57.
30 Kenneth D. Brown, *A Social History of the Nonconformist Ministry in England and Wales, 1800–1930* (Oxford: Clarendon Press, 1988), 54–55.

where that is a plausible interpretation.[31] There is, however, no evidence to support that theory in the present sample. There are, on the other hand, different precipitants such as uttering an oath when casting a fishing net and recoiling in horror.[32] We are, of necessity, largely in the dark about the motives hidden in the internal recesses of the soul, but it is likely that sexuality was only one element, albeit an important one, in the psychological *mélange* that adolescents experienced in orientating themselves for life. But what is clear is that there was a high proportion of youthful conversions in the Evangelical world of the late eighteenth and early nineteenth centuries.

Another factor to consider is gender. The female proportion of the sample was 44 percent, a high figure considering the large number of male ministers memorialized. That, however, is a feature of the record rather than of what actually happened. The important question is whether women had the same experience of conversion as men. The accounts suggest that they did. There is for each sex the same normative pattern of early heedlessness, conviction of sin, acceptance of salvation and the discovery of joy and peace in believing. The issue can in some measure be tested by comparing the age distribution of women with that of the opposite sex. Of thirty women whose age at conversion is given, only four were 15 or under, by contrast with ten men, and that seems low. The numbers however, are so small as not to be statistically significant. More important, fifteen of the thirty, exactly half, were converted between 16 and 20; and 80 percent had the experience at 25 or under. This pattern is similar to the distribution for men: fourteen of the thirty-three, that is 42 percent, were between 16 and 20; and 84 percent were 25 or under. There is no major gender difference in the age structure at conversion. That is exactly what Watts establishes.[33] It tends to confirm the fundamental sameness of the conversion experience for the two sexes. This appears to have been a long established feature, for C. L. Cohen remarks on the uniformity of phrasing between men and women in Puritan spiritual autobiographies of the seventeenth century.[34] The research of Linda Wilson on the spirituality of Evangelical Nonconformist women between 1825–1875 reaches the same conclusion, that there was no substantial difference between the religious experience of the two sexes.[35] It may well be

---

31 Watts, *Dissenters*, 2:49–50.
32 *EM*, September 1794, 381.
33 Watts, *Dissenters*, 2:57.
34 Charles L. Cohen, *God's Caress: The Psychology of Puritan Religious Experience* (New York: Oxford University Press, 1986), 222.
35 Linda Wilson, *Constrained by Zeal: Female Spirituality amongst Nonconformists, 1825–1875* (Carlisle: Paternoster Press, 2000), 225.

that in a patriarchal society the Evangelical insistence on the identical needs of men and women to enter by the straight gate was a major force tending towards gender equality.

Indications of status occur in only about a quarter of the cases in the sample. They arise chiefly through mention of the occupation of the subject or of the subject's father. It emerges that a few individuals enjoyed quite a high standing. There are men in business houses, one the son of a Sheffield master cutler. There are a ship's master, an affluent artist and several ministers who must have been reasonably well-to-do. A larger number, though less prosperous, were nevertheless, in the language of the time, highly respectable. There were a number of farmers and children of farmers, a yeoman, an estate steward, the son of a grocer, a draper and several clerks. These people were drawn from the ranks that later in the nineteenth century would have been called lower middle classes. There are also a skilled craftsman, a builder, a copper miner, a copper plate printer, a shoemaker, a coachman and a surgeon—who, as a manual worker, then occupied a much lower status than his successors in the profession would enjoy. The strength of the group among the lower middle classes and the upper working classes might give the impression that Evangelical Nonconformity was disproportionately drawn from these sections of society. That is the conclusion that, from similar evidence, historians have often drawn.[36] It has been established, however, that the extent of the involvement of the poor has been seriously underestimated. Laborers were numerously and increasingly represented in the meeting houses of the period.[37] The lower ranks of society are certainly to be found in the sample. There are a farm servant and a poor laborer, a factory worker, several common soldiers and an illiterate. Yet this handful of individuals is not proportionate to their strength among Evangelical Nonconformists. It is in regard to status that the sample has been most distorted by the sieve of selectivity through which it has passed. Smout's Cambuslang converts, among whom two-thirds were from a background of small tenants or low-status craftsmen, and Werner's Primitive Methodists, among whom more than half were servants, laborers, or in poverty, were both of lower average status than the group chosen for insertion in the *Evangelical Magazine* and

---

36 For example, Alan D. Gilbert, *Religion and Society in Industrial England: Church, Chapel and Social Change, 1740–1914* (London: Longman, 1976), 62–67.

37 Watts, *Dissenters*, 2:303–27; Lilian M. Wildman, "Changes in Membership, Recruitment and Social Composition in Ten Rural Old Dissent Churches in the South-East Midlands, 1718–1851," *Baptist Quarterly* 35 (1994), 343–45.

the two Baptist magazines.[38] But what is most significant for our purpose is that the poor as much as the prosperous were expected to pass through conversion. A man who "moved in the humble sphere, labouring for the support of his family," for example, was in as much need of renouncing his pharisaic self-righteousness and of praying until he received saving grace as his social superiors.[39] The summons to repentance and faith was a great social leveler.

When the place of conversion is investigated, it turns out that, as might be expected, the great majority of the instances were in England. Most of the counties and all the regions appear in the sample, although, as is inevitable given the strength of the denomination in the region, the East Midlands are particularly strongly represented among the General Baptists. Wales contributed only a pair of sisters from Montgomeryshire and a married woman from Gwent. This paucity was no doubt chiefly a consequence of the language barrier that inhibited the transmission of information from much of Wales to English-language periodicals based in London, and was certainly not a reflection of the true distribution of conversions. Further flung instances, however, do have their own significance. One was from Ireland, where, in Limerick, a serving soldier was converted through the Methodists.[40] Another was from Newfoundland. A boy was sent out at the age of twelve to serve in a shop in the capital, St John's. When rather older, finding the Anglican church in the severe climate "cold and dreary" but the Independent meeting house warmly heated, he was gradually illuminated as he was drawn into the worshiping congregation.[41] These cases are reminders that Evangelical conversion was the core of a movement that flourished beyond Britain, extending through the English-speaking world. Two subjects even responded to the gospel preached by missionaries. While serving with the forces of the East India Company, one was converted under the preaching of William Ward, Baptist missionary at Serampore.[42] Again, a woman born of British parents in Sumatra, having been orphaned and then educated at the Serampore school, was converted under the ministry of a recently arrived missionary there in 1837.[43] The same experience was now as possible on the banks of the Ganges as

---

38 Smout, "Born Again at Cambuslang," 117; Werner, *Primitive Methodist Connexion*, 155.
39 *BM*, August 1819, 372.
40 *BM*, August 1810, 430.
41 *EM*, May 1850, 226–27.
42 *BM*, July 1810, 389.
43 *BM*, July 1850, 140.

on the banks of the Trent. Conversion was a bond that united a growing international movement.

Most of the sample naturally comes from the denominations whose journals have been examined. At least 44 percent were converted among the Particular Baptists, 22 percent among the Independents and 11 percent among the General Baptists. The lesser Calvinistic Evangelical groupings are also covered: the Calvinistic Methodists and Lady Huntingdon's Connexion. There are also instances from the Church of England and the Wesleyans, and even a case—in fact the mother of William Ward of Serampore—who received her permanent religious impressions in about 1773 through the preaching of a female member of the Society of Friends in Derby, though subsequently worshiping with the Calvinistic Methodists.[44] Mrs Ward had previously attended an Arian meeting, but that phase had not led her into the path of salvation. There is no instance of conversion to vital religion among those professing an Arian or Socinian theology, whether of the English Presbyterian or the Old Connexion General Baptist variety. There is, however, an account in the *Evangelical Magazine* of "The Conversion of a Socinian." A Northamptonshire farmer was drawn away by reading Socinian authors from the ministry of his meeting house. The minister tried to bring him back, but for long there was no response. Only when the farmer was lying on his deathbed suffering from tuberculosis—indeed only three day before his death—did he receive the joy of salvation.[45] This case is instructive because it is an instance of conversion not from nominal Christianity, the normal pattern, but from different religious opinions. Socinianism is presented as a non-Christian option. True conversions were not to be expected under its sway. The occurrence of authentic commitments to vital religion is reported only among denominations created, touched or transformed by Evangelicalism. The experience was evidently regarded as unique to the Evangelical movement.

Evangelical Traits

A striking feature of the conversion narratives is therefore their association with aspects of Evangelical religion. The prominence of the Bible, in the first place, is reflected in the sample. In 6 percent of the cases reading the Bible, as distinguished from hearing sermons expounding the scriptures, is mentioned explicitly as one of the factors leading to conversion, but that figure is misleadingly low. It is artificial to separate Bible reading from hearing sermons since preaching was so deeply rooted in scripture. Thus Anne

---

44 *BM*, November 1810, 575.
45 *EM*, Supplement for 1793, 293–94.

Prangnell of Lockerly, Hampshire, recalled the texts of successive sermons as the milestones of her spiritual pilgrimage during the 1760s. Persuaded by her husband to attend the Baptist meeting, she first heard a sermon on Revelation 3:20 ("Behold I stand at the door and knock") and concluded that Christ was knocking at the door of her heart through her afflictions. Then she listened to an exposition of Colossians 3:3 ("For ye are dead, and your life is hid with Christ in God"), inferring that she was entitled to believe. Finally she was established in her new-found faith by a sermon on Hebrews 6:17, 18 (which refers to "the immutability of his counsel").[46] The Bible as it was explained from the pulpit formed the guidance for her progress through a long drawn out conversion. Preaching by settled ministers is included as a cause of conversion in as many as 27 percent of the sample, and by evangelists or visiting preachers in another 14 percent. In fact preaching is by far the most important of the precipitating factors mentioned. The Bible, furthermore, shaped the language of those who subsequently testified to conversion. Thus John Dando of Dursley, Gloucestershire, having been affected by a sermon, declared that "his soul became like the chariots of Amminadib."[47] Moreover, absorbing the Bible was a consequence as well as a cause of conversion. Master Joseph Thornton of Market Harborough, for example, though dying in 1794 at the age of only eight, having been led to a change of disposition through a sermon on "Search the Scriptures," afterward read the Bible at stated hours every day.[48] Conversion, itself one of the marked characteristics of the Evangelical movement, was intimately connected with biblicism, another of them.

The heart of the Evangelical doctrinal system was the atonement achieved by Christ on the cross. Consequently it features prominently in the conversion narratives. The cross is rarely isolated as a theme on which the subjects meditated before conversion, and so it cannot be identified as a statistically significant precipitant of the experience. Yet phraseology evoking the power of Christ crucified recurs frequently in the accounts, especially at the crisis of conversion. A young woman aged twenty-one of the name of Walker, who lived near High Wycombe, may be taken as an example. Having contracted a disease that would soon prove fatal, she became distressed over her sins. During December 1793, while she was sitting by the fireside bemoaning her situation, "Christ manifested himself to her soul as a bleeding, dying Saviour, making atonement for sin, with surprising clearness, and sweetness of

---

46   *BM*, October 1810, 519–20.
47   *BM*, May 1810, 301. An allusion to Song of Solomon 6:12.
48   *EM*, October 1794, 429–30.

application."[49] As in so many other cases, it is impossible to disentangle the language of the obituarist from the experience of the subject, but it would be hard to suppose that Christ crucified was not at the heart of Miss Walker's entry into faith. Likewise an anonymous living minister presenting his autobiography in the supplement to the first volume of the *Evangelical Magazine*, evidently as something of a model, describes how he sought liberty through Christ. "I was led," he recounts, "to behold him as wounded for my transgressions, and bruised for my iniquities."[50] The atonement is by no means universally mentioned in the obituaries, but its common occurrence suggests that it was the doctrine most closely bound up with conversion.

An intense orientation towards practical effort to spread the gospel and its blessings was another fundamental characteristic of the Evangelical movement. This activism was evident in the influence exerted by others to bring the subjects to a living faith. Mothers are sometimes named in this connection. Thus Thomas Reader, who, like another brother, became an Independent minister in later life, was sometimes taken as a boy by his mother into her room. Holding her son's hand, she would announce: "My dear child, I cannot be at rest till I see a work of grace begun in your heart." The boy, not surprisingly, would burst into a flood of tears.[51] Yet in this sample the mother alone is mentioned as a significant influence on conversion in only 6 percent of the cases, a smaller proportion than the 9 percent which alluded to both parents or to the father alone. The mother is therefore relatively less prominent than in Watts' sample,[52] perhaps because a significant number of the present group were children of the manse, where the religious authority of the father was reinforced by his role as a minister. But other relations also went out of their way to influence the subjects for Christ: brothers, sisters, a brother-in-law, a mother-in-law, an aunt, a son, even a granddaughter. Friends were often persuasive too: a girlfriend, a boyfriend, fellow clerks or "Blind Sally" of Dover, one of those women who figure so largely in Evangelical history as soul-winners. Though blind from birth, Sally Johnson spoke so winningly from texts of scripture that she was the means by which Elizabeth Wood was brought both soul concern and soul comfort.[53] All these friends and relations were active in the cause of the gospel, but so were the subjects once they had been converted. Andrew Kinsman of Tavistock, for instance, having laid to rest tormenting fears about

---

49 *EM*, July 1794, 297–98.
50 *EM*, Supplement for 1793, 271.
51 *EM*, November 1794, 443.
52 Watts, *Dissenters*, 2:53–56.
53 *BM*, August 1810, 433–34.

his own salvation, "was soon impressed with an ardent concern, to interest the attention of his relations to these important objects."[54] One young convert gathered his friends for a weekly prayer meeting for the advance of the gospel, a factory lad was set delivering devotional addresses when he was only fifteen and one later minister heard the call to future service in the same sermon that led him into the way of salvation.[55] The quest for conversions was the spur to activity; and activism was the result of the dynamic released by conversions.

The narratives refer to a variety of other circumstances that preceded conversion. Devotional works, family prayers and hymns are mentioned: "Jesu, lover of my soul" was the specific means by which the Norwich ex-prostitute first found rest, eclipsing both text and sermon.[56] A passage of scripture could be impressed on the mind of a person anxious for salvation in a way that might in a later day have been called a revelation.[57] And there were dreams. A dissolute man befuddled by drink is said to have dreamed of a nine-headed serpent ready to seize him during the night before an acquaintance asked him, without knowing of the dream, whether he would like to attend a meeting to hear a sermon on the old serpent; and the man's heart was duly changed.[58] Again, in 1804, a Liverpool clerk was awakened three times by a voice calling him, "John! John! John!" and the following night he saw "a most beautiful figure" who urged him to seek the Lord.[59] It was not only the Magic Methodists of Delamere Forest who in this period saw visions. Death and illness, however, formed the second most common precipitating factor after sermons: 13 percent of the sample included one or the other. Funeral sermons in particular, blending bereavement with proclamation, often provoked serious thought that led to change of heart. Watts draws attention to the importance of disease and death as causes of the fear that preceded conversion, but he lays most stress on the fear of hell.[60] The subject does occur in this sample too. Thus Ann Anderson, a seventeen-year-old in the last days of tuberculosis, was convinced that after death she would "*burn in hell for ever.*"[61] Less vivid phrases such as "endless perdition" crop up more frequently.[62] But what was emphasized, in

---

54   EM, August 1793, 45.
55   *EM*, Supplement for 1850, 705; October 1850, 507; April 1850, 170.
56   Supplement for 1793, 267.
57   *GBR*, April 1822, 140.
58   *EM*, March 1794, 116–17.
59   *EM*, November 1850, 567–68.
60   Watts, *Dissenters*, 2:72–80.
61   *EM*, January 1794, 34.
62   *EM*, Supplement for 1850, 708.

the obituaries and apparently in Evangelical teaching, was not so much the prospect of future punishment as the guilt of the sinner before God. An article on "Conviction of Sin" in the *Evangelical Magazine* for December 1793 distinguished delusive from real conviction. The first of the symptoms of the delusive variety was fear of the *danger* of sin; the contrasting attributes of real conviction were a sense of the *desert* of hell and of the *evil* of sin.[63] Sometimes, as in this article, it was insisted that conviction of sin is an essential preliminary to conversion, but at other times it was taught explicitly that never having felt the "*terrors of the Almighty*" was common among true Christians.[64] Terror "from a fear of divine wrath" was deliberately played down in pre-conversion spiritual counseling in order to concentrate on human responsibility for sin and the kindly promises of the gospel.[65] Maria Prudence Brassington of Burslem was said to have been "one of those who seem to be drawn by the cords of love rather than by the terrors of the law."[66] The two approaches are treated as equally valid. Fear of hell was undoubtedly associated with conversion in many instances, but the evidence of this material would imply that it was not as prominent a factor leading to conversion as Watts suggests.

Divine and Human Agency

How did conversion change over time? The sample is too small to draw statistical conclusions about shifts in any of the areas that have been considered; but trends are nevertheless apparent in the material, especially when it is seen against the backdrop of the theological literature of the period. The fundamental change was in the understanding of the balance between divine and human agency. Theologically the point was explained by the relationship between regeneration and conversion. Puritan divines, to whom eighteenth-century Evangelicals turned for guidance on the subject, distinguished between regeneration as the divine action whereby a person became a Christian and conversion as, in some sense, the human action which accomplished the same transition. John Rippon, the Baptist minister at Carter Lane, Southwark, included a valuable discussion of the subject in the "Theological Dictionary" that he inserted in his *Baptist Annual Register* for 1801–2. Regeneration is defined as "the MOTION OF GOD in the heart of a sinner." Conversion on the other hand is "the MOTION OF THE HEART of a sinner towards God."

---

63   *EM*, December 1793, 233.
64   *EM*, September 1794, 354.
65   *EM*, September 1794, 383.
66   *BM*, July 1850, 436.

"In Regeneration," he explains, "men are wholly passive—in Conversion, they become active." Here the distinction seems stark: conversion, by contrast with regeneration, is a solely human work. Yet Rippon has just defined conversion as consisting "both of God's act upon men in turning them, and of acts done by men under the influence of converting grace: they turn, being turned." Here the contrast is located within conversion: it is both a divine transformation and a human achievement. There is an ambiguity in Rippon's expression about whether or not the Almighty is at work in conversion. As though aware of his confusion, Rippon tries to illustrate his position by quoting a series of antitheses between regeneration and conversion from the "*most judicious*" Puritan Stephen Charnock. Here again, however, there is ambiguity. In some of Charnock's axioms, conversion seems to be wholly human, but in others it is both divine and human. "In Conversion," the Puritan concludes, "the sinner is active, but it is NOT FROM THE POWER *of* MAN, although it is from a POWER *in* MAN, not growing up from the FEEBLE ROOT of nature, but SETTLED THERE by the almighty spirit of God."[67] In that complex statement the great change is twice said to be human, twice not human, and once divine. Both Rippon and before him Charnock were wrestling with an intractable problem in theology, the sense in which human autonomy is compatible with divine agency. The ultimate grounding of the problem is the issue of freedom against necessity. Eighteenth-century Evangelicals such as Rippon were concerned to maintain the divine element even while admitting human freedom. The trend in the nineteenth century was for the human component to become greater so that divine participation in conversion tended to diminish. The structure erected by Rippon, perhaps inherently unstable, gradually disintegrated.

The change expressed itself, for one thing, in an increase of human planning. It was a hallmark of eighteenth-century Evangelicals to believe that the Almighty and human beings both used what were called "means," that is mundane instruments, to bring about conversions. The world had already been used in this sense by seventeenth-century Puritans such as William Ames,[68] but in stressing the concept, eighteenth-century Evangelicals differed from their high Calvinist contemporaries, who believed that conversion happened as a result of an unanticipated exercise of divine sovereignty, a shaft from the blue. On the high Calvinist view, conversion had to be waited for rather than contrived. William Carey attacked this position in his celebrated work, *An Enquiry into the Obligations of Christians to Use Means for the Conversion of*

---

67 John Rippon, *Baptist Annual Register for 1801 and 1802* (London: no pub., 1802), 664–65. I am grateful to Susan Mills for drawing my attention to this passage.
68 Cohen, *God's Caress*, 220.

the Heathens (1792). There should be no delay until God was pleased to act because means, in this case a missionary society, ought to be used to fulfill the known divine purposes.[69] The word "means" crops up in this sense in the obituaries. A woman among the General Baptists, for example, was stirred by the death of a friend in about 1815 to seek salvation and, as her memorialist puts it, "in the use of means, she was enabled to trust in Christ as an all sufficient Saviour."[70] The tendency over time was for the use of such means to increase.

The process can be illustrated from the field of religious education. Traditionally the catechism had been taught to lay the foundations of Christian knowledge. An instance occurs in the obituary of Mrs D. Smith, born in 1747 the daughter of a Suffolk farmer:

> Her father being a grave steady man, who kept up the old custom of catechising his children and servants, and praying with them on Lord's day evenings; some very serious impressions respecting soul concerns began in very early life.[71]

The expectation was that, as in this case, seeds would be sown that, under divine providence, might later germinate. Catechetical training was conceived as preparation of the soil, not as a forcing house for conversion. Very different, however, were the Sunday schools that first became popular in the 1780s and increasingly became associated with particular congregations during the nineteenth century. In the latter phase they generally aimed for conversions. Sunday schools constituted a means that could deliberately be used for that end. Thus four of the fifteen General Baptists in the sample were swayed by Sunday school. In a similar way other means were arranged to promote conversion. The sample includes instances of the phenomenon at a Sunday morning young men's prayer meeting in Market Harborough and at a Sunday evening cottage meeting in Fareham, Hampshire.[72] In another case an experience meeting at Redruth Baptist Church in Cornwall was where a man was able to give vent to the anxiety of soul that preceded his enlightenment.[73] This gathering seems to be an example of the copying of a Methodist class meeting in the most Methodist of counties. The followers of John Wesley, with their itinerancy and their love-feasts, were long the exemplars of pragmatic innovation for the sake of the gospel, but by the 1830s and

---

69 William Carey, *An Enquiry into the Obligations of Christians to Use Means for the Conversion of the Heathens* [1792] (London: Carey Kingsgate Press, 1961), sect. 1.
70 *GBR*, April 1822, 139.
71 *BM*, September 1810, 122.
72 *EM*, Supplement for 1850, 708; *BM*, June 1810, 346–47.
73 *BM*, April 1809, 147.

1840s a school of "instrumentalists" had arisen who copied the more elaborate American methods. The evangelists of the Baptist Home Missionary Society and their counterparts among the Independents both imitated the "new measures" pioneered in the United States by Charles Finney, notably the protracted meeting at which burdened souls could be prayed through to the new birth.[74] There was a trend over time towards deliberately creating the most favorable circumstances for turning to God.

Human timing, like human planning, came gradually more into fashion. It was increasingly believed that the sinner did not have to wait until the moment of divine appointment for conversion. In the seventeenth century it had been common for conviction of sin to last for years before a soul found rest in believing.[75] As late as the end of the eighteenth century the same pattern is clear in the experience of many Calvinists. In 1798 a man who was awakened by an Independent field preacher did not close with Christ immediately but rather spent "considerable time" in conviction of sin.[76] In 1789 another continued for four or five months "in the pangs of new birth;" and in 1795 a third occupied a full two years doubting his personal interest in redemption.[77] Among the Arminian General Baptists there was often much more Methodist-style earnest seeking after salvation, but, again, the time allocated to persevering prayer delayed the climax of conversion. Thus in around 1800 Mrs Elizabeth Johnson of Quorndon, Leicestershire, did not give up her heart to the Savior until some years after marriage. "In her first attempts, she was much perplexed with an evil heart of unbelief; but steadily pursuing the subject, her views became rectified, and she was enabled to say, 'I know in whom I have believed.'"[78] As the nineteenth century advanced, however, the approach to timing altered. Finney in the United States was once more the pace-setter, urging immediate surrender to Christ. His admirers in Britain during the 1830s and 1840s adopted the same technique. George Redford, a prominent Independent minister deeply influenced by Finney, issued a tract called *The Great Change* (1844), in which a chapter is given over to "Reasons why your conversion should take place now."[79] Likewise James Morison, the founder of the Evangelical Union denomination in Scotland in 1843, argued that people were guilty of a very great

---

74 Richard Carwardine, *Transatlantic Revivalism: Popular Evangelicalism in Britain and America, 1790–1865* (Westport, CT: Greenwood Press, 1978), chap. 2.
75 Cohen, *God's Caress*, 205.
76 *BM*, March 1810, 118–19.
77 *EM*, March 1794, 117; March 1850, 114.
78 *GBR*, April 1822, 141.
79 Redford, *Great Change*, chap. 7.

crime if they did not believe immediately on hearing the gospel.[80] There could be no plea for a moment's delay. In progressive Evangelical circles around the middle of the nineteenth century sinners were thought to be able to come to Christ at a time of their own choosing.

There was a similar development of opinion about human conviction. Expectations shifted about how confidently people could know that they had been converted. Reformed piety in the seventeenth century had deliberately fostered anxieties about whether or not a person was of the elect in order to ensure that each sinner persevered in ensuring that faith was real rather than counterfeit. Assurance of salvation was not regarded as a standard possession of the believer. The Evangelical Revival encouraged greater confidence in one's eternal destiny as a result of stronger assumptions about the capacity of human beings to achieve knowledge.[81] Yet the older Calvinist tradition still powerfully influenced late eighteenth-century Evangelicals. John Newton, the slavetrader turned clergyman, insisted that assurance was not of the essence of faith and portrayed the earliest phase of Christian experience as typically lacking any certainty of salvation.[82] Many Calvinist Dissenters continued to experience worries of the old type in the years around 1800. Thus Elizabeth Bowden, daughter of the Independent minister at Tooting, Surrey, fell seriously ill at the age of seventeen in the early 1790s. Aware of her danger, she was anxious and despondent. "I want more comfort in my soul," she told her father, "... I want to *know* my interest in the *covenant*."[83] Elizabeth evidently lacked assurance—though, since her last word as she died was "Joys!," she presumably found it at the end. Comparable uncertainty about one's spiritual state occurs several times in the sample. If the piety shows the continuing legacy of the seventeenth century, the counseling given in such circumstances was now different. Puritan pastors would not readily have calmed the anxieties for fear of giving ungrounded hope. The newer attitude in such a case was expressed in an authoritative footnote to a spiritual biography in the *Evangelical Magazine* for 1794. The subject, not remembering the start of God's work in her soul, sometimes questioned whether she had been effectually called to Christian discipleship. To doubt the sincerity of one's religion because of inability to recall the

---

80 James Morison, *Saving Faith: Or the Simple Belief of the Gospel* (Kilmarnock: J. Davie, 1842), 14.
81 David W. Bebbington, *Evangelicalism in Modern Britain: A History from the 1730s to the 1980s* (London: Unwin Hyman, 1989), 42–50.
82 Bruce Hindmarsh, *John Newton and the English Evangelical Tradition: Between the Conversions of Wesley and Wilberforce* (Oxford: Clarendon Press, 1996), 66, 251–52.
83 *EM*, March 1794, 121.

circumstances of one's conversion, according to the weighty editorial opinion, was "unreasonable and unscriptural." Fears could safely be set aside.[84] It was no longer supposed to be beneficial to welter in uncertainty. Accordingly the obituaries in the sample discussing experiences after about 1820 reveal no such lack of confidence in the validity of personal faith. By 1842 James Morison was teaching, like the early Wesley, that assurance is actually essential to faith. "Every man who believes the gospel," he asserted, "knows that he believes it."[85] Similarly the Independent R. W. Dale of Birmingham, when beginning his ministry in mid-century, had no qualms about the proper stance on the question of assurance: "it should be the aim of the Christian teacher so to represent the power and grace of the Lord Jesus, and the unconditional freeness of His gospel, that the troubled and guilty heart, forgetting itself altogether, shall trust everything to Christ."[86] There was now no need for introspection because confidence in one's spiritual state depends on Christ, not on one's response to him. The doctrine of assurance had become much more robust.

Alongside rising confidence in human conviction went a growing belief in human ability. High Calvinists of the eighteenth century taught that only God, by an irresistible exercise of his grace, can bring about the great change. The human contribution was minimal or nonexistent. The Evangelical mainstream, by contrast, learned from Jonathan Edwards to distinguish between natural and moral inability. Natural inability operated when human beings could not do what they wanted to do; moral inability operated when they did not do something because they did not want to do it. The latter was true of those rejecting the gospel, who therefore bore the culpability of their decision.[87] There was an obligation to believe, what came to be called "duty faith." This stance was shared by Andrew Fuller for the Baptists, Edward Williams for the Independents and Thomas Chalmers for the Presbyterians: it was the prevailing Evangelical theology of the early nineteenth century. Thus John Angell James, Dale's predecessor at Birmingham, could write of avoiding the antinomianism of the high Calvinists as much as the Arminianism of the Methodists.[88] His version of Calvinism was in the middle between the two. In parts of England and Wales, especially in East Anglia, as in the remoter parts of the

---

84 *EM*, September 1794, 354.
85 Morison, *Saving Faith*, 11.
86 Robert W. Dale, *The Life and Letters of John Angell James* (London: James Nisbet, 1861), 302.
87 Hindmarsh, *John Newton*, 153–54, offers a particularly clear exposition of the distinction.
88 Dale, *James*, 283.

United States, the Baptists split on this issue. The high Calvinists became the Strict and Particular body while the bulk of Baptists followed Fuller. It was a topic of sufficient gravity to divide brethren into separate denominations.

What has been less noticed, at least for Britain, is that there was a further shift on the question of human ability during the early nineteenth century. In the United States, where the process is much better known, the change was expressed in the New Haven theology associated particularly with Nathaniel W. Taylor. Starting with the principle of duty faith that a person has an obligation to believe the gospel, Taylor applied the Kantian maxim, "No ought without can." He inferred that all human beings have a free capacity to believe. Conversion was within the sinner's will. Taylor's theology, first extensively promoted in 1818, was to be the foundation for Finney's practice in revivalism, but it was stoutly resisted by the Old Presbyterians of Princeton as derogating from the divine prerogative.[89] The debate did not rage on the other side of the Atlantic, though it was known in Britain, for example by John Angell James.[90] There were, however, echoes of the controversy in discussions about the role of the Holy Spirit in conversion. John Howard Hinton, the son of the respected Baptist minister at Oxford, argued in a book of 1830 that human beings had power to repent without the aid of the Spirit.[91] The contention found little favor, but Hinton was able to assume a leading place in his denomination without recanting. Finney accepted that the Holy Spirit is always at work in conversion, but only as a moral influence, that is, merely in a persuasive role. The evangelist's major change in received theology was to collapse the distinction between regeneration and conversion altogether. Each term, according to Finney, described the same divine and human action, but the human being held the whip hand. "Neither God," he wrote, "nor any other being, can regenerate him, if he will not turn."[92] The prestige of the revivalist, who toured England in 1849-50, ensured his views a wide audience. In Scotland James Morison, who was deeply influenced by Finney, taught that there was nothing miraculous about conversion, "for if turning to God be a miracle, it cannot be the duty of any sinner to turn himself from his evil ways."[93] The intense moralism that was dominant in theology led to a minimizing of the divine part in the

---

89 Sidney E. Mead, *Nathaniel William Taylor, 1786-1858: A Connecticut Liberal* (Chicago: University of Chicago Press, 1942).
90 Dale, *James*, 261-62.
91 John Howard Hinton, *The Work of the Holy Spirit in Conversion* (London: Holdsworth and Ball, 1830); Carwardine, *Transatlantic Revivalism*, 63-64.
92 Charles G. Finney, *Lectures on Systematic Theology*, ed. George Redford (London: W. Tegg & Co., 1851), 411, 407, 413.
93 Morison, *Saving Faith*, 49.

transformation of sinners. It was such teaching that brought about Morison's condemnation by the United Secession Synod and his founding of the Evangelical Union. Here again was a theological disagreement about the balance of the divine and human in conversion that was capable of causing denominational division. Just as in the United States, a much stronger view of human ability entered British theology as the standpoint of revivalists who wanted to maximize conversions.

The prevailing trend in the understanding of conversion in the period therefore consisted in an elevation of the human element—in planning, timing, conviction and ability. The fine tension maintained by Chamock between divine and human activity was gradually relaxed. Why was the Puritan inheritance modified? All the changes may be traced to the spreading influence of Enlightenment patterns of thought, not external to the Evangelical movement, but in and through it. Since the Enlightenment was the dominant cultural form, it necessarily shaped the appreciation of the gospel. Its typical motifs of progress, pragmatism and shedding the metaphysical obscurities of the past are evident in the processes of adaptation that have been discussed. Finney voiced many of its characteristic themes in the introduction to the British edition of his *Lectures on Systematic Theology* (1851). The gospel, he contended, must no longer be hidden by a "false philosophy;" in this age of science the "spirit of enquiry" demands theological reformulation; only so can there be "improvements" suited to the nineteenth century.[94] As a result, conversion became a simpler, shallower experience, less a wrestling with the angel and more a scientific experiment. John Angell James described the British scene to an American correspondent in 1828. "Conversions," he wrote, "at least supposed conversions, are not unknown, nor unfrequent in many congregations, but the work, in most instances, is not of a decisive or impressive character."[95] Quality, it might be said, was being sacrificed to quantity. This was the legacy transmitted to the later nineteenth century.[96]

---

94 Finney, *Lectures*, vii, viii, x.
95 J. A. James to Dr W. B. Sprague, 15 December 1828, in Dale, *James*, 250.
96 Cf. Phyllis D. Airhart, "'What Must I Do to Be Saved?' Two Paths to Evangelical Conversion in Late Victorian Canada," *Church History* 59:3 (1990), 372-85.

Conclusions

A number of overall conclusions can be drawn from this study. First, conversion, though not necessarily a crisis experience, was regarded as essential in the Evangelical movement of this period. The situation of around the start of the twentieth century, when even candidates for the ministry were not necessarily expected to be able to testify to a great change of life, had not yet arrived.[97] The experience, secondly, was concentrated chiefly in a particular age group, those of twenty-five and under. Yet it was common to both sexes and widespread in terms of status, place and denomination. These findings correspond closely to those of Watts and others. Conversion, thirdly, was associated with the other main features of the Evangelical movement, the Bible, the cross and activism. Although the prospect of hell was a stimulus to conversion, an awareness of guilt was more significant. Finally, the direction of change, under the influence of the Enlightenment's categories of thought, was towards stressing the human dimension of the experience rather than the divine. Conversion, even mass conversion, was increasingly being seen as a matter of free choice. Already by the mid-nineteenth century the Evangelical movement had moved a long way towards the stance of some Nottingham Baptists who in the 1880s recorded the following resolution of church meeting: "that after the Bazaar we go in for a revival."[98]

---

97 Brown, *Nonconformist Ministry*, 50–53.
98 David W. Bebbington, *A History of Queensberry Street Baptist Church, Old Basford, Nottingham* (Nottingham: For the Church, 1977), 17.

10

Holiness in the Evangelical Tradition

Evangelicalism is the prevailing form of Protestantism in the modern world. In English-speaking lands, the tradition encompasses members of most denominations except the Unitarians and other bodies disavowing historic orthodoxy. In the Church of England, Evangelicalism has been the third option alongside High and Broad Churchmanship. Together with the Evangelical party in the Church of England, however, the tradition takes in the whole popular movement that ranges from the traditionalist Free Church of Scotland to innovative Pentecostalism. Although there is a worldwide movement possessing similar characteristics, this chapter concentrates on its British expression. It arose virtually simultaneously in the 1730s in Wales, England, Scotland and the British colonies in America. It created the new phenomenon of Methodism, but it also reinvigorated the established churches and the Old Dissent. It increased its impact at all social levels up to the middle of the nineteenth century, when it reached the peak of its influence. It remolded the language of the other Christian traditions, so that Victorian High and Broad Churchmen spoke very much like Evangelicals. By the early twentieth century, however, the movement had fallen on evil days: its numbers decreased, it tended to split into theologically opposed camps and it became socially marginalized. There was a resurgence in the later twentieth century within the churches, though hardly within society at large. This chapter examines Evangelical holiness over the centuries, dwelling on its main characteristics and its changing cultural affinities.

Evangelical Holiness Characterized

Evangelical versions of holiness were rooted in the distinctive features of the movement. First was its insistence on conversion as the start of the Christian life. Conversion could be instant or gradual, but in either case it was essential. For the Evangelical, the world was divided into two groups, believers and unbelievers, and the line of separation was a decisive turning from darkness to light. A measure of sanctity was a presumptive indication that the change had taken place. Thus Hannah More, an Evangelical bluestocking at the end of the eighteenth century, wrote that, "[h]oliness of life is the only true evidence of a saving faith."[1] Without the emergence of holiness, the process of sanctification, it could be judged that a sinner was still unconverted. Theologically the event of conversion was described as justification, the putting right of the sinner by God. There was no doubt about the relationship of justification and sanctification. "Sanctification is a fruit of justification," John Clayton, a London Congregational minister, declared in 1813. "It never exists without justification."[2] The insistence that sanctification came second was a corollary of justification by faith. Holiness entailed good works; but good works could not earn salvation. A right relationship with God was his gift to those who put their trust in Christ. Therefore holiness must follow, not precede, justification. It was a fundamental belief of Evangelicals that holiness was only for the converted.

A second characteristic was a stress on the doctrine of the atonement. It was not the teaching or example of Christ that brought salvation to the soul. Rather it was the work of Christ in dying on the cross that conveyed the forgiveness of sins. Charles Simeon, the leader of the Evangelicals in the Church of England at the start of the nineteenth century, published a sermon entitled "Christ Crucified, or Evangelical Religion Described." In it he urged that by appeal to the cross "holiness in all its branches must be enforced and a sense of Christ's love in dying for us . . . inculcated as the main spring of all our obedience."[3] The quest for sanctity was to be an expression of gratitude for the atonement. There was a sense in which the cross eclipsed the life of discipleship altogether. A person could never achieve assurance of salvation through obedience to the Almighty. That experience could come only through the death of the Savior. "Sanctification," according to William Goode, a leading Evangelical clergyman, in 1804, "is not the ground of our comfort. The work of Christ is the only ground of comfort."[4] The pursuit of holiness should never

---

1 James M. Gordon, *Evangelical Spirituality: From the Wesleys to John Stott* (London: SPCK, 1991), 107.
2 *The Thought of the Evangelical Leaders*, ed. John H. Pratt (Edinburgh: Banner of Truth Trust, 1978), 20.
3 Gordon, *Evangelical Spirituality*, 97.
4 *Thought of the Evangelical Leaders*, ed. Pratt, 314.

lead believers to place their confidence elsewhere than in the cross. The atonement was to be the foundation of all spiritual experience.

The Bible, thirdly, was the guide to the nature of holiness. Evangelicals were Bible people. Scripture was the kernel of their private devotional reading as well as, through preaching, the central element in public worship. In his book on *God's Way of Holiness* (1874), the Scottish Presbyterian Horatius Bonar recommended that "the whole soul be fed by the study of the whole Bible."[5] The absorption of scripture teaching was equated with the cultivation of godliness. The Bible thus provided more than a specification of what the Christian life entailed: it also imparted the power to fulfill the divine requirements. C. H. Spurgeon, the celebrated Baptist minister of the Metropolitan Tabernacle in London, put the principle in a nutshell: "It is the Word of God which sanctifies the soul."[6] The Bible was the chief instrument in the living of a holy life.

The result of holiness, finally, was vigorous activity. The Evangelical ideal of sanctity was much closer to that of Martha than to that of Mary in the gospel story: it was less concerned with contemplation than with busyness. "Activity for God," according to the American Methodist holiness preacher James Caughey, "is a consequence of a healthy soul, as green to a healthy leaf."[7] The logic was impeccable: once converted to God, any individual should try to bring the same momentous experience to others. Mission was therefore the lifeblood of the Evangelical movement. At home John Wesley was celebrated for spending his life in constant travel to preach the gospel through the British Isles. Abroad Evangelicalism gave rise to the modern missionary movement. But activism, as the work of the missionaries themselves reveals, was not confined to pioneering evangelism. From the start, missionaries were preoccupied with the temporal welfare of the lands they entered, as William Carey's campaign against widow burning in India illustrates. As time went on, an increasing proportion of missionaries concentrated on education, medicine and industrial development. Equivalent charitable effort was the central aim of many of the great domestic Evangelical agencies such as the Ragged School Society. Rank-and-file members were caught up in the flurry of doing. Sophia Nixon, for example, a Wesleyan convert in 1835, confided to her diary her eagerness to be holy; her obituarist recounts that she lived "in the healthy and

---

5   Gordon, *Evangelical Spirituality*, 140.
6   Charles H. Spurgeon, *Twelve Sermons on Sanctification* (London: Passmore & Alabaster, n.d.), 94.
7   James Caughey, *Earnest Christianity Illustrated* (London: Partridge & Co., 1857), 103.

bracing breeze of incessant employment and activity."[8] Evangelicals believed that devotional exercises must always issue in concrete deeds.

These, then, were the most salient features of the holy life in the Evangelical tradition. It would be quite wrong, however, to portray so diverse a movement as having a single understanding of anything, let alone so protean a concept as holiness. On the contrary, Evangelicals differed sharply among themselves over questions surrounding sanctification. So the main task here is to survey the various strands in Evangelicalism for their contrasting views in the field. Four chief sub-traditions are readily identifiable: the Reformed, the Wesleyan, the Keswick and the charismatic. Each will be explored in turn. The aim will be not only to bring out the most striking elements in their perceptions of sanctity, but also to diagnose their cultural affinities. That exercise goes a long way towards explaining why there have been different understandings of holiness.

Calvinist Holiness

The first sub-tradition was the Calvinist or Reformed strand. In the eighteenth century, nearly all Anglican Evangelicals other than Wesley's followers adopted Reformed teaching, but they tended to play it down because Calvinism seemed tainted with memories of the Puritan revolution. Simeon eventually publicly repudiated Calvinism altogether. Most Anglican Evangelicals thereafter sat loose to distinctively Reformed views, but their theology continued to be molded more by it than by any other source and a few, including the redoubtable J. C. Ryle, first bishop of Liverpool from 1880, remained self-conscious Calvinists.[9] Evangelical Dissenters, both Congregationalists and Baptists, were tied to their Calvinist moorings for longer, but gradually cast them off during the later nineteenth century. Presbyterians in Scotland and Calvinistic Methodists in Wales were confessionally Reformed, and so retained more of their doctrinal legacy than English Nonconformists, but followed broadly the same path. By the first half of the twentieth century Calvinism was at a low ebb. In its second half, however, the distinguished Welsh minister of Westminster Chapel, Martyn Lloyd-Jones, propagated a revival of Reformed teaching, especially through his sponsorship of the Banner of Truth Trust that republished Calvinist classics. What was the understanding of holiness in these circles?

Calvinist Evangelicals were constantly aware of two traps into which the unwary might stumble. One was the legalist snare: the notion, condemned in

---

8   *Methodist Magazine*, 1871, 287, quoted by Linda Wilson, *Constrained by Zeal: Female Spirituality amongst Nonconformists, 1825–1875* (Carlisle: Paternoster Press, 2000), 55.

9   On Ryle, see 2:2: "Bishop J. C. Ryle: Holiness, Mission and Churchmanship."

the New Testament by the apostle Paul, that human beings could obtain acceptance by the Almighty through fulfilling the demands of God's law. People might suppose that they could become holy by their own effort, independent of divine grace. The early Evangelicals saw this opinion propagated in the eighteenth century by many latitudinarian churchmen. The other threat was the assertion that believers were exempt from obeying the law of God and so need not exert themselves to obtain holiness. A handful of hyper-Calvinists took this ground, at least in theory. The best known were Robert Hawker, a Plymouth clergyman around the turn of the nineteenth century, and William Huntington, a former coalheaver who became an Independent preacher in London and delighted to place "S.S.," denoting "Sinner Saved," after his name. These men taught imputed sanctification, that is the idea that a person is wholly sanctified from conversion onwards, and contended that the need for holiness of life should not be mentioned in preaching. Mainstream Evangelicals such as Simeon were horrified at this view, which seemed calculated to foster immoral behavior. They insisted that, just as holiness is unattainable without divine help, so it must be sought through human endeavor. The achievement of sanctity was a result of synergy, divine and human. It was, furthermore, a gradual process. Over time, progress was to be expected in the Christian life. "A man," remarked Ryle, "may climb from one step to another in holiness."[10] Slowly old motives were transformed and new habits consolidated. There could nevertheless be a falling back into sinful ways—what Evangelicals called backsliding—but the remedy was to break with sin and return to the paths of righteousness. The whole business necessarily took time. "The new heart of a saint of God," according to an eminent Scottish Presbyterian minister at the turn of the twentieth century, Alexander Whyte, "was never attained at a bound."[11] Steady progress was the best that could be expected.

Spiritual development did not mean that a believer escaped from the blandishments of sin. There was always, even after a long pilgrimage, an enemy within, what John Newton, the eighteenth-century Anglican clergyman and hymn writer, called "the inseparable remnants of a fallen nature."[12] The flesh, in Pauline terms, always contended with the spirit. The hostility between the two aspects of human nature remained down to the grave. Not until death and the entrance on glory was the tension relieved. Hence there was a need for constant vigilance, dedication and effort. The Christian life was an arena of

---

10 John C. Ryle, *Holiness*, 3rd ed. (London: William Hunt & Co., 1887), 29.
11 Gordon, *Evangelical Spirituality*, 246.
12 Bruce Hindmarsh, *John Newton and the English Evangelical Tradition: Between the Conversions of Wesley and Wilberforce* (Oxford: Clarendon Press, 1996), 256.

perpetual conflict. Calvinists readily employed military imagery in their exposition of spirituality. "A holy violence," declared Ryle, "a conflict, a warfare, a fight, a soldier's life, a wrestling, are spoken of as characteristic of the true Christian."[13] Ryle was drawing on the long Christian tradition that depicted the quest for sanctity as a *pugna spiritualis*, a spiritual battle. The Calvinist approach was not far removed from that of the bulk of Christendom, Eastern as well as Western.

The Reformed understanding of holiness, in fact, had deep roots in the epoch before the rise of Evangelicalism. Its classic texts were not from the revival period at all, but from the previous century. John Goode, a Dissenting minister at an Evangelical discussion group in 1809, naturally appealed to the definition of sanctification in the catechism of the Westminster Assembly.[14] Ryle in the late nineteenth century included among his authorities on the subject Richard Sibbes, Thomas Manton, John Owen and Thomas Brooks—all Puritan divines.[15] These were still the authors being republished by the Banner of Truth Trust at the end of the twentieth century. There was, therefore, a strong sense of continuity with the past about the Calvinist advocates of holiness.

Nevertheless one element of the Puritan attitude was firmly repudiated. Seventeenth-century Calvinist authors had encouraged their readers to doubt their salvation. Only if they were aroused to be seekers, it was assumed, would they be likely to find. Hence authentic spirituality in the seventeenth century entailed intense introspection to discover whether there were any green shoots of a harvest of grace in the field of the soul. Evangelical Calvinists of the eighteenth century onwards, however, would have nothing of that. Except in the most conservative circles of English Strict Baptists and Scottish Free Churchmen, they held that assurance of salvation, though by no means certain for believers, was at least to be coveted. Only if they possessed an assured hope would they turn from spiritual hypochondriacs into dedicated participants in mission: "assurance is to be desired," according to Ryle, "because it tends to make a Christian an active working Christian."[16] The confident knowledge of God, which was the essence of assurance, formed an Evangelical species of the Enlightenment's characteristic preoccupation with epistemology. Calvinism had been sufficiently adapted to the times to take up a much stronger estimate of the knowability of the Almighty. The conception of the holy life current among Evangelical Calvinists was powerfully molded by long-standing

---

13   Ryle, *Holiness*, xxvi.
14   *The Thought of the Evangelical Leaders*, ed. Pratt, 464.
15   Ryle, *Holiness*, xxix, 48n, 460–71.
16   Ryle, *Holiness*, 163.

Christian tradition, especially in its Protestant variant, but adapted to the intellectual environment created by the Enlightenment.

Wesleyan Holiness

The second strand for consideration is that associated with John Wesley. The Wesleyan teaching contrasted with the Reformed position by asserting that before death a state of perfect holiness is attainable on earth. This was one of the distinctive views that brought eighteenth-century Methodists into conflict with their Calvinist contemporaries. It was part of the Wesleyan theological package labeled Arminianism, after the seventeenth-century continental opponent of Reformed doctrine, Jacobus Arminius. The central conviction setting Arminians apart from Calvinists was the belief that all might be saved: not, of course, that all would be saved but that all had the power to respond to the gospel. Yet Wesleyan holiness teaching should not be seen as a corollary of Arminianism. For one thing Arminius himself had not upheld it; for another the General Baptists, who, like Wesley, were Arminians, did not embrace his view of sanctification. All branches of Methodism, however, officially maintained the Wesleyan position during the nineteenth century.[17] Although in practice the holiness tradition within Methodism gradually decayed, it enjoyed a resurgence in the 1870s. This so-called "holiness revival" was much weaker in Britain than in the United States but it did give rise to a number of small holiness bodies including, in its early days, the Salvation Army. By the twentieth century, however, Wesleyan teaching had become marginal, being sustained in the later part of the century only by the Church of the Nazarene and a small number of Methodists. The Wesleyan tradition has largely fallen by the wayside.

The outstanding primary source is John Wesley's *Plain Account of Christian Perfection* (1766–89). In it Wesley teaches the possibility of entire sanctification, what he prefers to call "perfect love." This was held to be a state in which the believer commits no sin. It is not just that sinful acts have ceased; it is also that there is no longer any stimulus to sin. The condition was described in questions and answers summarizing the proceedings of the first Methodist Conference in 1744:

Q. What is it to be *sanctified*?

A. To be renewed in the image of God, in *righteousness and true holiness*.

---

17 See 2:3: "Entire Sanctification in Methodism during the Nineteenth Century."

Q. What is implied in being a *perfect Christian*?

A. The loving God with all our heart, and mind, and soul (Deut. 6:5)

Q. Does this imply that *all inward sin* is taken away?

A. Undoubtedly: or how can we be said to be *saved from all our uncleanness*? (Ezek. 36:29)[18]

The doctrine spread in the much more palatable form of the hymns of John Wesley's brother, Charles:

> Answer that gracious end in me
> > For which thy precious life was given:
> Redeem from *all iniquity*,
> > Restore and make me meet for heaven.
> Unless thou purge my *every stain*,
> > Thy suffering and my faith is vain.[19]

Here was a direct challenge to Reformed teaching. Far from the Christian life being a perennial struggle between the implanted spirit and the sinful flesh, it was possible to break free from sin altogether. This was strong meat, and it turned the stomachs of Calvinists.

The Wesleyan conception focused on what its opponents often called "the second blessing." After conversion, on this view, there was a fresh crisis in which the believer entered on a state of perfect blessedness. It was received instantaneously. Before that point, Wesley found, converts often struggled for years in the search for sanctity. Most, including Wesley himself, never professed to have discovered the blessed state at all. Those who did entered on it by faith alone. Sanctification, like justification, was given to faith, not achieved as a result of works. The Calvinist supposition that there must be sustained effort in the struggle against sin was rejected. On the contrary, there could be a serene reliance on Christ as the guarantor of Christian perfection. Peace, according to its advocates, had superseded the state of war in the soul. Nevertheless, Wesley and his followers readily admitted that perfect love could be lost. The condition of sanctity could be attained and forfeited repeatedly as a person lapsed into deliberate wrong. Errors that were not deliberate, however,

---

18 *John and Charles Wesley: Selected Prayers, Hymns, Journal, Notes, Sermons, Letters and Treatises*, ed. Frank Whaling (London: SPCK, 1981), 319.
19 *John and Charles Wesley*, ed. Whaling, 317.

were not classified as sins at all. They were merely "infirmities." For that reason Wesley denied that there was such a thing as "any *absolute perfection* on earth."[20] It was a concession that made the experience seem attainable. Wesley was nevertheless portraying a state of sanctity far higher than that envisaged by his Calvinist opponents.

Although Wesley always remained the leading authority in the Methodist holiness tradition, there were significant modifications in its content over time. In the middle years of the nineteenth century there was a process of American democratization. Visiting preachers from the United States, James Caughey and Phoebe Palmer, proclaimed a version of Wesleyan holiness for the masses. Wanting to maximize the numbers enjoying the experience, they tried to make the way of securing the blessing easier. There was no need to wait, as earlier Methodists had supposed, until a believer wrestled through to full salvation. Instead it was possible to believe for entire sanctification on the spot. By contrast with Wesley, they claimed that no feeling of confirmation— "the witness of the Spirit"—was necessarily to be expected. Faith would always be honored by God. Consequently numbers professing entire sanctification increased under their preaching; but the experience was normally less deeply rooted. At the same time, and on into the twentieth century, another factor came into operation. Exponents of the Wesleyan tradition smoothed away its sharp edges. William Arthur, a Wesleyan connexional official, for example, published *The Tongue of Fire* (1856) to urge entire sanctification, but wrapped up his subject in such oblique genteel language as to tone down the distinctiveness of the experience. He was catering for a Methodist public that was upwardly socially mobile. Professions of perfection seemed out of place in Victorian suburbia. Growing respectability dictated that talk about instantaneous holiness should be either modified or abandoned. Consequently the tradition fell into decay.

The decreasing popularity of holiness on Wesleyan lines was also partly the result of the fading of the intellectual context in which it had originally been created. It was the product of the Enlightenment of the eighteenth century. John Wesley has increasingly been recognized in recent years as an Enlightenment thinker. Although he retained a streak of superstition and credulity, he was a persistent assertor of the claims of reason in religion. Doctrine, he argued, should be accepted only if it was reasonable. The New Testament, in the first Epistle of John, taught that "[w]hosoever is born of God doth not commit sin."[21] It was a rational inference, Wesley insisted, that freedom from

20 *John and Charles Wesley*, ed. Whaling, 307.
21 1 John 3:9.

sin was possible. In keeping with the spirit of the age, Wesley was committed to empirical method. He therefore investigated the cases of Methodists claiming entire sanctification, and in many instances concluded that their claims were valid. He, like his era, was an optimist about human potential. Why should not human beings be capable of rising to sublime heights of sanctity? The result was an understanding of holiness cast in an Enlightenment mold. It is true that some late Victorian Methodists injected the Romantic style of thinking into Wesleyan teaching and so caught the wind of later cultural trends. There was, however, a more thorough Romantic revamping of holiness available in the alternative Keswick tradition which gained far more influence than its Wesleyan counterpart. As the legacy of the Enlightenment in the exaltation of reason, empiricism and optimism weakened in society, so Wesley's ideal of holiness ceased to exert a powerful appeal.

The Keswick Holiness Tradition

The Keswick movement that has just been mentioned forms the third strand of Evangelical holiness teaching. Its central contention, like Wesley's, was that sanctification is possible by faith. Unlike Wesley, however, it maintained that the sinful nature is never extinguished during life on earth. Keswick teaching was so called because it was the message of the annual convention held from 1875 in the Lake District town. The immediate source of the novel theory was an American couple, Robert and Hannah Pearsall Smith, who toured Britain in the early 1870s propagating what was often called "the higher life." Conferences in Oxford in 1874 and Brighton in 1875 laid the foundations for Keswick. The whole movement was nearly wrecked through an indiscretion by Robert Pearsall Smith at Brighton: he offered spiritual guidance to a young woman privately in a hotel room and had to be hurriedly shipped back to America. Once the annual convention had been launched, however, it went from strength to strength. Its journal, the *Life of Faith*, gained a mass circulation. Keswick sanctification doctrine became the norm in conservative Evangelical circles during the first half of the twentieth century, fading only in the 1950s and 1960s. For nearly a century it enjoyed considerable support.

Sanctification, on the Keswick understanding, was originally received in a moment. This belief shows the debt of Keswick, through the Pearsall Smiths and others, to the Wesleyan tradition before it. Every annual convention came to the point where a speaker would call on his hearers to receive entire consecration. Ryle, from his unreconstructed Reformed perspective, protested against "the theory of a sudden, mysterious transition of a believer into a state of blessedness . . . at one mighty bound."²² Faith, according to Keswick, was the only initial condition of embracing the higher spiritual life. Faith, furthermore, had to be exercised permanently. Only if a person continued to trust the Almighty would sin continue to be defeated. There had to be what was often termed a "moment-by-moment" form of dependence on God. By this means sin was not eradicated, as contemporaries in the Wesleyan succession claimed, but repressed. "The flesh," in the words of Evan Hopkins, the movement's leading theological exponent down to the First World War, "is . . . effectively counteracted by . . . the Holy Ghost within us, so that we can walk in the paths of continuous deliverance from it."²³ Hence there was no persisting struggle between spirit and flesh, as traditional Calvinists believed, but rather an experience of "victory," a common Keswick slogan. The whole convention position can best be understood as an attempt to remodel Wesley's teaching so as to make it palatable to those possessing a Reformed inheritance. Consecration was available in an instant through faith, as Wesley had contended; but there was no question of the elimination of sin from human life. Keswickers were always hot in denial of the charge that they were "perfectionists."

Like the Wesleyan approach, Keswick teaching underwent change over time. In its early days it remained particularly malleable. It was the achievement of Evan Hopkins and Handley Moule, bishop of Durham from 1901 to 1920, to formulate it in acceptable theological terms. Moule's commentary on the book of Romans was an important text. In the 1879 edition, written before the time of his spiritual consecration, Moule expounds chapter 7 as an account of the apostle Paul's experience as a mature believer of internal conflict between the flesh and the spirit—the standard Reformed view. In a revision published in 1894, after he gave his allegiance to Keswick, however, he reinterprets the passage as an account of the tensions in the life of someone yet to reach the moment of personal sanctification.²⁴ Only in chapter 8, on this view, does the apostle describe the life of victory. Here was a scholarly apologia intelligible to the theologically literate.

Subsequently, however, others put a different spin on the Keswick message. In the interwar years, Graham Scroggie, a Scottish Baptist minister, provided more careful biblical exegesis than had been customary on the convention platform. He also presented the difference between the unconsecrated and the consecrated believer as that between those who take Christ as Savior only and

---

22 Ryle, *Holiness*, xxiv.
23 Evan H. Hopkins, *Hidden Yet Possessed* (London: Marshall Brothers, 1894), 63.
24 Gordon, *Evangelical Spirituality*, 210–11.

those who accept him as Lord as well.[25] The Lordship of Christ involved no complexities about interior pneumatological repression: it was an altogether simpler message. At the same period another group whose members were attracted to Keswick spirituality, but who found its conservative theology and undenominational ethos repellent, established an alternative convention at Cromer on the Norfolk coast. The addresses at Cromer tended to pantheism but still called for the utmost spiritual dedication. The message of Keswick was adapted in different ways so as to have a wider appeal.

The people most drawn in during the earlier years of the movement were the educated, the prosperous and the young. Keswick was closely associated with the rise of the InterVarsity Fellowship of Christian Unions that consisted of undergraduates with precisely such characteristics. These students were young people possessing sufficient wealth to be able to attend conventions and a reading habit that allowed them to absorb Keswick literature. They were part of the sector of society most likely to be influenced by the gradually spreading Romantic cultural mood of the later nineteenth century. Keswick's appeal was grounded in its penetration by the spirit of the age. Its epicenter in the town of Keswick, symbolically, was in the Lake District, the home of Wordsworth and Coleridge. Those poets were in vogue among convention-goers, who descanted in the manner of Wordsworth on the "chastening and purifying effect" of "nature's panorama."[26] The serene side of the Romantic ethos, Wordsworth's beloved tranquility, was also reflected in the atmosphere of the movement, dwelling on the peace and rest enjoyed by the consecrated soul. There were also Romantic affinities in Keswick's doctrinal approach. On the one hand, its adherents tended to be less precise in dogmatic formulation than other Evangelicals, so mirroring the intellectual influence of Coleridge on Anglican Broad Churchmanship. On the other, they were almost unanimous in embracing the premillennial advent hope, the doctrine of the imminent Second Coming of Christ, which was closely related to Romantic thought. The heavy debt of the Oxford Movement and the succeeding style of High Churchmanship to the Romantic temper of the age is generally acknowledged. Keswick should be seen as an Evangelical parallel to that High Church idiom. Both enjoyed growing appeal in the period of the dissemination of Romantic cultural norms to a wider public, the later nineteenth and early twentieth centuries, and both faded afterwards. Keswick's brand of holiness should be diagnosed as an adaptation of the Evangelical tradition to a Romantic cultural setting.

25 Ian M. Randall, *Evangelical Experiences: A Study in the Spirituality of English Evangelicalism, 1918–1939* (Carlisle: Paternoster Press, 1999), 26–28.
26 *Christian*, 25 July 1895, 14.

Charismatic Renewal

The final strand of Evangelical holiness teaching is that associated with charismatic renewal.[27] Its exuberant style of worship has transformed much of the Evangelical world, and its influence has extended far beyond those boundaries into, for example, the Roman Catholic Church. Yet, as Roman Catholic participants have declared, the movement has drawn them into embracing customary Evangelical priorities such as detailed Bible study. Renewal sprang originally from the Pentecostal sector of Evangelicalism, its most distinctive feature in the early days being speaking in tongues. Nevertheless, the charismatic movement was not simply an extension of classic Pentecostalism. Leaders of the Pentecostal movement looked on the outgrowth of renewal in the historic churches with reserve and sometimes with dismay. They were aware that charismatic spokesmen failed to accept standard Pentecostal doctrine, and were uneasily conscious of a tangible difference in ethos. There is more of a similarity, in fact, between charismatic renewal and the interwar Oxford Group movement led by Frank Buchman.[28] Both cast aside inherited ways in order to minimize the cultural distance between adherents of the movements and their secular contemporaries. Both, for instance, eagerly used the slang of their times in preference to the accepted language of Zion. The great upsurge of the charismatic movement came in the 1960s, was simultaneous with the rise of youth culture and had close affinities with it. It took two forms: renewal in the historic denominations, fostered until 1980 by the Fountain Trust; and the creation of fresh bodies, usually called house churches until they started buying disused cinemas to accommodate their throngs of worshipers, and later normally called "New Churches." Charismatic renewal became a vigorously growing sector of British Christianity.

The charismatic conception of holiness is in some ways elusive, because the term itself has not been favored since it savors of off-putting religious language. Even the words "sin" and "salvation" have been much rarer in charismatic-influenced worship songs than in traditional hymnody. An approved phrase, however, was "spirituality in depth."[29] What were its salient features? In the first place the movement brought the physical into prominence, a point illustrated, for example, by the characteristic raising of the hands in worship. Hence spiritual wholeness and physical health were often linked. There have been many expressions of the ministry of healing. Most typical, however, was concern for the welfare of the place where the physical and the spiritual most

---

27 See 2:16: "The Rise of Charismatic Renewal in Britain."
28 See 2:15: "The Oxford Group."
29 *Anglicans for Renewal* 24 (1985), 26.

obviously intersect, the human consciousness. "Inner healing" was in vogue. Psychological healing was so generally practiced in the earlier days of renewal, according to Michael Harper, the organizer of the Fountain Trust, that it actually diverted the movement from trying to reach the unconverted.[30] Holiness meant a well-adjusted mind, complete with unpolluted depths.

Salvation was also often reinterpreted, in charismatic circles, in terms of relationships. Progress in salvation, what traditionally would have been called sanctification, was understood as advance in relationship with God and with fellow Christians. The principle of community was baptized into use. Christian communities, sometimes semimonastic though rarely celibate, sprang up in many parts of the country. House churches insisted on close bonds between individual believers, often entailing the subordination of those judged to be less advanced in the faith. "Everywhere," according to a leader of the Isca Christian Fellowship, "everything is based on relationships."[31] Holiness was embodied in right relationships.

Perhaps the supreme feature of charismatic spirituality, however, was what can appropriately be termed holy worldliness. By contrast with received Evangelical Nonconformist inhibitions, Gerald Coates, one of the most prominent New Church leaders, considered it a virtue to declare that one drank alcohol.[32] Coates' teaching was evaluated by a Calvinist to be formally antinomian.[33] There must be no pretense; one should follow one's real feelings; the public self should mirror the inner self. There should be authenticity. A former Durham vicar and future archbishop of Canterbury, George Carey, declared in 1985 that through renewal he discovered liberty. "It shattered," he explained, "my evangelical rigidity."[34] The charismatic movement undermined previous assumptions about how the Christians ought to behave. There was to be no retreat from the world for the sake of sanctity.

Like the Keswick movement of the late nineteenth century, charismatic renewal in the late twentieth century disproportionately attracted the educated, the prosperous and the young. Its adherents were overwhelmingly graduates rather than the masses. This was the section of British society most affected by fresh cultural currents. From the 1960s the rising intellectual tide was what has come to be labeled Postmodernism, although its lineage can be traced back to

---

30   Edward England, *The Spirit of Renewal* (Eastbourne: Kingsway, 1982), 159.
31   Roger Forster, *Ten New Churches* (Bromley: MARC Europe, 1986), 125.
32   Andrew Walker, *Restoring the Kingdom* (London: Hodder & Stoughton, 1985), 89.
33   Andrew Munden, "Encountering the House Church Movement: A Different Kind of Christianity," *Anvil* 1 (1984), 211.
34   *Anglicans for Renewal* 21 (1985), 8.

the Modernist avant-garde of the early twentieth century. The prominent features of charismatic spirituality are discernibly Postmodernist in style. Inner healing was predicated on the depth psychology stemming from Freud and Jung that steadily came into its own as the twentieth century advanced. The exaltation of relationships among charismatics had also been typified in the Bloomsbury Group and had become normal in the advanced circles of the late twentieth century. And holy worldliness entailed an erosion of boundaries that is perhaps the most striking feature of Postmodernist discourse. Insofar as there existed a concept of holiness in the renewal movement, it was strongly tinctured by the rising cultural mood of its time. Postmodernism shaped charismatic versions of spirituality.

Conclusion

These four strands show that the scrutiny of holiness has to take into account the social context of ideas. It must be, in a strong sense, a study in the relationship of gospel and culture. The Evangelical tradition has given rise to an approach to the holy life that is recognizably distinctive, displaying the characteristic marks of conversion, cross, Bible and activism. These elements have endured from the early eighteenth century down to the present day. Yet the tradition has been repeatedly transformed by its environment. The inherited Calvinist doctrine of gradual sanctification by works was challenged in the eighteenth century by Wesleyan teaching about a crisis of sanctification by faith. Wesley's new version of holiness reflected his immersion in the thought of the Enlightenment. In the late nineteenth century Keswick offered a fresh presentation of sanctification by faith in terms more acceptable to Calvinists by adopting Romantic categories of thought. A century later charismatic renewal built on Postmodernist premises as it formulated its understanding of the Christian life. The resurgence of Reformed teaching in the late twentieth century meant that by the early years of the following century the Evangelical world was increasingly polarized between the Calvinist and the charismatic views. The Wesleyan and Keswick interpretations had become negligible as the cultural forces with which they were associated had faded away. What survived were the stance with the longest pedigree, which tended to attract those of a reading and conservative inclination, and that with the greatest contemporary resonance, which drew on a much larger constituency. Sanctity has been understood in different ways in accordance with the changing assumptions of the age. Without doubt, therefore, holiness in the Evangelical tradition has been shaped by its cultural setting.

11

The Deathbed Piety of Evangelical Nonconformists in the Nineteenth Century

Over the last forty years or so the subject of death has become much more central to historical investigation. A landmark was the publication in France in 1977 of Philippe Ariès' overview of the various stages of attitudes to death in Western civilization.[1] Although the book was criticized as over-schematic and selective in its sources, Ariès' work stimulated much further research in his own country. France is also brilliantly treated in John McManners' *Death and the Enlightenment*.[2] The study of death in Britain lagged somewhat behind, but Ralph Houlbrooke edited a collection of essays on the subject in 1989 and published an authoritative monograph on the early modern period in England in 1998.[3] Central in that period was the ideal of "the good death:" subjects occupied their last days in distributing goods, arranging the funeral, making their peace with God and setting an example to their survivors.[4] It was still a question in 1989 how far this ideal survived into the nineteenth century. Was it reinvigorated, Houlbrooke asked in that year, by the Evangelical Revival?[5]

---

1 Philippe Ariès, *The Hour of Our Death* (London: Allen Lane, 1981).
2 John McManners, *Death and the Enlightenment: Changing Attitudes to Death among Christians and Unbelievers in Eighteenth-Century France* (Oxford: Clarendon Press, 1981).
3 *Death, Ritual and Bereavement*, ed. Ralph Houlbrooke (London: Routledge, 1989), and Ralph Houlbrooke, *Death, Religion and the Family in England, 1480–1750* (Oxford: Oxford University Press, 1998).
4 Lucinda M. Beier, "The Good Death in Seventeenth-Century England," in *Death, Ritual and Bereavement*, ed. Houlbrooke, 45–59, at 45.
5 Ralph Houlbrooke, "Introduction," in *Death, Ritual and Bereavement*, ed. Houlbrooke, 11.

A powerful answer was provided in Pat Jalland's *Death in the Victorian Family* (1996). Jalland demonstrated that the Victorian way of death was strongly molded by Evangelical religion. It is a particularly instructive part of her case, however, that the ideal contrasted with the reality. Evangelicals might look for a good death, a calm approach to the end in conscious enjoyment of fellowship with Christ, but private papers reveal that the last days of life usually involved moral failure, physical decline and behavior of which relatives were ashamed.[6] Yet Jalland examined only well-to-do families that have bequeathed a cache of documents for historians to investigate; and those families were exclusively Anglican. The experience of Evangelical Nonconformists in the face of death remained unilluminated. Linda Wilson, however, made an admirable start on exploring this subject in her book *Constrained by Zeal* (2000), a study of all aspects of female spirituality among Nonconformists. She provided quantified analyses of the abundant obituaries in the Nonconformist periodicals of the mid-nineteenth century, supplying comparative instances of male experience to set alongside her main female sample. She demonstrated, for example, that heaven figured more prominently in their consciousness than has previously been supposed.[7] That is the starting point of the present study. It tries to complement Linda Wilson's book by examining (without quantification) how Evangelical Nonconformists approached the frontier between this life and the heaven they confidently expected beyond.

The period under scrutiny, the Victorian era, is commonly thought to have been heavily preoccupied with death. Michael Wheeler, for instance, in his *Death and the Future Life in Victorian Literature and Theology* (1990), writes of "the Victorians' obsessive interest in death."[8] Since the work of the sociologist Geoffrey Gorer on death in modern Britain, published in 1965, it has been appreciated that later generations tried to marginalize the experience.[9] By contrast, it is usually held, the Victorians indulged themselves in the celebration of death with anguished grief, resplendent funerals and protracted mourning. Pat Jalland has argued, however, that part of this impression is based on false generalization from the case of Queen Victoria herself, whose pathologically profound sense of bereavement at the death of

6   Pat Jalland, *Death in the Victorian Family* (Oxford: Oxford University Press, 1996), 26.
7   Linda Wilson, *Constrained by Zeal: Female Spirituality among Nonconformists, 1825–1875* (Carlisle: Paternoster Press, 2000), 59–63.
8   Michael Wheeler, *Death and the Future Life in Victorian Literature and Theology* (Cambridge: Cambridge University Press, 1990), 25.
9   Geoffrey Gorer, *Death, Grief and Mourning in Contemporary Britain* (London: Cresset Press, 1965).

Prince Albert was unique. The queen's subjects, according to Jalland, generally had a much healthier approach, actually curbing undue spending on funerals before the reign was over.[10] Nevertheless it is true that death was much more central in Victorian culture than in ours. That was partly because mortality was much higher. The death rate in England and Wales in 1868 was twenty-two in every thousand. By 1928 it was already only twelve in every thousand and falling rapidly.[11] Consequently in the Victorian era people encountered death, especially of infants, far more frequently. Medicine had no remedy for many scourges such as tuberculosis that can now be readily cured in Western societies. All physicians could do was provide pain relief for the dying. Devout Christians sometimes seem to have avoided opium, the chief anaesthetic, and could regard any effort at alleviation as an affront to the ways of God.[12] Hence sufferers often passed through intense agonies on their deathbeds. Death was not only far more common than in later years: it was also more terrible.

Nonconformist Deathbeds

How did Evangelical Nonconformists cope with the experience? In this study the obituaries carried by the monthly denominational magazines are virtually the sole source. They varied enormously in length, ranging from full appraisals covering several pages to tiny notices of only two or three lines. Occasionally in the shorter records the passing of the subject was ignored altogether, but it is remarkable that, at least in the years down to the 1870s, the normal pattern was to allow significant space, often as much as a third of the account, for a description of the closing days of the person memorialized. The obituaries therefore contain ample material for the study of dying. The denominations selected, the three largest, are the Wesleyans, the Congregationalists and the Baptists. The *Wesleyan Methodist Magazine* was an official connexional journal and so carried what the leaders of the denomination wanted to appear. The *Christian Witness*, which circulated among Congregationalists, was more of a personal venture by its editor, the strong-minded John Campbell, minister of Tottenham Court Road Chapel in London, though he aspired to make it the mouthpiece of the Congregational Union. From the start of the magazine in 1844, Campbell included biographies and obituaries as illustrations

---

10 Pat Jalland, "Death, Grief and Mourning in the Upper-Class Family," in *Death, Ritual and Bereavement*, ed. Houlbrooke, 175–86, at 186.
11 Jalland, *Death in the Victorian Family*, 5.
12 Jalland, *Death in the Victorian Family*, 87; *Christian Witness* [hereafter *CW*], 1852, 369.

of what he called "grace reigning in life, grace triumphing in death."[13] The *Baptist Magazine*, though a private venture, reflected mainstream denominational opinion. The main sample of issues examined comes from the middle of the century: the whole of the year 1850 for the *Baptist Magazine*, only the first five months of that year for the *Wesleyan Methodist Magazine* (since its articles were far more numerous) and 1850 and the two following years as well for the *Christian Witness* (since its articles were far fewer, though generally much longer). A number of later issues, especially from the 1880s, have been consulted in order to establish the way in which views altered as the century wore on. The resulting group of some two hundred cases is sufficiently large to make generalizations possible. Yet several imbalances in the database need to be noted. In terms of gender, there are more men than women. That is largely because of the desire to commemorate ministers and leading lay officials, who were uniformly male in this period. In terms of age, no children are included. That is a serious misrepresentation of the pattern of death, because children were much more likely to die than adults. Infant mortality, however, was the greatest scourge, and the dying experiences of small children were beyond recovery. In terms of geography, all the cases, apart from a few missionaries, lived in the United Kingdom, mostly in England and Wales. Despite these limitations, the sample reflects its constituency fairly well. It provides a window on the deathbed scenes of Evangelical Nonconformity.

The sources dictate that a preliminary question should be addressed. Are the accounts in the denominational periodicals so distorted as to be worthless as transcripts of experience? Jalland's finding of a gulf between ideal and reality should be borne in mind. There is evidence of discrepancy even within the sample. In an obituary of W. S. Palmer, minister of Hare Court Congregational Church, London, who died in 1852, for example, it is remarked that, despite difficulty in breathing, "still no murmuring escaped his lips." Palmer is presented as a patient sufferer, a model for others to imitate. Yet a few lines below it is recorded that among the scraps of paper that Palmer wrote on his deathbed was one that ran, "Oh, my God... pardon every murmuring thought or word."[14] The true situation of the dying man was that he did murmur against his lot. In this case convention seems to have propelled a hasty obituarist into misrepresentation. Nor was it only the writers of the accounts in the periodicals who could manipulate the story for the sake of edification. The subjects

---

13   Albert Peel, *These Hundred Years: A History of the Congregational Union of England and Wales, 1831–1931* (London: Congregational Union of England and Wales, 1931), 130.
14   *CW*, 1852, 256.

themselves could act up to the parts they knew they were supposed to play. Thus Thomas Lewis, minister of Union Chapel, Islington, was given a cup of water as he lay moribund. "'How refreshing it is!,'" he cried; "it is an emblem of the purifying and sanctifying grace of the Holy Spirit; *and, as such, I take it!*"[15] Here was an artificial turning of an episode to practical Christian purposes, a sign that the preacher's instincts were not yet dead. Others made obvious efforts to fulfill the expectations of those gathered around them. A Baptist deacon of the Eagle Street Church in London, it was said, showed "all the composure and resignation to the divine will that those who loved him best could desire to witness."[16] Powerful family anticipations—he was visiting his son in the ministry—molded how the deacon behaved. The actual experience of being on the brink of heaven could definitely be affected by conventions in the acting and the telling.

Nevertheless it is possible to gain access to something like how people felt in the shadow of death. Their actual words, sometimes disarmingly frank and surely not invented, were frequently recorded. Their minutest gestures were faithfully chronicled. We know about raisings of hands and flickerings of eyelids. In some instances, therefore, we can penetrate to the sentiments of the dying closer than to the emotions of those in other phases of life. The further problem of sincerity is always there for the historian. Social expectations shaped behavior in any past setting so that individuals may not have expressed the feelings of their hearts. The difficulty may be at its most acute in relation to deathbeds, but is neither unique nor insurmountable. In one respect there was a supreme motive for sincerity among the dying. The near approach of the end of life meant that honesty was the best policy. A Congregational obituarist noted this point in relation to death: "It is generally the only hour—at least, the chief—in their lives, when their true condition is made fully apparent."[17] The conventions of deathbed literature may be a greater obstacle to circumvent. There is, for example, a suspicious frequency with which certain phrases, such as those about "victory" among the Wesleyans, are put in the mouths of the dying.[18] Yet it may be that the representation is as important as the reality of what was said. The expectations embodied in the phraseology of the obituaries represent the communal attitudes of Nonconformity towards death. The sources, even when using phrases that may not represent the whole truth or even in some cases the truth at all, reveal the social construction of death in

15 *CW*, 1852, 368.
16 *Baptist Magazine* [hereafter *BM*], 1850, 434 (John Penny).
17 *CW*, 1851, 318 (Edward Baines).
18 E.g., *Wesleyan Methodist Magazine* [hereafter *WMM*], 1850, 94 (William Scott).

the chapels. In the last resort it may be impossible to draw a line between actual experience and its mode of depiction, but the resulting vision of mortality is perhaps what is of greatest historical significance.

Resources for the Journey to Heaven

The material in the obituaries relating to death falls into three broad categories. There were in the first place resources for the journey to heaven. What forms of support, we may ask, did Evangelical Nonconformists enjoy on their deathbeds? Secondly, there was preparation for the entry to heaven. How did the soul get ready to move on to what lay beyond the grave? In the third place there were expectations of heaven. What were the anticipations of the afterlife? Deathbed piety will be discussed under each of these three headings in turn.

The most obvious support for deathbed spirituality was the Bible. It was common for others to read appropriate passages of scripture in the room of sickness. The Psalms were a favorite, especially those touching on the theme of death: "Precious in the sight of the Lord is the death of his saints" (Ps. 116: 15);[19] "Though I walk through the valley of the shadow of death, I will fear no evil: for thou art with me" (Ps. 23:4).[20] Sufferers themselves would quote verses or even repeat whole chapters that they knew by heart.[21] They might draw on the Old Testament, especially the Psalms and Isaiah, but mainly they used the New Testament, less the gospels than the epistles and Revelation. The favorite verse in the sample was 2 Timothy 1:12: "I know whom I have believed and am persuaded that he is able to keep that which I have committed unto him against that day."[22] Because the dying were familiar with the text of scripture, such passages sprang readily to their lips. Before victims of ill health were too indisposed to read, they might long persist in Bible study.[23] They were even sometimes capable of capping quotations put to them. "He is able," said a family member to a Congregational layman on his deathbed, "to save to the uttermost all that come unto God by Him." "And what is more," put in the dying man, "He is *willing*."[24] Knowing only the Authorized Version of the Bible, both visitors and victims naturally slipped into its idiom. A rich young Jewish girl, Leila Ada, who had been converted and become a Congregationalist, referred casually in the words of Psalm 23 to passing through the valley of the shadow

---

19 *BM*, 1850, 435 (Margaret Robinson); *WMM*, 1850, 91 (Mary Dudbridge).
20 *BM*, 1850, 435 (Margaret Robinson); *WMM*, 1850, 429 (Helen Sheldon).
21 *CW*, 1852, 256 (W. S. Palmer).
22 *BM*, 1850, 30 (Mrs John Stock); 32 (Thomas Wren); *CW*, 1850, 321 (John King).
23 *WMM*, 1850, 431 (Mary Tewson).
24 *CW*, 1851, 321 (Edward Baines).

of death.[25] The Bible conditioned the thought and language of these Nonconformists as the end approached, giving them consolation and hope.

Almost equally familiar to most Nonconformists was the hymnbook. William Rooker, a Congregational minister, often repeated on his deathbed verses of a hymn he had learned in childhood.[26] A Welsh Baptist recalled items from John Rippon's *Selection of Hymns*, the chief collection of hymnody used in the denomination.[27] Methodists were devoted to the compositions of Charles Wesley.[28] Apart from Wesley's writings, hymns mentioned more than once in the sample were Isaac Watts' "I'll praise my maker while I've breath," with its apposite second line "And when my voice is lost in death;"[29] and William Cowper's "There is a fountain filled with blood," with its reference to "this poor lisping stammering tongue" lying "silent in the grave."[30] By far the most frequently quoted hymn, however, was Wesley's "Jesus, lover of my soul." Baptists and Congregationalists found it as appealing as Methodists, though the version in use among Congregationalists had been bowdlerised to "Jesus, refuge of my soul."[31] Its lines "Safe into the haven guide, / O receive my soul at last" again had a direct bearing on the circumstances of the dying. As with scripture, the vocabulary of the hymnbook shaped the conversation of those on their sickbeds. One, while talking to his family, echoed Augustus Toplady in describing the rock of ages as being "cleft for you;" another spoke of his experience in Wesley's language as "'Tis mercy all."[32] Hymns undergirded the dying days of these people.

Other books receive far fewer allusions than the Bible and the hymn book. A Congregational minister read Richard Baxter's *Saint's Everlasting Rest* alongside the Bible.[33] In Cape Colony sermons by pulpit masters—John Howe, Robert Hall, William Jay—were read to the dying London Missionary Society representative John Philip.[34] One Wesleyan widow was said to have died unexpectedly just after reading a set of obituaries in an old issue of the connexional magazine.[35] The book—Bible and hymn book apart—with most sway over the

---

25 *CW*, 1852, 322.
26 *CW*, 1852, 370.
27 *BM*, 1850, 139 (John James).
28 E.g., *WMM*, 1850, 320 (Martha Newton).
29 *WMM*, 1850, 206 (John Stray); 319 (Sarah Crowe).
30 *BM*, 1850, 139 (John James); *CW*, 1850, 513 (William Atherton).
31 *CW*, 1851, 594 (Mrs John Gibson); 1852, 517 (Maria Atkins).
32 *CW*, 1851, 320 (Edward Baines); *WMM*, 1850, 429 (Letitia M'Turk).
33 *CW*, 1851, 510 (John Jerard).
34 *CW*, 1852, 210.
35 *WMM*, 1850, 206 (Sarah Kaye).

minds of those awaiting death, however, was John Bunyan's *Pilgrim's Progress*. A Baptist woman saw herself as a pilgrim nearing home; and a Congregational minister referred in Bunyan's phrase to the Delectable Mountains.[36] In this case the speaker actually told his daughter that he did not yet feel he was on the mountains, but it may be surmised that in many cases the familiar landscape of Bunyan was a distinct comfort.

Basic Christian teaching provided a further resource. By far the most frequent doctrinal reference was to the work of Christ on the cross. "I am trusting in the atonement," declared a Wesleyan class leader and circuit steward from Cornwall; and, he went on, "this is all my plea. What else have I now to lay hold of?"[37] The cross was prominent in the minds of many as the token that they would be admitted to heaven. Often they mentioned the blood—the blood that released, the blood that redeemed, the blood that had efficacy.[38] The subject was considered so important that it could be introduced artificially. A visiting friend noticed that the pillow of a Congregational minister lying on his bed was uncomfortable. "*But*," answered the dying man, "comfortable thoughts arise from the bleeding sacrifice!"[39] The reliance on the work of Christ on the cross was deeply felt. Another Congregational minister, who was said at times to be completely absorbed in the atonement, declared as his last words, "Nothing will do but the blood and righteousness of Christ."[40] The cross was at the core of the salvation that brought hope to those whose powers were failing.

A bulwark of a different kind was prayer. Relatives naturally prayed with those close to them who were dying. A Baptist husband, for example, asked his wife what he should request for her. "Pray," she replied, "*that I may be faithful unto death*."[41] Sufferers would ask visitors to read and pray with them.[42] They would also pray themselves—in brief expressions of praise, for deliverance from pain, for the conversion of their children.[43] A thirty-four-year-old Wesleyan married woman of Worksop, Nottinghamshire, Mary Levick, was said to have been delivered from an attack of Satan while her friends prayed for her.

---

36 *BM*, 1850, 168 (Elizabeth Ferris); *CW*, 1852, 370 (William Rooker).
37 *WMM*, 1850, 318 (Joseph Mayne).
38 *BM*, 1850, 30 (Mrs John Stock); 302 (Benjamin Coombs); *CW*, 1852, 370 (William Rooker).
39 *CW*, 1852, 257 (W. S. Palmer).
40 *CW*, 1850, 513 (William Atherton).
41 *BM*, 1850, 101 (Elizabeth May).
42 *BM*, 1850, 436 (Maria Prudence Mayer).
43 *CW*, 1852, 256 (W. S. Palmer); 1850, 111 (William Jones); *WMM*, 1850, 205 (Mary Ann Adcock).

"For fourteen hours before her departure," the account continues, "her room was like a sea of glory, in which all who entered it were bathed. Mr Levick, perceiving that she was earnestly pleading with God, asked what it was for. 'I am struggling,' she said, 'to get a little nearer the throne.'"[44] Mary Levick evidently found prayer—her own and that of her fellow believers—a profoundly effective resource as she moved towards the close of her earthly journey.

A sense of the divine presence, sometimes realised through prayer, lent further support to the dying. Commonly it is described simply as the presence of God. Thus an elderly Welsh Baptist minister spoke of enjoying "much rich communion with God" during his affliction.[45] The Holy Spirit is mentioned in this context only once in this set of obituaries. A Plymouth Congregational minister, William Rooker, declared that he now greatly valued "the promise of the Comforter, to show Christ to the soul."[46] It is significant that Rooker described the role of the Spirit as to illuminate Christ, because the references to divine companionship are overwhelmingly to the second person of the Trinity. Christ, affirmed a married Irish Wesleyan woman, "is walking with me through the dark valley of the shadow of death."[47] Christ was said to be "all to me," "all in all," "a panacea."[48] Most frequently Christ was described as "precious." Perhaps the commonest inquiry put by others concerning the spiritual welfare of the sufferer was, "Is Christ precious?"[49] The allusion is to 1 Peter 2:7, which announces that to those who believe he is precious. So the avowal that Christ was indeed precious was a confirmation of believing. Here was a profoundly Christocentric spirituality.

The question put by others is a reminder that death was not a private matter. Traditionally in early modern Europe a deathbed was a public place with members of the community gathered around. Visitors came and went, to observe and to learn. The custom had passed away, according to Pat Jalland, by the Victorian period.[50] That had no doubt become true of the well-to-do Anglican families that Jalland has studied, but it was not the case among midcentury Nonconformists. While helpless for fourteen weeks, for instance, Mary Cowell, a member of Old Sampford Baptist Church, Essex, who was dying of

---

44   *WMM*, 1850, 431.
45   *BM*, 1850, 138 (John James).
46   *CW*, 1852, 371.
47   *WMM*, 1850, 541 (Louisa Rowe).
48   *CW*, 1852, 368 (Thomas Lewis); *WMM*, 1867, 517 (Charles Roger Kelvey); *BM*, 1850, 36 (James Harington Evans).
49   *CW*, 1851, 513 (Joseph Tattersfield); 1852, 372 (William Rooker); *WMM*, 1850, 92 (Ann Burrows).
50   Jalland, *Death in the Victorian Family*, 26.

tuberculosis, welcomed visitors to her bedside. They were, however, "Christian visitors," friends from the chapel world.[51] That was the norm. Moribund Nonconformists were attended by a procession of people: ministers, church members, believing friends from a distance. A typical account of "the death-bed of a saint" notes incidentally that "[f]riends wept around."[52] The community concerned in this and other cases, however, was not the people of the vicinity at large. The community, rather, was the society of the converted, those who shared the faith of the dying and who came to offer Christian solidarity. To them the doors were normally open.

The nucleus of those around a dying believer, however, consisted of members of the family. The husband or wife of the sufferer, if still alive, would normally be the principal attendant. The role of the spouse was not only to provide physical care and emotional support but also to convey spiritual nourishment. If the accounts are to be believed, husbands and wives could discuss the religious experience of their partners with unflagging zeal. Death was faced together. "My dear," the wife of the minister of Whitchurch Baptist Church, Hampshire, told him, "we have often together sung, 'Thy will be done,' 'tis now for you to *live* this sentiment, and for me to *die* it; pray we may do so like Christians."[53] Other female members of the family, especially sisters and daughters, would help in nursing and would offer edifying remarks or catechize the dying relation. A sister, for example, asked a married Wesleyan woman if she loved Jesus and an aunt inquired if she was happy.[54] Perhaps, because she was a minister's wife, they were confident she would reply acceptably, and they were not disappointed. Again a son might read to a sufferer, as did the adult son of the missionary John Philip.[55] Even children of a tender age might be present at the bedside, for there was little if any attempt to shield the young from the reality of death. They might well be brought into the room for a final farewell. Thus three grandchildren of the Congregational newspaper magnate Edward Baines of Leeds were solemnly ushered into his presence.[56] Consequently those who were dying were often surrounded by their close relations. The family provided yet another type of support in their time of trial. There was thus a wide range of resources available to Evangelical Nonconformists in their final days.

51 *BM*, 1850, 501.
52 *BM*, 1850, 221 (William Secker).
53 *BM*, 1850, 633 (Mrs Smith).
54 *WMM*, 1850, 312 (Hannah Greenwood).
55 *CW*, 1852, 210.
56 *CW*, 1851, 321.

Preparation for the Entry to Heaven

A second dimension of the experience of dying was preparation for passing to another world. Deathbeds formed, as it were, a transitional state between earth and heaven. Lying in one's own room was an opportunity for putting one's soul in order. A Baptist missionary's wife who was dying in Calcutta at the age of twenty-nine "acknowledged the mercy of her heavenly Father in giving her so much time to think of heaven before she went there."[57] A sufferer might pass through a variety of experiences. They can usefully be analyzed one by one, but first a couple of preliminary factors need to be noted.

One preliminary is to recognize that sometimes there was no opportunity for preparation because the end could come suddenly. Thus a Congregational shipmaster from Sunderland was swept overboard while rounding the Horn;[58] and a Wesleyan minister was struck down while administering the Lord's supper. Of the second, though he lingered for about nineteen hours, it was said, in the words of a Charles Wesley hymn, that "he ceased at once to work and live."[59] A sudden death of this kind was sometimes recounted with dismay because it did not permit the opportunities offered by a protracted deathbed. The family of a Lowestoft Wesleyan woman who died of a heart attack was reported to "deplore her removal under circumstances which allowed no dying testimony."[60] Yet, as Linda Wilson has noted, unexpected death was not uniformly regretted.[61] Indeed such an event could be turned to advantage. The loss at sea of the Sunderland shipmaster, for example, was publicized so as to induce "careless sinners to prepare for sudden death."[62] A Wesleyan surgeon in Edinburgh actually adopted Charles Wesley's words and so prayed that he might "cease at once to work and live." In the event his wish to end his days in active Christian service was fulfilled.[63] So death arriving unheralded was ambiguous. On the one hand it did not permit preparation for the end, but on the other it held no terrors for the soul already thoroughly prepared.

The second preliminary consideration is that long-term preparation was expected of a believer. Thus a Wesleyan local preacher at Leake in Lincolnshire always kept death in view even though he was only forty-three years old. About two minutes before he died while walking along a road, he told a

---

57 *BM*, 1850, 435 (Margaret Robinson).
58 *CW*, 1852, 125 (John Young).
59 *WMM*, 1850, 432 (George Hambly Rowe).
60 *WMM*, 1850, 91 (Elizabeth Carr).
61 Wilson, *Constrained by Zeal*, 163.
62 *CW*, 1852, 125 (John Young).
63 *WMM*, 1850, 230 (Dr Coldstream).

man he met, "I am ripening for glory."⁶⁴ Again a sixty-eight-year-old Wesleyan woman from Bewdley in Worcestershire was asked if she was afraid of death. "Why should I fear?" she replied. "More than forty years I have been preparing for this."⁶⁵ Sometimes premonitions made people especially conscious of the approach of the end. A female member of Moorfields Tabernacle, though only twenty-one and recently married, told her husband when visiting her brother's grave that she would be the first to cause the flowers on it to be removed for a fresh burial. Shortly afterwards she collapsed on the stairs in her home, suffered an acute attack of pain in the head and had blood gush from her mouth before expiring.⁶⁶ Again a Wesleyan Cornishwoman received an impression that she would die suddenly and so lived in a state of constant preparedness.⁶⁷ Looking to immortality was not confined to the deathbed. Often it was an attitude of mind cultivated over a much longer period.

The experience of dying, however, was a time when sufferers could prepare their souls in a more concentrated manner. The first essential was conversion, an event that could sometimes take place in the last days of life. A twenty-two-year-old woman of Ashbourne, Derbyshire, whose earlier spiritual negligence was illustrated by her habit of reading novels, developed a severe illness and was visited by fellow attenders of Sion Chapel. Through conversation and reading a different kind of book, she came to faith before dying a model death.⁶⁸ After conversion, sanctification could proceed. A symptom was often what was called "humiliation," a deep-seated loathing of the sinfulness that the sufferers found within themselves. Thus a notable Baptist pastor, James Harington Evans, lamented the "hellishness" of his soul.⁶⁹ An elderly minister of the same denomination felt himself to be "a poor creature" and a prominent Leeds Congregational layman was characterized in his last illness by "self-distrust."⁷⁰ Usually self was decried in order to exalt the role of Christ in salvation and so led to an increased sense of devotion to him. Pain actually helped the quest for holiness because it operated as a purgative of self. Another Baptist minister, latterly at Bridport in Dorset, exclaimed when he was suffering from exceptional pain, "Oh, this refining process . . . is to take away sin."⁷¹ Likewise a Wesleyan woman at

64 *WMM*, 1850, 204 (Mr Taylor).
65 *WMM*, 1850, 319 (Sarah Crowe).
66 *CW*, 1852, 589 (Mrs Harris).
67 *WMM*, 1850, 430 (Elizabeth Martin).
68 *CW*, 1852, 516 (Maria Atkins).
69 *BM*, 1850, 36.
70 *BM*, 1850, 402 (John Elliott); *CW*, 1851, 319 (Edward Baines).
71 *BM*, 1850, 303 (Benjamin Coombs).

Ashton-under-Lyne was said to see her sufferings as "the chastening of her heavenly Father, designed to make her a partaker of His holiness."[72] The agonies that were often a prelude to dying were therefore given meaning as the character matured for heaven. For some of the victims that must have afforded a measure of relief.

The deathbed, however, could also be a scene of struggle. Thus Matthew Binks, a Wesleyan of Colburn in the North Riding of Yorkshire, experienced a short time before his death "a severe conflict with the powers of darkness."[73] The temptation to fall into sin sometimes seemed acute. Usually this crisis is described as taking place not immediately before death but some time before—for example, in the first of two weeks spent in bed before the subject breathed her last.[74] Often, particularly in Wesleyan accounts, the struggle is with Satan himself: "the enemy," "the adversary," "the spiritual adversary."[75] This last assault was, in Methodist thinking, Satan's final chance to bring the soul to perdition. A converted sinner could be snatched back to the kingdom of darkness even from the deathbed since there was no doctrine of the eternal security of the believer in the Arminian theology of the Methodists. In published accounts, however, Satan is always thwarted and the believer triumphs. The form a Satanic attack could take is illustrated by the experience of a Cornish Wesleyan circuit steward: "His affliction was protracted and depressing, and he was powerfully assaulted by the adversary of his soul."[76] Here the cosmic conflict is decoded as a case of depression. Whatever the cause, dying could entail a hard-fought spiritual battle.

The specific problem facing several individuals in the sample was doubt about their faith. This experience is sometimes recorded with surprising candor. A Congregational minister confessed to having had many dark doubts in his sick room. "Lord, I believe!" he cried. "Help thou my unbelief!"[77] After several pious affirmations, a Baptist pastor's wife in Devon paused and asked, "But suppose it should be all a delusion?"[78] A number of Baptists expressed traditional Calvinist doubts not about the substance of their faith but about whether they were numbered among those accepted by God. "Do you think," asked the missionary's wife in Calcutta, "that I am a Christian, indeed?"[79]

72   *WMM*, 1850, 203 (Mrs Swain).
73   *WMM*, 1850, 204.
74   *WMM*, 1850, 431 (Mary Levick).
75   *WMM*, 1850, 320 (Martha Newton); 317 (Hannah Rabone); 94 (William Scott).
76   *WMM*, 1850, 318 (James Mayne).
77   *CW*, 1852, 256 (W. S. Palmer).
78   *BM*, 1850, 101 (Elizabeth May).
79   *BM*, 1850, 435 (Margaret Robinson).

Religious hope, it was observed, could become "clouded."[80] The opposite of these doubts was assurance. After self-examination, those in the Calvinist tradition could often reach this stage. A Baptist pastor's wife from Desborough in Northamptonshire eventually decided that, as she had a high priest who sympathized with her infirmities, she "could not doubt of his love being unchanging."[81] Methodists, by contrast, required no such self-examination. Since for them assurance was bound up with faith, they knew that believing guaranteed their future. "I am quite satisfied," declared a Blackpool Wesleyan, "that I am going to heaven."[82] Among all these Nonconformists assurance was looked for, but doubt was often encountered on the way.

Another pitfall for the dying Christian was complaint. Murmuring, repining and complaining itself were often mentioned by obituarists, but usually to remark that, despite their sufferings, the unwell did not express themselves in these ways. Murmuring was distinguished from groaning. Whereas groaning, a reaction to physical pain, was regarded as legitimate, murmuring, the questioning of God's purposes, was not.[83] Occasionally there are hints in the accounts of last days that there were complaints. The words of Jesus in the garden of Gethsemane requesting that the cup should pass from him constituted, because they were a scriptural description of the words of the Son of God, an acceptable way of seeking a respite from pain.[84] If there were any regret or dissatisfaction, it was said in one case, it was "instantly repressed by faith."[85] The opposite frame of mind, however, was celebrated in many an obituary. Submission, patience, resignation formed the kernel of the attitude expected of the dying believer. The Almighty had the right to do as he willed. It was the duty of his servants to accept his will, even if it entailed suffering. Thus the Cardigan Baptist minister, dying of "mortification of the feet," "bore his excruciating pains with Christian patience, and at last died without a groan."[86] The suffering, more than one reflected, was much less than what the Savior endured for their salvation.[87] Resignation to the will of the Lord, according to a female Irish Wesleyan, was a difficult lesson, but she had learned it.[88] Complaints certainly existed, but they were regarded as a sign of human rebellion.

80 *CW*, 1852, 420 ('GB').
81 *BM*, 1850, 228 (Mary Clements).
82 *WMM*, 1850, 318 (Robert Baird).
83 *CW*, 1852, 512 (Joseph Tattersfield).
84 *BM*, 1850, 101 (Elizabeth May).
85 *CW*, 1852, 368 (Thomas Lewis).
86 *BM*, 1850, 561 (David Rees).
87 *BM*, 1850, 772 (Joseph Davies); *WMM*, 1850, 315 (Thomas Sawtell).
88 *WMM*, 1850, 206 (Eliza Conway).

The other major temptation was fear, which came in several forms. There was fear of the process of dying. A young Baptist wife asked her husband anxiously whether Christ would let her sink; and a Wesleyan woman at Manchester dreaded losing her reason through the severity of her suffering.[89] Then there was the fear of what might lie beyond the grave. The Calcutta missionary's wife, for example, confessed to "very great fear" over what awaited her.[90] And there was the specific fear of judgment. A Baptist minister's wife was alarmed on this score because of the contrast between her sinful ways and divine purity.[91] What is often recorded, however, is not that fears were weighing down the subjects of the obituaries but that their anxiety for the future was over. "In her life she feared death," it was said of another Baptist wife, "[but] in her death she had no fear."[92] Believers were delivered into an opposite temper, one of peace, calm or tranquility. Fewer comments are more common than that believers enjoyed a sense of peace as they awaited death. Alexander Dewar, Congregational pastor at Avoch in Ross-shire, for example, enjoyed a frame of mind that was "peaceful."[93] Several obituaries contain echoes of the description of an upright man in Psalm 37:37: "The end of that man is peace."[94] Calm in the face of death was an indication of conscience at rest. The transcending of fear was of the essence of a good death.

Accounts of some deaths, however, were set in a different key. The events were not so much tranquil as triumphant. Many sufferers are described near the end as being simply happy. James Elsom, a Wesleyan of Owston Ferry in Lincolnshire, lost his voice during his final illness but shortly before he died, to the surprise of his family, he waved his hand three times and exclaimed "Happy—Happy—Happy!"[95] Several are said to have had an overpowering sense of joy. Lucy Sheppard, a member of Towcester Baptist Church, Northamptonshire, felt joy that was "literally 'unspeakable and full of glory.'"[96] Methodists were often given to the most exuberant expressions of triumph. A female Wesleyan class leader, for example, cried on the evening before she died, "Victory! Shout! Shout! Victory!"[97] There were even experiences that fall in the ecstatic category. A Wesleyan woman at Bramley in the West Riding of

89 *BM*, 1850, 694 (Mary Croxton); *WMM*, 1850, 92 (Ann Burrows).
90 *BM*, 1850, 435 (Margaret Robinson).
91 *BM*, 1850, 30 (Mrs John Stock).
92 *BM*, 1850, 169 (Mary Jackson).
93 *CW*, 1850, 17.
94 E.g., *CW*, 1851, 207 (T. B. Evans).
95 *WMM*, 1850, 92.
96 *BM*, 1850, 302 (Lucy Elizabeth Sheppard).
97 *WMM*, 1850, 320 (Martha Newton).

Yorkshire a few hours before her death had an extraordinary awareness of the divine presence, whispering only, "I can't express! I can't express!"[98] The wife of a Congregational minister who had taken a Presbyterian charge in Australia seems to have had a consciousness of reaching heaven but then returning. "What a pity I lost the glory!," she declared, "What a pity to come back again!"[99] And a London Wesleyan widow, a relation by marriage of John Wesley, was eager to see the splendor of Christ. She was described as being "rapt into an ecstasy of unspeakable joy for several minutes," after which she announced, "I have seen my Saviour."[100] These experiences were not general. Sometimes obituarists commented that their subjects could not lay claim to them.[101] Yet when they did take place they were reported as apparent vindications of Christian claims that death was swallowed up in victory.

Even if they were not usually exuberant, many Nonconformists were far from passive on their deathbeds. Making arrangements for the settling of one's affairs was part of the standard expectation of what should happen. Thus the Jewish convert made a careful distribution of some of her possessions and did the detailed planning for her funeral.[102] The dying would send messages to relatives, to church members or to ministerial colleagues.[103] Those restricted to the bedroom would ask friends and relations to visit them, sometimes to give them exhortations. A Congregational minister at Idle in the West Riding of Yorkshire, though periodically suffering from delirium, spoke "in solemn words" to his friends and pleaded with his sister to give her heart to God.[104] Again an ordinary Wesleyan woman, though seventy-eight years old, "earnestly preached Christ to her family."[105] In some cases there was a formal gathering of relations around the deathbed. Thus Edward Baines, proprietor of the *Leeds Mercury* and a former Member of Parliament, summoned his family after chapel on Sunday morning and spoke individually to each of them with "patriarchal dignity."[106] Such set pieces were far from universal. Indeed one Congregational minister declared that he did not want "a scene got up" with all his children

98 *WMM*, 1850, 542 (Eliza Smithson).
99 *CW*, 1851, 593 (Mrs John Gibson).
100 *WMM*, 1850, 94 (Jane Vazeille).
101 E.g., *BM*, 1850, 694 (Joseph Campton).
102 *CW*, 1851, 322–23.
103 *BM*, 1850, 634 (Mrs Smith), 36 (James Harington Evans); *CW*, 1852, 371 (William Rooker).
104 *CW*, 1850, 512–13 (William Atherton).
105 *WMM*, 1850, 92 (Mrs Cheesman).
106 *CW*, 1851, 321.

and grandchildren.¹⁰⁷ Yet, if the obituaries are to be believed, it was normal to proffer spiritual guidance from the brink of the grave. On their deathbeds, Evangelicals, who were habitually activist, did not cease to be active.

Words of testimony were what most sufferers could provide most readily. Even when they could no longer easily speak, they might affirm their convictions by raising their hands or making expressive looks.¹⁰⁸ The purpose of the testimony was twofold. One aim was edification, to give spiritual help to those who could be influenced. The widow of a naval captain, Mrs Chick, is a good instance. Before her marriage she had attended New Road Independent Chapel in London, but her husband had been "pleasure-loving." "The calm and sacred service of the Independent chapel was now superseded by the trill of the gay assembly, the box at the opera, or the fashionable dinner-party. Her life became a whirl of exciting pleasure."¹⁰⁹ Afterwards, however, she was converted and became a church member. On her deathbed she expressed deep regret over her earlier worldliness and spent the time urging her visitors to avoid her bad example. The second purpose was consolation. It was a help to the bereaved to retain a memory of the strong faith of the person who had passed away. A piece of negative evidence makes the point. Sarah Paul, a London Wesleyan Sunday school teacher, was struck down suddenly and her speech became inaudible; and so, comments her obituarist, "she had not the power of cheering her disconsolate relatives with her dying testimony."¹¹⁰ The normal hope was that dying believers would express confidence in their future state and so provide reassurance to friends and relatives.

Because testimony was so important, it was common practice to put questions to the dying about their spiritual condition. This pattern, for understandable reasons, was not the universal rule. Thus while it was hoped that a Baptist woman's liver complaint might not prove fatal, relatives refrained from asking about her state of mind for fear of damaging her chances of recovery.¹¹¹ Nevertheless such delicacy was usually swept aside by the eagerness of hearers to learn from the dying. An Edinburgh tradesman who was a member of Albany Street Independent Chapel suffered from feverish mental wanderings, but was "always able to give an answer when asked a question."¹¹² The Baptist wife lying in Calcutta was interrogated by her husband

---

107 *CW*, 1852, 369 (Thomas Lewis).
108 *WMM*, 1850, 95 (James Johnston); 206 (Thomas Powell).
109 *CW*, 1850, 65.
110 *WMM*, 1850, 318.
111 *BM*, 1850, 101 (Elizabeth May).
112 *CW*, 1852, 419 (Andrew Jack).

even though she was dying as the result of an epidemic. "One thing more," he said: "may I hope you sleep in Jesus and are blessed?" She replied, "*Yes*—there is no doubt of it." "And at the last day," he added, "will you stand at the right hand of the Judge?" "Yes, I hope you will see me there."[113] Although, as in this case, the questions were sometimes made easier because, like certain Latin forms of inquiry, they expected the answer yes, this type of catechizing must have been something of an ordeal. Occasionally, too, the answers could be unsatisfactory. A Sunday school teacher visiting one of his oldest girls who was dying of tuberculosis in Stoke-by-Clare, Suffolk, asked her to tell him the state of her mind. "So much hesitation and doubt were mingled with her replies," we are informed, "that he felt greatly discouraged."[114] There was nevertheless a happy ending. The girl was only fearful and died in her teacher's arms expressing her secret discipleship. It is clear that interrogation was no formality. It was designed to elicit the truth in particularly serious circumstances.

If all the remarks uttered on a deathbed were solemnized by the approach of the end, the very last words carried special significance. They were what would linger most in the memory; and they were the views of the person on the very verge of heaven. Accordingly they were carefully recorded. Some carry peculiar poignancy. A tradesman at Cromford, Derbyshire, a member of Lady Glenorchy's Chapel at Matlock Bath, was not a success in business. "Want of energy and of adaptation to the taste of the times," according to the obituarist, "were the chief defects of his character as a tradesman." He evidently lived in embarrassed circumstances. His last words were, "The Lord is faithful."[115] One female member of Burslem Baptist Church, in a desire to avoid self-dramatization, declared that she did not wish to say anything for posterity.[116] That attitude, however, was abnormal. A dramatic summing up was what many aimed to express. "All is right!" confessed a Baptist; "Praise the Lord! Glory! Hallelujah!" cried a Wesleyan.[117] Some final statements nevertheless seem to be entirely accurate transcriptions of the inner lives of the subjects. The last intelligible words of a Baptist minister were: "Lord, if it please thee, if it please thee, dismiss me. These are the toils of death—sin—sin—precious Jesus."[118] The very disjointedness of these remarks adds to their authenticity.

113 *BM*, 1850, 435–36 (Margaret Robinson).
114 *CW*, 1850, 320 (John King).
115 *CW*, 1851, 208 (Samuel Moore White).
116 *BM*, 1850, 436 (Maria Prudence Mayer).
117 *BM*, 1850, 139 (John James); *WMM*, 1850, 431 (Mary Levick).
118 *BM*, 1850, 303 (Benjamin Coombs).

The last words were an indication that life had meaning right down to its end, the final act in the drama of preparing for heaven.

Expectations of the Life in Heaven

The third aspect of deathbed piety for consideration here is the expectation of heaven itself. Nonconformists had lively anticipations of what lay beyond the grave, often expressing a wish to depart from this life to the next. Nobody seemed to doubt that access to heaven was immediate after death. There was no trace of belief in the soul being asleep until the day of judgment or until the resurrection of the body. Rather Nonconformists looked forward to translation from life on earth to life in heaven without any intermission. The idea was perhaps most movingly expressed by Elizabeth Cooper, a twenty-five-year-old Congregationalist whose new baby had died shortly before she herself faced death. "One little pledge in heaven," she remarked: "I shall soon, soon be there too."[119] Hence there was no frightening prospect between death and full enjoyment of the life to come. It is perhaps not surprising then that the female member of Towcester Baptist Church was said to have "longings to depart" that became "every day more ardent."[120] The desire was reinforced by the knowledge that the aspiration was scriptural. The apostle Paul had spoken approvingly in Philippians 1:23 of "a desire to depart, to be with Christ." And it was also a properly unworldly attitude. "I can give up everything now," avowed a minister's wife, "the world has no charms for me!"[121] The commonest restraint on the wish to depart, at least in this sample, was a longing to remain with spouse and family.[122] It was regarded as a sign of spirituality, however, to be willing to leave even children behind, trusting that they would be cared for. A Baptist missionary to Africa with a wife and a daughter named Rosanna died on board ship while returning to England. "I leave you," he told his wife, "and Rosanna, and all near and dear to me, to Christ."[123] The eagerness to move on to the afterlife, though often occasioned by physical weakness, was regarded as a symptom of spiritual health.

An associated belief was a strong sense of the nearness of heaven. Often it was expressed in metaphor. "I shall soon," said a Baptist minister's wife, "eat of the fruit of the heavenly Canaan."[124] "I shall soon," echoed an Irish Wesleyan

---

119 *CW*, 1850, 209.
120 *BM*, 1850, 302 (Lucy Elizabeth Sheppard).
121 *CW*, 1851, 593 (Mrs John Gibson).
122 *CW*, 1851, 463 (Mrs Thomas Spalding).
123 *BM*, 1850, 269 (Joseph Merrick).
124 *BM*, 1850, 30 (Mrs John Stock).

woman shortly after receiving communion wine, "drink it new in the kingdom of my God."[125] Some spoke figuratively of "seeing" the land ahead of them. A Welsh Baptist minister had "a glimpse of the heavenly Canaan."[126] A Wesleyan minister's wife even reported seeing angels.[127] Others, however, could be prosaic or even deflating. "I suppose," a venerable Congregational minister told his daughter, "... you expected to have found me in the land of Beulah, ... with my glass in my hand, telling the towers of the heavenly city...; but no, ... here is poor old William Rooker just creeping into heaven."[128] Nevertheless relations liked to fancy they could perceive in the countenances of their loved ones the reflected glory of the land they were entering.[129] The faces of the dead in repose might show a calm or a smile that seemed to reveal the rest that they were now enjoying—though it was more probably the result of the contraction of the facial muscles after death.[130] A minister and a deacon were said to be already experiencing something of the communion of saints on their deathbeds, the deacon holding imaginary conversations with friends long dead.[131] There was a sense in which the thin veil between earth and heaven was thought to be pierced in the last moments of life.

What image of the afterlife did Nonconformists entertain? It has been shown by Michael Wheeler that there is no orthodox definition of the heavenly state so that the Christian imagination is free to portray the future life in an infinite variety of ways.[132] The predominant manner in this sample of obituaries was by contrast with the present. "This is a dark world," said an elderly Wesleyan class leader from Bury, Lancashire; "but I shall soon be in a bright one!"[133] Heaven was often bright, light or glorious, but it was easiest to describe it negatively. It was, according to a Congregational estimate, "a world where there is not a sorrow, or a fear, or a cross ... where sin and death are known only by report or recollection."[134] Crucially, as sufferers often anticipated, there was no pain. "My sufferings are great," confessed a Wesleyan who had been an invalid for thirty-three years, "but what are they when compared with the joys

---

125 *WMM*, 1850, 541 (Louisa Rowe).
126 *BM*, 1850, 139 (John James).
127 *WMM*, 1850, 92 (Jane Miller).
128 *CW*, 1852, 370.
129 E.g., *WMM*, 1850, 92 (Jane Miller).
130 E.g., *BM*, 1850, 302 (Lucy Elizabeth Sheppard).
131 *CW*, 1852, 162 (Thomas Lewis); *BM*, 1850, 302 (Thomas Collier).
132 Wheeler, *Death and the Future Life*, chap. 3.
133 *WMM*, 1850, 428 (George Mills).
134 *CW*, 1852, 420 ("G. B.").

that I shall soon realise?"[135] Hence heaven was a happy place, the happiness being unmixed.[136] Unlike earth, it would be a scene of rest and perfect love.[137] Heaven was attractive because it was different.

It has been suggested by Colleen McDannell and Bernhard Lang in their history of ideas of heaven that a "modern" understanding of the future state reached its peak in the nineteenth century. Although there was still an element of rest in the way heaven was conceived, one of its leading features was activity. Believers expected to be more involved in doing in the future life.[138] One aspect, according to McDannell and Lang, was progress in the other world. Souls were expected, on this view, to advance steadily in spiritual awareness. That understanding of the future life was not apparent among Evangelical Nonconformists of the mid-nineteenth century. It is true that James Baldwin Brown, one of the most theologically liberal of Congregationalists, voiced such opinions later on. Life in heaven, declared Baldwin Brown in 1877, was not a place of rest but instead would give scope for "fruitful sunlit activity," in continuity with life on earth.[139] There was no trace of such notions a quarter of a century earlier. There was not even talk of heaven as an opportunity for service. This novel element was to appear soon afterwards. In 1857 Charles Haddon Spurgeon, the eminent Baptist preacher, announced in his iconoclastic youth that to consider heaven as a place of rest was suitable only for the indolent. Rather it was "a place of uninterrupted service."[140] That idea became a commonplace in the obituaries of Nonconformists only in the 1860s and afterwards. The chief attraction of heaven for a distinguished Wesleyan minister, he declared in 1867, was "that I shall still serve Him."[141] Around 1850, however, activity in heaven, as anticipated by the dying, took only one form: singing. A Wesleyan girl spoke of going to join the angel choir; a Congregational minister expected to be singing the song of Moses and the Lamb.[142] The Redeemer would be honored in song. The great activity of the world to come was praise.

---

135 *WMM*, 1850, 90 (Mary Dudbridge).
136 *CW*, 1851, 320 (Edward Baines).
137 *CW*, 1851, 510 (J[ohn] Jerard); 1852, 323 (Leila Ada).
138 Colleen McDannell and Bernhard Lang, *Heaven: A History* (New Haven, CT: Yale University Press, 1988), 183.
139 James Baldwin Brown in "The Soul and Future Life," *Nineteenth Century* 2 (1877), 511–17, quoted in Jalland, *Death in the Victorian Family*, 267–68.
140 McDannell and Lang, *Heaven*, 278–79.
141 E.g., *WMM*, 1867, 513 (Michael Coulson Taylor). Cf. *BM*, 1881, 479 (Samuel Manning).
142 *WMM*, 1850, 430 (Christina Crook); *CW*, 1852, 368 (Thomas Lewis).

Another aspect of the "modern" understanding of heaven predicated by McDanneell and Lang, however, does occupy a prominent place in the sample of obituaries. That is the anticipation of meeting friends and family once more in the hereafter. The subjects of the obituaries often spoke of going home;[143] and in the home there would be reunion. An elderly Wesleyan in Dudley assured her daughter that she would meet her "where there will be no more separations."[144] Edward Baines, the patriarchal figure in Leeds, trusted that his family would be "reunited in a world of eternal blessedness and glory."[145] The expectation often extended beyond the family to servants and friends,[146] for the hope of reunion encompassed all Christian believers. A Welsh Baptist minister sent a message to an elderly member of his church, remarking that he would "never again see her this side of Jordan, but we shall soon meet in heaven."[147] The expectation of meeting again was therefore more than a sanctified version of Victorian domesticity. Rather it was an expression of the solidarity of believers that would endure beyond the grave.

The most frequent feature of the anticipation of heaven in the obituaries is a looking forward to being in the divine presence. Occasionally the reference is simply to God or the heavenly Father, indicating the first person of the Trinity.[148] Far more often, however, the hope centers on Christ. James Harington Evans, for instance, spoke of soon being "with Jesus, whom I love; who loved me before I loved him."[149] In the future world, according to a Baptist spinster, "we shall see and dwell with our Saviour."[150] Commonly sufferers spoke of Christ coming to them at the moment of death. The prayer "Come, Lord Jesus," applied in Revelation 22:20 to the second coming, was standardly used to invite Christ to fetch a believer to heaven.[151] The dying Jewish convert wrote on the flyleaf of her Bible, "Christ is Heaven!"[152] It was a sentiment that reflected a strong conviction among her fellow believers. Heaven was supremely a place made welcoming by the presence of the Savior. The prospect of being with Christ was for many the most important dimension in expectations of the afterlife.

143 E.g., *WMM*, 1850, 91 (Mary Dudbridge), 204 (Thomas Briggs).
144 *WMM*, 1850, 317 (Hannah Rabone).
145 *CW*, 1851, 321.
146 *BM*, 1850, 30 (Mrs John Stock); *WMM*, 1850, 315 (Thomas Sawtell).
147 *BM*, 1850, 138 (John James).
148 *WMM*, 1850, 427 (George Mills); 205 (Mary Fair).
149 *BM*, 1850, 36.
150 *BM*, 1850, 500 (Mary Cowell).
151 E.g., *BM*, 1850, 269 (Joseph Merrick). Cf. Wilson, *Constrained by Zeal*, 163.
152 *CW*, 1852, 323 (Leila Ada).

The Decay of Deathbed Spirituality

The elements of Evangelical Nonconformist spirituality that have been reviewed were in flux. The growth of the idea that heaven was a place of activity rather than of rest has already illustrated one direction of change. More drastic alteration took place before the end of the century. A contributor to the *Baptist Magazine* in 1880 reported the belief that too much had been made by a past generation of deathbed experiences.[153] In that year the journal published no obituaries whatsoever. In the following year, it is true, a new editor reintroduced them, but the descriptions of the process of dying were shorter than in the past and there were no records at all of last words. Although the *Wesleyan Methodist Magazine* was still carrying accounts of last words during the 1880s, its reports of death were less ample than in earlier years. The *Christian Witness* had ceased publication in 1871,[154] and its successor the *Congregationalist* printed no records of deathbeds. Why did publicizing end-of-life piety go out of fashion?

One explanation is the growth of respectability. As the economy prospered, personal wealth was increasing. Well-to-do Nonconformists tended to be more reticent about their faith. Already in 1850 there were signs of the tendency at work. One of the most successful men memorialized in the magazines for that year, James Lomax, a Baptist wholesale and retail grocer of Nottingham, was said to be "remarkably reserved on the subject of his own religious experience."[155] The idea that it was vulgar to pry into sacred personal territory spread more widely over subsequent years. The contributor to the *Baptist Magazine* in 1880 considered it "very repugnant to refinement of feeling for the still utterances of the chamber of death to be noised abroad and made the theme of rude religious declamation."[156] A second reason was the broadening of Nonconformist theology during the second half of the nineteenth century. New ideas, sometimes derived from Anglican Broad Churchmen, eroded the sharp lines of the Evangelical scheme of salvation. A kindly Father, it was increasingly believed, would welcome those who showed signs of goodness into the heavenly home.[157] The fate of the soul no longer seemed to hang upon its state at the end of its earthly existence. Life seemed to matter more than death,

---

153 J. H. Cooke, "The Last Moments of Two Masters of Science," *BM*, 1880, 35.
154 Josef L. Altholz, *The Religious Press in Britain, 1760–1900* (New York: Greenwood Press, 1989), 186.
155 *BM*, 1850, 662.
156 Cooke, "Last Moments," *BM*, 1880, 35.
157 Mark Hopkins, *Nonconformity's Romantic Generation: Evangelical and Liberal Theologies in Victorian England* (Milton Keynes: Paternoster Press, 2004).

activity more than experience. "Words from his dying lips are not needed," declared the preacher at the funeral of a Sheffield Baptist minister in 1881. "His has been a speaking life."[158] The third reason was related to the second. The theological broadening largely reflected the spread of sensibility stemming from the Romantic movement. Language softened and fresh motifs rose to prominence. The sharpness of death was blunted by calling it "sleep," nature was supposed to mold human development and the appeal of the child became popular. All three of these typical cultural indicators are evident in a description of the last moments of a Coventry Baptist deacon in 1881. He spent a Friday afternoon gathering raspberries in the garden with his grandchildren: "The evening came on, and ... the children ... remained in the garden among the fruit-trees, but he—the fine old man—with the child-heart, went to his quiet room, not to die, but to SLEEP in Christ."[159] In such sentimental accounts there was no room for stout avowals of personal faith. For all these reasons deathbed scenes such as those of the mid-century ceased to appear before the end of the reign of Victoria. The marginalization of death, so crucial a dimension of social life in the twentieth century, was already under way.

Conclusion

In the high Victorian years around 1850, however, there was still a remarkable willingness among Nonconformists to face the issues of eternity. They enjoyed ample resources. All the facilities of Evangelical religion were at the disposal of the dying. Bible and cross, key Evangelical emphases, were prominent in their minds. Hymns, books, prayer and a sense of the divine presence fortified the believer. The primary Evangelical social units, church and family, provided support. Preparation for death, though not always possible immediately before the end, was regarded as a long-term responsibility. In the final days the deathbed was an opportunity for spiritual progress. There were temptations to doubt, complaint and fear, but they were expected to be superseded by calmness or even triumph. Evangelical activism was still possible on the deathbed. The dying offered spiritual guidance, bore public testimony, submitted to questioning and uttered profitable last words. And there were definite anticipations of heaven. It was thought to be the destination of the soul straight after death and to be close at hand even before the end. Heaven was often contrasted with the sorrows of earthly existence. It was a place of praise rather than any other activity, of reunion with other believers and of fellowship with Christ. Unlike in subsequent years, when last days were no longer

---

158 *BM*, 1881, 539.
159 *BM*, 1881, 441 (Richard Bassett).

described, death was Christianized. The experience was made meaningful in the light of Evangelical faith. Family and friends could draw consolation from the reflection that the death of their loved ones was not futile. Individuals were prepared for the often terrible process of dying themselves. Their anticipations were transformed by the hope of heaven so that, in a sense, the last enemy was defeated. As an obituary of 1850 put it, these Evangelical Nonconformists were "cheered by the prospect of a blessed immortality."[160]

---

160 *BM*, 1850, 692 (Richard Freeman).

IV

Evangelicals, History and Science

12

Calvin and British Evangelicalism in the Nineteenth and Twentieth Centuries

The legacy of John Calvin to the Protestants of Great Britain was immense. His version of Reformed theology became virtually universal in the Elizabethan Church of England and remained the norm during the earlier years of the seventeenth century.[1] The Puritans who wished to press further with the task of reformation upheld the same doctrinal scheme, which was codified by the Westminster Assembly during the 1640s. Their heirs who left the established church, either voluntarily or compulsorily, formed Dissenting denominations that were overwhelmingly Calvinist in profession: the Presbyterians, the Independents and the Baptists.[2] The teaching of Calvin was also warmly embraced in Scotland, where the structures of church life were remodeled much more drastically than in England. By means of its kirk sessions, Presbyterianism created what has been called "a Puritan nation" in early modern Scotland.[3] The people of Britain turned into Calvinists. In Scotland they remained so, all Presbyterian ministers having to profess their allegiance to the theology of the Westminster Assembly down the years into the nineteenth century. In England, on the other hand, the Calvinism of the established church evaporated in the later seventeenth century and the Presbyterian variety faded during the eighteenth. Only the small communities of Independents and Baptists retained their loyalty to Calvin's convictions. The Evangelical Revival of the eighteenth century, however, put the process

---

1 Patrick Collinson, *The Religion of Protestants: The Church in English Society, 1559–1625* (Oxford: Clarendon Press, 1982).
2 Michael R. Watts, *The Dissenters from the Reformation to the French Revolution* (Oxford: Clarendon Press, 1978).
3 Margo Todd, *The Culture of Protestantism in Early Modern Scotland* (New Haven, CT: Yale University Press, 2002), 405.

into reverse. Independents and Baptists grew in numbers and distinctive Reformed convictions were planted once more in the Church of England. As the nineteenth century wore on and Evangelicals continued to expand, therefore, Protestantism increasingly owed some allegiance to John Calvin. In Evangelical circles, as an Independent divine put it at the tercentenary of Calvin's death in 1864, "it is the spirit of Calvin, more than any other man, which breathes and works."[4]

The Limits of Attention to Calvin

Nevertheless for a number of reasons the extent of the Calvinist commitment of Evangelicals during the nineteenth century needs to be qualified. In the first place, the type of theology upheld by most of the Reformed differed significantly from the doctrines maintained by Calvin and their Puritan ancestors. The eminent American theologian Jonathan Edwards had introduced a crucial distinction between natural and moral inability. Sinners suffered from no natural inability, imposed on them by their Creator, to believe the gospel; rather they exercised a moral inability, a refusal to repent of their sins, for which they alone were culpable. The Almighty had not created them merely to punish them for their unavoidable failures. This milder form of Calvinism, a species of determinism compatible with human liberty to choose, was the type embraced by most British Evangelicals. Among Baptists Andrew Fuller was its champion, among the Independents Edward Williams and among Scottish Presbyterians Thomas Chalmers.[5] The exponents of this point of view sat loose to Calvin's writings. A contributor to the *Evangelical Magazine* in March 1809 was typical. "I avow myself," he wrote, "a Calvinist. . . . Do I make the *Institutions* and *Comments* of Calvin the directory of my faith?" The answer was that he certainly did not: the writer merely held the leading doctrines of "that illustrious man."[6] Calvin was still respected: many of the moderate Calvinists, including Andrew Fuller and Edward Williams, subscribed to the first of the nineteenth-century lives of the Reformer published in 1809 by John Mackenzie, an Anglican who himself shared the views of Edwards.[7] The theologians of this school nevertheless felt entirely at liberty to diverge from the Reformer's teaching. Thus

---

4   Alexander Thomson, *John Calvin: The Man and the Doctrine: A Tercentenary Memorial* (London: Jackson, Walford and Hodder, 1864), 5.
5   See 1:5: "The Legacy of Jonathan Edwards in Britain."
6   S., "On Names of Religious Distinction," *Evangelical Magazine*, March 1809, 101.
7   John Mackenzie, *Memoirs of the Life and Writings of John Calvin* (London: For Williams and Smith, 1809), x, xiii, 246–49.

the Independent Alexander Thomson, even when in 1864 celebrating Calvin's achievement, expressed regret at his decree of reprobation.[8] The moderates were denounced by the much smaller number who retained more robust views as "Bastard Calvinists,"[9] but their views came to dominate the Reformed communities. That opened a doctrinal gulf between most Calvinist Evangelicals and John Calvin himself.

There were, secondly, reasons why members of particular denominations felt distanced from Calvin. The Reformer of Geneva suffered in the eyes of an insular people from being a foreigner. Members of the Church of England usually preferred to appeal to the authority of the English Reformers of the sixteenth century who were unequivocally their own. On occasion they would defend Calvin, as did the leading Anglican Evangelical Daniel Wilson, later bishop of Calcutta, who in an account of a continental tour in 1823 described the Reformer as a "sober, practical holy writer."[10] In general, however, they regarded themselves as being in continuity with those who had undertaken the reformation of the Church of England in the sixteenth century. In *Light from Old Times* (1890), for instance, Bishop John Charles Ryle, though the most outspokenly Calvinist of Anglican bishops during the nineteenth century, ignored the Reformer in favor of such men as Bishops Hooper, Latimer and Ridley, the glories of early Protestantism in England.[11] Similarly in Scotland John Calvin was eclipsed by his disciple John Knox. For a few, such as William Cunningham, the principal of New College, Edinburgh, who loved systematic theology, Calvin was "the man who, next to St. Paul, has done most good to mankind."[12] But for a larger number Calvin was a remote figure with unappealing characteristics who, unlike Knox, had no direct connection with Scotland. In an assessment of Calvin delivered in a series of lectures in Edinburgh on "The Evangelical Succession" in 1882, J. S. Candlish, a leading figure in the Free Church of Scotland, contrasted the "sternness and determination" of Calvin with the "geniality" of Knox that was reminiscent of the same quality

---

8   Thomson, *Calvin*, 34.
9   "On Exhortations to Unconverted Sinners," *Evangelical Magazine*, November 1814, 424.
10 Daniel Wilson, *Letters from an Absent Brother*, 2 vols., 3rd ed. (London: For G. Wilson), 1:291, quoted in James Rigney, "John Calvin and English Travellers in Geneva," in *Sober, Strict, and Scriptural: Collective Memories of John Calvin, 1800–2000*, ed. Johan de Niet, Herman Paul and Bart Wallet (Leiden: Brill, 2009), 329.
11 John C. Ryle, *Light from Old Times* (London: W. Hunt & Co., 1891). On Ryle, see 2:2, "Bishop J. C. Ryle: Holiness, Mission and Churchmanship."
12 Quoted by Jean Henri Merle d'Aubigné, *History of the Reformation in the Time of Calvin*, 8 vols. (London: Longman, Roberts & Green, 1863–78), 3:ix.

in Luther.[13] To the Dissenters of England and Wales Calvin was not only foreign but also a champion of the principle that the church was coextensive with the state. Their very existence was predicated on the opposite conviction that religion was a matter for voluntary choice. Hence, as the Independent John Kelly put it in an otherwise appreciative lecture on Calvin, the Reformer was guilty of "forcing religious habits on those who were not prepared to receive them."[14] Anglicans, Presbyterians and Dissenters alike therefore usually lauded their own heroes rather than Calvin.

Some within the Evangelical community, in the third place, actually repudiated Calvin altogether. Methodists, the followers of the eighteenth-century John Wesley, agreed with their founder in rejecting Calvinism in favor of Arminianism. It is true that one independent-minded Wesleyan minister, Samuel Dunn, published in 1837 a warm account of Calvin's theology, quoting copiously from his commentaries and sermons, but Dunn was exceptional.[15] W. B. Pope, the greatest of Victorian Methodist theologians, took Calvin's distinguishing points into account in order to refute them at various points in his three-volume *Compendium of Christian Theology* (1880), characterizing divine sovereignty, for example, as "despotic."[16] Others outside the Methodist fold agreed in attacking Calvin. Thus Edward Smyth, an Anglican Evangelical minister who gloried in being an Arminian, wrote a book in 1809 contrasting the apostle Paul with Calvin, censuring the Reformer's "eternal irrevocable decree, assigning to particular men salvation or damnation, antecedent to any foreseen faith or unbelief, good or evil works."[17] Some were more equivocal. Andrew Fairbairn was brought up in the tiny Scottish Evangelical Union that was explicitly anti-Calvinist, but, as the best-known theologian of the English Free Churches at the end of the century, he was required to deal even-handedly with Calvin. His solution, extraordinarily, was to turn Calvin into as much of an Arminian as he dared. Calvin's harsh doctrines were blamed on Augustine, but, according to Fairbairn, "while the system held and awed Calvin's reason

---

13 James S. Candlish, "John Calvin," in *The Evangelical Succession*, 2nd series (Edinburgh: Macniven & Wallace, 1885), 18.
14 John Kelly, *John Calvin* (Liverpool: R. Smith, n.d.), 24.
15 Samuel Dunn, *Christian Theology: By John Calvin* (London: Tegg and Son, 1837).
16 William B. Pope, *A Compendium of Christian Theology*, 3 vols., 2nd ed. (London: Wesleyan Methodist Book Room, 1880), 2:352.
17 Edward Smyth, *St. Paul or Calvin: Or a Full Exposition and Elucidation of the Ninth Chapter of His Epistle to the Romans: Whereby the False Glosses of the Calvinists, on That Particular Portion of Scripture, Are Clearly Refuted* (London: W. Baynes, 1809), xxxii.

it did not yet win his heart."[18] Anglican Evangelicals had found themselves in an even more difficult position over Calvin in the early years of the century because the bishop of Lincoln, George Pretyman Tomline, a pillar of the establishment, argued in a book of 1799 that the Thirty-Nine Articles of the Church of England could not be interpreted in a Calvinist sense, following it up twelve years later with *A Refutation of Calvinism*.[19] The aim of branding Calvinism an alien creed was to drive the Evangelicals out of the church. One Evangelical response was to reaffirm the rightness of Reformed convictions: John Allen, an Anglican schoolmaster, published an edition of Calvin's *Institutes* in 1813 for that reason.[20] Charles Simeon, the judicious leader of the Evangelical section of the clergy, took a different line. Believing there was truth in both Calvinism and Arminianism, but supposing that the Bible rose above such "human systems," Simeon eventually, in 1822, decided to try to disarm anti-Evangelical prejudice by publicly disavowing Calvinism altogether.[21] Thereafter many Anglican Evangelicals regarded themselves not as indebted to Calvin but as simple "Bible Christians." So substantial sections of Evangelicalism were outside the Calvinist ranks.

During the nineteenth century, fourthly, there was a gradual undermining of Calvinism in circles where it had been upheld. The chief agency was the spread of influences derived from the Enlightenment, with its exaltation of reason and empiricist technique. At first, during the eighteenth and early nineteenth centuries, there was a firm marriage between characteristic ideas of the Enlightenment and the doctrines of the gospel. Both were spreading light and civilization.[22] The ideas of the age of reason were even read back by Evangelicals into the career of Calvin. Thus in 1809 John Mackenzie praised the Reformer for being a dispassionate commentator: "Disavowing all authority but that of the Scriptures ... his investigations were conducted [in a] spirit of free enquiry."[23] The same temper, however, as the example of Simeon has

---

18   Andrew M. Fairbairn, "Calvin and the Reformed Church," in *The Cambridge Modern History*, ed. A. W. Ward, 14 vols. (Cambridge: Cambridge University Press, 1903), 2:365.
19   Grayson M. Ditchfield, "Sir George Pretyman Tomline," *The Oxford Dictionary of National Biography*, http://www.oxforddnb.com/view/article/27520, accessed 8 May 2009.
20   John Calvin, *Institutes of the Christian Religion*, trans. John Allen, 3 vols. (London: For John Walker, 1813), 1:xi.
21   *Memoirs of the Life of the Rev. Charles Simeon, M.A.*, ed. William Carus, 2nd ed. (London: J. Hatchard & Son, 1847), 66.
22   See 1:32: "Revival and Enlightenment in Eighteenth-Century England."
23   Mackenzie, *Memoirs*, 178.

already illustrated, was unfriendly to inherited doctrinal systems such as Calvinism. "Make your own system," was the advice to candidates for the ministry regularly given by James Acworth, principal of the Baptists' Horton Academy, in the middle years of the century.[24] The effect was to make preachers in denominations with a Reformed tradition, even when wholly Evangelical in outlook, averse to proclaiming distinctive Calvinist doctrine. In Scotland the United Presbyterians and the Free Church passed Declaratory Acts in 1879 and 1892 allowing divergence from some doctrinal positions of the Westminster Assembly so long as there was no departure from the substance of the faith.[25] Gradually more liberal theological opinion was being tolerated, especially among Congregationalists, the newer term for Independents. When, at the first International Congregational Council in 1891, a preacher, E. P. Goodwin of Chicago, called his coreligionists back to a Calvinist profession, there was a sharp reaction from Joseph Parker, the angular minister of the City Temple, where the meetings were being held. He must have his pulpit fumigated, declared Parker. "By this time Calvinism stinketh," he said, "for it hath been dead these two centuries."[26] It was not as lifeless as Parker suggested, but its vitality had been sapped by assumptions stemming from the Enlightenment.

Members of the Protestant denominations, in the fifth place, were propelled further in a liberal theological direction by the newer body of ideas associated with the Romantic cultural revolution. The fresh mood encouraged greater attention to history, and so made Calvin and the Puritan inheritance more highly valued, but also fostered a love of the natural, the imaginative and the personal at the expense of received doctrinal views, especially Calvinism. Thomas Carlyle, the greatest Romantic prose writer of the age, epitomized the shift in sensibility, recommending moral earnestness as a replacement for sterile orthodoxy.[27] The Carlylean theme of heroism is apparent, for instance, in a study of the leaders of the Reformation by John Tulloch, a broad-minded Presbyterian theologian of the University of St Andrews, first published in 1859 and revised in 1883. He praises "all the moral heroism in Puritanism" but contrasts Calvin unfavorably with Luther because, as an organizer rather than a man of action, he was less heroic. Calvin was like "a Doric column, chaste, grand, and

---

24 William Medley, *Rawdon Baptist College: Centenary Memorial* (London: Kingsgate Press, 1904), 26.
25 Alexander C. Cheyne, *The Transforming of the Kirk: Victorian Scotland's Religious Revolution* (Edinburgh: Saint Andrew Press, 1983), chap. 3.
26 *Peace and Truth* [hereafter *P&T*], January 1937, 3.
27 Mark Hopkins, *Nonconformity's Romantic Generation: Evangelical and Liberal Theologies in Victorian England* (Milton Keynes: Paternoster Press, 2004), 249–50.

sublime in the very simplicity and inflexibility of its mouldings;" Luther was like "a Gothic dome, with its fertile contrasts and ample space."[28] The taste of the age preferred the Gothic aesthetic, so that Calvin and his system seemed altogether too fixed and confined. In particular the Romantic shift towards conceptualizing the Almighty as a benevolent Father often led to moral revulsion against Calvinism during the Victorian era. It was vigorously expressed in 1892 by an unusually liberal Baptist minister, Charles Aked. Like Tulloch, he was willing to admire the effects of Calvin's ideas in forging "grand, strong, and heroic servants of the living God," but the content of Calvin's teaching, what Aked called "the doctrine of the gloomy fanatic of Geneva," was no better than "the poison of the rattlesnake and the blood-lust of the tiger."[29] For Aked, original sin and predestination summed up the whole of Calvin's theology, and he hated it. Romantic attitudes, often carrying their exponents beyond the bounds of Evangelical belief, tended to corrode the Calvinist legacy further.

The result of these various factors was that Calvin did not occupy a prominent place in the Evangelical memory during the nineteenth century. Perhaps the most significant episode of homage to the Reformer was the visit to Geneva in 1816–17 by Robert Haldane, a doughty Scottish laird who had sponsored widespread itinerant evangelism in his homeland. Drawn by Romantic expectations of the city of Calvin and encountering a small group friendly to Evangelical religion, Haldane expounded there the epistle to the Romans and so sparked off the *Réveil* in Switzerland.[30] Few of Haldane's contemporaries shared his degree of enthusiasm for Calvin. Between 1800 and the 1830s there were only six translations of works by the Reformer published in Britain. By contrast, however, in the single decade of the 1840s there were as many as twenty-three.[31] The upsurge of interest was partly a symptom of the rising tide of historical concern associated with Romantic taste, but half the titles were the fruit of a particular venture, the Calvin Translation Society, which was founded in May 1843, the same month as the Disruption split the Church of Scotland.[32] The Evangelicals who left, forming the Free Church of Scotland, supported the

---

28 John Tulloch, *Luther and Other Leaders of the Reformation*, 3rd ed. (Edinburgh: William Blackwood and Sons, 1883), 264, 177, 237.
29 Charles F. Aked, *Calvin and Calvinism* (London: James Clarke and Co., 1891), 18, 11, 7.
30 Timothy C. F. Stunt, *From Awakening to Secession: Radical Evangelicals in Switzerland and Britain, 1815–35* (Edinburgh: T&T Clark, 2000), 31–37.
31 *Bibliographia Calviniana*, ed. Alfred Erichson, 3rd impr. (Nieuwkoop: B. de Graaf, 1960), 58–67.
32 E.g., John Calvin, *Institutes of the Christian Religion*, trans. Henry Beveridge, 3 vols. (Edinburgh: For the Calvin Translation Society, 1845), 1:ii.

publishing scheme because it promised to recruit the memory of the Reformer to their cause. Thirteen works of the Reformer were issued during the 1850s, ten of them by the Calvin Translation Society. When the society had fulfilled its ambition of publishing translations of most of Calvin's works, however, the demand for new titles fell away. Between 1860 and the end of the century there were only three.[33] At the mid-century peak of interest in the Reformer, three biographies of Calvin were published in swift succession. One, a version of the German life by Paul Henry, pastor of the French Reformed congregation in Berlin, was, as its translator observed, marked by "profound admiration for Calvin;" the second, a translation of a Catholic work by Jean Marie Vincent Audin, was an exercise in outright denigration; the third, written by a sober Anglican, Thomas Dyer, provided, according to a reviewer, "a judicious and very readable summary" but claimed originality only for its coverage of Calvin's dealings with the Church of England.[34] No subsequent lives other than popular sketches were published during the century, for no scholar arose to pursue Calvin studies in depth. The Calvin Translation Society represented an isolated peak of interest in the Reformer.

Calvin and Politics

Hence there was much less scope for Calvin to mold the political role of Evangelicals than might be imagined. His attitudes that verged on public affairs were more a subject for debate than a spur to action. In one of the most widely circulated presentations of Calvin, the translation of the vivid unfinished account by the Genevan professor of church history J. H. Merle d'Aubigné, Calvin is depicted as a lover of liberty but also as a champion of order.[35] The central question for Evangelicals was whether the element of order had unduly repressed the element of liberty. John Kelly, an Independent advocate of Calvin, spoke for many when he contended that the Reformer had exerted a profound influence "in the direction both of spiritual religion and civil liberty."[36] But that assessment was about the long-term effects of Calvinism. When it came to evaluating Calvin himself, there was much more criticism. The Reformer had been wrong, declared Tulloch, to expect the state to suppress vice; Calvin was equally wrong, according to an article in the journal of the interdenomi-

---

33 *Bibliographia Calviniana*, ed. Erichson, 58–67.
34 Paul Henry, *The Life and Times of John Calvin, the Great Reformer*, trans. Henry Stebbing (London: Whittaker and Co., 1849), vi; *Quarterly Review*, March 1851, 533; Thomas H. Dyer, *The Life of John Calvin* (London: John Murray, 1850), viii.
35 Merle d'Aubigné, *Reformation*, 1:x-xi.
36 Kelly, *Calvin*, 25.

national Evangelical Alliance in 1864, to expect the state to suppress heresy.[37] That observation raised the specter of Servetus. A succession of Unitarians challenged Evangelicals over the years, alleging that Calvin's responsibility for the execution of Servetus on the grounds of his anti-Trinitarianism revealed the dark implications of orthodoxy.[38] Defenses of Calvin's behavior in the affair varied. It was common to argue that the standards of his age differed from those of the more enlightened nineteenth century; that the policy was a carryover from popish persecution; or that Calvin was taking his virtue of concern for the truth to an unwarranted extreme.[39] One Strict Baptist admirer who wrote a popular biography in 1851 describing Calvin's "glorious doctrines" solved the problem by simply leaving out the execution of Servetus.[40] Others, however, did not wish to excuse the Reformer. Henry Stebbing, the translator of Paul Henry's life of Calvin, deplored Henry's efforts at extenuation; and Thomas Dyer agreed.[41] Calvin therefore bore an ambiguous reputation in a land that prided itself on a long history of toleration. The intolerant Reformer did not make an attractive political hero.

Calvin also suffered from the burden of association with republicanism. In America, the republican credentials added to his reputation, but in firmly monarchist Britain they did not. Merle d'Aubigné mused that the republican constitution of Geneva might have told against the appeal of his narrative, remarking delphically that his own preference was for monarchy.[42] English Evangelicals were all too aware that they were tainted in the popular mind by association with the Puritans, the Calvinists who had killed King Charles I. This was a particular problem for the Independents, who in the seventeenth century had numbered in their ranks Oliver Cromwell, the military leader of the revolution that had established a republic with himself as Lord Protector. In the earlier years of the nineteenth century their attitude to Cromwell was extremely reserved. Robert Vaughan, the leading historian among the Independents, treated Cromwell in a book of 1831 as a wily politician,

---

37 Tulloch, *Luther*, 13; *Evangelical Christendom*, June 1864, 268.
38 Richard Wright, *An Apology for Dr. Michael Servetus* (Wisbech: F. B. Wright, 1806); Edward Tagart, *Sketches of the Lives and Characters of the Leading Reformers of the Sixteenth Century* (London: John Green, 1843), 37; Robert Willis, *Servetus and Calvin: A Study of an Important Epoch in the Early History of the Reformation* (London: Henry S. King & Co., 1877).
39 Mackenzie, *Memoirs*, 91, 92, 144.
40 Charles W. Banks, *The Life and Times of John Calvin: With an Earnest Appeal for the Adoption of Open-Air Preaching* (London: Houlston & Stoneman, 1851).
41 Henry, *Life*, vi; Dyer, *Life*, 536.
42 Merle d'Aubigné, *Reformation*, 3:xiv.

given to "circuitousness and insincerity." Cromwell had injured religious Independency by identifying it with "revolution and republicanism."[43] In this phase Calvin suffered from guilt by association with his seventeenth-century English disciple. There was, however, a transformation in the reputation of Cromwell in the 1840s. Thomas Carlyle presented the Lord Protector as an archetypal hero, publishing in 1845 an edition of his letters and speeches that enjoyed enormous sales.[44] In the wake of the altered perception of Cromwell, the Independents began to take pride in his allegiance to their denomination. In a book of 1863, Vaughan praises Cromwell's "signal service" and "transcendent capacity."[45] The Lord Protector turned into an idol not only of Cromwell's immediate coreligionists but of all the Nonconformists, the newer name in the Victorian period for the Dissenters. John Clifford, the Baptist minister who gave leadership to Nonconformity in public affairs around the close of the century, appealed repeatedly to Cromwell as an inspiration for campaigns in his own day.[46] The chief political Calvinist of the English past had been rehabilitated. It did not follow, however, that the political stock of Calvin himself rose in these years. Because Calvinism as a theological system was in such serious decay, Cromwell's new prestige did not rub off on his theological mentor. At this juncture Cromwell, not Calvin, was the Nonconformists' political exemplar.

In consequence nineteenth-century Evangelicals were rarely roused by Calvin or his teaching for the political fray. It has been supposed that the Clapham Sect, the group of largely Anglican Evangelicals led by William Wilberforce who were responsible in the early years of the century for campaigns against the slave trade and other social evils, had Calvinism as its inspiration.[47] That estimate, however, is mistaken. The second most active member of the parliamentary group was William Smith, a Dissenter who adopted Socinian views and so deplored Calvinist theology; and Wilberforce himself recorded that "every year that I live I become more impressed

---

43 Robert Vaughan, *Memorials of the Stuart Dynasty*, 2 vols. (London: Houldsworth and Ball, 1831), 2:263, 260.
44 Blair Worden, "The Victorians and Oliver Cromwell," in *History, Religion and Culture: British Intellectual History, 1750-1950*, ed. Stefan Collini, Richard Whatmore and B. W. Young (Cambridge: Cambridge University Press, 2001), 112-35.
45 Robert Vaughan, *Revolutions in English History*, 3 vols. (London: John W. Parker, 1859-63), 3:395.
46 David W. Bebbington, *The Nonconformist Conscience: Chapel and Politics, 1870-1914* (London: George Allen & Unwin, 1982), 145.
47 William T. Whitley, *Calvinism and Evangelism in England* (London: Kingsgate Press, [1933]), 12.

with the unscriptural character of the Calvinistic system."[48] On the other hand, the most outspoken Calvinists, Dissenters such as William Gadsby in Manchester and Joseph Irons in London, were undoubtedly champions of the urban poor in their day, but they drew no connection between their public activities and their distinguishing doctrines, let alone Calvin himself.[49] The Evangelical Nonconformists who in the second half of the century became the shock troops of Liberalism included large denominations hostile to Calvinism and so as a body did not consider appealing to the memory of the Reformer. Even Charles Haddon Spurgeon, a doughty Calvinist who was generally acknowledged to be the greatest preacher of the age, did not make the link. Although the Baptist minister urged support for Liberal policies and candidates,[50] he did not see the Reformed faith as a sanction for participation in public affairs. It was only in Presbyterian Scotland that there were political applications of Calvinism. During the 1830s John Brown, a scholarly minister of the United Secession Church, elaborated his denomination's belief in the separation of church and state. Brown led a campaign for refusal of the annuity tax that was payable in Edinburgh to the Established Church. Quoting sixteenth- and seventeenth-century texts by Calvinist resistance theorists, he argued that Romans 13 did not require absolute obedience to the authorities. That would be to endorse "slavish principles."[51] The Free Church of Scotland created in 1843, on the other hand, upheld in its early years the principle of establishment. "The civil magistrate is bound," according to William Cunningham, ". . . to aim at the promotion of religion and the welfare of the church."[52] He saw that axiom as being an outworking of Reformed doctrine. Around the middle years of the century, therefore, Scotland did generate Calvinist political perspectives, albeit contradicting each other about whether the state should grant recognition to the church. But an explicitly Reformed view of politics was limited to Scotland, and Calvin himself was little, if ever, invoked as its inspirer.

---

48 Robert I. and Samuel Wilberforce, *The Life of William Wilberforce*, 5 vols. (London: J. Murray, 1838), 5:162.
49 Ian J. Shaw, *High Calvinists in Action: Calvinism and the City: Manchester and London, c. 1810–1860* (Oxford: Oxford University Press, 2002).
50 David W. Bebbington, "Spurgeon and the Common Man," *Baptist Review of Theology*, 5:1 (1995), 63–75, at 71–72.
51 John Brown, *The Law of Christ Respecting Civil Obedience, Especially in the Payment of Tribute*, 3rd ed. (London: William Ball, 1839), 5, 65, 83, ix.
52 William Cunningham, *Discussions on Church Principles* (Edinburgh: T&T Clark, 1863), 209.

If the memory of Calvin played only a marginal part in public affairs, there was an exception in the area of anti-Catholicism. Militant Protestantism had been bound up with national identity in England and Scotland alike during the sixteenth and seventeenth centuries, and in the eighteenth had been perhaps the strongest factor in uniting the two nations as Great Britain.[53] Hostility to Catholicism began to fade under the influence of the Enlightenment, but it was vigorously revived between the 1830s and the 1850s by circumstances in Catholic Ireland, by the Oxford Movement that seemed to point the Church of England in a Catholic direction and especially by Evangelicals themselves, hostile to the claims of Rome.[54] In this revival the name of Calvin loomed much larger than in other contexts. The evaluation of Calvin by Samuel Dunn in 1837, for example, concludes that to him and his helpers in "the glorious cause of the reformation from Popery, we owe that Scripture light and liberty which we now enjoy."[55] Merle d'Aubigné sustained similar views in the next generation by his vigorous account of the Reformation as a conflict between truth and error with Calvin as "his hero."[56] So did homegrown authors. J. A. Wylie, a lecturer at the Protestant Institute in Edinburgh, published an oft reprinted three-volume illustrated history of Protestantism in the 1870s that delighted in simple antitheses. Thus he contrasted Calvin's ascendancy in Geneva with the mediaeval authority of Pope Innocent III: "Calvin governed *by* God; Innocent governed *as* God."[57] Again Thomas Lawson, the editor of the monthly magazine the *Protestant Echo*, published in 1885 a popular life of Calvin designed for young people in which he spent a whole chapter fulminating against priests, the confessional and absolution as making up "a great fraud."[58] Political Protestantism impinged in major ways on contemporary issues, playing, for instance, a large part in the mobilization of opposition to W. E. Gladstone's proposal of Home Rule for Ireland in 1886.[59] The reputation of Calvin as the great antagonist of the papacy did contribute to public affairs.

---

53 Linda Colley, *Britons: Forging the Nation, 1707–1837* (New Haven, CT: Yale University Press, 1992), chap. 1.
54 John R. Wolffe, *The Protestant Crusade in Great Britain, 1829–1860* (Oxford: Clarendon Press, 1991).
55 Dunn, *Christian Theology*, 74.
56 Merle d'Aubigné, *Reformation*, 6:vii.
57 James A. Wylie, *The History of Protestantism*, 3 vols. (London: Cassell & Co., 1874), 1:347.
58 Thomas Lawson, *The Life of John Calvin* (London: W. Wileman, 1885), chap. 5.
59 Bebbington, *Nonconformist Conscience*, 89–93.

The Calvin Quatercentenary

The events of 1909 marking the quatercentenary of Calvin's birth form a useful prism through which some of the developments in the Reformer's image over the previous century can be viewed. H. R. Mackintosh, professor of systematic theology at New College, Edinburgh, went in July as a delegate to the international celebrations at Geneva, noting, "Calvinistically," as he put it, that "the corruption of human nature came out in the unpardonable length of the speeches."[60] He reported that there was significant support from Britain, with representatives of Scotland, England and the Welsh Calvinistic Methodists, who took pride in being alone among the world's denominations in calling themselves Calvinistic.[61] Yet in England the degree of enthusiasm for the occasion was muted. Only the small Presbyterian Church of England organized a public meeting, at which the evident affection for Calvin of the visiting Dutch theologian Herman Bavinck contrasted with the reserve of the English Presbyterian Oswald Dykes, who "did not attempt to portray Calvin as a lovable or a gracious personality" but merely claimed in Carlylean fashion that the Reformer's doctrines had "bred up a generation of heroes."[62] There was, it was admitted, "gross ignorance" about Calvin, even in Presbyterian communities.[63] A popular but solid biography published by C. H. Irwin in time for the commemorations illustrates why there was such neglect. Writing from the viewpoint that Calvinism and Arminianism could be reconciled, Irwin, like Dykes, praises the effects rather than the content of Calvin's theology. "His doctrines have their defects," he claims, "but they moulded men."[64] In Scotland there was rather more effort to remember the Reformer, with both local and national events being organized. The General Assemblies of the two main Presbyterian churches, the Church of Scotland and the United Free Church, combined to hold a celebration in St Giles' Cathedral attended by the lord provost of Edinburgh and the councilors in their robes. It was a grand occasion, but it was as much an excuse to bring the churches together for the first time in "longing for reunion" as an expression of zeal for Calvin. Repeatedly in the commemorations, Calvin was put into the shade by Knox, who loomed far larger

---

60   Hugh R. M[ackintosh], "Calvin's Quatercentenary," *British Weekly*, 8 July 1909, 332.
61   Hugh R. M[ackintosh], "The Geneva Celebrations," *British Weekly*, 15 July 1909, 347, 349.
62   *British Weekly*, 13 May 1909, 129.
63   *Quarterly Register* [of the Alliance of the Reformed and Presbyterian Churches throughout the World], May 1909, 224.
64   Clarke H. Irwin, *John Calvin: The Man and His Work*, 2nd ed. (London: Religious Tract Society, 1909), 57.

in the Scottish memory.[65] The political significance of the Reformer was not wholly forgotten, for the prayers at St Giles' included thanks for what Calvin did "towards establishing civil and religious freedom."[66] But his main remembered role in public affairs was brought out in a poem in the magazine of the Church of Scotland that celebrated his triumph over "Romish hate."[67] By the opening of the twentieth century, we may conclude, Calvin was only weakly recalled, though more strongly in Scotland than in England; his disciples were respected more than the man; his theology seemed superseded; and his political significance, except as a champion against Catholicism, was minimal.

There was one individual, however, who stood apart from the prevailing tone of merely formal acknowledgment of Calvin during the 1909 commemorations. At the English Presbyterians' public meeting, an address by Charles Silvester Horne, the Congregational minister of the central London Whitefield's Tabernacle, "dwelt on the Calvinistic element in the Puritan period of English history."[68] Horne, though forty-four years old, retained the effervescence of youth and put his considerable scholarship into making the Reformed inheritance attractive. Although he was a historian, in the past he had not been an enthusiast for Calvin. Horne's *Popular History of the Free Churches* (1903) mentions the Reformer only once, as an influence that retarded the development of church song in England.[69] But Horne had been asked to contribute to *Mansfield College Essays*, a volume that appeared in 1909 to mark the intellectual attainments of former members of the Nonconformist postgraduate college at the University of Oxford, and selected "Calvin in his Letters" as his theme. The writer set himself the task of doing for Calvin what Carlyle had done for Cromwell, of restoring his subject's reputation. A nontraditional Calvin emerged, combining "great courtesy, chivalry, and kindliness of spirit." The essayist argued against received opinion that Calvin was on the side of liberty. The tight social discipline of Geneva, according to Horne, was merely a reflection of the practice of mediaeval cities; Calvin was not as extreme as his followers; his letters reveal him as human, flexible, a peacemaker. He was "one of the greatest of men, and truest friends of freedom." Furthermore, possessing a "statesmanlike mind," Calvin, though a Christian minister, played a

---

65 *British Weekly*, 15 July 1909, 347, 349.
66 Lady Frances Balfour, "John Calvin," *British Weekly*, 27 May 1909, 188.
67 Lauchlan MacLean Watt, "Calvin," *Life & Work*, July 1909, 165.
68 *Quarterly Register*, August 1909, 248.
69 Charles Silvester Horne, *A Popular History of the Free Churches* (London: James Clark & Co., 1903), 249.

part in public affairs.[70] He had inspired, Horne declared at the public meeting, "an inquisitive, democratic, insubordinate spirit."[71] That clearly appealed to the speaker, who, as a leader of the Brotherhood movement that combined religion with progressive politics, was becoming eager to join the political fray himself. In the following year he was returned to parliament as a Liberal, the first man to serve in the House of Commons while in pastoral charge.[72] The demands of the two roles proved too great a burden, leading to Horne's early death in 1914, but it is evident that a strongly favorable interpretation of Calvin helped propel this charismatic representative of the Evangelical Free Churches into public life. Silvester Horne was an exceptional figure.

Aversion and Neglect

In the earlier years of the twentieth century the attitude towards Calvin in British society at large was harshly critical. There were lingering memories of Victorian sages such as J. A. Froude, who had pronounced in favor of Calvin's influence over posterity, but the man himself, as Froude had said, was associated "only with gloom and austerity."[73] John Morley, a Liberal politician and man of letters, was unusual in praising Calvin, in his *Oliver Cromwell* (1900), for many of his qualities, yet also highlighted "his unbending will, his pride, his severity" and assumed his theology was a version of fatalism.[74] Ecclesiastical developments did not help. The current within the main churches was running forcefully in a high and broad direction, away from Evangelicalism and towards, in the Church of England, a dominant liberal Catholicism. Churchmen often made pronouncements hostile to Calvin and his teaching. Percy Dearmer, the editor of the two most popular Anglican hymn books of the period, asserted in 1924 that Calvinists worshiped a being who was "cruel beyond human words;" C. A. Alington, dean of Durham, published in 1937 an article in a daily newspaper headed "A Doctrine Which Breeds Atheism: Calvin's Travesty of Christianity."[75] Even in Scotland the sense that Calvin had bequeathed an honorable legacy to the nation was fading. The Scottish literary Renaissance around Hugh MacDiarmid regarded Calvinism as a blight on

---

70 Charles Silvester Horne, "Calvin in His Letters," in *Mansfield College Essays* (London: Hodder and Stoughton, 1909), 11, 20, 15.
71 *British Weekly*, 13 May 1909, 129.
72 William B. Selbie, *The Life of Charles Silvester Horne, M.A.* (London: Hodder and Stoughton, 1920).
73 James A. Froude, *Calvinism* (London: Longmans, Green and Co., 1871), 53.
74 John Morley, *Oliver Cromwell* (London: Macmillan and Co., 1900), 48, 51.
75 Quoted in *P&T*, April 1925, 37; July 1937, 74.

the land. Thus in 1933 Eric Linklater, a prolific author in this circle, declared in a radio broadcast that Scotland was "still crippled by Calvinism."[76] One of the most striking instances of this entrenched anti-Calvinism was an episode during the First World War. In March 1918, during the German offensive in northern France, Maurice Bowra, later to be a celebrated warden of Wadham College, Oxford, but then a callow artillery officer of nineteen, found himself on a hill above Noyon, where the enemy had occupied the cathedral. At first he felt qualms about firing on a historic building, but then he remembered that Noyon was the birthplace of Calvin. He immediately opened fire, feeling that "nothing could be too bad, even after some four centuries, for this enemy of the human race."[77] With this sort of prejudice entrenched in the intellectual elite, twentieth-century defenders of Calvin had an uphill task.

Within Evangelicalism the earlier twentieth century was marked by a continuation of the earlier trend towards a more liberal theology. Mainstream churches were broadening the bounds of permissible doctrine, welcoming critical study of the Bible and forgetting the terrors of hell. The effects on the appreciation of Calvin were twofold. On the one hand he could be recast in a new image that molded him in accordance with the spirit of the age. Thus Hugh Reyburn, a young Scottish Presbyterian minister who was willing to approach a doctrine of universal salvation, published a full life of Calvin in 1914 that recognized the importance of the *Institutes* but in the end supposed that predestination should be seen only as an expression of evolution. "Darwin," he wrote in his last sentence, "unites with Calvin to guide us."[78] On the other hand Calvin could be seen as superseded. "The dogmatism of the sixteenth century," declared a lady member of the council of the Presbyterian Historical Society of England, "has been largely modified."[79] Hence, she contended, religious questions were no longer approached in the manner of Calvin's day. Where such attitudes prevailed, the Reformer was largely ignored. Emile Doumergue's seven-volume biography of Calvin, published in French between 1899 and 1927, was not translated into English at all. An essay on Calvin by Doumergue was translated in 1909, but it appeared in New York, not London.[80] When the

---

76 Quoted in *P&T*, January 1934, 13.
77 Cecil Maurice Bowra, *Memories, 1898–1939* (London: Weidenfeld and Nicolson, 1966), 83.
78 Hugh Y. Reyburn, *John Calvin: His Life, Letters and Work* (London: Hodder & Stoughton, 1914), 369, 39, 371.
79 Mrs W. W. D. Campbell, "Early English Presbyterianism and the Reformed Church of France," *Journal of the Presbyterian Historical Society of England* 2 (1922), 133.
80 Emile Doumergue et al., *Calvin and the Reformation: Four Studies* (New York: Fleming H. Revell Co., 1909).

home of the Reformer was rebuilt after the wartime bombardment of Noyon, the United States gave nearly 10,000 francs and France almost 34,000. By contrast Scotland gave only some 1,330 francs, together with a few pounds, and England gave as little as 140 francs and a handful of pounds.[81] The memory of the Reformer was not salient in Britain among the most likely donors, people who had embraced a liberal form of Evangelicalism.

There was, however, a conservative reaction against the growth of theological liberalism, rather as in America there was a Fundamentalist backlash against Modernism. In Britain the phenomenon was milder and consequently the polarization was less acute, but it might have been expected that the more conservative would turn to Calvin for inspiration. In general, however, that was not the case. The twin primary theological impulses on the conservative side, the premillennial hope of the imminent return of Jesus to earth and the holiness message of the availability of a higher Christian life, were not conducive to Calvinism. The Keswick movement, which constituted the backbone of conservative Evangelicalism in these years, was the main expression of holiness teaching in Britain, and its platforms welcomed the message of the premillennial advent. It is true that Evan Hopkins, the guarding theologian of Keswick, insisted that its teaching must remain compatible with the core of Reformed doctrine, but the central emphasis on sanctification by faith diverged from traditional Calvinist insistence that growth in grace required struggle.[82] A staunch Calvinist attended the Keswick convention in 1930 solely in order to distribute hundreds of pamphlets entitled *Keswick Teaching—Weighed in the Balance and Found Wanting*.[83] Consequently authentic upholders of Reformed teaching often felt isolated. A student in a Welsh theological college reported that "I am looked down upon because I believe and maintain that Calvin was right." Most of his contemporaries, he said, acknowledged that Calvin was a man of God, but they thought the Reformer too extreme; some supposed that Calvin taught pagan ideas; and even the strongest Fundamentalist in the college would not accept the doctrine of election. His friends gave the student the nickname "Calvin."[84] The prevailing ethos on the conservative wing of Evangelicalism was unfriendly to full-blooded Calvinism.

---

81 "Dons reçus de 1923 à 1929 pour la maison de Calvin et la musée Calvin à Noyon," *Bulletin de la Société de l'Histoire du Protestantisme Français* 79 (1930), 352. I am grateful to Sébastien Fath for this reference.
82 David W. Bebbington, *Holiness in Nineteenth-Century England* (Carlisle: Paternoster Press, 2000), chap. 4. See also 1:10: "Holiness in the Evangelical Tradition."
83 *P&T*, October 1930, 74.
84 *P&T*, January 1929, 14.

Calvin Revivals

There was nevertheless a small organization in interwar Britain that championed the Calvinist cause, the Sovereign Grace Union. Its beleaguered mentality is brought out by its aims: "to reaffirm the old truths in these days of apostacy [sic] and declension" and "to raise a Testimony against Romanism, Ritualism, Rationalism, Arminianism and other evils in religion."[85] The energetic general secretary from the foundation of the Union in 1914 down to 1931 was Henry Atherton, minister of Grove Chapel, Camberwell, an independent congregation in south London, but its main support came from Strict Baptists and the most conservative of Anglican churches. Much of its activity consisted in holding lectures up and down the country, often on historical themes. It might be expected that Calvin would figure large in the Union's program, but that was not the case. The strong preference was for topics from English history, such as Oliver Cromwell or the Glorious Revolution of 1688. A sixpenny tract on the life of Calvin written by Thomas Lawson, the anti-Catholic biographer of the Reformer in the previous century, was on sale by the Union in 1918 but soon went out of print and was not reissued.[86] In a lecture on "The Invincible Reformation" of 1923, Atherton talked in general terms about Calvin's theological priorities, but the purpose of the speech is apparent from its description as "a stirring Protestant address."[87] The Sovereign Grace Union was part of the network of small organizations that existed during the period to denounce Rome and resist the advance of Anglo-Catholicism in the Church of England. They complained that ritualist clergy were imitating Roman Catholic practices such as the reservation of the sacrament and so undermining the Protestant character of the established church. The threat was as much to national identity as to doctrinal rectitude, and so the reaction often had a political edge. Hence the leaders of the Union, including Atherton, were commonly associated with the Orange Order, an organization with Irish roots designed to oppose the public influence of Roman Catholicism.[88] So the Union illustrates that Calvinism still had its chief political expression in anti-Catholicism.

In the 1930s, however, the Sovereign Grace Union changed. It became caught up in a Dutch initiative in 1929 to form an International Calvinistic Federation. Atherton responded, leading a tour of the Netherlands that opened his eyes to the possibilities of a Calvinist culture. He was amazed by the numbers flocking to the congregations of the *Gereformeerde Kerken* (Rere-

---

85 *P&T*, January 1937, x.
86 *P&T*, January 1918, 16.
87 *P&T*, July 1923, 28.
88 *P&T*, January 1928, 9.

formed Churches) and by the power of the Calvinist political party founded by Abraham Kuyper. Burgomasters were not ashamed to be called Calvinists and "even on a crowded railway station would not hesitate to speak quite openly of the doctrines of Free Grace."[89] Atherton went on to organize an international Calvinist conference in London in May 1932 with representatives from the Netherlands, Germany, France, Ireland and South Africa.[90] Several, such as the French Calvin scholar and right-wing activist August Lecerf, were men of weight, and the international federation founded in 1932 was to prove a significant body. Its second conference, held in Amsterdam two years later, attracted the Dutch Prime Minister, Hendrik Colijn, and the third and fourth, in Geneva in 1936 and Edinburgh in 1938, offered a variety of capable papers. The effects on British Calvinism, as represented by the Sovereign Grace Union, were striking. Calvin himself came into much greater prominence. It was symptomatic that a small Calvin plaque designed in the Netherlands for home display was put on sale.[91] In 1936 the Union advertised an edition of Calvin's sermons published in Germany.[92] At the same time the standard of scholarship in the Union rose sharply. Its magazine editor, S. Leigh Hunt, who had once been a candidate for the Catholic priesthood, published perceptive articles on Calvin and Calvinism, eventually acknowledging in this staunch anti-Catholic periodical the Reformer's honor for the Virgin Mary.[93] Scottish churchmen were drawn in to give solid papers on dogmatics, ecclesiology and even economics.[94] Calvinism was now seen, in Kuyperian fashion, as a worldview and not just a theology. Kuyper's Stone Lectures of 1900, previously little known in Britain, were circulated.[95] Consequently there was some embryonic formulation of Calvinist political principles, leading, for example, in the magazine to an incidental repudiation of pacifism at the height of its popularity in Britain.[96] In the 1930s a section of British Calvinism was drawn into the international Calvin revival.

The fullest exponent of the political theory of this phase was Donald Maclean, professor of church history for the Free Church of Scotland and

---

89 *P&T*, October 1929, 84.
90 *The Reformed Faith Commonly Called Calvinism: Report of the International Conference Held in May, 1932* (London: Sovereign Grace Union, 1932), 6.
91 *P&T*, October 1931, 67.
92 *P&T*, October 1936, vi.
93 *P&T*, March 1947, 28.
94 E.g., at the Edinburgh 1938 conference: Alexander Ross, G. T. Thomson and J. H. S. Burleigh, *P&T*, July 1938, 100–1.
95 *P&T*, July 1933, 3; April 1929, 39.
96 *P&T*, January 1936, 35.

president of the Sovereign Grace Union from 1935.[97] Maclean often represented the Free Church at the General Synods of the *Gereformeerde Kerken* in the Netherlands, developing an admiration for the achievements of their members in public life.[98] In 1927 he was invited to give the first series of Calvin Lectures at the Free University of Amsterdam on aspects of Scottish church history. "Calvin," he contended, "without ever setting foot on Scottish soil, contributed more than any other person to the formation of Scottish character."[99] Maclean set out the political implications of this thesis in a related set of lectures at the Free Church College later in the year. Sovereignty on Calvin's principles, he insisted, derives from the Almighty. The king therefore receives authority from above, but the people, who are his equals as priests before God, can challenge his commands whenever he promotes ungodliness or tyranny. In those circumstances the monarch rather than the people is the revolutionary agent, subverting true principles of civil government. Hence, unlike the French Revolution, the Glorious Revolution of 1688 against a Catholic tyrant in Britain was a legitimate conservative response by the people. Scotland was as opposed as Kuyper's Dutch Anti-Revolutionary Party to "mob rule, violent revolt and uncontrollable anarchy."[100] Nine years later, in 1938, Maclean elaborated his theme, applying it to contemporary circumstances. The continent had been torn by irrational revolutions and the dictators who behaved like the absolutist rulers of seventeenth-century Scotland had to be resisted. The remedy was to be found in the revival of the Reformed faith and its application, on the Dutch model, to all departments of life.[101] As the editor of the *Evangelical Quarterly*, a journal circulating in Reformed circles worldwide, Maclean was already trying to propagate that vision. The Second World War, however, extinguished it. Maclean died before the war was over and he had no successor as an intellectual intermediary between the Netherlands and his own land. Maclean's was the most remarkable expression of political Calvinism in Britain during the twentieth century.

---

97   *P&T*, January 1935, 3.
98   George N. M. Collins, *Donald Maclean, D.D.* (Edinburgh: Lindsay & Co., 1944), 73; *Monthly Record of the Free Church of Scotland*, November 1928, 270.
99   Donald Maclean, *Aspects of Scottish Church History* (Edinburgh: T&T Clark, 1927), 29.
100 Donald Maclean, "Influence of Calvinism on Scottish Politics," *Monthly Record of the Free Church of Scotland*, December 1927, 291, 292; March 1929, 64; April 1929, 85, 87. I am grateful to Ken Roxburgh for drawing my attention to this source.
101 Donald M. Maclean, *The Revival of the Reformed Faith* (London: InterVarsity Fellowship, 1938), 6, 13–14.

There was nevertheless a very different instance of the application of Calvinism to public affairs in the interwar years. The two major Presbyterian churches of Scotland wished to merge, but there was a problem because, though they shared allegiance to the same confessional documents, they had different relationships to the state. The Church of Scotland was the established church of the nation, enjoying privileges and responsibilities in areas such as the justice system; the United Free Church, on the other hand, had no such involvement, and some of its members were opposed in principle to the state connection. The resolution of the difficulty was found in an appeal to the principle of "spiritual independence." The notion meant that the church and the state should give recognition and assistance to each other, but that the church should remain immune to state interference within its own bounds. "Spiritual independence" arose chiefly from the debates preceding the Disruption of the nineteenth century, but it was read back into earlier Scottish history and, to clinch the case, attributed to Calvin himself. Thus Alexander Smellie, in an able study of the Reformation in 1925, claimed that Calvin espoused the principle in opposition to the Erastians among the magistrates of Geneva. The Reformer's attitude to church and state, according to Smellie, was that "each has its sphere and each is under obligation to Christ."[102] David Cairns, principal of the United Free Church College at Aberdeen, writing in the same year, argued that Calvin endorsed the Old Testament view that nations are responsible to God. The Reformer was notably original, however, in drawing from the New Testament the principle of spiritual independence. That perception, according to Cairns, allowed a blending of national religion and ecclesiastical freedom.[103] The "articles declaratory" of a united Scottish church, formulated in 1921 and embodied in legislation in 1929, followed this pattern.[104] The principle of spiritual independence, allegedly derived from Calvin, was incorporated in the constitutional arrangements of Great Britain.

There were comparable efforts to appropriate Calvin for other causes. During the earlier years of the century some depicted the Reformer as a church leader who wanted to relate the Christian faith to social questions. "Calvin," declared a bold English Presbyterian minister in 1930, "was an exponent of

---

102 Alexander Smellie, *The Reformation in Its Literature* (London: Andrew Melrose, 1925), 186.
103 David S. Cairns, *Life and Times of Alexander Robertson MacEwan, D.D.* (London: Hodder & Stoughton, 1925), 167.
104 Douglas Murray, *Freedom to Reform: The "Articles Declaratory" of the Church of Scotland, 1921* (Edinburgh: T&T Clark, 1993), 144.

what to-day is sometimes called the 'social Gospel.'"[105] When, in the 1930s, however, there was a reaction against dwelling on the social implications of the faith, Calvin was represented as an opponent of this approach. In 1938 G. T. Thomson of Edinburgh condemned the social gospel as a handicap to effective Protestantism and saw Calvinism as standing instead for "true doctrine."[106] In a similar way the role of Calvin was a factor in contemporary economic debate. Arthur Dakin, president of Bristol Baptist College, argued in a scholarly study of Calvinism published just after the opening of the Second World War that the Reformer had stood for self-denial, hard work and private property. Dakin was less sure that Calvin's sanction extended to capitalism, at least in its recent forms.[107] Others were even more wary of making this connection. In the atmosphere of the period, when staple industries were collapsing and the Labour Party was mounting a powerful critique of traditional free enterprise, it seemed unwise to bind Calvinism to the contemporary economic system. When Dean Inge, a right-wing clergyman outside the ranks of Evangelicalism, claimed in 1924 that "John Calvin is the spiritual father of the modern business man," the journal of the Sovereign Grace Union tried to distance the Reformer from modern industrial conditions.[108] There was similar reserve over the contention of the German sociologist Max Weber that Calvinism had been responsible for the emergence of capitalism. In 1927 Donald Maclean used the recent research of the historian R. H. Tawney to show that Weber's case was one-sided.[109] Similarly in 1938 the Scottish church historian J. H. S. Burleigh spent the whole of his paper on "Calvinism and Economics" at the Calvinist congress in Edinburgh arguing that capitalism was older than the Reformation and so Calvinism could not have generated its defects.[110] In an ideological age there was often more effort to secure praise or avoid blame for Calvin than to discover his actual views.

There also developed a powerful association between Calvin and modern liberal democracy. This attitude was shared by all who looked on Calvin with any degree of sympathy. C. H. Irwin ended his biography of 1909 with the rhetorical claim, not based on previous reasoning, that to the nations influenced by the Reformer's teaching it had brought "the priceless boon of civil

---

105 F. J. Smithers in *Journal of the Presbyterian Church of England* 4 (1930), 183.
106 *P&T*, July 1938, 101.
107 Arthur Dakin, *Calvinism* (London: Duckworth, 1940), 211–12, 223–29.
108 *P&T*, April 1925, 34–35, quoted at 34.
109 Maclean, *Aspects*, 113–14.
110 *P&T*, July 1938, 101.

and religious liberty."[111] The conclusion was the more surprising since Irwin had earlier admitted that Calvin's civil legislation at Geneva had overlooked individual liberty and had spent a chapter wrestling with perennial problem of the Reformer's responsibility for the execution of Servetus.[112] The claim was therefore based not on Calvin's life but on his legacy. The common perception of his subsequent influence was summarized in the following year by James Orr, a prolific theologian of the United Free Church, in an article on "Calvinism" in the widely used *Encyclopaedia of Religion and Ethics* edited by James Hastings. Calvin's system, he declared, "became the soul of Puritanism in England, of Republicanism in Holland, of the Covenanting struggle in Scotland, of democratic institutions in America, identifying itself in every land to which it went with the undying principles of civil freedom."[113] The movements he named had all championed liberty in their nation-building efforts. Calvin himself had to be twisted in the popular memory to fit this paradigm. Thus A. M. Hunter, a young Scottish minister writing in 1920, conceded that Calvin might be aristocratic in sympathies and autocratic in behavior, but he was "democratic in his fundamental convictions."[114] The democratic credentials of Calvinism became a major theme of the twentieth century. Calvinists, according to Dakin in 1940, had been driven by persecution to more explicitly democratic theories, but the seeds had already been sown in their church order, which was based on "the rights of the individual." The legacy of Calvin could therefore contribute rights, freedom and democracy to "the urgent task of creating a truly Christian civilization" after the Second World War.[115] Calvin was almost a recruit to the war effort.

Even before the Second World War, however, the theological climate had begun to change. Two movements in the mainstream British churches shifted thinking towards still greater sympathy for Calvin. The first was the electrifying message of Karl Barth about the radical transcendence of God, which was initially articulated in Britain in 1930 by J. E. Daniel, a young Welsh Independent theologian.[116] By 1938 Maclean was able to note that several theological

---

111 Irwin, *Calvin*, 197.
112 Irwin, *Calvin*, 142, chap. xi.
113 James Orr, "Calvinism," in *Encyclopaedia of Religion and Ethics*, ed. James Hastings, 12 vols. (Edinburgh: T&T Clark, 1910), 3:148.
114 Adam M. Hunter, *The Teaching of Calvin: A Modern Interpretation* (Glasgow: Maclehose, Jackson and Co., 1920), 3.
115 Dakin, *Calvinism*, 235–36.
116 Dafydd Densil Morgan, *The Span of the Cross: Christian Religion and Society in Wales, 1914–2000* (Cardiff: University of Wales Press, 1999), 203–4.

chairs in Scottish universities were occupied by Barthians.[117] The central figure was Thomas Torrance, a professor at Edinburgh only from 1950 but, having personally studied under Barth, already a force in Scottish theology a decade earlier.[118] Torrance believed that Calvinism had been damaged by hardening into a system, and so turned attention back to the Reformer himself: "in John Calvin the Reformed Church has had a theologian, with magnitude in mind and depth in understanding, second to none in the history of the Christian Church."[119] Torrance took the lead in creating a much warmer Scottish Presbyterian appreciation of Calvin during the later twentieth century. The second movement was a reaction against theological liberalism within Congregationalism that earned the label "Genevan" by its enthusiasm for Calvin. In December 1936, J. S. Whale, president of Cheshunt College, Cambridge, delivered a lecture on the Reformer praising his personal religion, "rooted in faith in divine sovereignty and predestinating grace."[120] In the following month, Nathaniel Micklem, principal of Mansfield College, Oxford, published an article on "The Genevan Inheritance of Protestant Dissent—The Present Need to Affirm It."[121] This was a movement of intellectuals swayed by the Anglican ethos of the ancient English universities. Their assertion was that Calvin was an embodiment of Catholic tradition. Whale's *Christian Doctrine* (1941) called the Reformer "the Cyprian of the XVIth century;" Micklem pointed out that his *Institutes* was a commentary on the Apostles' Creed.[122] The next generation of Congregational ministers was deeply swayed by this higher estimate of Calvin. The turn away from a broader theology in circles where liberal Evangelicalism had prevailed meant that in the postwar era Calvin was restored to a place among the great theologians.

The most resolutely Calvinist movement, however, was among conservative Evangelicals. The pivotal figure was Martyn Lloyd-Jones, a Welsh Calvinistic Methodist who, partly under the influence of Donald Maclean, gradually came to adopt an explicitly Reformed theology. From 1938 Lloyd-Jones was assistant and from 1943 the minister at Westminster Chapel, where he exercised a powerful preaching ministry at the heart of London. Although he was

---

117 Maclean, *Revival*, 9–10.
118 Alister E. McGrath, *T. F. Torrance: An Intellectual Biography* (Edinburgh: T&T Clark, 1999).
119 Thomas F. Torrance, *Calvin's Doctrine of Man* (London: Lutterworth Press, 1949), 8.
120 *P&T*, January 1937, 3.
121 Nathaniel Micklem, "The Genevan Inheritance of Protestant Dissent—The Present Need to Affirm It," *Hibbert Journal* 35 (1937), 193–204.
122 Quoted from John S. Whale, *Christian Doctrine* (1941) in *P&T*, January 1943, 15; Micklem, "Genevan Inheritance," 200.

aware of continental forms of Calvinism, attending in 1948 a conference in Amsterdam on "Calvin and the Modern Mind,"[123] his own style was molded by the Puritans of England and Wales. Lloyd-Jones praised Calvin as a preacher and arranged for the republication of the *Institutes*,[124] but his ambition was to use Puritan teaching to kindle a fresh revival such as the one that had swept Wales in the eighteenth century. Calvinism must not degenerate into dry doctrinal teaching divorced from Christian experience or remote from the text of scripture. "Calvin's main feature," Lloyd-Jones wrote, "is that he bases everything on the Bible."[125] From 1950 the Welshman presided at an annual Puritan Conference at his chapel that grew by the 1960s into a gathering of some 350, mostly of a younger generation.[126] It was the focus of a developing resurgence of Calvinist teaching in British Evangelicalism. There were also an Evangelical Library designed to sow "the seeds of a fresh Awakening to-day,"[127] the *Banner of Truth* magazine founded in 1955 by Lloyd-Jones' assistant at Westminster Chapel, Iain Murray, together with its associated publishing house, the Banner of Truth Trust,[128] and the predominantly Calvinistic Evangelical Movement of Wales, first launched in 1948.[129] The organizer of the Puritan conferences was J. I. Packer, a young Anglican who was to become an influential theologian. In 1964, the four hundredth anniversary of Calvin's death, Packer arranged that the papers should be devoted to aspects of the Reformer. In a highly accessible account of Calvin's significance for the times, Packer suggested that the integrating concept of his theology was the "Knowledge of God."[130] Packer was to choose "Knowing God" as the title of a subsequent book that was to prove one of the most popular texts in global Evangelicalism.[131] The Calvinistic revival associated with Lloyd-Jones and Packer was one with wide appeal.

---

123 *P&T*, July 1948, 76.
124 David Martyn Lloyd-Jones, *The Puritans: Their Origins and Successors* (Edinburgh: Banner of Truth Trust, 1987), 379; Iain H. Murray, *David Martyn Lloyd-Jones: The Fight of Faith, 1939–1981* (Edinburgh: Banner of Truth Trust, 1990), 194.
125 Martyn Lloyd-Jones, *Knowing the Times*, 35, quoted in Murray, *Lloyd-Jones*, 195.
126 *Church of England Newspaper*, 4 January 1963, 3.
127 Geoffrey Williams, "The Revival of Nations. Flames Worth Fanning," *Cylchgrawn Cymdeithas Hanes y Methodistiad Calfinaidd* [Journal of the Calvinistic Methodist Historical Society of Wales], June 1943, 70.
128 "Introduction," in Lloyd-Jones, *Puritans*, ix.
129 Noel Gibbard, *The First Fifty Years: The History of the Evangelical Movement of Wales, 1948–98* (Bridgend: Bryntirion Press, 2002).
130 James I. Packer, "Calvin: A Servant of the Word," in *Able Ministers of the New Testament: Papers Read at the Puritan and Reformed Studies Conference, December 1964* (London: Evangelical Magazine, 1965), 36–55, at 44.
131 James I. Packer, *Knowing God* (London: Hodder and Stoughton, 1973).

The Later Twentieth Century

The resurgence of Calvinist teaching was initially concerned with churchly issues, but in due course it also became associated with Christian sociopolitical engagement. In the era when conservative Evangelicalism had been dominated by the Keswick message of holiness, withdrawal from the world to preserve the believer's purity had been a common theme. When, however, in the 1960s the Keswick hegemony waned, there was a fresh impetus towards involvement with the problems of the world. The seedbed for the change was the InterVarsity Fellowship (IVF) of Christian Unions, a network of conservative Evangelical societies in the universities and colleges of Britain. One of the figures most active in the IVF, Fred Catherwood, who was a son-in-law of Martyn Lloyd-Jones, published in 1964 *The Christian in Industrial Society*, a pioneering discussion of the weekday responsibilities of the contemporary believer. While not directly appealing to Calvin, the book was undergirded by a Reformed theology and showed great respect for the "Protestant ethic."[132] The general secretary of the IVF, Oliver Barclay, who tried to read through the *Institutes* annually, published in 1970 an appeal for Christians to claim the world as God's.[133] The authoritative Evangelical perspective on social questions emerged in 1984 in *Issues Facing Christians Today* by John Stott, the most prominent leader of Evangelical Anglicans in England: "[N]ow we are convinced," he explained, "that God has given us social as well as evangelistic responsibilities in his world."[134] Stott did not parade a Calvinist allegiance, but others were more prepared to avow a Reformed stance. Alan Storkey, a sociologist who in 1969 launched the Shaftesbury Project on the fringe of the IVF in order to encourage Christian social thought and action, was influenced by the Dutch Reformed thinking of Herman Dooyeweerd.[135] There was a Christian Studies Unit dedicated to the propagation of the perspective of Kuyper and Dooyeweerd.[136] Storkey stood several times as a parliamentary candidate for a Christian party, but the influence of these developments on public affairs was generally through more established channels. Catherwood, for instance, became a Member of Parliament and then Member of the European Parlia-

---

132 Henry Frederick R. Catherwood, *The Christian in Industrial Society* (London: Tyndale Press, 1964), 6, appendix.
133 A. N. Triton [Oliver Barclay], *Whose World?* (London: InterVarsity Press, 1970).
134 John Stott, *Issues Facing Christians Today* (Basingstoke: Marshalls, 1984), xi.
135 Alan Storkey, *A Christian Social Perspective* (Leicester: InterVarsity Press, 1979), 133–34.
136 "CSU Booklist," typescript (n.p., 1984).

ment as a Conservative.[137] But Evangelicals, let alone the Calvinists among them, did not become a significant force in political life. Evangelicalism itself was transformed far more than British politics.

Meanwhile in the later twentieth century Evangelical scholarship on Calvin showed a broader appreciation of his role. With the relaxation of interconfessional tension in the wake of the Second Vatican Council, Calvin was no longer seen primarily as a standard-bearer of Protestantism. T. H. L. Parker, an Anglican clergyman close to the Evangelical party who had been introduced to the study of Calvin by J. S. Whale,[138] wrote a series of studies on the Reformer between 1947 and 1995, including a new standard biography in 1975. Calvin, he contended, was not just a Reformer but also a doctor of the universal church.[139] Likewise Paul Helm, an academic philosopher of Reformed convictions, depicted Calvin's mind from an article of 1984 onwards as strongly formed by late medieval theology.[140] The theologian Alister McGrath also insisted in 1987 on Calvin's "remarkable continuity with the leading features of academic Augustinianism characteristic of the late mediaeval period."[141] There no longer seemed a need to stress the break of the Reformation. The old role of Calvin as a sanction for anti-Catholic political campaigning had disappeared. Instead Calvin was depicted more neutrally, by Parker, for instance, as a conservative whose ideas were turned into revolutionary channels.[142] The anti-Catholic Calvin had been deployed in order to reinforce a Protestant national identity, but from the 1960s that, too, had vanished.[143] Calvin was therefore disengaged from his role in molding individuals in the British past. In a life of Calvin published in 1990, McGrath presented the Reformer with academic detachment but as a major figure in the history of the world. In an extensive discussion of the Weber thesis, McGrath, while inconclusive, leans towards seeing Calvinism as favoring capitalism. There was no longer, after a decade

---

137 "The Papers of Sir Frederick Catherwood," http://janus.lib.cam.ac.uk/db/node.xsp?id=EAD%2FGBR%2F0014%2FCATH, accessed 18 May 2009.
138 Thomas H. L. Parker, *The Oracles of God: An Introduction to the Preaching of John Calvin* (London: Lutterworth Press, 1947), 11.
139 Thomas H. L. Parker, *John Calvin: A Biography* (London: J. M. Dent & Sons, 1975), vi, xi.
140 Paul Helm, "Calvin and Natural Law," *Scottish Bulletin of Evangelical Theology* 2 (1984), 5–22; *John Calvin's Ideas* (Oxford: Oxford University Press, 2004), vii, 1–9.
141 Alister McGrath, *The Intellectual Origins of the European Reformation* (Oxford: Blackwell, 1987), 107.
142 Parker, *Calvin*, xi.
143 Callum G. Brown, *The Death of Christian Britain: Understanding Secularisation, 1800–1900* (London: Routledge, 2000), chap. 8.

of the ascendancy of free market principles under Mrs Thatcher, any reason to deny the connection for apologetic reasons. But McGrath makes greater claims, considering Calvinism to have promoted artistic creativity and scientific research as well as human rights: "If any religious movement of the sixteenth century was world-affirming, it was Calvinism."[144] Calvin was no longer seen through the prism of earlier British history, but as a shaper of the whole of Western culture.

By the last years of the twentieth century, however, the legacy of Calvin in British life was relatively small. The chief reason was the decline of the churches over the previous century, a process that accelerated from the 1960s. United Kingdom church membership had fallen from roughly 33 percent of the population in 1900 to a mere 12 percent in 2000.[145] Attendance was even worse, with only some 7.5 percent of the population of England and 11 percent of the population of Scotland at worship on a given Sunday at the end of the century. Only approximately a third of the attenders in each country were Evangelicals.[146] In England no survey identified the proportion who were Calvinists, but in Scotland about a third of the Evangelicals attended congregations that described themselves as "Reformed."[147] Only a tiny proportion, therefore, looked to the tradition stemming from Calvin for their Christian sustenance. Nevertheless the tradition had not been extinguished. On two occasions, in 1968 and 1983, the Church of Scotland had declined to alter its formal adhesion to the confessional statements of the Westminster Assembly.[148] Some ministers of the Scottish Church, such as James Philip of Holyrood Abbey Church, were distinguished exponents of Reformed teaching.[149] In Wales the Evangelical Movement guarded its inheritance from Martyn Lloyd-Jones while in England several smaller denominations such as the Grace Baptists cherished a Calvinist position. In the Church of England a movement called Reform, begun in 1993, aimed to make the institutions of the established church more suited to

---

144 Alister E. McGrath, *A Life of John Calvin: A Study in the Shaping of Western Culture* (Oxford: Blackwell, 1990), chaps 11, 12, quoted at 219.
145 *UK Christian Handbook Religious Trends No. 2*, ed. Peter Brierley (London: Christian Research, 1999), 8, 17.
146 Peter Brierley, *The Tide Is Running Out: What the English Church Attendance Survey Reveals* (London: Christian Research, 2000), 27; Peter Brierley, *Turning the Tide: The Challenge Ahead* (London: Christian Research, 2003), 15, 65; *UK Christian Handbook Religious Trends No. 2*, ed. Brierley, 12.3.
147 Brierley, *Turning the Tide*, 66.
148 Murray, *Freedom to Reform*, chap. 6.
149 https://www.scotsman.com/news/obituaries/james-philip-2444034, accessed 19 May 2009.

effective evangelism. It was rarely assertive about Calvinism, but its corporate allegiance was to the theological position of J. I. Packer.[150] One of its most vigorous congregations, Jesmond Parish Church in Newcastle-upon-Tyne, was associated with a Christian Institute designed to exert "Christian influence in a secular world" by briefing its supporters nationwide on public issues.[151] Political action, however, was not the aim of any of these Calvinist groupings, which saw the defense and propagation of the faith as their priorities. As in earlier periods, the political impact of Calvinism was marginal.

Conclusion

The memory of John Calvin among British Evangelicals was not, therefore, as potent a force as might be imagined. In the nineteenth century his image was dimmed by a form of moderate Calvinism, by the tendency of British Evangelicals to prefer their own heroes and by his total repudiation in many quarters. The advance of theological liberalism arising from the Enlightenment and from Romanticism pushed Calvin further into the background. Only around mid-century was there a temporary upsurge of interest in the Reformer. His political potential was limited by his reputation for intolerant policies and his identification with republican revolution. Consequently in general he did not function as an inspiration for political movements, the one significant exception being the fervent anti-Catholicism that ran through much of British life. In both centuries it was in Scotland, with its Presbyterian dominance, that Calvin loomed largest, being invoked by the early Free Church of Scotland, by all the Presbyterians in 1909, by Donald Maclean in the interwar years and by the architects of the Scottish settlement between church and state in 1929. Despite Silvester Horne's advocacy, an aversion to Calvin was widespread during the twentieth century and in general neither liberal nor conservative Evangelicals were attracted to him. The Sovereign Grace Union, however, rose from obscurity in the 1920s to become a partner in the international Calvin revival of the 1930s. In these years Calvin was appropriated for various sociopolitical causes, especially the defense of liberal democracy against dictatorship. The endorsement of Calvin by Barthians and Genevans from the 1930s gave him more favorable treatment, but most crucial was the adoption of his teaching by Martyn Lloyd-Jones, J. I. Packer and their circle, a recovery that gave rise to a number of sociopolitical ripples in the 1960s and afterwards. Scholarship on Calvin no longer saw him as a patron for anti-Catholic campaigns but as

---

150 http://www.reform.org.uk/pages/covenant/intro.php, accessed 19 May 2009.
151 Alan Munden, *A Light in a Dark Place: Jesmond Parish Church, Newcastle upon Tyne* (Newcastle-upon-Tyne: Clayton Publications, 2006), 228–29.

a more significant actor on the world stage. Although in a land of declining church attendance Calvin had a low salience by the end of the century, there were still groups that, while not regarding him as a political example, firmly upheld his theology. That was the prevailing pattern throughout the period. Calvin was not a major personality; his doctrinal position was shared by some but not all Evangelicals; and he inspired relatively little political activity. The situation was therefore very different from that in the Netherlands, Hungary or even the United States, where Calvin came to be treated by a section of the population as a political icon.[152] During the 1909 Calvin celebration in London an English Presbyterian leader, Monro Gibson, remarked that many thought of the Reformer as "a somewhat unlettered and bigoted Scotsman."[153] The remark, though made in jest, illustrates the distance between most Evangelicals in Britain and an understanding of John Calvin.

---

152 *Sober, Strict and Scriptural*, ed. De Niet, Paul and Wallet, 11, 14.
153 *British Weekly*, 13 May 1909, 129.

13

The Evangelical Discovery of History

"From some modern perspectives," wrote James Belich, a leading historian of New Zealand, in 1996, "the evangelicals are hard to like. They dressed like crows; seemed joyless, humourless and sometimes hypocritical; [and] they embalmed the evidence poor historians need to read in tedious preaching."[1] Similar views have often been expressed in the historiography of Evangelical Protestantism, the subject of this chapter.[2] It covers such disapproving appraisals of the Evangelical past, but also, because a high proportion of the writing about the movement was by insiders, it has more to say about studies by Evangelicals of their own history. Evangelicals are taken to be those who placed particular stress on the value of the Bible, the doctrine of the cross, an experience of conversion and a responsibility for activism. They were to be found in the Church of England and its sister provinces of the Anglican communion, forming an Evangelical party that rivaled the High Church and Broad Church tendencies, and also in the denominations that stemmed from Nonconformity in England and Wales and the Protestant churches of Scotland. Evangelicals were strong, often overwhelmingly so, within Methodism and Congregationalism and among the Baptists and the Presbyterians. Some bodies that arose later on, including the (so-called Plymouth) Brethren, the Churches of Christ and the Pentecostals (the last two primarily American

---

1   James Belich, *Making Peoples: A History of the New Zealanders: From Polynesian Settlement to the End of the Nineteenth Century* (Auckland: Penguin, 1996), 35.
2   This paper was originally delivered at the summer conference of the Ecclesiastical History Society in 2011, when the society was considering developments in the historiography of its field over the fifty years of its existence. I am very grateful to Mark Noll for his comments on a draft of the paper and to other friends for discussion of topics in this field.

in origin), joined the Evangelical coalition. These dynamic groupings spread over the parts of the globe inhabited by people of British stock. From the outbreak of the Evangelical Revival in the eighteenth century onwards, they obeyed their own imperative of preaching the gospel. By the second half of the nineteenth century they were culturally dominant in Britain, the United States and other lands of British settlement. Although their ascendancy subsequently decayed in most areas of the British Isles, there was ample compensation in the extension of their influence into many other regions of the world through the missionary movement.[3] Evangelicals also penetrated the European continent, affecting the religious life of most of its countries. Excellent work has been done on some branches of the Evangelical movement on the continent,[4] but this paper concentrates on history written about its adherents in the English-speaking world and the missions it generated. It offers an evaluation of the work written about Evangelicals of all types during the period since the foundation of the Ecclesiastical History Society in 1961.

Around that time Evangelicals were generally averse to history. Many of them suffered from a disinclination to explore the life of the mind, preferring to concentrate on the more pressing task of evangelism.[5] The present, not the past, was the time in which people were converted. The eschatology most favored among conservative Evangelicals, a form of premillennialism, encouraged belief in the imminent return of Christ to earth. If the second advent was likely at any time, scholarly enterprise appeared a waste of energy.[6] Furthermore there was an aspect of the Evangelical worldview that inhibited specifically historical work. The time that mattered was that of the earliest church. The first century provided, through the New Testament, authoritative

---

3   The series "A History of Evangelicalism" is the most convenient source for an overview: Mark A. Noll, *The Rise of Evangelicalism: The Age of Edwards, Whitefield and the Wesleys* (Leicester: InterVarsity Press, 2004); John Wolffe, *The Expansion of Evangelicalism: The Age of Wilberforce, More, Chalmers and Finney* (Nottingham: InterVarsity Press, 2006); David W. Bebbington, *The Dominance of Evangelicalism: The Age of Spurgeon and Moody* (Leicester: InterVarsity Press, 2005); Geoffrey R. Treloar, *The Disruption of Evangelicalism: The Age of Torrey, Mott, McPherson and Hammond* (London: InterVarsity Press, 2016); and Brian Stanley, *The Global Diffusion of Evangelicalism: The Age of Billy Graham and John Stott* (Nottingham: InterVarsity Press, 2013).
4   E.g. Sébastien Fath, *Une autre manière d'être chrétien en France: Socio-histoire de l'implantation baptiste (1810–1950)* (Geneva: Labor et Fides, 2001).
5   Mark A. Noll, *The Scandal of the Evangelical Mind* (Grand Rapids, MI: Eerdmans, 1994).
6   Timothy P. Weber, *Living in the Shadow of the Second Coming: American Premillennialism, 1875–1925* (New York: Oxford University Press, 1979). The same school of thought predominated long after 1925. See 1:8: "The Advent Hope in British Evangelicalism since 1800."

teachings to obey and noble examples to follow. Subsequent Christian generations were notoriously inclined to degeneration and so, for many, were barely worth attention. Consequently when in the 1940s a group of British Evangelicals did create a center for scholarly research, Tyndale House, Cambridge, it concentrated on biblical studies and effectively excluded church history from its purview.[7] Its moving spirit, F. F. Bruce, who was to go on to occupy the Rylands Chair in Biblical Criticism and Exegesis at Manchester from 1959, was exceptional in writing three historical volumes on early Christianity, but even he had declared ten years before that "if Church History teaches one thing more than another, it is that there is a constant tendency to deterioration."[8] History was, if anything, at more of a discount in the United States, where a strident Fundamentalism displaying overt hostility towards the academy had made a far greater impact on the Evangelical world. Although by the 1940s a number of "neo-Evangelicals" were inching their way back towards greater engagement with scholarship, progress was especially slow in the discipline of history. As late as 1982 Mark Noll, a leading American Evangelical historian, was deploring "the generally weak sense of history among most evangelical groups."[9] Even the past of the Evangelical movement itself was alien territory.

Yet over the years beginning in 1961 the situation was transformed. Evangelicals—or at least a growing number of scholars in their ranks—became interested in their own past. Books were published, organizations formed and conferences held. By 1994 Harry S. Stout, professor of history at Yale, could claim that, whereas in the 1970s "evangelicalism was not a field of scholarly inquiry," by 1994, when he was writing, "it certainly has become one."[10] Stout was considering the United States alone, but his comment applied also to Britain, Australia and elsewhere. Although there were important contributions from outside the Evangelical movement, the achievement was largely the fruit of exploration by Evangelicals of their own past. They had made a discovery of history. This chapter examines that process. It considers first the state of the historiography of the Evangelical movement in the years preceding

---

7   Thomas A. Noble, *Research for the Academy and Church: Tyndale House and Fellowship: The First Sixty Years* (Leicester: InterVarsity Press, 2006).
8   Frederick F. Bruce, "Church History and Its Lessons," in *The Church*, ed. Joseph B. Watson (London: Pickering & Inglis, 1949), 178, quoted in Tim Grass, *F. F. Bruce: A Life* (Milton Keynes: Paternoster, 2011), 73.
9   "Proposal for a Planning Grant: An Institute for the Study of American Evangelicalism" (TS, Wheaton, IL, 1982), 1. Copy in archives of the Institute for the Study of American Evangelicals, Billy Graham Center, Wheaton College, Wheaton, IL [hereafter "ISAE"]. I am grateful to Eric Brandt for his assistance with research in these archives.
10 Harry S. Stout to ISAE Advisors, 29 May 1994, ISAE.

the upsurge of interest. Earlier historical work on aspects of the Evangelical world did exist, but much of what was produced was popular and unscholarly. The second theme is the ways in which the existing patterns of writing were changed from the 1960s onwards. The general trend was towards markedly higher standards of scholarship. There will be a discussion of the major innovations in writing about the Evangelical movement over the period. So thirdly there will be assessment of the impact of religious developments on Evangelical historiography. That will be followed by the fourth section of the paper, providing analysis of changes in historical fashion that affected the subject. The overall aim will be to explain the reasons for the growth and character of Evangelical historical studies over the last half-century.

Earlier Evangelical Historiography

In the first place the prevailing model in the study of the Evangelical past before 1961 was denominational history. In Britain history societies had existed within the various Nonconformist bodies since around the opening of the twentieth century. The Baptist Historical Society, for example, had been founded in 1908 for the purpose, among others, of "holding Meetings to Discuss Obscure Points."[11] There was a similar pattern in America, where the equivalent Baptist organization had been formed as long ago as 1853. Methodists, Congregationalists, Presbyterians and even Huguenots possessed their counterparts. Quakers, on the fringe of Evangelical movement, and Unitarians, definitely beyond the fringe, had their own organizations too. The aim of these historical agencies was to defend the principles of their parent bodies. Anglican Evangelicals, though possessing no historical society, fitted the mold by reissuing in 1951 G. R. Balleine's history of the Evangelical party, first published in 1908, with a preface expressing the hope that the book would remain "a vindication of the historic Evangelical tradition in the Church of England."[12] There was therefore a long-standing custom of, as it were, slicing the history of Protestantism longitudinally, by denomination. The rarity of horizontal slicing into different periods meant that the common ground occupied by Evangelicals in the relatively recent past was obscured. Methodists, who owed their existence to the Evangelical Revival, focused their historical interest almost exclusively on John Wesley, with perhaps a side-glance for his brother Charles.

---

11 Circular announcing meeting to establish Baptist Historical Society, April 1908, quoted in Faith Bowers, "Centenary History of the Baptist Historical Society: Part 1: 1908–2008," *Baptist Quarterly*, 42 (2008), 325–39, quoted at 325.

12 George R. Balleine, *A History of the Evangelical Party in the Church of England* (London: Longmans, Green and Co., 1951), v.

Thus the Methodist denominational association was (and is) called the Wesley Historical Society. Consequently, at least down to the 1950s, there was little attention to the decades after Wesley's death in 1791. The chief exceptions were the four groundbreaking but rather uncritical studies of the relationship of Methodism to labor history by the minister Robert Wearmouth published between 1937 and 1957.[13] In America William Warren Sweet, though himself a Methodist minister, deliberately tried to counteract the same dominance of confessional history by refusing to allow his graduate students at the University of Chicago to write dissertations about their own denominations, thereby producing a generation of scholars with a broader vision who flourished in the third quarter of the twentieth century—Robert Handy, Winthrop Hudson, Sidney Mead.[14] Among them there were signs, as in Handy's volume about the United States and Canada in the Oxford History of the Christian Church series, that religious history could be illuminated by treating Evangelicals as a distinct sector.[15] Yet the institutional pattern of higher education in America, whereby most church history was taught and written in seminaries and departments affiliated to specific religious bodies, meant that the subject retained its overwhelmingly confessional stance. History was treated as a branch of denominational apologetics.

Biography was another common feature of Evangelical historical work in the middle years of the twentieth century. The practice of commemorating the recently dead persisted, often generating anecdotal volumes with such titles as *Passion for Souls*.[16] Figures from the remoter past attracted some attention, with Wesley predictably looming large. Wesley was manipulated to fit the preconceptions of his Methodist biographers so that their twentieth-century priorities could bask in the glow of his authority. Thus the most popular American biography of Wesley in the 1950s was written by Francis J. McConnell, a

---

13 Robert F. Wearmouth, *Methodism and the Working-Class Movements of England, 1800–1850* (London: Epworth Press, 1937); *Methodism and the Common People of the Eighteenth Century* (London: Epworth Press, 1945); *Methodism and the Struggle of the Working Classes, 1850–1900* (Leicester: Edgar Backus, 1954); *The Social and Political Influence of Methodism in the Twentieth Century* (London: Epworth Press, 1957).
14 Sidney E. Mead, "Professor Sweet's Religion and Culture in America: A Review Article," *Church History* 32 (1953), 33–49, at 41–42; James L. Ash, Jr, *Protestantism and the American University: An Intellectual Biography of William Warren Sweet* (Dallas, TX: SMU Press, 1982), 103.
15 Robert T. Handy, *A History of the Churches in the United States and Canada* (Oxford: Oxford University Press, 1976).
16 Kenneth Hulbert, *Passion for Souls: The Story of Charles H. Hulbert, Methodist Missioner* (London: Epworth Press, 1959).

bishop in the Methodist Episcopal Church whose mind had been molded by the school of philosophy sometimes labeled "personalism." Accordingly Wesley is described as having been "profoundly interested in human values" and eager for the "release of higher human possibilities."[17] Even when historical work aspired to higher scholarly standards, it was often cast in biographical form. The most telling study of Anglican Evangelicalism published around mid-century, though not presented as a biography, illustrates the point. G. C. B. Davies' book *The Early Cornish Evangelicals* (1951), despite its title, was almost exclusively concerned with Samuel Walker of Truro.[18] There were symptoms of change, for there was already the start of a tendency to examine the theology of Wesley in its intellectual context. Harald Lindström's *Wesley and Sanctification* (1946), though concentrating again on the single individual, is an early instance of a series of fruitful studies of the thought of the founder of Methodism.[19] When L. E. Elliott-Binns, a broad-minded Evangelical clergyman who had also written on Erasmus and Innocent III, published in 1953 an account of the eighteenth-century revival, he expressed dismay that his source biographies were often "the works of pious admirers, lacking in critical ability and with no apparent desire to verify their statements."[20] He was not going to add to their number, but his scrupulosity was unusual. Biography, often tending to hagiography, remained a living genre among Evangelicals.

That was true of a specific department of Evangelical historical writing, missionary studies. Biographies depicting the heroic deeds of their pioneering subjects were almost as much the norm in the middle of the twentieth century as they had been in the middle of the nineteenth. In 1947 A. G. Pouncy published an account of the career of Henry Martyn, the scholar who left Cambridge at the opening of the nineteenth century in order to blaze a gospel trail into Iran. An Evangelical publisher issued it with the subtitle "The First Modern Apostle to the Mohammedan."[21] Complementing the biographies were institutional histories published by the various agencies, denominational and undenominational. The Bible Churchmen's Missionary Society, for example, published a record, again in 1947, of its first quarter century. The tone

17 Francis J. McConnell, *John Wesley* (New York: Abingdon Press, 1939), 310, quoted in Richard P. Heitzenrater, *The Elusive Mr. Wesley*, 2 vols. (Nashville: Abingdon Press, 1984), 2:203.
18 George C. B. Davies, *The Early Cornish Evangelicals, 1735–60* (London: SPCK, 1951).
19 Harald Lindström, *Wesley and Sanctification* (London: Epworth Press, 1946).
20 Leonard E. Elliott-Binns, *The Early Evangelicals: A Religious and Social Study* (London: Lutterworth Press, 1953), 5.
21 Anthony G. Pouncy, *Henry Martyn, 1781–1812: The First Modern Apostle to the Mohammedan* (London: Church Book Room Press, 1947).

of the book can be gauged from the foreword's explanation that the society's missionaries were eager to "get to grips with the devil in the strongholds of paganism by unsheathing therein the sword of the Spirit."[22] Although the book did include descriptions of setbacks, it was primarily a story of successive triumphs designed to foster further support for the society. The one major work that broke out of the constrictions of missionary advocacy was Kenneth Scott Latourette's magisterial *History of the Expansion of Christianity* (1937-47). Latourette, a Baptist minister on the faculty of Yale Divinity School, discussed the advance of the faith over its two thousand years in seven volumes, allocating the sixth to the nineteenth century and the seventh to the twentieth century.[23] His expertise in Chinese history ensured that he treated missions in the context of their host cultures far more than his contemporaries. In general, however, the history of the worldwide spread of Evangelical religion remained an intellectual backwater.

The place of Evangelicalism in mainstream historiography was marginal, particularly in Britain. It is true that the Evangelical Revival claimed a place in British textbooks just as the Great Awakening was discussed in their American equivalents. G. M. Young, a fellow of All Souls College, Oxford, also gave weight to the formative influence of Evangelical religion over Victorian England in his luminous study, *Portrait of an Age* (1936). A boy born in 1810, he pointed out on his opening page, "found himself at every turn controlled, and animated, by the imponderable pressure of the Evangelical discipline."[24] It became conventional to acknowledge the role of Evangelical faith in the temper of the era. A postwar collection of B.B.C. talks on the Victorian age included two, by Charles Smyth of Cambridge and Gordon Rupp, later of the same university, on the Anglican and Nonconformist varieties of Evangelicalism.[25] Acknowledgment, however, did not lead on to analysis. In the 1950s the Victorian era, still languishing under a shadow of sneering disapproval, was accorded only limited academic scrutiny. The place of Evangelicals in nineteenth-century Britain remained shrouded in obscurity, with few apart

---

22 Daniel H. C. Bartlett, "Foreword," in Walter S. Hooton and J. Stafford Wright, *The First Twenty-Five Years of the Bible Churchmen's Missionary Society (1922-47)* (London: Bible Churchmen's Missionary Society, 1947), ix.
23 Kenneth S. Latourette, *A History of the Expansion of Christianity*, 7 vols. (New York: Harper and Bros, 1937-47).
24 George M. Young, *Victorian England: Portrait of an Age*, 2nd ed. (London: Oxford University Press, 1957), 1.
25 Charles Smyth, "The Evangelical Discipline," and Gordon Rupp, "Evangelicalism of the Nonconformists," in *Ideas and Beliefs of the Victorians* (London: Sylvan Press, 1949), 97-104, 105-12.

from Lord Shaftesbury receiving attention.[26] The twentieth century, according to leaders of historical opinion, was a period for recollection rather than record. Since the United States possessed so much shorter a past, the centuries when Evangelicals were active were more carefully researched. Eminent historians such as Richard Hofstadter of Columbia University could not fail to take account of the movement, so that, for example, his study of *Anti-Intellectualism in American Life* (1963) treats the Evangelical spirit as "the most powerful carrier" of the phenomenon he examines.[27] More sympathetic accounts could also be found in mainstream history. In 1959 William G. McLoughlin Jr of Brown University successfully argued in his *Modern Revivalism* that the religious revivals beloved by Evangelicals had been "more significant than social historians have yet acknowledged."[28] The most thorough coverage of Evangelicalism in a national history, however, was to be found in the first volume of Manning Clark's massive *History of Australia*, appearing in 1962.[29] Clark, as the unbelieving son of an angular Evangelical Anglican clergyman,[30] saw Evangelicalism as one of the three great contending forces in the Australian past, alongside the Enlightenment and Roman Catholicism. Yet the internal history of the movement was little illuminated either in Clark's volumes or elsewhere. Although in lands outside Britain there was rather more recognition of the role of the Evangelical movement in the national past, the detail of its life usually seemed beneath serious academic notice.

Higher Scholarly Standards

The second section of the paper can usefully address the ways in which the mid-twentieth century legacy of historiography relating to Evangelicalism was adapted in later years. The existing pattern—high on denominational history, life stories and missionary successes but low in mainstream history—certainly persisted in the decades from the 1960s onwards, but with striking modifications. Denominational studies became notably more scholarly. The transformation was most obvious in Methodist history, where a new edition of Wes-

---

26 The frequently reprinted John L. and Barbara Hammond, *Lord Shaftesbury* (London: Constable, 1923), had put Shaftesbury on the intellectual map.
27 Richard Hofstadter, *Anti-Intellectualism in American Life* (London: Knopf Publishing Group, 1964), 47.
28 William G. McLoughlin, Jr, *Modern Revivalism: Charles Grandison Finney to Billy Graham* (New York: Ronald Press, 1959), vi.
29 Manning Clark, *The History of Australia*, 6 vols. (Parkville, VIC: Melbourne University Press, 1962–87).
30 Manning Clark, *A Historian's Apprenticeship* (Parkville, VIC: Melbourne University Press, 1992), chap. 1.

ley's works achieved much higher standards of precision from the appearance of the first volume in 1975.[31] Reg Ward, the editor of the journals in Wesley's works, John Wigger, David Hempton and others wrote works that put Methodism—British, American and global—squarely within the parameters of conventional history.[32] *A History of the Methodist Church in Great Britain*, published in four volumes between 1965 and 1988, included chapters of great quality, perhaps the most valuable being a study in volume 1 by John Walsh of Jesus College, Oxford, who also wrote illuminatingly on the broader Evangelical movement.[33] Congregationalism was similarly served in England by Clyde Binfield, whose long editorship of the *Journal of the United Reformed Church Historical Society* ensured a succession of perceptive articles. There were authoritative monographs on the Presbyterians of North America by, for example, Mark Noll on the leaders of Princeton Seminary and Richard Vaudry on the Free Church in Canada.[34] Baptists were particularly well served by a series of nearly twenty publications on the Baptist Heritage in Atlantic Canada issued from 1979 under the inspiration of Jarold K. Zeman, who had received an academic formation at Charles University in Prague before the Communist takeover of Czechoslovakia forced him to emigrate.[35] Newer religious bodies also began to attract their historians: Harold Rowdon on the Brethren in England, Edwin Harrell on the Disciples of Christ in America and Walter Hollenweger on the Pentecostals worldwide opened fresh paths where others have

---

31 *The Works of John Wesley*, vol. 11: *The Appeals to Men of Reason and Religion and Certain Related Open Letters*, ed. Gerald R. Cragg (Oxford: Clarendon Press, 1975). The series continues.

32 William Reginald Ward, *Religion and Society in England, 1790–1850* (London: Batsford, 1972); John H. Wigger, *Taking Heaven by Storm: Methodism and the Rise of Popular Christianity in America* (New York: Oxford University Press, 1998); David Hempton, *Methodism: Empire of the Spirit* (New Haven, CT: Yale University Press, 2005).

33 John Walsh, "Methodism at the End of the Eighteenth Century," in *A History of the Methodist Church in Great Britain*, ed. Rupert Davies, A. Raymond George and Gordon Rupp, 4 vols. (London: Epworth Press, 1965–88), 1:275–315; John D. Walsh, "Origins of the Evangelical Revival," in *Essays in Modern English Church History in Memory of Norman Sykes*, ed. Gareth V. Bennett and John D. Walsh (London: Adam and Charles Black, 1966), 32–62.

34 Mark A. Noll, *Princeton and the Republic, 1768–1822: The Search for a Christian Enlightenment in the Era of Samuel Stanhope* (Princeton, NJ: Princeton University Press, 1989); Richard W. Vaudry, *The Free Church in Victorian Canada, 1844–1861* (Waterloo, ON: Wilfrid Laurier University Press, 1989).

35 The series included Jarold K. Zeman, *Open Doors: Canadian Baptists, 1950–1990* (Hantsport, NS: Lancelot Press, 1992).

followed.[36] At the same time denominational loyalties were fading,[37] so that Evangelical history relating to more than one denomination seemed a more natural unit of historical study. Yet writing about specific denominations did survive, and, while much of it continued to be designed for internal consumption and some of it tolerated low standards of research, several historians were engaging powerfully with the issues raised by a wider historiography.

Biography has also been affected by an improvement in scholarly standards. It must be admitted once more that a great deal of more popular writing has remained immune to the trend. A biography of Charles Haddon Spurgeon, the Victorian Baptist preacher at the Metropolitan Tabernacle in London, appeared in 1992. The author, Lewis Drummond, formerly president of Southeastern Baptist Theological Seminary in North Carolina, provided a full scholarly apparatus and conceded that his subject had weaknesses, but he was eager to draw lessons, turned aside to vindicate the miracle of the feeding of the five thousand and even gave an account, without any sense of anomaly, of the entry of Spurgeon into heaven.[38] Yet a growing number of biographers have illuminated whole areas by writing about individuals. One of them, John Pollock, an Evangelical Anglican clergyman, managed to bridge the gulf between the popular and the academic in his well-rounded study of William Wilberforce.[39] Henry Rack of the University of Manchester performed the same feat to produce the standard life of John Wesley in 1989.[40] Eighteenth-century Methodists have fared better than most other categories of Evangelical: Charles Wesley, John Fletcher and Francis Asbury have all received penetrating biographical treatment.[41] The high proportion of attention to the eighteenth century, in some measure reflecting a general

---

36 Harold H. Rowdon, *The Origins of the Brethren, 1825–1850* (London: Pickering and Inglis, 1967); David Edwin Harrell, Jr, *A Social History of the Disciples of Christ*, vol. 1: *Quest for a Christian America: The Disciples of Christ and American Society to 1966* (Nashville, TN: Disciples of Christ Historical Society, 1966); Walter J. Hollenweger, *The Pentecostals* (London: S.C.M. Press, 1972).
37 Robert Wuthnow, *The Restructuring of American Religion: Society and Faith since World War II* (Princeton, NJ: Princeton University Press, 1988).
38 Lewis Drummond, *Spurgeon: Prince of Preachers* (Grand Rapids, MI: Kregel Publications, 1992), 715, 44, 771.
39 John Pollock, *Wilberforce* (London: Constable, 1977).
40 Henry D. Rack, *Reasonable Enthusiast: John Wesley and the Rise of Methodism* (London: Epworth Press, 1989).
41 Gareth Lloyd, *Charles Wesley and the Struggle for Methodist Identity* (Oxford: Oxford University Press, 2007); Patrick Streiff, *Reluctant Saint? A Theological Biography of Fletcher of Madeley* (Peterborough: Epworth Press, 2001); John H. Wigger, *American Saint: Francis Asbury and the Methodists* (Oxford: Oxford University Press, 2009).

preoccupation of historians in the early twenty-first century, is nowhere better illustrated than in the scholarship lavished on Jonathan Edwards, the New England Puritan divine who is often hailed as "America's theologian." The Yale edition of his works, begun in 1959, spawned a cottage industry of conferences, colloquia and collections on Edwards, culminating in the masterly biography by George Marsden.[42] There are also excellent biographies of later figures such as the leader of the Free Church of Scotland, Thomas Chalmers, the nineteenth-century American evangelist D. L. Moody, his twentieth-century successor Oral Roberts and the British social gospeler Hugh Price Hughes, but they are less thick on the ground than for the earlier period.[43] Biographical work, especially on the eighteenth century, has greatly improved over the last fifty years.

The academic revolution in the historiography of Evangelicals is nowhere more evident than in missionary studies. The prime agent of change was Andrew Walls, successively of Aberdeen, Edinburgh and Liverpool Hope Universities, who, as a church historian who had served in Africa, realized the need to remodel the history of Christian missions. Its focus was to be less on the missionaries than on the peoples being evangelized and their subsequent creation of an indigenous Christian culture. Walls did not compose monographs, his favored form of expression being the essay, but the two collections of his short pieces, in conjunction with his supervision of postgraduates, his sponsorship of the biennial Yale-Edinburgh conferences on missionary history and his collection of an archive of primary sources at Edinburgh, laid the foundations for the turning of missionary history into a thoroughly academic subdiscipline.[44] Much of the superstructure was added during the 1990s by the North Atlantic Missiology Project and its successor the Currents in World Christianity project, funded by the Pew Charitable Trust in the United States. Both projects sponsored sequences of seminars and larger international con-

---

42 George M. Marsden, *Jonathan Edwards: A Life* (New Haven, CT: Yale University Press, 2003).
43 Stewart J. Brown, *Thomas Chalmers and the Godly Commonwealth in Scotland* (Oxford: Oxford University Press, 1982); James F. Findlay, Jr, *Dwight L. Moody: American Evangelist* (Chicago: University of Chicago Press, 1969); David Edwin Harrell, *Oral Roberts: An American Life* (Bloomington, IN: Indiana University Press, 1985); Christopher Oldstone-Moore, *Hugh Price Hughes: Founder of a New Methodism, Conscience of a New Nonconformity* (Cardiff: University of Wales Press, 1999).
44 Andrew F. Walls, *The Missionary Movement in Christian History: Studies in the Transmission of Faith* (New York: Orbis Books, 1996); *The Cross-Cultural Process in Christian History: Studies in the Transmission and Appropriation of Faith* (New York: Orbis Books, 2002).

ferences that led to published collections of papers. Perhaps the most significant outcome was the account of the world missionary conference of 1910 by Brian Stanley, the coordinator of the projects and Walls' successor but one at Edinburgh.[45] Meanwhile Andrew Porter, Rhodes Professor of Imperial History at King's College, London, was examining the rapports between missions and overseas expansion, the result being his telling *Religion versus Empire?* (2004).[46] Twentieth-century world Christianity, drawn to general attention by Philip Jenkins' *The Next Christendom* (2002), has become a vibrant research field.[47] This upsurge of scholarship embraced Roman Catholic, Anglo-Catholic and liberal Protestant missions, but its chief focus was on Evangelical agencies and the churches they created.

Over the last fifty years mainstream history has sometimes given the Evangelical movement its due, though often it has not. Even accomplished church historians have at times misrepresented Evangelicals. Thus Adrian Hastings, once a colleague of Walls at Aberdeen before moving to the chair of theology at Leeds, marred his otherwise admirable volume of the Oxford History of the Christian Church on Africa by presenting early nineteenth-century Evangelicals as making "millennialist assertions," whereas in reality, as postmillennialists, they were almost uniformly opposed to expectations of the imminent end of the world.[48] Perhaps the most influential study giving prominence to Evangelicals has been *The Age of Atonement* (1988) by Boyd Hilton of Trinity College, Cambridge. Although Hilton disclaimed any wish to examine Evangelicals themselves, he aimed to give much greater depth to the generalizations made in the wake of G. M. Young about the sway of the movement over the culture of the earlier Victorian years. Hilton persuasively argued that attitudes relating to the central Evangelical teaching about the cross conditioned social thought and public policy.[49] The role of Evangelicalism in molding public affairs in North America has also received greater attention. Richard Carwardine, of Sheffield and then Oxford, showed how, as he put it, "evangelical Protestants were amongst the principal shapers of American political culture

---

45   Brian Stanley, *The World Missionary Conference, Edinburgh, 1910* (Grand Rapids, MI: Eerdmans, 2009).
46   Andrew Porter, *Religion versus Empire? Protestant Missionaries and Overseas Expansion, 1700–1914* (Manchester: Manchester University Press, 2004).
47   Philip Jenkins, *The Next Christendom: The Coming of Global Christianity* (Oxford: Oxford University Press, 2002).
48   Adrian Hastings, *The Church in Africa, 1450–1950* (Oxford: Oxford University Press, 1994), 271.
49   Boyd Hilton, *The Age of Atonement: The Influence of Evangelicalism on Social and Economic Thought, 1785–1865* (Oxford: Oxford University Press, 1988).

in the middle years of the nineteenth century."⁵⁰ In Canada, partly because of Richard Allen's book *The Social Passion* (1971), it became historical orthodoxy that the shift of Evangelical religion towards the social gospel was the primary factor in the move in the direction of welfare legislation of the earlier twentieth century.[51] Thus general historians have contributed to putting the role of Evangelical religion on the map of broader affairs. It is another way in which the treatment of Evangelicals has rolled forward during the last fifty years.

Religious Developments

In many respects, however, there have been more fundamental changes in the historiography of the Evangelical movement. It is not merely that the subject has become more academically serious; it is also that alterations in the ecclesiastical landscape have affected writing about the movement, especially by Evangelicals themselves. The third section of the paper will accordingly be devoted to innovations flowing from religious developments of the postwar era. A basic conditioning factor was the growing strength of Evangelicalism. That may sound odd as a comment on a period in British history marked by a collapse of churchgoing. In the single decade between 1989 and 1998 the proportion of the English population worshiping on a given Sunday fell from 9.9 percent to 7.5 percent. Over the same years, however, the Evangelical share of churchgoers increased from 30 to 37 percent.[52] Although there was a decline in absolute numbers of Evangelical worshipers, they had become a larger proportion of the Christian community at prayer. Likewise in the United States the mainline churches lost ground to those identifying themselves as Evangelical. Awareness of Evangelicals as a sector of the American population made rapid strides after Jimmy Carter, elected president in 1976, was identified as coming from their ranks. Evangelicals began to enjoy salience as a political constituency to be courted or reviled.[53] There was also a growing consciousness that the mushrooming Protestants of the third world, the long-term fruit of the missionary movement, were overwhelmingly Evangelical by conviction. Hence Evangelicals as a grouping enjoyed much more prominence than in the past. The public, especially in America, wanted to read about them and

50 Richard J. Carwardine, *Evangelicals and Politics in Antebellum America* (New Haven, CT: Yale University Press, 1993).
51 Richard Allen, *The Social Passion: Religion and Social Reform in Canada, 1914–28* (Toronto: University of Toronto Press, 1971).
52 Peter Brierley, *The Tide Is Running Out: What the English Church Attendance Survey Reveals* (London: Christian Research, 2000), 27; *UK Christian Handbook Religious Trends No. 2*, ed. Peter Brierley (London: Christian Research, 1999), 12.3.
53 Wuthnow, *Restructuring of American Religion*, chap. 8.

mainstream publishers became keen to issue books on Evangelical themes. A milestone was the publication in 1980 by Oxford University Press in New York of George Marsden's *Fundamentalism and American Culture*, a study of the warping of popular Evangelicalism into hardline Fundamentalism in the United States.[54] The huge success of Marsden's pathbreaking book helped ensure that Oxford in New York welcomed titles on Evangelical subjects for the rest of the period. Other academic presses followed suit, with McGill-Queen's University Press in Canada, for instance, generating a long sequence of "Studies in the History of Religion," many with Evangelical subject matter. The expansion of Evangelicalism in the later twentieth century undergirded the growth of historical work on the movement.

At the same time, Evangelicals discovered history as a career option. The movement had long fostered entry to the ministry and the other professions, but, with the expansion of higher education after the Second World War, rapid in North America but also happening elsewhere after some delay, academia offered fresh opportunities. A generation of American graduate students with backgrounds in conservative denominations pursued history as a vocation. Timothy L. Smith, who composed the first major work in the efflorescence of Evangelical historiography, *Revivalism and Social Reform* (1957), was a minister of the Church of the Nazarene, a Holiness denomination.[55] George Marsden was the son of a minister of the Orthodox Presbyterians who had split from mainline Presbyterianism in the wake of the Fundamentalist disputes chronicled by the historian. Mark Noll came from a Conservative Baptist home.[56] Martin Marty at Chicago, William Hutchinson at Harvard and Sydney Ahlstrom at Yale all provided supervision on Evangelical topics for doctoral candidates, who in due course went on to mentor a further generation of aspirants in the field. In Britain a key agency was the InterVarsity Fellowship that bound together Christian Unions, groups of Evangelical students in the universities. It launched professional groups for graduates, the Christian Medical Fellowship being the largest, but added one in the early 1960s for historians. Although for many years the Historians' Study Group did little more than hold a couple of small gatherings a year, it fostered the idea that

---

54 George M. Marsden, *Fundamentalism and American Culture: The Shaping of Twentieth-Century Evangelicalism, 1870–1925* (New York: Oxford University Press, 1980).
55 Timothy L. Smith, *Revivalism and Social Reform: American Protestantism on the Eve of the Civil War* (New York: Harper and Row, 1957).
56 Maxie B. Burch, *The Evangelical Historians: The Historiography of George Marsden, Nathan Hatch and Mark Noll* (Lanham, MD: University Press of America, 1996), 5, 3.

historical research and teaching could be a sphere for Christian enterprise. One of the earliest pieces of writing to explore Evangelical history as a distinct genre was an unpublished Cambridge prize essay of 1962 by Haddon Willmer, later professor of theology at Leeds, on the movement in England between 1785 and 1835.[57] Again Willmer, the son of a conservative Baptist minister, was active at university in the Cambridge Inter-Collegiate Christian Union. The InterVarsity Fellowship, which established equivalents in most other countries in the Commonwealth and some beyond, nurtured scholars in other parts of the world. At an international conference on Evangelical history in Sydney in 1997, nearly all the dozen people round the table found that they had IVF backgrounds.[58] The rise of Evangelical historical scholarship, which was parallel to the advance of conservative Protestants in several other academic disciplines, was a global phenomenon.[59]

Their enterprise established a number of institutional bases. The Historians' Study Group in Britain evolved into the autonomous Christianity and History Forum with its own bulletin, its sixth issue publishing in 2010 articles on Evangelical interactions with the Huguenots, the novel and the empire.[60] The forum paled in significance, however, by comparison with its sister organization in North America, the Conference on Faith and History, founded in 1968 by Richard V. Pierard and Robert D. Linder, graduate students at the University of Iowa. The conference could draw on the network of Christian colleges in North America as well as the smaller number of Evangelicals holding posts in secular institutions and so grew to number over six hundred members.[61] Its periodical, *Fides et Historia*, existed primarily to "stimulate or provoke dialogue among evangelical Christian historians" rather than to encourage research on any sector of religious history,[62] but from its earliest years it generated papers on the history of the Evangelical movement and their proportion grew over time. In Australia an Evangelical History Association, sharing the American organization's concern with fellowship but more centrally focused on the history of the movement, was launched in 1987 under Stuart Piggin, soon to become master of Robert Menzies College at Macquarie

---

57 Haddon Willmer, "Evangelicalism, 1785 to 1835" (Hulsean Prize Essay, University of Cambridge, 1962).
58 Personal experience.
59 D. Michael Lindsay, *Faith in the Halls of Power: How Evangelicals Joined the American Elite* (New York: Oxford University Press, 2007), chaps. 3 and 4.
60 *Christianity and History Bulletin* 6 (2010), 7–43.
61 "The Conference on Faith and History," http://www.huntington.edu/cfh/fides.htm, accessed 1 August 2011.
62 Robert D. Linder, "Editorial," *Fides et Historia* 2 (1969), 2.

University.⁶³ It issued the periodical *Lucas*, produced an *Australian Dictionary of Evangelical Biography* and published collected volumes of papers. Most important of all was the Institute for the Study of American Evangelicals at Wheaton College, Illinois. Originating as no more than informal meetings between young friends in academia such as Mark Noll and Nathan Hatch, in 1979 the group held a successful conference at Wheaton on the Bible in America, afterward publishing the papers, and three years later set up the institute to organize more gatherings.⁶⁴ The momentum of the series of conferences, which regularly led to volumes published with academic imprints, was sustained by annual consultations that doubled as holidays *en famille* on the coast of New England complete with games of softball. The result, as George Marsden put it, was the creation of "an informal network of colleagues who have become the closest of friends and hence have accomplished by concerted effort what none of them could have done alone."⁶⁵ The emergence of Evangelical history probably owes as much to family games as to high-level intellectual developments.

Nevertheless innovations in the sphere of theology did have an impact on historical studies. Evangelicals had been accustomed to repudiating tradition, seeing it as a sinister force undermining a pure biblicism. Gradually during the period some of their leaders became more friendly towards the idea. F. F. Bruce realized "the prevalence of tradition" among Brethren assemblies which believed themselves to be free from its influence and so expounded the value of early Christian traditions in a lecture series of 1968.⁶⁶ The Baptist Barrie White, principal of Regent's Park College, Oxford, was willing, in a booklet of 1976, to treat tradition as a condensing of the work of the Holy Spirit in the past and as such carrying a measure of authority for subsequent practice.⁶⁷ In the United States, where the Evangelical school in the Episcopal Church had long been in eclipse, there was from the 1970s a novel upsurge of enthusiasm for liturgy that drew many towards the traditional. Robert E. Webber of Wheaton College was the central figure, joining an Episcopal church and

---

63 Geoffrey R. Treloar, "History as Vocation: Stuart Piggin as Evangelical Historian and Historian of Evangelicalism," in *Making History for God: Essays on Evangelicalism, Revival and Mission in Honour of Stuart Piggin, Master of Robert Menzies College, 1990-2004*, ed. Geoffrey R. Treloar and Robert D. Linder (Sydney: Robert Menzies College, 2004), 3-34.

64 *The Bible in America: Essays in Cultural History*, ed. Nathan O. Hatch and Mark A. Noll (New York: Oxford University Press, 1982).

65 George Marsden, "ISAE: Retrospect and Prospect—June 1994," ISAE.

66 Frederick F. Bruce, *Tradition Old and New* (Grand Rapids, MI: Zondervan, 1970), 9.

67 Barrington R. White, *Authority: A Baptist View* (London: Baptist Publications, 1976), 23-6.

urging a rediscovery of the common roots that bound Evangelicals to the past of the universal church.[68] Although he was the son-in-law of Harold Lindsell, the author of *The Battle for the Bible* (1976) and champion of a stern inerrancy designed to buttress the sole authority of the Bible, Webber published an influential series of books commending High Church worship as the correct complement to Evangelical belief. Addressing the common fear of Evangelicals that the venture might elevate tradition over scripture, he pointed out that tradition meant no more than "passing on," whether a truth or a practice. The proper perspective on Christ, the church, worship and spirituality was within what Webber called "the paradigms of history," how each of them had been viewed in the past.[69] A fascination for the links between the New Testament and the present, a form of history-mindedness, was springing up. In such a context the Evangelical past itself could not fail to exert a stronger appeal over minds associated with the movement.

A more specific set of intellectual influences played over the growth of Evangelical historiography. The Conference on Faith and History, together with its organizational equivalents in other lands, was centrally preoccupied in its early years with the relationship of theology to the discipline of history. "Is there a Christian approach to history?" asked an article in the second volume of *Fides et Historia* in 1969.[70] The aim was to bridge the gulf between an Evangelical allegiance and the academic enterprise. At one level the object was the typical Evangelical desire to witness to the faith; at another it was to develop what came to be called a "Christian mind." The most significant theological stimulus in this direction came, perhaps remarkably, from the Netherlands. A number of Dutch neo-Calvinist theologians developed a school of thought that called for the subjection of all areas of human activity to the Lordship of Christ. Its leading exponent, Abraham Kuyper, founder of the *Gereformeerde Kerken* (Rereformed Churches) in 1892 and prime minister of the Netherlands from 1901 to 1905, set out his vision in the Stone Lectures of 1898 at Princeton Seminary, published as *Lectures on Calvinism*.[71] The impact of this point of view on English speakers was hugely reinforced by American exponents, especially the theologian Cornelius Van Til, a son of Dutch immigrants to the

---

68 Robert E. Webber, *Common Roots: A Call to Evangelical Maturity* (Grand Rapids, MI: Zondervan, 1978).
69 Robert Webber, *Ancient-Future Faith: Rethinking Evangelicalism for a Postmodern World* (Grand Rapids, MI: Baker Books, 1999), 180–1, chaps. 4, 8, 11, 14.
70 Charles J. Miller, "Is There a Christian Approach to History?" *Fides et Historia* 2 (1969), 3–15.
71 Abraham Kuyper, *Lectures on Calvinism* (Grand Rapids, MI: Eerdmans, 1931).

United States who contended for the importance of presuppositions in intellectual exploration. It followed that believers must adopt distinctively Christian premises when undertaking any discipline such as history.[72] The school of Kuyper shaped the thought of C. T. McIntire of the Institute for Christian Studies at Toronto, at one time a leading theorist of history in Evangelical circles.[73] Van Til deeply swayed George Marsden, who believed that "the very facts of history differ for the Christian and the non-Christian historian."[74] Calvin College, where Marsden taught, was a bastion of this point of view. During the 1970s a small Christian Studies Unit propagated the same standpoint in Britain, but its deepest influence was always felt in the Netherlands itself, helping in 1989 to inspire the creation there of an Association of Christian Historians.[75] Although this ideological position was applicable to all genres of history, political and economic as much as religious, and although several advocates, including Marsden, modified their loyalties over time, it fostered self-confidence among Evangelical historians. They came to believe that they could study their own past with an emphasis on what they themselves considered important, the theological and the spiritual. Neo-Calvinism was a potent reinforcer of Evangelical history.

Yet Calvinism also generated opposition to the rise of academic historiography among Evangelicals. During the second half of the twentieth century there was a striking resurgence of specifically Reformed theology in the English-speaking world. Under the leadership of Martyn Lloyd-Jones and J. I. Packer, confessional Calvinism gathered force, first in Britain, and then, partly through the *Banner of Truth* magazine and publishing house, across the globe. The editor of the magazine, Iain Murray, once Lloyd-Jones' assistant minister, believed that history books ought to subserve the twin causes of advancing spiritual religion and promoting Reformed orthodoxy. He preferred history with heroes—as a book of his with that title published in 2009 confirmed.[76] Murray was championing a more traditional style of Evangelical historiography. In 1994–95 there was an instructive controversy about how history should be written. In a review in the *Banner of Truth*, Murray censured Harry S. Stout of Yale, a regular participant in the programs of the Institute for the Study

72 John Frame, *Cornelius Van Til: An Analysis of His Thought* (Phillipsburg, NJ: Presbyterian & Reformed, 1995).
73 C. Thomas McIntire, "The Focus of Historical Study: A Christian View," *Fides et Historia* 14 (1981), 6–17, spec. 10, 11.
74 George M. Marsden, "The Spiritual Vision of History," *Fides et Historia* 14 (1981), 55–66.
75 *Christianity and History: An International Newsletter* 2 (1991), 1–3.
76 Iain H. Murray, *Heroes* (Edinburgh: Banner of Truth Trust, 2009).

of American Evangelicals, for having embraced the norms of social and cultural history and so having surrendered to the "unregenerate mind."[77] Another reviewer in the magazine criticized Stout's biography of the evangelist George Whitefield for "being obsessed with finding the slightest flaw in the character of a spiritual giant."[78] Stout, himself a firm Calvinist, replied vigorously that he and professionals like him followed the evidence, not dwelling on "devotional or hagiographic themes." The Bible itself did not hide the faults of its characters. If social and cultural history was illegitimate, "there is no room for Christians in the secular academy."[79] Murray responded that "to write the lives of eminent Christians with minimum notice of the things which meant *most* to them, and without which their lives cannot be understood, is to mislead."[80] It was an issue of priorities. For Murray, selecting the achievements of Evangelicals was designed to edify and evangelize; for Stout, portraying Evangelicals in their totality was a contribution to scholarship. By 1995 there was no doubt that the second brand of Evangelical historiography had come to stay.

Ecclesiastical Context

Ecclesiastical developments of the period also conditioned the type of writing produced by scholarly historians. Among the most important phenomena of the later twentieth century was the ecumenical movement. The organized rapprochement between the churches had long been suspect in most Evangelical eyes because it neglected the existing unity of true believers and seemed to augur compromise with Rome. From the 1960s, however, there was a thaw in the ecclesiastical climate. The Second Vatican Council showed that Rome was not, after all, *semper eadem*. Ecumenical contacts, multiplying from that decade onwards, steadily reduced suspicions. For a few Evangelical historians the Ecclesiastical History Society was one of the agencies that disarmed their fears. Joint historical efforts, however, were easiest where there was least ecclesiastical distance to bridge. In 1993, for example, Alan Sell, a dedicated ecumenist in the United Reformed Church, brought together previously separate English and Welsh Nonconformist bodies in the quaintly named Association of Denominational Historical Societies and Cognate Libraries.[81] The Dr Williams's Centre for Dissenting Studies, set up in 2004, fulfilled a similar

---

77   Iain H. Murray in *Banner of Truth*, July 1994, 8.
78   David White in *Banner of Truth*, March 1994, 29.
79   Harry S. Stout in *Banner of Truth*, March 1995, 7–10, at 7, 8.
80   Iain H. Murray in *Banner of Truth*, March 1995, 10–11, at 11.
81   "Association of Denominational Historical Societies and Cognate Libraries," http://www.adhscl.org.uk/, accessed 2 August 2011.

function in promoting the history of all the Nonconformist denominations, Evangelical and non-Evangelical. Both Association and Centre were responsible for publishing several valuable collections of papers. The ecumenical climate, however, undoubtedly had wider results, affecting the style of writing about Roman Catholics and Anglo-Catholics. In the past Evangelical historians would have concentrated on chronicling Protestant resistance to Catholic designs, and in 1979 Peter Toon still wrote a book celebrating the Evangelical critique of the Oxford Movement. Evangelicals, however, were now capable of writing dispassionately about their own anti-Catholic past, as in John Wolffe's *The Protestant Crusade in Great Britain* (1991).[82] John Maiden's study of the Prayer Book controversy of 1927–28 discussed the two sides, the Catholicizing forces and their Evangelical opponents, with scrupulous even-handedness.[83] For most Evangelicals who were attracted to historical writing, the Catholic Church and its Anglican imitators no longer constituted the opposition.

The ecumenical impulse meant not just closer interdenominational relations but also stronger international awareness. Advances in communications, especially flights by air and messages by e-mail, revolutionized possibilities of global cooperation during the period. This trend was reflected in Evangelical historiography too. The World Methodist Historical Society, affiliated to the World Methodist Council, held three-yearly conferences in various countries.[84] Similar series of peripatetic Baptist, Brethren and Pentecostal world conferences, largely historical in their concerns, were launched. For generic Evangelical history a crucial event was a conference on Transatlantic Evangelicalism at Wheaton College, Illinois, in 1992, giving rise to two collections of published essays, *Evangelicalism* and *Amazing Grace*.[85] Representatives from much of the English-speaking world attended, setting up a short-lived International Association for the Study of Christianity and History. Although this fledgling body managed to do little more than circulate a newsletter, bonds

---

82 Peter Toon, *Evangelical Theology, 1833–1856: A Response to Tractarianism* (London: Marshall, Morgan and Scott, 1979); John R. Wolffe, *The Protestant Crusade in Great Britain, 1829–1860* (Oxford: Clarendon Press, 1991).

83 John Maiden, *National Religion and the Prayer Book Controversy, 1927–1928* (Woodbridge, Suffolk: Boydell Press, 2009).

84 "World Methodist Historical Society," http://www.gcah.org/site/pp.aspx?c=ghKJI0PHIoE&b=3761527, accessed 2 August 2011.

85 *Evangelicalism: Comparative Studies of Popular Protestantism in North America, the British Isles and Beyond, 1700–1990*, ed. Mark A. Noll, David W. Bebbington and George A. Rawlyk (New York: Oxford University, Press, 1994); *Amazing Grace: Evangelicalism in Australia, Britain, Canada and the United States*, ed. George A. Rawlyk and Mark A. Noll (Montreal and Kingston: McGill-Queen's University Press, 1994).

forged at the Wheaton conference remained strong and led to other ventures.[86] The same international approach led to the publication by InterVarsity Press, an Evangelical imprint, of a five-volume "History of Evangelicalism."[87] The oeuvre of one individual was probably the most valuable contribution to scholarship arising from the internationalization of Evangelical history. Reg Ward, professor of history at Durham until 1986, wrote in retirement *The Protestant Evangelical Awakening* (1992), delineating for the first time some of the rapports between continental revivals and the subsequent developments in North America and the United Kingdom. He followed it up fourteen years later with *Early Evangelicalism: A Global Intellectual History*.[88] His appreciation of pan-European linkages, possible because of Ward's command of German, unusual among English-speaking historians, transformed the context in which the genesis of the Evangelical movement must be situated.[89] Reg Ward demonstrated that Evangelical history has to be international in scope.

A further tendency in the churches of the period, especially strong among Evangelicals, was a rising eagerness to relate the Christian gospel to its cultural setting. Missiologists, among whom Andrew Walls was the most historically informed, took the initiative in relating the spread of the faith to the attitudes of its recipients, hoping to reveal the best ways of maximizing converts.[90] It was the genius of Lesslie Newbigin, a United Reformed Church minister who had served as a bishop in the Church of South India, to relate this body of thinking to the circumstances of the West. In his brief but powerful book, *The Other Side of 1984*, published by the British Council of Churches in 1984, Newbigin argued that the Western churches must penetrate behind the debilitating effects of the Enlightenment if they are to recover their missionary vigor in articulating public truth.[91] His summons led to the "Gospel and Our Culture" movement, which held a conference at Swanwick in 1992, published the conference papers and maintained an ongoing network.[92] The interaction of

---

86 *Christianity and History: An International Newsletter* 1–8 (1992–94).
87 See n. 3 above.
88 William Reginald Ward, *The Protestant Evangelical Awakening* (Cambridge: Cambridge University Press, 1992); *Early Evangelicalism: A Global Intellectual History, 1670–1789* (Cambridge: Cambridge University Press, 2006).
89 See John Walsh, "Profile: W. R. Ward: Methodist Historian and Historian of Methodism," *Epworth Review* 22 (1995), 41–46.
90 See n. 44 above.
91 Lesslie Newbigin, *The Other Side of 1984: Questions for the Churches* (Geneva: World Council of Churches, 1983).
92 *The Gospel and Contemporary Culture*, ed. Hugh Montefiore (London: Mowbray, 1992); "The Gospel and Our Culture," http://gospel-culture.org.uk/intro.htm, accessed 3 August 2011.

gospel and culture was becoming a central topic for reflection among Evangelicals and a wider Christian constituency. Historiography displayed similar symptoms. George Marsden's *Fundamentalism and American Culture* had already, in 1980, shown by its very title an appreciation of the need to locate Evangelical developments in their broad setting.[93] Hymns attracted attention, notably in Sandra Sizer's *Gospel Hymns and Social Religion* (1978), as a key way in which Evangelicals expressed themselves in an art form.[94] On the other side of the Atlantic, my *Evangelicalism in Modern Britain* (1989), though perhaps best known for its effort to state the meaning of "Evangelical," attempted to show how the movement had been shaped by the changing cultural ambience.[95] Regent's Park College, Oxford, set up a Centre for the Study of Christianity and Culture, its first conference in 1996 taking "Culture and the Nonconformist Tradition" as its theme. The resulting book, according to one of the editors, reported on the experience of Nonconformists in "balancing their absorption of the culture of their time, with the creation of their own distinctive subcultures."[96] Popular culture was not neglected in subsequent writing, with such studies as an account of the enormously popular Cornish Methodist fiction by the three Hocking siblings, Silas, Joseph and Salome.[97] The two-way process of culture influencing religion and religion influencing culture became a common historical theme.

A final trend in the churches took place in the area of spirituality. Its normative form among many Evangelicals had long been that propagated by the Keswick movement, according to which holiness was to be discovered through the exercise of faith. The hold of Keswick teaching, however, slackened during the 1960s, when there arose an entirely different model of piety associated with charismatic renewal, encouraging free expression in worship, a search for bodily wholeness, close personal relationships and a willingness to embrace

93 See n. 54 above.
94 Sandra S. Sizer, *Gospel Hymns and Social Religion: The Rhetoric of Nineteenth-Century Revivalism* (Philadelphia: Temple University Press, 1978).
95 David W. Bebbington, *Evangelicalism in Modern Britain: A History from the 1730s to the 1980s* (London: Routledge, 1989). On the thesis of chapter 1 of this book, see *The Emergence of Evangelicalism: Exploring Historical Continuities*, ed. Michael G. Haykin and Kenneth J. Stewart (Nottingham: InterVarsity Press, 1988), published in the United States as *The Advent of Evangelicalism: Exploring Historical Continuities* (Nashville: B & H Academic, 2008).
96 Jane Shaw, "Introduction: Why 'Culture and the Nonconformist Tradition'?" in *Culture and the Nonconformist Tradition*, ed. Jane Shaw and Alan Kreider (Cardiff: University of Wales Press, 1999), 6.
97 Alan M. Kent, *Pulp Methodism: The Lives and Literature of Silas, Joseph and Salome Hocking, Three Cornish Novelists* (St Austell, Cornwall: Cornish Hillside Publications, 2002).

authentic living in the secular world.[98] The topic of spiritual practice became a major preoccupation. A whole series of pamphlets, the Grove Spirituality booklets, explored the subject from an Anglican Evangelical standpoint from 1982 onwards.[99] Historians affected by renewal naturally paid attention to religious experience in the past. Ian Randall, tutor at the Baptist Spurgeon's College in London and the author of *Evangelical Experiences* (1999), an account of interwar English Evangelical spirituality, had himself been touched by the charismatic movement.[100] Likewise in America a new and thorough account of the Great Awakening was written by Thomas S. Kidd, a member of a Baptist church with a distinctly charismatic ethos. Unlike many previous commentators, Kidd laid particular stress on the radical Evangelicals who went in for dreams and portents.[101] Revivalism was increasingly studied for its own sake rather than for the light it cast on such themes as social control. A leading historian of eighteenth-century Canada, George Rawlyk, drew attention to the formative role of the revivalist Henry Alline in the Maritime provinces.[102] Rawlyk, who was a core member of the circle around the Institute for the Study of American Evangelicals, became fascinated by religious experience in the past and wrote *Canada Fire* (1994) to show the radical credentials of revivalists from his home country.[103] Janice Holmes demonstrated the importance of revivals in late nineteenth-century Britain and Ireland and a range of scholars of Evangelicalism swamped the 2008 volume of "Studies in Church History" with accounts of revivalism in the modern period.[104] Spirituality and revival were in the air; they also appeared

---

98 See 1:10 and 2:16: "Holiness in the Evangelical Tradition" and "The Rise of Charismatic Renewal in Britain."
99 The first was Peter Adam, *Living the Trinity* (Bramcote: Grove Books 1982).
100 Ian Randall, *Evangelical Experiences: A Study in the Spirituality of English Evangelicalism, 1918–1939* (Carlisle: Paternoster Press, 1999).
101 Thomas S. Kidd, *The Great Awakening: The Roots of Evangelical Christianity in Colonial America* (New Haven, CT: Yale University Press, 2007).
102 George A. Rawlyk, *Ravished by the Spirit: Religious Revivals, Baptists and Henry Alline* (Montreal and Kingston: McGill-Queen's University Press, 1984); *Henry Alline: Selected Writings* (New York: Paulist Press 1987).
103 George A. Rawlyk, *The Canada Fire: Radical Evangelicalism in British North America* (Montreal and Kingston: McGill-Queen's University Press, 1984). On Rawlyk, see Mark A. Noll, "George Rawlyk's Contribution to Canadian History as a Contribution to United States History: A Preliminary Probe," *Fides et Historia* 32 (2000), 1–17; and also in *Revivals, Baptists, and George Rawlyk*, ed. Daniel C. Goodwin (Wolfville, NS: Acadia Divinity College, 2000), 29–51.
104 Janice Holmes, *Religious Revivals in Britain and Ireland, 1859–1905* (Dublin: Irish Academic Press, 2000); *Revival and Resurgence in Christian History*, ed. Kate Cooper and Jeremy Gregory, *Studies in Church History*, vol. 44 (Woodbridge, Suffolk: Boydell Press, 2008).

increasingly in the historiography. It was another way in which religious developments affected the writing of Evangelical history in the period.

Mainstream Historiography

The historiography of the movement, however, was also shaped by broader trends in the world of scholarship. To this, the fourth aspect of the subject, we can now turn. The long-term twentieth-century shift of history towards techniques and concepts drawn from the social sciences necessarily had a major impact. Some of the best work on religion in the modern world was achieved by applying sociological methods. In England the oeuvre of Hugh McLeod, beginning with *Class and Religion in the Late Victorian City* (1974), showed how much could be revealed about religion when the central category of analysis was class and there was copious use of statistics.[105] Few Evangelical historians practised this type of history, though one, Nigel Scotland, contributed to the adjacent subdiscipline of labor history by writing a study of agricultural laborers' trade unionism in East Anglia in the later nineteenth century. It was notable for giving ample space, as labor historians rarely did, to the ideas of the Primitive Methodists who formed the trade union vanguard.[106] A social scientific theory much in vogue during the 1960s and 1970s, the notion of manipulation of the lower classes by the upper classes, was applied to Evangelical religion. "Revivals," wrote Paul E. Johnson in an influential study of early nineteenth-century Rochester, New York, that appeared in 1978, "provided entrepreneurs with a means of imposing new standards of work discipline and personal comportment upon themselves and the men who worked for them, and thus they functioned as powerful social controls."[107] Likewise an account of the Clapham Sect around William Wilberforce by Ford K. Brown, published in 1961, dwelt on its efforts to discipline the lower orders and, most famously, E. P. Thompson, in his *Making of the English Working Class* two years later depicted Methodist preachers as using "emotional violence" to turn converts into docile workers and loyal subjects.[108] Those with Evangelical sympathies

---

105 Hugh McLeod, *Class and Religion in the Late Victorian City* (London: Croom Helm, 1974).
106 Nigel Scotland, *Methodism and the Revolt of the Field: A Study of the Methodist Contribution to Agricultural Trade Unionism in East Anglia, 1872–1896* (Gloucester: Alan Sutton, 1981).
107 Paul E. Johnson, *A Shopkeeper's Millennium: Society and Revivals in Rochester, New York, 1815–1837* (New York: Hill and Wang, 1978), 138.
108 Ford K. Brown, *Fathers of the Victorians: The Age of Wilberforce* (Cambridge: Cambridge University Press, 1961); Edward P. Thompson, *The Making of the English Working Class* (Harmondsworth, Middlesex: Penguin Books, 1968), 418.

found this picture far from compelling. Two of them were responsible for powerful ripostes. Reg Ward showed in *Religion and Society in England, 1790–1850* (1972) the extent to which Methodism in early industrial England was a radical force, sapping the foundations of church and state, and Nathan O. Hatch, in his book *The Democratization of American Christianity* (1989), laid bare the populism of Evangelical and related movements in the early national period of the United States that caused alarm to the new country's elites.[109] Although the first of these works was less effective than the second in redirecting the flow of historical writing, both struck powerful blows at the model of social manipulation by religion.

The theory of social control was a symptom of the permeation of Marxist ideas into academia. E. P. Thompson, though coming from a Methodist background, had embraced a sophisticated form of Marxism with a strong cultural component.[110] A few other British historians with Marxist convictions wrote about aspects of the Evangelical movement. Allan MacLaren, for example, published in 1974 a study of religion in Aberdeen at the time of the Disruption of the Scottish Church from that standpoint.[111] Its claims about the dearth of working-class involvement in Presbyterianism were later to be undermined by Peter Hillis.[112] Although research findings molded by Marxist premises rarely endured, the legacy of Karl Marx played a significant role in the emergence of Evangelical historiography. Perhaps surprisingly, Marxism acted as a beacon for Evangelical historians. Those Evangelicals who gave any thought to historical theory in the 1960s and even in the 1970s normally accepted uncritically the prevailing objectivist model of history being the patient collection of brute facts from relevant sources.[113] According to John Warwick Montgomery of Trinity Evangelical Divinity School, Deerfield, Illinois, probably the best known exponent of an Evangelical philosophy of history at the time, Marxist rewritings of history were "gross examples" of the solipsistic fallacy that "there

---

109 Ward, *Religion and Society*; Nathan O. Hatch, *The Democratization of American Christianity* (New Haven, CT: Yale University Press, 1989).
110 On Thompson, see David Hempton and John Walsh, "E. P. Thompson and Marxism," in *God and Mammon: Protestants, Money and the Market, 1790–1860*, ed. Mark A. Noll (New York: Oxford University Press, 2002), 99–120.
111 A. Allan MacLaren, *Religion and Class: The Disruption Years in Aberdeen* (London: Routledge and Kegan Paul, 1974).
112 Peter Hillis, "Presbyterianism and Social Class in Mid-Nineteenth-Century Glasgow: A Study of Nine Churches," *Journal of Ecclesiastical History* 32:1 (1981), 47–64.
113 Peter Novick, *That Noble Dream: The "Objectivity Question" and the American Historical Profession* (Cambridge: Cambridge University Press, 1988).

is no objective reality outside myself."[114] For the younger generation who were discovering history as a vocation, however, Marxist successes in the academy showed that committed history was acceptable. "If neo-Marxists can write neo-Marxist history," asked George Rawlyk in 1993, "why should not evangelical Christian historians . . . write from an evangelical Christian perspective?"[115] Marxist ideas began to be treated temperately in Evangelical writing about history. Thomas McIntire, for instance, wrote appreciatively of Marx's insight into human culture-making capacity and in my *Patterns in History* (1979) there is a sympathetic appraisal of the Marxist view of history.[116] Marxist historical scholarship blazed a trail where Evangelicals were eager to follow.

The rise of women's history, followed by gender history, was one of the most striking phenomena of historiography during the late twentieth century. Accounts of women's part in religious history began to flow from the press, though sometimes it was accused of being, especially in America, more committed to feminism than to scholarship. In Britain, however, the earliest significant study of an Evangelical topic was written by Olive Anderson of Westfield College, London, precisely to show that female preaching in the 1860s owed more to premillennialism than to feminism.[117] The best monograph in the field was actually by a man, Frank Prochaska, whose *Women and Philanthropy in Nineteenth-Century England* (1980) documented the work of Evangelical societies.[118] The publication of Leonore Davidoff and Catherine Hall's *Family Fortunes* (1987), examining religious as well as other roles of men and women in nineteenth-century households, already marked a shift towards a more sophisticated gender history.[119] Evangelicals themselves lagged behind in Britain, not publishing illuminating critical history about women until the eve of the twenty-first century.[120] Part of the explanation lay in the division of opinion among Evangelicals about the role

---

114 John Warwick Montgomery, *The Shape of the Past: A Christian Response to Secular Philosophies of History* (Minneapolis, MN: Bethany Fellowship, 1975), 8.
115 George A. Rawlyk, "Writing about Canadian Revivals," in *Modern Christian Revivals*, ed. Edith L. Blumhofer and Randall Balmer (Urbana, IL: University of Illinois Press, 1993), 208–26, quoted at 219.
116 McIntire, "Focus of Historical Study," 12–13; David Bebbington, *Patterns in History* (Leicester: InterVarsity Press, 1979), chap. 6.
117 Olive Anderson, "Women Preachers in Mid-Victorian Britain: Some Reflexions on Feminism, Popular Religion and Social Change," *Historical Journal* 12 (1969), 467–84.
118 Frank K. Prochaska, *Women and Philanthropy in Nineteenth-Century England* (Oxford: Oxford University Press, 1980).
119 Leonore Davidoff and Catherine Hall, *Family Fortunes: Men and Women of the English Middle Class, 1780–1850* (London: Hutchinson, 1987).
120 Linda Wilson, *Constrained by Zeal: Female Spirituality among Nonconformists, 1825–1875* (Carlisle: Paternoster Press, 2000).

of women, crystalized over the issue of female ordination. A commissioned article on nineteenth-century Evangelical women appearing in 1984 in the journal circulating among graduates from Christian Unions carefully avoided taking sides in the debate.[121] The theme first occurred on the conference schedule of the Institute for the Study of American Evangelicals in 1993.[122] In the following year there appeared Susan Juster's *Disorderly Women*, an account of the prominence of women among New England Free Baptists in the Revolutionary Era, and three years later Catherine Brekus' *Strangers and Pilgrims*, an exploration of female preaching in America down to 1845.[123] Women became and remained central to historiography about Evangelicals. Men considered as male fared less well, in that the rising theme of masculinity was rarely examined on either side of the Atlantic. Two studies of the representation of men in the writings of the Victorian preacher Charles Haddon Spurgeon and William Booth, the founder of the Salvation Army, are exceptions.[124] Despite the small inroads into masculinity, the content of writing about Evangelicalism was transformed in the area of gender during the period.

So was discussion of Evangelicals and race. In the United States the civil rights movement prompted a sustained reassessment of the place of racial divisions in the national past. The scrutiny of slave religion led to novel findings such as the extent of black preaching to whites and the prevalence of mixed black and white worship before the Civil War.[125] The intertwining of the subsequent racial discrimination in the South with the Evangelical religion of the oppressors and of the oppressed was freshly explored.[126] Perhaps

---

121 David W. Bebbington, "Evangelicals and the Role of Women, 1800-1930," *Christian Arena* 37 (1984), 19-23.
122 "ISAE History Research: Consultations," 14-15, ISAE.
123 Susan Juster, *Disorderly Women: Sexual Politics and Evangelicalism in Revolutionary New England* (Ithaca, NY: Cornell University Press, 1994).
124 Laura Lauer, "Soul-Saving Partnerships and Pacifist Soldiers: The Ideal of Masculinity in the Salvation Army," and Andrew Bradstock, "'A Man of God Is a Manly Man': Spurgeon, Luther and 'Holy Boldness,'" in *Masculinity and Spirituality in Victorian Culture*, ed. Andrew Bradstock et al. (Basingstoke: Macmillan, 2000), 194-208, 209-25.
125 Mechal Sobel, *Trabelin' On: The Slave Journey to an Afro-Baptist Faith* (Princeton, NJ: Princeton University Press, 1979), 190-99; *Masters and Slaves in the House of the Lord: Race and Religion in the American South, 1740-1870*, ed. John B. Boles (Lexington, KY: University Press of Kentucky, 1988).
126 Paul Harvey, *Redeeming the South: Religious Cultures and Racial Identities among Southern Baptists, 1865-1925* (Chapel Hill, NC: University of North Carolina Press, 1997); *Freedom's Coming: Religious Culture and the Shaping of the American South from the Civil War through the Civil Rights Era* (Chapel Hill, NC: University of North Carolina Press, 2005).

the most striking development in the historiography was a turn from treating the civil rights movement as a largely secular phenomenon to emphasizing, as Mark Noll put it in 2008, "the strength of the African-American religion that drove the movement."[127] More generally black studies became more widespread, producing such classics as Evelyn Brooks Higginbotham's *Righteous Discontent: The Women's Movement in the Black Baptist Church, 1880–1920* (1993).[128] Works on indigenous peoples, including Native Americans and Australian Aborigines, increasingly engaged with the role of Evangelical missionaries among them.[129] In British historiography the issue of race focused mainly on the subject of the abolition of the slave trade. Traditionally this was a topic where the Evangelicals came to the fore as the leaders, under Wilberforce, of the campaign against the trade. They still appeared in that role in a probing analysis by Roger Anstey, professor at the University of Kent at Canterbury and a Methodist, in 1975.[130] The subsequent growth of coverage of the topic, however, had the effect of stressing the agency of other groups and circumstances, even in a collection of essays in memory of Anstey.[131] It was only with the appearance of Christopher Leslie Brown's *Moral Capital* (2006) in time for the bicentenary of abolition that the Evangelicals were reinstated to prominence, though it was now an earlier group and with more carefully delineated motives.[132] At a more popular level William Hague's biography of Wilberforce (2007), with the subtitle "The Life of the Great Anti-Slave Trade Campaigner," and even more the film *Amazing Grace* helped consolidate the place of Evangelical religion in the process of abolition.[133] The Evangelical record on issues surrounding race relations was increasingly valued in America and intermittently stressed in Britain.

127 Mark A. Noll, *God and Race in American Politics: A Short History* (Princeton, NJ: Princeton University Press, 2008), 135.
128 Evelyn Brooks Higginbotham, *Righteous Discontent: The Women's Movement in the Black Baptist Church, 1880–1920* (Cambridge, MA: Harvard University Press, 1993).
129 E.g., William G. McLoughlin, Jr, *Cherokees and Missionaries, 1789–1839* (New Haven, CT: Yale University Press, 1984), and John W. Harris, *One Blood: 200 Years of Aboriginal Encounter with Christianity: A Story of Hope*, 2nd ed. (Sutherland, NSW: Albatross Books, 1994).
130 Roger Anstey, *The Atlantic Slave Trade and British Abolition, 1760–1810* (London: Macmillan, 1975).
131 *Anti-Slavery, Religion and Reform: Essays in Memory of Roger Anstey*, ed. Christine Bolt and Seymour Drescher (Folkestone: Archon Books, 1980).
132 Christopher Leslie Brown, *Moral Capital: Foundations of British Abolitionism* (Chapel Hill, NC: University of North Carolina Press, 2006).
133 William Hague, *William Wilberforce: The Life of the Great Anti-Slave Trade Campaigner* (London: Harper Perennial, 2007).

There was again a transatlantic difference over the theme of nationhood. For Americans, the question of how the diverse elements in a new land were forged into a nation was a matter of perennial importance. British historians of the recent past, by contrast, long left the equivalent issue to the medievalists and early modernists. A long-standing American tradition saw Evangelical religion as an agent of social integration in the early republic. Its hold on the historiography was, if anything, strengthened during the period. Mark Noll's *America's God* (2002) recounted how the Second Great Awakening exercised a pervasive influence on the society, so that, for example, in 1840 there were more than twice as many Methodist sermons heard per capita as letters delivered.[134] Daniel Walker Howe's volume on the years 1815–1848 in the Oxford History of the United States confirmed the general verdict that the Evangelical movement brought "civilization and order" to America.[135] In Britain the subject of national identity became a popular theme only as the devolution debate gathered momentum and particularly after the publication of Linda Colley's *Britons* (1992), a book which attributed a primary role to Protestantism in integrating the diverse parts of the United Kingdom during the eighteenth century.[136] Already, however, the question had been broached in volume 18 of *Studies in Church History*, which was devoted to *Religion and National Identity* (1982).[137] The president of the Ecclesiastical History Society who chose that theme, Keith Robbins, subsequently delivered a series of Ford Lectures that touched on the topic, issued a collection of essays about it and wrote the volume of the Oxford History of the Christian Church on twentieth-century Britain with the title *England, Ireland, Scotland, Wales* (2008).[138] Evangelicalism had its place in Robbins' analyses, but it was far more prominent in R. Tudur Jones' study of Wales between 1890 and 1914, *Faith and the Crisis of a Nation* (1981–82; ET 2004).[139]

---

134 Mark A. Noll, *America's God: From Jonathan Edwards to Abraham Lincoln* (New York: Oxford University Press, 2002), 201.
135 Daniel Walker Howe, *What God Hath Wrought: The Transformation of America, 1815-1848* (New York: Oxford University Press, 2007), 188.
136 Linda Colley, *Britons: Forging the Nation, 1707–1837* (New Haven, CT: Yale University Press, 1992).
137 *Religion and National Identity*, ed. Stuart Mews, *Studies in Church History*, vol. 18 (Oxford: Blackwell, 1982).
138 Keith Robbins, *Nineteenth-Century Britain: Integration and Diversity* (Oxford: Clarendon Press, 1988); *History, Religion and Identity in Modern Britain* (London: Hambledon Press, 1993); *England, Ireland, Scotland, Wales: The Christian Church, 1900-2000* (Oxford: Oxford University Press, 2008).
139 Robert Tudur Jones, *Faith and the Crisis of a Nation: Wales, 1890–1914* (Cardiff: University of Wales Press, 2004).

A collection of essays on religion and national identity in Wales and Scotland confirmed that Evangelicalism was closely bound up with the sense of nationhood in each.[140] The amplest treatment of the Evangelical factor in nationhood, however, was in Callum Brown's book *The Death of Christian Britain* (2000). In a work of marked originality, Brown contended that Evangelicalism shaped the discourse, and therefore the identity, of the British people between 1800 and the sudden onset of secularization in the 1960s.[141] At a single bound, British historiography caught up with its American counterpart in relating Evangelical religion to national identity.

Advances in the history of ideas also impinged on Evangelical historiography. The discussion of Evangelical theology was in a backward state for much of the period. Bernard Reardon of the University of Newcastle, the author of the most frequently used text on nineteenth-century religious thought in Britain, confined Evangelicalism to an introductory section, pointing out its "weaknesses." "Intellectually it was narrow," he wrote, "and naïvely reactionary."[142] That judgment reflected the paucity of research that had hitherto been undertaken in the field. America had been better served in the past with a series of monographs on the decline of Calvinism, but even in the United States there was a dearth of up-to-date studies until Bruce Kuklick's *Philosophers and Churchmen* (1985).[143] Stimulus to further work came chiefly from three directions. In the first place, the historians of science found it essential to engage with theology. Thus in 1991 John Hedley Brooke, in pushing forward the study of religion and science in the eighteenth and nineteenth centuries, explored Evangelical themes in some detail.[144] Four years later a conference under the auspices of the Institute for the Study of American Evangelicals brought together historians of science, including Brooke and historians of theology, to produce a collection of essays on *Evangelicals and Science in Historical Perspective* (1999).[145] Secondly, the history of political thought, the main genre in the study of ideas

---

140 *Religion and National Identity: Wales and Scotland, c.1700–2000*, ed. Robert Pope (Cardiff: University of Wales Press, 2001).
141 Callum Brown, *The Death of Christian Britain: Understanding Secularisation, 1800–2000* (London: Routledge, 2000).
142 Bernard M. G. Reardon, *Religious Thought in the Victorian Age: A Survey from Coleridge to Gore* (London: Longman, 1980), 29.
143 Bruce Kuklick, *Philosophers and Churchmen: From Jonathan Edwards to John Dewey* (New Haven, CT: Yale University Press, 1985).
144 John Hedley Brooke, *Science and Religion: Some Historical Perspectives* (Cambridge: Cambridge University Press, 1991).
145 *Evangelicals and Science in Historical Perspective*, ed. David N. Livingstone, D. G. Hart and Mark A. Noll (New York: Oxford University Press, 1999).

normally encountered by historians, prompted some of them to take a parallel interest in the history of religious thought. In particular, the novel methods in the history of political thought championed by Quentin Skinner at Cambridge inspired a few to apply similar techniques to Evangelical theologians. A collection of papers on the subject, showing an awareness of the limitations as well as the potential of Skinnerian methods in the intellectual history of religion, appeared in 2009.[146] And thirdly some historical theologians, with Alan Sell prominent among them in Britain and E. Brooks Holifield in America, laid bare hitherto unexplored dimensions of Evangelical thought.[147] One of the most illuminating, because opening up non-Anglican Evangelical theology with unprecedented clarity, was Mark Hopkins' *Nonconformity's Romantic Generation* (2004).[148] Sell, Hopkins and others began to fill up the gaps left by Reardon. Past Evangelical ideas were at last coming into their own.

It has to be admitted that the most radical historical approaches of the age did not take root in Evangelical studies. Apart from Callum Brown, few students of Evangelical history drew on postmodernist practice. That is primarily because so many of the specialists in the field were themselves Evangelicals. In general the Evangelical world reacted with horror to the challenge of postmodernism to cherished assumptions. In particular its characteristic denial of any single intended meaning in texts alarmed those who saw the Almighty as the primary author of scripture. Evangelicals published such works as *Truth Decay: Defending Christianity against the Challenges of Postmodernism*.[149] Only a handful of bolder souls in the Evangelical movement, such as Robert Webber, were willing to endorse a postmodern understanding of the world and virtually none of them was a historian.[150] Nevertheless the postmodern questioning of received practice constituted a stirring of the historiographical

---

146 *Seeing Things Their Way: Intellectual History and the Return of Religion*, ed. Alister Chapman, John Coffey and Brad S. Gregory (Notre Dame, IN: University of Notre Dame Press, 2009).

147 Alan P. F. Sell, *Defending and Declaring the Faith: Some Scottish Examples, 1860–1920* (Exeter: Paternoster Press, 1987), and many subsequent titles; E. Brooks Holifield, *Theology in America: Christian Thought from the Age of the Puritans to the Civil War* (New Haven, CT: Yale University Press, 2003).

148 Mark Hopkins, *Nonconformity's Romantic Generation: Evangelical and Liberal Theologies in Victorian England* (Carlisle: Paternoster Press, 2004).

149 Douglas Groothuis, *Truth Decay: Defending Christianity against the Challenges of Postmodernism* (Downers Grove, IL: InterVarsity Press, 2000).

150 Webber, *Ancient-Future Faith*, spec. 29–34. An exception was Stanley Grenz, an Evangelical who was sympathetic to postmodernism and, though primarily a theologian, also wrote history.

waters. In 2010 there appeared a collection of essays, *Confessing History*, which asked whether faith needed to be applied more drastically to the study of the past. Perhaps, the authors suggested, history had been unduly limited by its confinement to a professional straitjacket.[151] In due course that point of view was likely to produce more drastic reassessments of the Evangelical past. The period under review, however, had already, as we have seen, witnessed at least two significant advances in method associated with the Evangelical discovery of history. One was a recognition that history is a matter of perspectives on the past; the other was fresh attention to culture as a subject for historical investigation. Both innovations, though showing little or no postmodern inspiration, were parallel to the postmodernist enthusiasms for perspectives and culture, and sometimes they were put into practice even in advance of contemporary fashion. So the practitioners in the Evangelical school of history were by no means retrogressive in their methodological assumptions.

Conclusion

There was therefore a transformation of Evangelical history over the half-century between 1961 and 2011. At the opening of the period Evangelicals themselves neglected their history, producing chiefly denominational apologias, edifying biographies and missionary hagiographies. Evangelicals in Britain, and in some measure those elsewhere, did not figure prominently in mainstream historical literature. These patterns altered over the fifty years, with denominational, biographical and missionary studies all becoming much more scholarly and Evangelicalism sometimes (though by no means consistently) occupying an enhanced position in general histories. Religious changes affected the volume of Evangelical history, with Evangelicals increasing as a proportion of the churchgoing population, adherents of the movement pursuing careers in history and some of them creating effective institutional bases. The acceptance of tradition and the influence of neo-Calvinism helped promote their study of the past, though not without criticism from the Calvinist camp. Broader religious developments impinged on the type of history they wrote: the ecumenical imperative led to more cooperative studies and less anti-Catholic content, global links fostered international coverage, the theme of gospel and culture rose to prominence and equally spirituality came to the fore. At the same time scholarly trends shaped the way the history of Evan-

---

151 Eric Miller, "Introduction: A Tradition Renewed? The Challenge of a Generation," in *Confessing History: Explorations in the Christian Faith and the Historian's Vocation*, ed. John Fea, Jay Green and Eric Miller (Notre Dame, IN: University of Notre Dame Press, 2010), 9. I am grateful to Andy Tooley for this reference.

gelical movements was written. Methods and models from the social sciences were applied to the Evangelical past while Marxism both impinged on written history and showed that committed scholarship was possible. The rise of women's and gender history, race issues and national identity changed the content of Evangelical studies, each of these themes attracting historians from outside the movement to explore aspects of its record. The history of Evangelical ideas began to be nourished by advances in the history of science, the history of political thought and historical theology. And if postmodernism exerted little effect, Evangelical historians could claim to have anticipated its twin concerns for perspectives and culture. By the end of the period, historians in general paid growing attention to the history of the Evangelical movement, though there was much scope for further growth. Among Evangelical scholars themselves, the previous neglect of their past was over: they had made a discovery of history.

14

Science and Evangelical Theology in Britain from Wesley to Orr

Evangelicals, in Britain as elsewhere, have often been seen as wary of science. The movement springing from the Evangelical Revival, it has been supposed, generated a species of religion alien to painstaking research. The hothouse atmosphere of Evangelicalism, marked by intense feeling and sudden conversions, seemed unlikely to nurture the calm, reflective temper of scientific investigation. Historians have pointed out that it was not Evangelicals but liberal Anglicans of the Broad Church school, often seconded by Unitarians, who were at the heart of British science.[1] Evangelicals, by contrast, appeared the defenders of a literal interpretation of the Bible that made them suspicious of advances in the understanding of nature. It has been suggested, furthermore, that their antiscientific stance was theologically grounded. They so exalted biblical revelation as to cast aspersions on other sources of religious knowledge. Hence Evangelicals, it has been argued, were marked by a "rejection of the natural theology" that bound together science and religion during the eighteenth century.[2] The idea that the Creator could be known through his works, on this view, was dismissed as a vain human fancy. "For an evangelical minister," Adrian Desmond has written, "revelation overshadowed natural

---

1 Walter F. Cannon, "Scientists and Broad Churchmen: An Early Victorian Intellectual Network," *Journal of British Studies* 4:1 (1964), 65–88; Jack Morrell and Arnold Thackray, *Gentlemen of Science: Early Years of the British Association for the Advancement of Science* (Oxford: Clarendon Press, 1981), 224–45.
2 John Gascoigne, *Cambridge in the Age of the Enlightenment: Science, Religion and Politics from the Restoration to the French Revolution* (Cambridge: Cambridge University Press, 1989), 262. Similarly, the invaluable biography of Michael Faraday comments that natural theology was attacked by Evangelicals alongside Tractarians and Scriptural Geologists: Geoffrey Cantor, *Michael Faraday: Sandemanian and Scientist* (London: Macmillan, 1991), 137.

theology; it made any attempt to prove God's actions from nature not only redundant but actually pernicious."[3] The belief has become widespread that Evangelicals were hostile to natural theology because of their fundamental religious convictions. Their characteristic devotion to the Bible ranged them among the opponents of scientific progress.

Suspicions of Science

It must be conceded at the outset that there is an element of truth in this picture. Since Evangelicals were constantly aware of the illumination they derived from scripture, they tended to minimize the role of other sources of light. Thus in the later eighteenth century Thomas Haweis, a leading Anglican Evangelical and associate of the Countess of Huntingdon, contrasted the glowworm ray of human reason with the glory of the Sun of righteousness.[4] Haweis' contemporary, the influential clergyman John Newton, drew out the stern implication for the examination of creation. "The study of the works of God," he wrote, "independent of his word, though dignified with the name of *philosophy*, is not better than an elaborate trifling and waste of time."[5] It is hardly surprising that John Foster, a later Baptist essayist who was personally much better disposed towards scientific endeavor, complained that among serious persons there was an irreligious neglect of the works of the Almighty, which they tended to deprecate in relation to his word.[6] Likewise it was noted that in Scotland many Christians raised an outcry against any coverage in the pulpit of topics relating to the work of God in nature because they were thought to be remote from the doctrines of grace.[7] The Evangelicals' preoccupation with issues of salvation goes a long way towards explaining their reservations about giving a larger place to natural philosophy, but another reason was doubt about its epistemological status. The Bible, according to a correspondent of the Evangelical Anglican *Christian Observer* in 1839, "ought not to be bended and conformed to philosophy, but more plastic science should rather be assimilated to . . .

---

[3] Adrian Desmond, *The Politics of Evolution: Morphology, Medicine and Reform in Radical London* (Chicago: University of Chicago Press, 1989), 64.

[4] Thomas Haweis, *Essays on the Evidence, Characteristic Doctrines, and Influence of Christianity* (Bath: S. Hazard, 1790), iv, v, quoted in Arthur Skevington Wood, *Thomas Haweis, 1734-1820* (London: SPCK, 1957), 176.

[5] John Newton, "A Plan of a Compendious Christian Library," in *The Works of the Rev. John Newton*, 6 vols. (London: For the Author's Nephew, 1808), 1:215. Cf. Doreen Rosman, *Evangelicals and Culture* (London: Croom Helm, 1984), 228.

[6] John Foster, "Astronomy and Christian Revelation," *Critical Essays Contributed to "The Eclectic Review"*, ed. J. E. Ryland, 2 vols. (London: George Bell and Sons, 1879-85), 2:367.

[7] Thomas Dick, *The Christian Philosopher*, 2 vols. (Glasgow: William Collins, 1846), 1:26.

Scripture."[8] Science was plastic because the investigators of the natural world were constantly changing their minds. Why should their results be treated with wholehearted deference? Certainly there seemed no good reason for preferring scientific findings to the assured teachings of the Bible. Accordingly there was a thread of skepticism running through Evangelical attitudes to the accomplishments of researchers. Science seemed shifting sands; the Bible was a solid rock.

Hence Evangelicals were sometimes lukewarm towards natural theology. For John Newton, to attempt to reason towards God from the phenomena of nature was in itself fruitless. "The works of creation," he wrote, "may be compared to a fair character in cipher, of which the Bible is the key; without this key they cannot be understood."[9] The evidence for this conclusion was plain to anyone acquainted with the classics: the ancients were not persuaded by arguments drawn from the natural world to believe in the true God. Their authors dwelt on the harmony and design of the universe, pointed out J. B. Sumner, later the first Evangelical archbishop of Canterbury, but to no avail. That left us "undisputable proof that the God of NATURAL THEOLOGY will never be anything more than the dumb idol of philosophy; neglected by the philosopher himself, and unknown to the multitude; acknowledged in the closet, and forgotten in the world."[10] Even if, on occasion, the arguments of the philosophers carried conviction to the intellect, that was not far enough. "The works of creation," commented Daniel Wilson, later bishop of Calcutta, "wonderful as they are, are incapable of changing the heart."[11] Even Thomas Chalmers, the leading early nineteenth-century Evangelical in the Church of Scotland who wrote extensively on natural theology, held that the discipline had only limited powers. It shed light on the being of God and the human predicament but had nothing to say about the way of salvation. "Natural theology," he declared, "might announce the problem, but cannot resolve it."[12] He was aware that some distrusted the whole enterprise as an apparent attempt to supplant the gospel by another system of belief.[13] That

---

8   F. S. to editor, *Christian Observer*, March 1839, 154.
9   Newton, "A Plan," 215.
10 John B. Sumner, *A Treatise on the Records of the Creation*, 2 vols., 5th ed. (London: T. Hatchard, 1833), 1:x.
11 *The Thought of the Evangelical Leaders: Notes of the Discussions of the Eclectic Society, London, during the Years 1798–1814*, ed. John H. Pratt (Edinburgh: Banner of Truth Trust, 1978), 496.
12 Thomas Chalmers, *Institutes of Theology*, 2 vols. (Edinburgh: Sutherland and Knox, 1849), 2:135.
13 Chalmers, *Institutes*, 2:133.

suspicion Chalmers deplored; but his own stance is a clear sign that even among its exponents Evangelicals imposed strict limits on what natural theology was supposed to achieve.

The exaltation of scripture and the downgrading of natural theology could issue in a marginalization of science. Although the evangelist George Whitefield might allude to astronomy in his preaching, he injected little learning into his gospel sermons and was accused by a Cambridge don of decrying human reasoning altogether.[14] John Newton was willing to admit that Christians, as opposed to unbelievers, might trace God's wisdom in his works, but only "if their inquiries are kept within due bounds, and in a proper subservience to things of greater importances." In any case, he added, "they are comparatively few who have leisure, capacity, or opportunity for these inquiries."[15] Likewise Thomas Robinson, vicar of St Mary's, Leicester, believed that though the investigation of God's wisdom in his works was legitimate, "we shall find much matter for devout admiration, rather than for curious research and critical explanation."[16] In 1780 John Venn, subsequently the spiritual mentor of the Clapham Sect, warned his Cambridge friend Francis Wollaston not to let a passion for chemistry eclipse his work as a minister of Christ. "What comparison," he exclaimed, "can there be between saving a soul and analysing a salt!"[17] It is hardly strange that a religious movement should make religion its priority, but it has to be acknowledged that it also gave rise to bad science. The school of "Scriptural Geology," beginning in 1826 with a book of that title by the Evangelical clergyman George Bugg, tried to eliminate the apparent threat to the early chapters of Genesis from practicing geologists. The British Association for the Advancement of Science, which gathered together many real practitioners in the 1830s, was denounced by another Evangelical, Frederick Nolan, for aiming at "the ascendancy of philosophy on the ruins of religion."[18] J. Mellor Brown, another of Bugg's school, was typical in denying that any particular expertise was needed for engaging with scientific questions. The natu-

14 William Jay, *Memoirs of the Life and Character of the Late Rev. Cornelius Winter*, 2nd ed. (London: For William Baynes, 1812), 31; Gascoigne, *Cambridge*, 261.
15 Newton, "A Plan," 215.
16 Thomas Robinson, *The Christian System Unfolded in a Course of Practical Essays on the Principal Doctrines and Duties of Christianity*, 3 vols. (London: For the Author, 1805), 1:41.
17 John Venn to F. J. H. Wollaston, 15 June 1789, quoted in Michael Hennell, *John Venn and the Clapham Sect* (London: Lutterworth Press, 1958), 52.
18 Frederick Nolan, *The Analogy of Revelation and Science* (Oxford: J. H. Parker, 1833), viii. On "Scriptural Geology," see Milton Millhauser, *Just before Darwin: Robert Chambers and Vestiges* (Middletown, CT: Wesleyan University Press, 1959), 46–57.

ral world could be sufficiently understood a priori by the devout reasoner from the pages of the Bible.[19] Such an opinion, though having a long lineage, was tottering towards extinction. The Scriptural Geologists illustrate that Evangelicals were capable of closing their eyes to empirical science altogether.

Sympathy for Science

The evidence reviewed so far shows why the idea has sprung up that Evangelicalism was inimical to science. Allegiance to the Bible could lead the movement's adherents to disparage natural theology and to neglect or distort scientific endeavor itself. Yet that is a very partial sampling of their attitudes. Many of these instances—such as the views of Thomas Haweis and John Newton—come from the early days of the revival when it was small and embattled, struggling to make an impression on the mass of unbelief around it by summoning hearers to conversion. The pressing need was for preachers of the gospel, not for academics in any field. Thus the curriculum of the Dissenting theological academies associated with Evangelicalism concentrated on giving men basic Bible knowledge, not on turning them into scholars.[20] The movement's apologists were inclined to set out their central doctrines rather than to pursue related matters. Thus in his *Essays on the Most Important Subjects in Religion* (1794), Thomas Scott, well known as a commentator on the Bible, deals with topics such as the inspiration of the scriptures and the deity of Christ, justification and regeneration, never touching on questions of natural theology.[21] As time passed, however, there was a tendency for intellectual curiosity, which had never been dead, to branch out in fresh directions. Evangelical authors became more numerous; Evangelical periodicals multiplied; and topics were treated for the first time from an Evangelical angle. In the first half of the nineteenth century ideas that had previously existed only in germ within the movement began to be elaborated more fully. Sympathy for science was voiced more often. Although there were sometimes worries about its implications, the prevailing attitude was one of confidence that God's works were in harmony with God's word. "Nature and Revelation," wrote the leading Congregational theologian John Pye Smith in 1839, "are both beams of light from the same Sun of eternal truth; and there

---

19 James Mellor Brown, *Reflections on Geology: Suggested by the Perusal of Dr. Buckland's Bridgewater Treatise* (London: James Nisbet, 1838), 52.
20 Geoffrey F. Nuttall, *The Significance of Trevecca College, 1768-91* (London: Epworth Press, 1969).
21 Thomas Scott, *Essays on the Most Important Subjects in Religion* (London: D. Jacques, 1794).

cannot be discordance between them."²² Evangelical theology revealed an alignment with the scientific enterprise.

Consequently the leaders of Evangelical thought were on the same side as the broader Anglicans who endorsed and practiced the science of the day. William Buckland, professor of geology at Oxford, received the backing of the Evangelicals J. B. Sumner and G. S. Faber.²³ William Whewell and Adam Sedgwick, the leading Cambridge authorities on science, were quoted deferentially by J. H. Pratt, the Evangelical archdeacon of Calcutta, in his *Scripture and Science Not at Variance* (1856).²⁴ W. D. Conybeare, with the editor's approval, defended what has been called "the liberal Anglican position" on geology in the pages of the *Christian Observer*, the magazine of the moderate Evangelicals in the Church of England.²⁵ Although it gave space to the fulminations of George Bugg against infidel tendencies in geology, the *Christian Observer*, unlike the more conservative Evangelical journal the *Christian Guardian*, came down consistently against Bugg and the other Scriptural Geologists.²⁶ So did Pye Smith, the most respected Dissenting theologian of the period.²⁷ Around Thomas Chalmers in Scotland there was a circle of distinguished men who blended Evangelical theology with scientific practice: Sir David Brewster, a specialist in optics and eventually principal of the University of Edinburgh; John Fleming, professor of natural history at King's College, Aberdeen, and afterwards professor of natural science at New College, Edinburgh; and, among amateurs, Hugh Miller, the stonemason turned *littérateur* who

---

22 John Pye Smith, *On the Relation between the Holy Scriptures and Some Parts of Geological Science* (London: Jackson and Walford, 1839), 168.
23 Nicolaas A. Rupke, *The Great Chain of History: William Buckland and the English School of Geology (1814–1849)* (Oxford: Clarendon Press, 1983), 14.
24 John H. Pratt, *Scripture and Science Not at Variance*, 3rd ed. (London: Thomas Hatchard, 1859), 25, 108, 87. Both Whewell and Sedgwick had Evangelical leanings, but neither was an adherent of the Evangelical party. See John H. Brooke, "Indications of a Creator: Whewell as Apologist and Priest," in *William Whewell: A Composite Portrait*, ed. Menachem Fisch and Simon Schaffer (Oxford: Clarendon Press, 1991), 161–62. The remaining distance between Sedgwick and Evangelicalism is indicated in the *Christian Observer*, June 1834, 371.
25 *Christian Observer*, May 1834, 306–9. Cf. Morrell and Thackray, *Gentlemen of Science*, 236.
26 *Christian Observer*, October 1829, 647–48; April 1834, 207; June 1834, 369–85; July 1834, 395; August 1834, 482. Cf. Boyd Hilton, *The Age of Atonement* (Oxford: Clarendon Press, 1988), 23.
27 Pye Smith, *On the Relation*, 172–97.

pursued and popularized geological investigation.[28] Cambridge produced a crop of eminent scientific Evangelicals, including Isaac Milner, Francis Wollaston and William Parish, successive occupants of the Jacksonian chair of natural and experimental philosophy.[29] The university's graduates, many Evangelicals among them, sometimes imbibed a taste for experiment. John Venn, despite his warning to Wollaston about the siren appeal of chemistry, filled his notebooks with diagrams on optics, astronomy, hydrostatics and mechanics.[30] Likewise John Ryland, principal of Bristol Baptist College, was said to delight in natural history, being "much assisted by the structure of his eyes which were a kind of natural microscope."[31] The passion for fossils of Philip Gosse, a member of the Brethren, has become enshrined in English literature.[32] Scientific pursuits could be little more than a hobby; but equally they could form the basis of a career. To uphold Evangelical theology was certainly no bar to scientific interests.

An Enlightenment Approach

It was not merely that the two—Evangelicalism and science—were compatible; rather, there was a tight bond between them. Both as they were pursued in the late eighteenth and early nineteenth centuries bore the marks of the Enlightenment. Few would doubt that the Newtonian framework of British science was associated with the Age of Reason: the enlightened ideal of free inquiry leading to greater understanding through empirical investigation was itself modeled on scientific method. Increasingly it has also been recognized that Evangelical thought shared the same values, with reason occupying the supreme place.[33] When, in 1801 and again in 1813, the Eclectic Society of leading Evangelicals

---

28   Paul Baxter, "Science and Belief in Scotland, 1805–1868: The Scottish Evangelicals" (Unpublished Ph.D. dissertation, University of Edinburgh, 1985).
29   Rosman, *Evangelicals and Culture*, 205.
30   Hennell, *Venn*, 2.
31   Robert Hall, *Sermon Occasioned by the Death of the Rev. John Ryland, D.D.* (London, 1825), 43, quoted in Herbert MacLachlan, *English Education under the Test Acts: Being the History of the Nonconformist Academies, 1662–1820* (Manchester: Manchester University Press, 1931), 97.
32   Edmund Gosse, *Father and Son* (London: William Heinemann, 1907), chap. 5.
33   Roger Anstey, *The Atlantic Slave Trade and British Abolition, 1760–1810* (London: Macmillan, 1975), chaps. 7 and 8; Bernard Semmel, *The Methodist Revolution* (London: Heinemann, 1974); Frederick Dreyer, "Faith and Experience in the Thought of John Wesley," *American Historical Review* 88:1 (1983), 12–30; David W. Bebbington, *Evangelicalism in Modern Britain: A History from the 1730s to the 1980s* (London: Unwin Hyman, 1989), chap. 2. See also 1:2: "Revival and Enlightenment in Eighteenth-Century England."

met to consider the province of reason in religion, they decided that it fulfilled a central role. "I do not oppose reason and revelation," declared Thomas Scott. "Reason is the eye, revelation the sun."[34] Hence there was no intrinsic antithesis between vital religion and learning. Cornelius Winter, a younger associate of George Whitefield, for instance, began his ministry without a classical education, yet valued erudition, gained skill in Greek and Hebrew, read and corresponded in Latin, and became proficient in French.[35] John Wesley was constantly urging his preachers to read and to promote reading among the early Methodists.[36] The scriptures themselves seemed to sanction the pursuit of natural philosophy in particular. "Though they give us no system of astronomy," wrote the Baptist divine Andrew Fuller, "yet they urge us to study the works of God, and teach us to adore him upon every discovery."[37] Wesley, who took a serious interest in scientific matters, issued a two-volume *Survey of the Wisdom of God in the Creation* (1763).[38] His central preoccupation, in typical Enlightenment fashion, was with the usefulness of new discoveries. In another work, *The Desideratum: Or Electricity Made Plain and Useful* (1760), he set out the therapeutic value of electrical current. It was, he remarked with his accustomed precision, a "general and rarely failing remedy, in nervous cases of every kind (old palsies excepted)."[39] Science, as an essential component of the Enlightenment worldview, came naturally to most Evangelicals.

The most striking exceptions in the Evangelical community confirm this analysis. By the 1820s the Romantic reaction against Enlightenment thought was making headway in society at large. Mediated through Coleridge and others, intellectual dispositions that had previously been more powerful in Germany began to penetrate the British Evangelical world. The values of the previous century—reason, utility, free inquiry—were eagerly discarded by a small number of individuals who began to dwell on dramatic religious themes such as the second advent and the revival of glossolalia. At their head was Edward

---

34 *Thought of the Evangelical Leaders*, ed. Pratt, 230–32, 523–24, spec. 231.
35 Jay, *Winter*, 249.
36 Horace F. Mathews, *Methodism and the Education of the People, 1791–1851* (London: Epworth Press, 1949).
37 Andrew Fuller, "The Gospel Its Own Witness," in *The Complete Works of the Rev. Andrew Fuller*, ed. Andrew G. Fuller, 5 vols. (London: Holdsworth and Ball, 1831), 1:121.
38 John Wesley, *A Survey of the Wisdom of God in the Creation*, 2 vols. (Bristol: William Pine, 1763). See John W. Haas, Jr, "Eighteenth Century Evangelical Responses to Science: John Wesley's Enduring Legacy," *Science and Christian Belief* 6 (1994), 83–102.
39 John Wesley, "The Desideratum: Or Electricity Made Plain and Useful," *The Works of the Rev. John Wesley, M.A.*, 32 vols. (Bristol: William Pine, 1773), 24:287.

Irving, minister of the Church of Scotland congregation in Hatton Gardens, London.[40] Scientific investigation soon fell under suspicion in this group. "Again," asked Irving in a lecture of 1828, "are you students and inquirers into any region of nature? [T]hen, be assured, that the understanding will blind the reason: the understanding which judgeth by the sense of the nature of things, will blind the reason, which judgeth by the conscience. And of all blinds and eclipses, this is the most helpless which hath darkened all our scientific men to the light of God."[41] Irving exploited the Coleridgean distinction between "understanding," mere sense perception, and "reason," with the peculiar meaning of moral intuition, in order to mount his blanket denunciation. Similarly his associate Henry Drummond condemned the habit of looking into secondary causes, as did scientists, instead of contemplating the first Cause of all things. This approach to the world, Drummond claimed, was to live by sight rather than by faith.[42] Some years later William Tarbet, a minister of the Catholic Apostolic Church created on Irving's principles by Drummond's circle, expounded some of the consequences. "It is by faith, then, and not by science that we can understand how God made the world. He has revealed it to us. And *He* ought to know."[43] Astronomy and geology must bow before the letter of the scriptures. Similar attitudes appeared in the diatribe against natural theology issued by the Tractarian William Irons in 1836.[44] Tractarians shared with the knot of radical Evangelicals around Irving a reverence for authority and an exaltation of faith that were profoundly hostile to free inquiry.[45] Here, in the church groupings most swayed by Romanticism, there were deep-seated antiscientific convictions. They were not present, however, among the mass of Evangelicals who remained faithful to the legacy of the Enlightenment.

That is evident in the widespread respect, almost amounting to adulation, for the memory of Sir Isaac Newton. Wesley led the way with a striking eulogy. "The immortal man," he wrote in his *Concise Ecclesiastical History* (1781),

---

40   Bebbington, *Evangelicalism in Modern Britain*, chap. 3.
41   Edward Irving, "Lectures on the Parable of the Sower," *Sermons, Lectures and Occasional Discourses*, 3 vols. (London: R. B. Seeley and W. Burnside, 1828), 2:709.
42   [Henry Drummond], *Dialogues on Prophecy* (London: James Nisbet, 1827), 346.
43   [William Tarbet], *Astronomy and Geology as Taught in the Holy Scriptures* (Liverpool: James Woollard, 1855), 17, quoted in Michael J. Crowe, *The Extraterrestrial Life Debate, 1750-1900: The Idea of a Plurality of Worlds from Kant to Lowell* (Cambridge: Cambridge University Press, 1986), 338.
44   William J. Irons, *On the Whole Doctrine of Final Causes* (London: J. G. & F. Rivington, 1836). See Pietro Corsi, *Science and Religion: Baden Powell and the Anglican Debate, 1800-1860* (Cambridge: Cambridge University Press, 1988), 179-80.
45   Rupke, *Great Chain of History*, chap. 20.

"to whose immense genius and indefatigable industry philosophy owed its greatest improvements, and who carried the lamp of knowledge into paths of knowledge that had been unexplored before, was Sir Isaac Newton, whose name was revered, and his genius admired, even by his warmest adversaries."[46] Later Methodists, including the polymath Adam Clarke and the theologian Richard Watson, treated Newton with deference.[47] So did the Anglican Evangelicals Joseph Milner, J. B. Sumner, and, later on, T. R. Birks, who referred to the "immortal writer of the Principia."[48] The Baptist Andrew Fuller yoked Newton's name with those of Bacon and Boyle as admirable examples of the combination of philosophy and Christianity.[49] In Scotland Thomas Chalmers contrasted Newton's sound reasoning with the "unfounded imaginations of Des Cartes" and devoted the second of his *Astronomical Discourses* (1817) to praise of the scientist.[50] Sir David Brewster wrote two separate lives of Newton, in 1831 and again in 1855.[51] Newton's Arianism, of which Chalmers and Brewster were both aware, did little in their eyes to detract from his greatness. Even the Scriptural Geologist George Bugg claimed to be a Newtonian.[52] It might be supposed that the rival Hutchinsonian scheme of natural philosophy drawn from the Hebrew text of the Bible would appeal to Evangelicals.[53] Certainly

46 John Wesley, *A Concise Ecclesiastical History from the Birth of Christ to the Beginning of the Present Century*, 3 vols. (London: Paramore, 1781), 3:332, quoted by John C. English, "John Wesley and Isaac Newton's 'System of the World,'" *Proceedings of the Wesley Historical Society* 48:3 (1991), 73.
47 Adam Clarke, "Some Observations on the Being and Providence of a God," *Discourses on Various Subjects Relative to the Being and Attributes of God and His Works in Creation, Providence and Grace*, 3 vols. (London: J. and T. Clarke, 1828–30), 2:385–86; Richard Watson, *Theological Institutes*, 14th ed., 4 vols. (London: Wesleyan Conference Office, 1865), 1:407.
48 Joseph Milner, "A Selection of Tracts and Essays, Theological and Historical," in *The Works of Joseph Milner*, ed. Isaac Milner, 8 vols. (London: For T. Cadell and W. Davies, 1810), 8:285; Sumner, *Treatise*, 1:325; Thomas R. Birks, *The Bible and Modern Thought* (London: Religious Tract Society, 1862), 310.
49 Fuller, "Gospel Its Own Witness," 117.
50 Thomas Chalmers, *The Evidence and Authority of the Christian Revelation* (Edinburgh: for William Blackwood, 1814), 189; Thomas Chalmers, *A Series of Discourses on the Christian Revelation Viewed in Connection with the Modern Astronomy*, 4th ed. (Glasgow: John Smith and Son, 1817), 56–93.
51 Sir David Brewster, *The Life of Sir Isaac Newton* (London: John Murray, 1831); *Memoirs of the Life, Writings and Discoveries of Sir Isaac Newton* (Edinburgh: T. Constable and Co., 1855).
52 *Christian Observer*, June 1828, 367.
53 On Hutchinsonianism, see Geoffrey N. Cantor, "Revelation and the Cyclical Cosmos of John Hutchinson," in *Images of the Earth: Essays in the History of the Environmental*

William Romaine, the earliest Evangelical Anglican to occupy a London pulpit, used his single series of lectures as Gresham Professor of Astronomy to assail Newtonian philosophy on Hutchinsonian lines.[54] As late as 1828 an Evangelical Oxford graduate, claiming that Newton's followers rather than the great man himself had made most of the mistakes, professed himself a Hutchinsonian.[55] But Thomas Haweis was more representative in being initially attracted by the devotional spirit of the Hutchinsonians but then alienated by their High Church sacramentarianism.[56] Wesley was fascinated by their strangely cabalistic scheme but found it untenable.[57] So it was Newtonianism that claimed the allegiance of nearly all the branches of the Evangelical community. Chalmers was an uncompromising champion of simple induction. "Nothing," he wrote, "can be more safe or more infallible than the procedure of inductive philosophy as applied to the phenomena of external nature. It is at liberty to classify appearances, but then in the work of classifying, it must be directed only by observation."[58] Similarly Wesley, whose *Survey of the Wisdom of God* (1770) included a history of empiricism, was so wedded to experience as the grand source of knowledge that he wished to banish hypotheses from experimentation altogether.[59] Others were more sophisticated. Brewster, under the influence of the Scottish common-sense philosophy of Thomas Reid and Dugald Stewart, believed that imaginative hypotheses were essential.[60] Pye Smith recognized that deduction had a place as well as induction. "In Physical Science," he explained, "the evidence of truth is obtained by drawing inferences from observations of facts made known by our senses; and confirmed in many cases, and those the most important, by the application of Mathematics."[61] His fellow Congregationalist Henry Rogers perceived the need for both induction and deduction in scientific activity but, like Pye Smith, gave induction the priority.[62] In the same way as scientists, Evangelicals habitually appealed to

---

Sciences, ed. Ludmilla J. Jordanova and Roy S. Porter (Chalfont St Giles, Bucks: British Society for the History of Science, 1979), 3-22.
54 William B. Cadogan, "The Life of the Rev. William Romaine, M.A.," in *Works of the Late Reverend William Romaine, A.M.*, 8 vols. (London: For T. Chapman, 1796), 7:34.
55 *Christian Observer*, October 1828, 631-32.
56 Wood, *Haweis*, 46-47.
57 English, "John Wesley and Isaac Newton's 'System,'" 84-85.
58 Chalmers, *Evidence and Authority*, 191.
59 John Wesley, "Primitive Physic," in *Works*, 25:8.
60 Baxter, "Science and Belief," 117.
61 Pye Smith, *On the Relation*, 21.
62 Alan P. F. Sell, "Henry Rogers and the Eclipse of Faith," in *Dissenting Thought and the Life of the Churches: Studies in an English Tradition* (San Francisco: Mellen Research University Press, 1990), 492-93.

observation and experience. Describing their faith as "experimental Christianity,"[63] they saw no difference between procedures in religion and science. "We are applying," declared Chalmers, "the very same principles to a system of theism, that we would do to a system of geology." In order to understand the ways of God in either salvation or creation there was but one requirement. "Give us the facts," demanded Chalmers.[64] The result of the application of empirical technique in either field was an assured grasp of reality. Although their formulations differed, Evangelicals accepted the standard method of the Enlightenment as the high road to knowledge.

Natural Theology

Because theology and science shared the same modus operandi, the two disciplines could be closely integrated with each other. Their intersection was chiefly in the field of natural theology, which therefore calls for more detailed examination. This department of divinity was succinctly defined by Thomas Gisborne, an Anglican Evangelical specialist in the subject, as "that knowledge concerning the Deity and our relations to Him, which by observation and natural reasoning man is capable of attaining."[65] It encompassed more than the semi-scientific province of what could be observed in creation of the Creator. It included as well the dimension of a priori reasoning for the existence of God. Although the Methodist Adam Clarke set out the five classic arguments presented by Aquinas and found them "powerfully convincing," he was unusual among Evangelicals in giving them substantial weight.[66] The Newtonianism of the Evangelicals normally predisposed them in favor of concentrating on the evidence of the Almighty in the natural world. They were aware of standing in a long tradition. The *Methodist Magazine*, for example, quoted Cicero's argument for a Creator at length in successive issues between February and June 1804.[67] Richard Watson and many others listed later authorities, almost always including John Ray's *The Wisdom of God Manifested in the Works of Creation* (1691) and William Derham's *Physico-Theology*

---

63 E.g., Edward Williams, *An Essay on the Equity of Divine Government and the Sovereignty of Divine Grace*, 3rd ed. (London: For Francis Westley, 1825), xlviii.
64 Chalmers, *Evidence and Authority*, 204.
65 Thomas Gisborne, *The Testimony of Natural Theology to Christianity* (London: For T. Cadell and W. Davies, 1818), 1.
66 Clarke, "On the Being and Attributes of God," *Discourses*, 1:6.
67 *Methodist Magazine*, February 1804, 78–81; March 1804, 127–28; April 1804, 168–71; May 1804, 217–20; June 1804, 265–68.

(1713).⁶⁸ The *Methodist Magazine* went out of its way to note Derham's evidence for a benevolent Deity from the fact that eyelashes grow only to a suitable length and so never need cutting.⁶⁹ There was a chorus of approval for the latest statement of the overall case in William Paley's *Natural Theology* (1802).⁷⁰ The theological tradition least enthusiastic about this strand of Christian apologetic, it has been pointed out, was High Churchmanship, where the Hutchinsonian leaven was still at work. William Van Mildert, in his Boyle Lectures for 1802–05, was extremely reserved about the light shed by nature on the Creator.⁷¹ Evangelicals, by contrast, were usually eager to avail themselves of the armory of natural theology.

What did they hope to achieve? John Brooke has drawn attention to the variety of purposes that natural theology was meant to serve.⁷² Within the heterogeneous Evangelical movement, virtually every suggested aim was pursued by at least a few. The small number of scientists, such as John Fleming, who after his time at King's College, Aberdeen, became first professor of natural science at New College, Edinburgh, found physico-theology a useful vehicle for the promotion of science and a source of regulative principles for the discipline.⁷³ Archdeacon Pratt wrote his *Scripture and Science Not at Variance* (1856) to provide reassurance for fellow believers and to indicate the most tenable apologetic positions.⁷⁴ Pye Smith, in putting down the Scriptural Geologists, was similarly showing a legitimate way of reconciling science and religion but was also taking the opportunity to celebrate the powers of reason against misdirected enthusiasm. There was sometimes an element of social conservatism about the enterprise: in 1803 a contributor to the *Christian*

---

68 Watson, *Theological Institutes*, 1:445; Pye Smith, *On the Relation*, 27; James McCosh, *The Method of the Divine Government Physical and Moral*, 11th ed. (London: Macmillan and Co., 1878), 3.
69 *Methodist Magazine*, April 1804, 167.
70 Sumner, *Treatise*, 1:30; Watson, *Theological Institutes*, 2:8–10, 51–55, 122–27; William Cunningham, *Theological Lectures on Subjects Connected with Natural Theology, Evidences of Christianity, the Canon and Inspiration of Scripture* (London: James Nisbet and Co., 1878), 107.
71 Elizabeth A. Varley, *The Last of the Prince Bishops: William Van Mildert and the High Church Movement of the Early Nineteenth Century* (Cambridge: Cambridge University Press, 1992), 39–45.
72 John H. Brooke, "The Natural Theology of the Geologists: Some Theological Strata," in *Theories of the Earth*, ed. Jordanova and Porter, spec. 40; Brooke, "Indications of a Creator," spec. 149–51.
73 John Fleming, *The Institutes of Natural Science* (Edinburgh: For the Author, 1846).
74 John H. Pratt, *Scripture and Science Not at Variance* (London: Thomas Hatchard, 1856).

Observer, probably William Wilberforce, contended that natural theology could counteract the atheism of France that had led to the revolutionary chaos of the previous decade.[75] A less epic form of social control was in the mind of Pye Smith when he remarked on the leisure enjoyed by young people in the evening. "The cultivation of Natural History and the Sciences," he observed, "will be a dignified means of excluding those modes of abusing time which are the sin and disgrace of many young persons."[76] Not only did natural theology provide common ground for church and chapel, as John Brooke has suggested, but it also mediated, within the Evangelical movement, between Arminians and Calvinists.[77] Arguments for God's existence drawn from nature were also valued as the stock-in-trade of the missionary. For pre-evangelism among the heathen, Gisborne pointed out, it was essential to gain access to their minds through natural theology.[78] By far its most important function, however, was the defense of Christianity against skepticism at home. "In these days," wrote Adam Clarke, "when blasphemy stalks abroad unmolested, and the Bible is treated with malicious and satanic indignity—every Christian, who has it in his power, and especially every Christian minister, should acquaint himself with these arguments!"[79] Thus equipped, the disciple could give a reason for the hope within him that might awaken the careless unbeliever. Natural theology was intrinsic to the missionary strategy of Evangelicalism.

The kernel of physico-theology was the argument for the existence of God from design in external nature. It rested, as Chalmers explained, on an analogy between human and divine craftsmanship. Just as a house, the result of contrivance, indicated a contriver, so the world, adapted to the welfare of its inhabitants, implied an architect.[80] The appropriate inference was the reality of a Being infinite in power, wisdom and goodness. References to the "final cause" of the created order illustrate the rooting of this mode of thinking in the scholastic tradition, but Evangelicals commonly presented this teleological argument in distinctively Newtonian guise.[81] Adam Clarke discussed elliptic orbits, Pye Smith traced the causes of motion and both J. B. Sumner and Richard Watson stressed the simplicity of gravitation as evidence for divine

---

75 *Christian Observer*, March 1803, 162. Wilberforce is known to have held the estimate of Paley contained in this review: Rosman, *Evangelicals and Culture*, 44.
76 Pye Smith, *On the Relation*, 327.
77 E.g., the Methodist Richard Watson cited writers from the Reformed tradition such as Thomas Gisborne in *Theological Institutes*, 2:134–43.
78 Gisborne, *Testimony of Natural Theology*, 2.
79 Clarke, "Experimental Religion and Its Fruits," *Discourses*, 1:129–30.
80 Chalmers, *Institutes*, 1:91.
81 Sumner, *Treatise*, 1:29; Watson, *Theological Institutes*, 2:109; Fleming, *Institutes*, 6.

wisdom.[82] The idea of adaptation—what Chalmers called contrivance—was pivotal to the argument. When plants were so formed as to be nourished by moisture and animals so constituted as to be nourished by plants, the whole structure of nature seemed to manifest design. The adaptations were the effects, the Designer the cause. The eighteenth century, however, had witnessed a powerful challenge to this mode of thinking from David Hume. Subsequent writers usually located the problem in his analysis of causation. Any cause, Hume held, was only contingently related to its alleged effect. If he was right, the design argument fell to the ground. The rebuttal of Hume, implicitly or explicitly, was therefore a standard element in the Evangelical case. The contention of Thomas Reid and Dugald Stewart that the concept of causation was part of the data of human experience was repeated by apologists in England as well as in their native Scotland.[83] Evangelicals adopted the same groundwork of reasoning as their British contemporaries.

Yet Evangelicals typically pressed the argument further than the other thinkers of their day.[84] Although they agreed with the thrust of William Paley's classic statement of the case, they found aspects of it unsatisfactory. The reviewer in the *Christian Observer*, probably Wilberforce, criticized Paley on the one hand for denying the inherent sinfulness of human nature and on the other for a shallow treatment of the problem of the existence of venomous and predatory animals. This dysfunctional aspect of creation could not be explained away, in the manner of Paley, as being outbalanced by the evidence of benevolence. Rather, along with the other signs of natural and moral evil, it was an indication that the world was in a state of degradation resulting from the fall of humanity. Natural theology taught the holiness of God, the sinfulness of human beings and even the need for redemption.[85] Likewise the Methodist Richard Watson, though following Paley about predatory animals, argued that "we see natural evils, and punitive acts of the divine administration, not because God is not good, but because he is just as well as good."[86] The geological strata illustrating past convulsions of the world, according to the *Methodist Magazine* for 1825, together with volcanoes, earthquakes,

---

82 Pye Smith, *On the Relation*, 25–26. Clarke, "Some Observations on the Being and Providence of God," *Discourses*, 2:384–87; Sumner, *Treatise*, 2:8; Watson, *Theological Institutes*, 2:111.
83 E.g. Sumner, *Treatise*, 1:300–16; Watson, *Theological Institutes*, 1:418–24.
84 Rosman, *Evangelicals and Culture*, 44–47; Hilton, *Age of Atonement*, 21–22; Daniel F. Rice, "Natural Theology and Scottish Philosophy in the Thought of Thomas Chalmers," *Scottish Journal of Theology* 24:1 (1971), 23–46, at 36–37.
85 *Christian Observer*, June 1803, 371–73, spec. 373.
86 Watson, *Theological Institutes*, 2:133.

thunderstorms, tempests and hurricanes, showed that human beings could not be innocent.[87] The irregularity and confusion of the earth, Thomas Gisborne similarly believed, revealed the holiness of the Almighty in punishing sin.[88] This type of theodicy was systematically stated by Chalmers. The miseries of life, he contended, could be explained only as a consequence of the displeasure of a righteous God. Since so much physical evil was the result of moral evil, the world would be happy if it were not depraved. Its present state taught that "while God loves the happiness of His children, He loves their virtue more."[89] Partly because of Chalmers' influence, and partly because it possessed the clear merit of grappling with the twin problems of suffering and evil, this version of natural theology spread. Inevitably it shaped the thinking of Chalmers' fellow Free Churchman William Cunningham, but hints of a similar approach can also be detected in the Anglican William Whewell.[90] The Evangelical modification of natural theology extended beyond the boundaries of the movement to become the prevailing attitude in the early Victorian years.

Challenges from Science

The tradition of reasoning from natural phenomena towards the Christian God, enriched by this Evangelical input, was nevertheless encountering fresh difficulties. One was the problem of the immensity of space. During the eighteenth century astronomers had discovered an ever-expanding array of stars. The increasing likelihood that other worlds were populated posed a question for faith. To believe that God created a plurality of inhabited worlds, according to the Deist Thomas Paine, was incompatible with Christian belief. The idea that the obscure earth was the scene of the death of the Son of God seemed ridiculous in light of the extent of the universe.[91] Andrew Fuller, the Baptist theologian, was early in responding to this assault on the central Evangelical doctrine of the atonement. There was no reason, Fuller contended, why one small part of creation should not be chosen as the theater of God's most glorious works, though the theologian treated life on other planets as no more than hypothetical.[92] Chalmers, who elaborated some of Fuller's points in his *Astronomical Discourses*, was less tentative. "Worlds roll in these distant regions,"

---

87 *Methodist Magazine*, April 1826, 240–44.
88 Gisborne, *Testimony of Natural Theology*, spec. 29, 69.
89 Chalmers, *Institutes*, 1:110.
90 Cunningham, *Theological Lectures*, 120; Brooke, "Indications of a Creator," 154.
91 Thomas Paine, "The Age of Reason: Part First," in *Thomas Paine: Political Writings*, ed. Bruce Kuklick (Cambridge: Cambridge University Press, 1989), 243.
92 Fuller, "Gospel Its Own Witness," 119, 118.

he declared; "and worlds must be the mansions of life and of intelligence."[93] Chalmers popularized among Evangelicals the idea of intelligent extraterrestrial life. The Baptist essayist John Foster, an Anglican Evangelical contributor to the *Christian Observer* and the Scottish Secessionist Thomas Dick all endorsed the opinion.[94] Sir David Brewster did battle for it in a celebrated exchange with Whewell.[95] Although, in deference to the view of Wesley, the Methodist *London Quarterly Review* was staunchly skeptical about Brewster's position, nearly three-quarters of non-Unitarian Protestant opinion took his side.[96] It seems remarkable that Evangelicals should hold a speculative notion that potentially endangered the atonement, but, as one of them put it, "the wisdom and goodness of God would be compromised by a material creation, stupendous and astounding as that which astronomy discloses, and yet wholly discontinuous from moral life."[97] If the galaxies lacked intelligent beings, the purposiveness of the universe would be undermined. The strength of the belief by Evangelicals in the plurality of inhabited worlds is a further sign of their commitment to the argument from design.

A second problem concerned not space, but time. In the early nineteenth century the rising science of geology posed insistent questions about the interpretation of the Bible. Fossils from rocks revealed extinct creatures that had roamed the earth in a remote and unimagined past. The fact that some had evidently been carnivorous challenged the belief, endorsed in the New Testament, that death entered the world through the fall of humanity. The biblical text was consequently reinterpreted as teaching that Adam's sin was responsible only for the introduction of the death of human beings.[98] Many Evangelicals were capable of taking the absence of evidence for Noah's flood equally in their stride. John Fleming, himself a practicing scientist, accepted as early as 1826 that, since the waters rose and fell gradually, it was unsurprising that there were no geological signs of catastrophe, and informed opinion followed his lead in seeing no disharmony between the biblical text and scientific discovery.[99] More intractable was the reconciliation of fresh evidence with the opening of Genesis. How could the vast eons of geological time be matched with the

93 Chalmers, *Modern Astronomy*, 41.
94 Foster, "Astronomy and Christian Revelation," spec. 359–60; *Christian Observer*, July 1834, 388–95; Dick, *Christian Philosopher*, 1:100.
95 John H. Brooke, "Natural Theology and the Plurality of Worlds: Observations on the Brewster-Whewell Debate," *Annals of Science* 34:3 (1977), 222–84.
96 Crowe, *Extraterrestrial Life Debate*, 338, 352.
97 *Christian Observer*, July 1834, 390.
98 Pye Smith, *On the Relation*, 294–98; Pratt, *Scripture and Science*, 41–43.
99 Pye Smith, 113 (quoting Fleming); Pratt, *Scripture and Science*, 45–46.

information that creation occupied a mere six days? One answer, retaining a literal interpretation of the six days, was to hypothesize an interval, perhaps of enormous duration, between the creation "in the beginning" recorded in the Bible's first verse and the ordering of the present state of the world described from the second verse onwards. Chalmers adopted this viewpoint in his pre-Evangelical period and propagated it steadily afterwards.[100] The theory became precarious, however, when Charles Lyell demonstrated that rocks laid down before the human era contained fossils of species still living, so undermining the idea of a break between the early tracts of the planet's history and the phase following the six days' work.[101] Despite ingenious attempts to shore up the tottering interpretation, many Evangelicals followed Hugh Miller in turning to the scheme earlier proposed by the French natural philosophers Buffon and Cuvier, according to which the "days" were to be understood figuratively as protracted epochs.[102] Although there was considerable difficulty in fitting the sequence of the strata into the order of the days in Genesis, this speculation gained ground during the later nineteenth century and was still being advanced by James Orr in the twentieth.[103] The two schemes of harmonization proved popular because they appeared to uphold the integrity of science as well as scripture. Unlike on the one hand the liberal Anglican Baden Powell, who resorted to treating Genesis as myth, and on the other the Scriptural Geologists, who closed their eyes to fresh discoveries, many Evangelicals ardently wished to believe in both. Their allegiance to the Bible is predictable; what is striking is the degree of their commitment to science.

A third, and ultimately the greatest, challenge to the synthesis of theology and science came from the idea of the transformation of species. If plants and animals could adapt themselves, the evidence for contrivance in the natural world vanished. The new doctrine, in the form of the evolutionary thought of the French naturalist Lamarck, became rooted by the 1830s in the radical circles of London medicine.[104] The discovery of the law of the conservation of energy in the following decade encouraged expectations that similar natural continuities awaited discovery elsewhere. The rising tide of a broadly Romantic temper, expressed in a vogue for German *Natürphilosophie*, undergirded

100 Baxter, "Science and Belief," 71–72.
101 Pratt, *Scripture and Science*, 63–65.
102 Hugh Miller, *The Two Records: Mosaic and Geological* ([London: J. Nisbet], 1854), 17–33. Cf. Hugh Miller, *The Testimony of the Rocks* (Edinburgh: Thomas Constable & Co., 1857).
103 James Orr, "Science and Christian Faith," in *The Fundamentals*, 12 vols. (Chicago: Testimony Publishing Co., 1910–15), 4:101.
104 Desmond, *Politics of Evolution*.

the drift of opinion.¹⁰⁵ The trends culminated in the appearance in 1859 of Charles Darwin's *Origin of Species*. There were Evangelicals who showed sympathy for this movement of thought. Pye Smith, for example, maintaining in 1839 the high probability of Laplace's nebular hypothesis, drew the inference that God originally created a small number of simple bodies, which, operating according to laws, produced "all the forms and changes of organic and inorganic natures."¹⁰⁶ The publication in 1844 of Robert Chambers' *Vestiges of the Natural History of Creation*, however, provoked a dismayed reaction. The book exploited Laplace to maintain the transformation of species as a universal law and so appeared to imply that everything in creation was ultimately material. Brewster, who, like Pye Smith, had previously endorsed the nebular hypothesis, now repudiated it; a chair of natural science was established at New College, Edinburgh, to counter erroneous theories; and Hugh Miller denounced *Vestiges* in his *Foot-Prints of the Creator* (1847).¹⁰⁷ Evangelicals tended to become more wary of development in the natural world, stressing instead the immediacy of divine intervention. That was to leave many of them more vulnerable to the coming Darwinian revolution. Yet the door was left open, at least by the far-sighted Miller, to a means of reconciling evolution with natural theology. "God," he wrote, "might as certainly have *originated* the species by a law of development, as he *maintains* it by a law of development;—the existence of a First Great Cause is as perfectly compatible with the one scheme as with the other."¹⁰⁸ It was along these lines that other Evangelicals were to come to terms with Darwin.

Those who anathematized Darwin and all his works were at first outspoken. A botanist who reviewed *The Origin of Species* in the *Christian Observer* condemned the book as biased, negligent of scripture, unsupported by facts and designed "to cast God out of His own creation."¹⁰⁹ The Nonconformist readers of the *Eclectic Review* were told that Darwin's thesis, while suffering from an absence of evidence, implicitly denied immortality and showed an "absolute incompatibility" with any faith in revelation.¹¹⁰ But as the new theory gained general approval in the scientific community, opinion mellowed. By the early 1870s much less outright resistance remained among Evangelical

105 Hilton, *Age of Atonement*, 309–11.
106 Pye Smith, *On the Relation*, 281–82.
107 Paul Baxter, "Deism and Development: Disruptive Forces in Scottish Natural Theology," in *Scotland in the Age of Disruption*, ed. Stewart J. Brown and Michael Fry (Edinburgh: Edinburgh University Press, 1993), 106–8.
108 Hugh Miller, *Foot-Prints of the Creator* (London: Johnstone and Hunter, 1849), 13.
109 *Christian Observer*, August 1860, 561, 562–63, 565, 570.
110 *Eclectic Review*, March 1860, 234, 230.

theologians. The most strident opponent was T. R. Birks, vicar of Holy Trinity Church, Cambridge, and from 1872 Knightbridge Professor of Moral Philosophy in the university there. Birks, like many contemporaries, closely associated the scientific understanding of evolution with Herbert Spencer's "social Darwinism" and attacked both for teaching that humanity was ultimately no different from the material world.[111] Against Darwin in particular he argued that the experience of the ages showed that like produced like. Only by overthrowing "the inductive principles of Bacon and Newton" could a false science maintain the transformation of species.[112] Evolution, he asserted, proposed a universe that was "nothing but a Proteus without reason or intelligence."[113] The theory, in Birks' mind, was simply an upstart rival to the Christian doctrine of creation.[114] The Wesleyan theologian W. B. Pope, though conceding (unlike Birks) that others might assume that the Creator used the method of evolution, argued strongly against that supposition. "No theory of evolution or development," he wrote, "that seems to trace a regular succession of forms through which organic existence has passed, in obedience to a plastic law originally impressed upon matter, can be made consistent with Scripture."[115] Still, in the early 1880s at the Baptist college founded by C. H. Spurgeon, the tutor in philosophy maintained a "protest against being considered a blood relation of the ape or the oyster."[116] There were circles where Darwinian evolution appeared unscientific, anti-scriptural and nonsensical.

111 Thomas R. Birks, *Modern Physical Fatalism and the Doctrine of Evolution* (London: Macmillan and Co., 1876).
112 Thomas R. Birks, *Supernatural Revelation: Or First Principles of Moral Theology* (London: Macmillan and Co., 1879), vi.
113 Birks, *Supernatural Revelation*, 136.
114 Thomas R. Birks, *The Scripture Doctrine of Creation* (London: SPCK, 1872), chap. 11.
115 William B. Pope, *A Compendium of Christian Theology*, 3 vols., 2nd ed. (London: For the Author at the Wesleyan Methodist Book Room, 1880), 1:398. David Livingstone has stressed Pope's concession, whereas John Kent treats his views as the epitome of conservatism on the issue: David N. Livingstone, *Darwin's Forgotten Defenders: The Encounter between Evangelical Theology and Evolutionary Thought* (Grand Rapids, MI: Eerdmans, 1987), 135–36; John Kent, *From Darwin to Blatchford: The Role of Darwinism in Christian Apologetic, 1875–1910* (London: Dr Williams's Trust, 1966), 11–14.
116 *Annual Paper Concerning the Lord's Work in Connection with the Pastors' College, Newington, London, 1881–82* (London: Alabaster, Passmore and Sons, 1882), 17. Some other persistent opponents of evolution are noted by Livingstone, *Darwin's Forgotten Defenders*, 131–32, and by James R. Moore, *The Post-Darwinian Controversies: A Study of the Protestant Struggle to Come to Terms with Darwin in Great Britain and America, 1870–1900* (Cambridge: Cambridge University Press, 1979), chap. 9.

Accommodation with Evolution

Yet during the last third of the nineteenth century it was more common to try to reach an accommodation with the new approach to science. Here natural theology came into its own, providing the intellectual framework within which the absorption of the Darwinian style of thinking could take place. Those who had been trained before the appearance of *The Origin of Species* did not abandon their belief in design but enlarged it to take account of the fresh evidence. Thus Robert Rainy, when delivering in 1874 his inaugural address as principal of New College, Edinburgh, contended that the conditions of the argument for the existence of God had not been altered by evolution. Each "stream of processes" revealed by the scientist had distinct value for the natural theologian.[117] Rainy's colleague John Duns, professor of natural science at New College, still asserted "the doctrine of final causes" even though he believed there must be a "frank acceptance of the law of development from lower to higher." The argument from design, he contended, must go beyond special adaptations of particular organisms in the manner of Paley to correspondences of whole systems, such as the bones in the skulls of carnivores.[118] James Orr, eventually to become professor of apologetics and theology at the United Free Church college in Glasgow, similarly held that when evolution was granted, the argument from design stood, but with its sphere extended.[119] There was disagreement about whether natural selection had to be rejected in the name of design. John Laidlaw, like Duns, believed that it did; James Iverach, like Orr, thought that it did not.[120] "Supposing natural selection true," wrote Iverach, "what is it but another way of indicating design."[121] So long as there were a directing power, purpose could be discerned in the process. Nor was this position restricted to Presbyterians with their Reformed heritage. The Wesleyan W. H. Dallinger, accepting "the Darwinian law of evolution," saw it as only a method of universal design.[122] The General Baptist John Clifford

---

117 Robert Rainy, *Evolution and Theology: Inaugural Address* (Edinburgh: Maclaren and Macniven, 1874), 9, 14.
118 John Duns, *Science and Christian Thought* (London: Religious Tract Society, 1866), 22, 122, 59–60.
119 James Orr, *The Christian View of God and the World as Centering in the Incarnation*, 2nd ed. (Edinburgh: Andrew Elliot, 1893), 119.
120 John Duns, *On the Theory of Natural Selection and the Theory of Design, Part II*, paper for Victoria Institute, 1887 (Author's copy, New College, Edinburgh), 1; John Laidlaw, *The Bible Doctrine of Man* (Edinburgh: T&T Clark, 1879), 39.
121 Orr, *Christian View*, 120; James Iverach, *Christianity and Evolution*, 3rd ed. (London: Hodder and Stoughton, 1900), 79.
122 William H. Dallinger, *The Creator and What We May Know of the Method of Creation* (London: T. Woolmer, 1887), 66, 61.

declared that evolution, if proved to be true, would not lessen the force of the witness to design of the physical nature of man.[123] Far from dying out in the 1860s and 1870s, natural theology discovered a new role. It became a means by which Evangelicals adjusted their faith to post-Darwinian science.

For those who wished to reach an accommodation with developmental thinking there were three potential sticking points. One such sticking point was before any willingness to surrender the idea of creation as something separate from evolution. Sir George Stokes, the Lucasian professor of mathematics at Cambridge and the leading Anglican Evangelical scientific thinker of the late nineteenth century, wanted to continue to distinguish exertions of creative power from the continuity of the evolutionary process.[124] Others, however, encouraged by the willingness of biblical scholars to treat Genesis metaphorically, agreed with Orr that the terms "evolution" and "special creation" could in some sense be synthesized. Certainly there was no contradiction between them.[125] A second sticking point was at the transition from the inorganic to the organic. Duns denounced the Lamarckian idea of latent vitality in matter because he was sure it would lead to materialism.[126] The danger of a materialistic philosophy was already patent in the thought of Spencer and in the exotic monism of the German Ernst Haeckel, whose system, as Orr pointed out, spelled the death of God, freedom and immortality.[127] Against them it was possible to recruit the authority of the militant agnostic scientist T. H. Huxley, who could see no link between the living and the not living.[128] Yet even on this issue there were those such as Rainy who claimed that if life were shown to derive from matter, the foundations of natural theology would remain undisturbed.[129] For a large number, among whom Orr was the most prominent, the greatest sticking point was the connection of humanity with the rest of the

---

123 John Clifford, "Charles Darwin or Evolution and Christianity," *Typical Christian Leaders* (London: Horace Marshall and Son, 1898), 233.
124 Sir George G. Stokes, *Natural Theology: The Gifford Lectures Delivered before the University of Edinburgh in 1893* (London: Adam and Charles Black, 1893), 150.
125 James Orr, *God's Image in Man and Its Defacement in the Light of Modern Denials* (London: Hodder and Stoughton, 1905), 87. For exegetical developments, see Richard A. Riesen, *Criticism and Faith in Late Victorian Scotland: A. B. Davidson, William Robertson Smith and George Adam Smith* (Lanham, MD: University Press of America, 1985), 383–88.
126 Duns, *Science and Christian Thought*, chap. 5.
127 Orr, *God's Image*, 5. On Haeckel, see Paul Weindling, "Ernst Haeckel, Darwinismus and the Secularisation of Nature," in *History, Humanity and Evolution: Essays for John C. Greene*, ed. James R. Moore (Cambridge: Cambridge University Press, 1989), 311–27.
128 Dallinger, *The Creator*, 32.
129 Rainy, *Evolution and Theology*, 9.

evolutionary series. Orr perceived in the assimilation of human beings to the animal world a threat to their rationality, moral freedom and religious capacity, and beyond that to the recognition of their sinfulness and ultimately to the need for atonement.[130] Yet many others—including Rainy, Dallinger and Clifford—saw no problem in accepting the physical continuity of the human race with the animal kingdom because a spiritual discontinuity could still be postulated.[131] At each point there were some who were willing to take the radical course. There was great diversity in the Evangelical responses to the Darwinian revolution, but perhaps what is most remarkable is the degree of novelty so many were willing to adopt.[132]

While their attitude towards science was being transformed, the Evangelicals' natural theology, though remaining in place, was inevitably modified. Since evolution entailed an immense extension of the reign of law, there was a move towards a broader style of teleological reasoning. The emphasis in the design argument shifted from special adaptation to cosmic order. "Teleology," wrote W. H. Dallinger, "does not now depend for its existence on Paleyan 'instances'; but all the universe, its whole progress in time and space, is one majestic evidence of teleology."[133] The older form of the case had argued *from* design, from the premise of adaptation to an intelligent Creator. The theistic conclusion, however, was no longer necessary when natural selection constituted an alternative and perhaps more plausible interpretation of the evidence for adaptation. Hence the revised form of the case had to argue *for* design, from the premise of order to the existence of a plan.[134] It was no longer an argument in favor of theism but merely an argument for the compatibility of the evidence with theism. It made no pretense to have demonstrated the being of God. In his Gifford Lectures for 1893 at Edinburgh, Sir George Stokes delivered an elaborate account of design in the human eye. Although he himself attributed its intricate structure to a directing power, he admitted that it was possible to explain the eye in terms of natural selection. The evidence, he conceded, in no sense compelled a verdict in favor of divine

---

130 Orr, *God's Image*, 146–50, 10; James Orr, *Sin as a Problem of To-day* (London: Hodder and Stoughton, 1910). Cf. Glen G. Scorgie, *A Call for Continuity: The Theological Contribution of James Orr* (Macon, GA: Mercer University Press, 1988), chap. 6.
131 Rainy, *Evolution and Theology*, 15; Dallinger, *The Creator*, 79–81; Clifford, "Charles Darwin," 234.
132 Moore, *Post-Darwinian Controversies*, part 3; Livingstone, *Darwin's Forgotten Defenders*, chap. 4.
133 Dallinger, *The Creator*, 74.
134 This analysis is indebted to Lewis E. Hicks, *A Critique of Design-Arguments* (New York: Charles Scribner's Sons, 1883), spec. 27.

superintendence.[135] Christians could now merely choose to believe what they could not prove. Since design had become a far less powerful weapon, they were thrown on to the defensive. The evidence of natural phenomena now had to be interpreted sympathetically if it was to match theological claims. Before Darwin, science had been an asset. After him, and throughout the twentieth century, there was a constant struggle to avoid its becoming a liability.

Nor could Evangelical theology itself escape the encounter with scientific evolution unaffected. Anglicans of the High and Broad Church schools already gave priority to the doctrine of the incarnation, and from *Lux Mundi* (1889) onwards High Churchmen normally stressed the immanence of God. The two themes became the hallmarks of Anglican thought down to the Second World War.[136] Both were deployed to incorporate an evolutionary perspective into theology. Orr was unusual in the Evangelical community in emphasizing incarnationalism,[137] but it was immanence that he, like many others, related directly to evolution. "Assume God," he wrote, ". . . to be immanent in the evolutionary process. . . . The real impelling force of evolution is now from *within*."[138] The most celebrated figure to take this course was the evangelist Henry Drummond, the author of the immensely popular *Natural Law in the Spiritual World* (1883), whose chief debt was to Herbert Spencer.[139] By 1894 he saw no need to reconcile Christianity and evolution because, as he ingenuously put it, "the two are one."[140] Another liberal thinker, the Congregationalist W. F. Adeney, was delighted that religion had turned to immanentism. "The great Gardener," he wrote, "is always moving about among His plants, fostering and feeding them." Perhaps, he

---

135 Stokes, *Natural Theology*, 62-108, 138-39, spec. 139. On Stokes' "directionism," see David B. Wilson, "A Physicist's Alternative to Materialism: The Religious Thought of George Gabriel Stokes," *Victorian Studies* 28:1 (1984), 69-96. Cf. Peter J. Bowler, *The Eclipse of Darwinism: Anti-Darwinian Evolution Theories in the Decades around 1900* (Baltimore: Johns Hopkins University Press, 1983), 45.
136 Arthur Michael Ramsey, *From Gore to Temple: The Development of Anglican Theology between "Lux Mundi" and the Second World War, 1889-1939* (London: Longmans, 1960).
137 Scorgie, *Call for Continuity*, 50-51.
138 Orr, *God's Image*, 96.
139 James R. Moore, "Evangelicals and Evolution: Henry Drummond, Herbert Spencer and the Naturalisation of the Spiritual World," *Scottish Journal of Theology* 38:3 (1985), 395-99. On Drummond, see 2:14: "Henry Drummond: A Presbyterian, Evangelicalism and Science."
140 Henry Drummond, *The Lowell Lectures on the Ascent of Man* (London: Hodder and Stoughton, 1894), 438.

added, Origen had been right that the eternal God was eternally creating.[141] Although the celebration of immanence as the true meaning of evolution is found in theologians less given to speculation, such as the Free Church of Scotland's James Iverach and A. B. Bruce,[142] there is no doubt that this theme pointed in a liberal direction. Vernon Storr, who was to be the inspiration of the liberal Evangelical movement in the interwar Church of England, restated natural theology in 1906 in terms of immanence.[143] The same idea was to be the burden of *Evolution and the Christian Concept of God* (1936) by Charles Raven, Regius Professor of Divinity at Cambridge and another leading liberal Evangelical.[144] Because immanence was not a traditional theme among Evangelicals, and because it was harder to relate the doctrine to their central preoccupation with the atonement than to other Anglicans' emphasis on the incarnation, its unaccustomed prominence changed the balance of their thinking. For good or ill, evolution had the effect broadening the Evangelical mind.

Conclusion

The conclusion must be that on the whole Evangelicalism in Britain was not hostile to science. Although there were some reservations about the value of natural philosophy, especially in the eighteenth century, the movement's adherents were not generally foes of learning, research and the intellect; and, even if they ranked these matters below conversion, revelation and the Spirit, they normally regarded scientific investigation in particular as bound up with the knowledge of God through natural theology. The worldview of the Enlightenment, fully shared by most of them, encouraged reverence for Newtonianism, induction and the argument for God from design in nature. They created a distinctive version of physico-theology that, like the atonement itself, took account of the pain and suffering of the world. Their presentation of the design argument, particularly as expounded by Chalmers, was the substance of the revitalization of natural theology around

---

141 Walter F. Adeney, *A Century's Progress in Religious Life and Thought* (London: James Clarke and Co., 1901), 102–3.
142 Iverach, *Christianity and Evolution*, 206; Alexander B. Bruce, *The Providential Order of the World* (London: Hodder and Stoughton, 1897), 57.
143 Vernon F. Storr, *Development and Divine Purpose* (London: Methuen and Co., 1906), spec. 132–34.
144 Charles E. Raven, *Evolution and the Christian Concept of God* (London: Oxford University Press, 1936).

the 1830s.[145] Endorsement by Evangelicals gave the British tradition of argument from design a new lease on life in a period when their assumptions tinctured the whole intellectual atmosphere. The style of reasoning proved flexible, accommodating the problems of space and time on the borders of science and religion, and, even when challenged by developmental thinking, enabled many Evangelicals to come to terms with Darwinism. If their theology altered in the process, finding a larger place for immanence, so did their attitude towards natural phenomena. The world examined by scientists, though compatible with theistic belief, no longer appeared to demonstrate the divine. Science itself turned into a potential threat, and Evangelicals in the twentieth century were often to be wary of it. Before then, however, the progress of discovery was usually hailed as an ally. In the era between Wesley and Orr science was a handmaid of Evangelical theology.

---

145 John Gascoigne, "From Bentley to the Victorians: The Rise and Fall of British Newtonian Natural Theology," *Science in Context* 2:2 (1988), 219–56, at 240–41. Gascoigne, however, does not recognize the Evangelical dimension of the revitalization (249).

V
Evangelicals into the Twenty-First Century

15

Evangelical Trends, 1959–2009

The foundation of *Anvil* in 1984 was the midway point in a process of drastic transformation within the Evangelical movement in Britain.[1] By no means all the novelties appeared in the quarter-century after that event; many of them took place in the earlier part of the period. The aim of this paper is to review the developments over the whole half-century. In 1959 change was afoot in the world at large. The first section of the M1 motorway was opened, General de Gaulle was declared president of the Fifth French Republic and Pope John XXIII announced the convening of the Second Vatican Council. Innovation was also touching the sphere of Evangelicals. In the same year there was an outbreak of speaking in tongues, then nearly unknown outside Pentecostalism, at a Methodist church in Congleton, Cheshire;[2] F. F. Bruce, the pioneering Brethren scholar, took up the Rylands Chair of Biblical Criticism and Exegesis at the University of Manchester;[3] and Maurice Wood, the vicar of St Mary's, Islington, told the annual Islington Conference of Anglican Evangelicals that there was a "new evangelical revival" in the church.[4] An editorial in the *Church of England Newspaper* applauded the spirit of modern Anglican Evangelicals. "By and large," it declared, "they are less inclined to be backward-looking ... and more ready to face current needs; less controversial and more positive in outlook; less narrow-minded and more tolerant towards

---

1   This article was originally commissioned by *Anvil*, an Anglican Evangelical journal, to mark the twenty-fifth anniversary of its foundation.
2   Peter Hocken, *Streams of Renewal: The Origins of Early Development of the Charismatic Movement in Great Britain* (Exeter: Paternoster Press, 1986), 64 n. 31.
3   Frederick F. Bruce, *In Retrospect: In Remembrance of Things Past* (London: Pickering & Inglis, 1980), 204.
4   *Church of England Newspaper* [hereafter *CEN*], 19 January 1959, 6.

those of other views; less afflicted by an inferiority complex and more aware of a sense of mission."[5] Some were aware of stirrings in the Evangelical camp.

Yet the older temper—backward-looking, controversial, narrow-minded and, in the opinion of the *Church of England Newspaper*, suffering from an inferiority complex—was by no means consigned to history. In November 1959 there was issued "A Memorial Addressed to Leaders of the Church of England in a Time of Crisis and Opportunity" signed by seventy-eight prominent laypeople and about five hundred clergy, all of them Evangelical. The crisis was the process of canon law revision being pushed through by Geoffrey Fisher, the tidy-minded former public-school headmaster who was archbishop of Canterbury, giving greater license to Anglo-Catholic practices within the Church of England. The urgent requests of the signatories were that vestments should no longer be required and that canon law revision should not raise unnecessary issues within the Church. The opportunity was for the Bible again to be "established in fact, as well as in theory, as the final and supreme authority in all matters of faith and doctrine." That would entail "a return to that simplicity of worship and Scriptural doctrine which has been characteristic of our Church since the Reformation," which meant Prayer Book services of morning and evening prayer. The result would be a remedy for falling church attendance and "weakened moral fibre" among the people of England. There was talk of "the British character" and "a firm foundation for national life."[6] Church and nation were closely identified in an outburst of Protestant patriotism. The whole episode seemed a minor rerun of the Prayer Book controversy of 1927–28, when an attempt to revise the basis of Anglican worship so as to permit greater latitude to Anglo-Catholics had been voted down in parliament after an upsurge of national concern led by Evangelicals. As though to confirm the link with the earlier affair, one of the honorary treasurers of the fund promoting the memorial was Viscount Brentford, the son of the home secretary who in 1927–28 had played a large part in the defeat of Prayer Book revision. As in the earlier case, the protest was endorsed by non-Anglican Evangelicals, this time including Sir John Laing, a Brethren building magnate, and Viscount Alexander of Hillsborough, a Baptist ex-cabinet minister. It also secured the support of men who were later to lead an alteration in the public face of Anglican Evangelicalism, such as John Stott, rector of All Souls, Langham Place, and Norman Anderson, director of the Institute of Advanced Legal Studies in the

---

5 *CEN*, 19 January 1959, 6.
6 "A Memorial Addressed to Leaders of the Church of England in a Time of Crisis and Opportunity," November 1959.

University of London and Stott's close friend. In 1959, therefore, the Evangelical movement in Britain was still steeped in the past.

Nor did everything about Evangelicals change during the succeeding half-century. The characteristics that had long marked adherents of the movement persisted down the years. The appeal to the authority of the Bible evident in the memorial of 1959 was part of a respect for the importance of scripture that never ceased to be a feature of Evangelicalism. At the 1967 Keele National Evangelical Anglican Congress, a milestone in the journey towards fresh attitudes in many fields, the place of the Bible was reaffirmed: "the Scriptures," according to the Congress statement, "are the wholly trustworthy oracles of God."[7] Again, the doctrinal centrality of the atonement was asserted in a series of books, including Stott's *The Cross of Christ* (1986) and Steve Holmes' *The Wondrous Cross* (2007).[8] Even though controversy surged around both scripture and atonement, the fundamental allegiance to these priorities was a consistent attribute of the movement over time. The insistence on the need for conversion was another continuing hallmark of Evangelicals. Billy Graham, with his unashamed calls for conversion, was a welcome figure in Britain on several occasions during the period. Notwithstanding his potentially off-putting Americanness, when a *Church of England Newspaper* questionnaire in 1965 asked its readers whether they approved of his methods of evangelism, a resounding 587 answered yes and a mere 47 said no.[9] Evangelicals also remained eager to be up and doing, taking evangelism as their focus but extending their mission to many other spheres. Thus in 1973 John Stott called for churches not to monopolize the weekday evenings of their members. The object was not to give Christians an easier time, for he urged that they should experience a "busy Sunday" with prayer, Bible study and business meetings supplementing regular worship. Rather the aim was to enable believers to engage in such weeknight activities as badminton where they could be witnesses.[10] So the typical Evangelical stance, involving emphasis upon Bible, cross, conversion and activism, endured throughout the period. The degree of weight attached to the four priorities varied from time to time and from group to group, but, despite occasional charges to the contrary, none of the four traits

---

7 Phillip Crowe, *Keele '67: The National Evangelical Anglican Congress Statement* (London: Falcon Books, 1967), 20.
8 John R. W. Stott, *The Cross of Christ* (Nottingham: InterVarsity Press, 1986); Stephen R. Holmes, *The Wondrous Cross: Atonement and Penal Substitution in the Bible and History* (Milton Keynes: Paternoster Press, 2007).
9 *CEN*, 1 October 1965, 6.
10 *CEN*, 2 February 1973, 16.

faded from view in any quarter. Like other fundamental characteristics shared with other Christians, this quartet remained in place down to 2009.

Characteristics in Decline

Nevertheless there were major modifications in the movement, and they form the substance of this article. Certain inherited qualities fell into decay. In the first place, the anti-Catholicism of which the resistance to ecclesiastical vestments was a symptom went into decline. Rome was the enemy that Protestants had resisted, politically as well as spiritually, ever since the Reformation, and deep-seated fears surrounding the threat to national identity from that quarter were very much alive at the opening of the period. The memorial of 1959, for example, fulminated against "Roman practices."[11] In the following year, when Jesmond Parish Church in Newcastle-upon-Tyne moved from a liberal Evangelical position that had accepted some features of High Church innovation to a conservative Evangelical stance, it dropped the seasonal changing of frontals on the holy table, flowers were kept in place during Lent and the clergyman ceased to raise his hand in giving the blessing.[12] Only occasionally would the chasm between Evangelicals and Roman Catholics be bridged during the 1960s. On one occasion Maurice Wood, by now principal of Oak Hill College, invited the Catholic prior of Cockfosters to dinner, but the consequence, as he remembered, was "an enormous turmoil in the college."[13] The palpable revolution in the Roman Catholic Church arising from the Second Vatican Council, however, transformed relations. Already Keele in 1967 rejoiced at the "signs of biblical reformation" in the Roman communion;[14] the Anglican Evangelical Assembly of 1983 resolved to "welcome" the final report of the Anglican-Roman Catholic International Commission;[15] and, famously, David Watson spoke in 1977 of the Reformation as one of the greatest tragedies in the history of the church.[16] The appearance of a section of Roman Catholic opinion willing to endorse the Lausanne Covenant, an international statement of Evangelical faith and practice, and even in 1990 to form a body called "Evangelical Catholics," largely drawn from charismatics, strengthened

---

11 "Memorial."
12 Alan F. Munden, *A Light in a Dark Place: Jesmond Parish Church, Newcastle upon Tyne* (Newcastle-upon-Tyne: Clayton Publications, 2006), 204.
13 Rudolph Heinze and David Wheaton, *Witness to the World: A History of Oak Hill College, 1932–2000* (Carlisle: Paternoster Press, 2002), 118.
14 Crowe, *Keele '67: The National Evangelical Anglican Congress Statement*, 39.
15 Andrew Atherstone, *An Anglican Evangelical Identity Crisis: The Churchman-Anvil Affair of 1981–84* (Cambridge: Latimer Trust, 2008), 11.
16 *CEN*, 22 April 1977, 8.

the general rapprochement.[17] There were Evangelicals, especially in the ranks of the Protestant Reformation Society, who looked askance at the trend and at times their voices were raised. Yet the publication of the *Alternative Service Book* (1980) put an end to the liturgical wars that had lasted for over a century in the Church of England. With its acceptance by Evangelicals, the chief casus belli with Anglo-Catholics disappeared. So there was a definite decline in anti-Catholicism during the period.

A second feature that weakened during the period was Keswick teaching. The annual convention at the Lake District town and its satellite gatherings had sustained the predominant style of Evangelical spirituality since the opening of the twentieth century. Keswick taught holiness by faith: there was to be a stage beyond conversion when a believer received a distinct form of sanctification that could be maintained through moment-by-moment trust. In any circumstances, through passive reliance on the Almighty, a Christian could enjoy the "victory."[18] The resulting tendency was to withdraw from anything tainted with wrongdoing, or even doubtful, such as the cinema. In 1955 J. I. Packer, then a stern critic of the traditions of the fathers, had condemned Keswick doctrine as a Pelagian denial of the doctrines of grace.[19] Keswick platform speakers themselves began to broaden, by 1960 allowing that there is a fight of faith as well as a rest of faith.[20] Soon Norman Anderson began to see the message as unhelpful because of its world-denying implications, wanting instead to emphasize the world-affirming dimensions of the faith.[21] The specific Keswick teaching did not immediately shrivel, and some of the branches of the convention maintained their witness long after the 1960s. Oak Hill College, for example, continued to be the venue for a North London Keswick Convention down to 1981.[22] But by the 1990s the distinctive Keswick paradigm for spirituality had shattered. Even at the main convention itself its former teaching was presented by 1996 as just one option among a range of several perspectives on sanctification.[23] The consequence was that the chief supposed biblical sanction

---

17 *"What Is an Evangelical Catholic?"* (Dublin: Evangelical Catholics, 1992).
18 Charles Price and Ian Randall, *Transforming Keswick: The Keswick Convention: Past, Present, Future* (Carlisle: OM Publishing, 2000). See also 1:10: "Holiness in the Evangelical Tradition."
19 James I. Packer, "'Keswick' and the Reformed Doctrine of Sanctification," *Evangelical Quarterly* 27:3 (1955), 153–67.
20 *CEN*, 29 July 1960, 2.
21 Norman Anderson, *An Adopted Son: The Story of My Life* (Leicester: InterVarsity Press, 1985), chap. 9.
22 Heinze and Wheaton, *Witness to the World*, 113.
23 Personal observation.

against participation in many activities was relaxed. Film-going became normal among Evangelicals, with reviews of movies forming a staple feature of magazines and even sermons. Worldliness seemed far less of a snare in the early twenty-first century than it had half a century before.

An associated decline took place in the field of eschatology. Evangelicals had commonly asserted a premillennial belief in the imminent return of Jesus to the earth, holding that the advent would take place before the millennium. The schematic version of premillennialism known as dispensationalism that was embodied in the notes of the Scofield Bible and championed by the Brethren exerted a remarkably pervasive influence in Britain as well as America as late as the 1960s.[24] In 1977, however, InterVarsity Press in the United States published a volume called *The Meaning of the Millennium: Four Views*, which set out expositions of other options alongside the dispensationalist teaching.[25] Postmillennialism, the belief that before the second advent the world would be transformed into a millennium of peace and plenty through the spread of the gospel, found new advocates. Iain Murray, representing the rising Reformed body of opinion within Evangelicalism, pointed out in *The Puritan Hope* (1971) that this expectation had once been normal in Britain, and some of the more radical charismatics embraced a similar confidence in *Restoration* magazine.[26] Others, without discarding their belief in the personal return of Jesus, adopted more generalized views about the future. Thus in his booklet of 1977 on *What Is an Evangelical?*, John Stott explained simply that Christ was coming back and that there would be a new world.[27] Many fell back on a more or less conscious dismissal of the whole notion of a future millennium. Hence the American series of Left Behind novels by Tim LaHaye and Jerry B. Jenkins postulating a scenario within the dispensationalist scheme, which attained over the seven years down to 2002 the astonishing sales of thirty-two million copies, achieved only a small circulation in Britain.[28] Even the more progressive Brethren cut adrift from their inherited views on prophetic matters. By

24 Timothy P. Weber, *Living in the Shadow of the Second Coming: American Premillennialism, 1875–1982* (New York: Oxford University Press, 1979). See 1:8: "The Advent Hope in British Evangelicalism since 1800."
25 Robert Clouse, *The Meaning of the Millennium: Four Views* (Downers Grove, IL: InterVarsity Press, 1977).
26 Iain Murray, *The Puritan Hope: A Study in Revival and the Interpretation of Prophecy* (London: Banner of Truth Trust, 1971); Andrew Walker, *Restoring the Kingdom* (London: Hodder & Stoughton, 1985), 126–29.
27 John Stott, *What Is an Evangelical?* (London: Church Pastoral Aid Society, 1977), 12.
28 Crawford Gribben, *Writing the Rapture: Prophecy Fiction in Evangelical America* (Oxford: Oxford University Press, 2009), 130.

2008 Spring Harvest, the annual holiday camps for Bible teaching associated with the Evangelical Alliance, issued a handbook on eschatology that had little time for traditional debates between postmillennialists and premillennialists, seeing the "promised end" as a time "when Jesus shall return and bring in his kingdom of justice and joy."[29] The normative Evangelical eschatology had crumbled.

The missionary impulse, at least in the form it had taken in earlier years, was also sapped during these years. The typical Evangelical around 1959 was "missionary-minded."[30] The final evening of the Keswick Convention was always devoted to overseas missions. "Consider," a typical chairman on that evening might have asked in the early 1960s, "the thin red line of missionaries, in contrast with the millions living and dying without Christ."[31] But with the end of empire, the attention of younger Britons was diverted away from many overseas mission fields. A life of evangelistic service in Africa seemed a less natural vocation. There were alternatives nearer home. In 1981, for example, the Evangelical Coalition for Urban Mission was inaugurated, providing new opportunities for radical discipleship among the deprived within Britain.[32] The faith missions such as the Overseas Missionary Society (formerly the China Inland Mission) that had once channeled much Evangelical enthusiasm abroad found it harder to recruit personnel or to raise money for their support. They even abandoned their traditional conviction that the Lord would supply all the needs of their missionaries, requiring them instead to raise sufficient funds to cover their support in advance. With the expansion of air travel, short-term visits overseas became possible and popular, but the effect was to diminish the number of those who possessed a sense of vocation to a lifetime of service. There were still long-term missionaries, but when, for example, in the late 1990s the Baptist Missionary Society had an increase in recruitment, most were volunteers and short-term workers.[33] Many missionary societies engaged in a flurry of rebranding in order to enhance their appeal: the Bible and Medical Missionary Fellowship became Interserve, the Bible Churchmen's Missionary

---

29 Stephen R. Holmes, "Introduction," in *What Are We Waiting For? Christian Hope and Contemporary Culture*, ed. Stephen Holmes and Russell Rook (Milton Keynes: Paternoster Press, 2008), 8.
30 *CEN*, 11 February 1977, 6.
31 John C. Pollock, *The Keswick Story: The Authorized History of the Keswick Conventions* (London: Hodder and Stoughton, 1964), 178.
32 Ian M. Randall, *The English Baptists of the Twentieth Century* (Didcot: Baptist Historical Society, 2005), 458.
33 Randall, *English Baptists of the Twentieth Century*, 531.

Society became Crosslinks and even the venerable Church Missionary Society became the Church Mission Society. The last of these alterations helped to signal a major shift of thinking away from a pattern of missionaries going from a sending country to a receiving country to a more multilateral model of mission. Traditional missionary approaches were transformed.

Another casualty of change was Evangelical unity. There had never been a time when Evangelicals as a whole had been without their divisions, and the era down to 1959 was no exception. Conservative Evangelicals in most denominations were at odds with their more liberal brethren. Within the conservative Evangelical community there was nevertheless a strong bond of common purpose, cemented during the 1950s by support for Billy Graham. The same unity found expression in the calling of two National Assemblies of Evangelicals in 1965 and 1966. At the second, however, there was an awkward stand-off between Martyn Lloyd-Jones, the doughty minister of Westminster Chapel, and John Stott. Lloyd-Jones called for a united Evangelical body that would entail the withdrawal of Evangelicals from their existing denominations, a pattern he had previously inaugurated through the Evangelical Movement of Wales. Already Stott saw the future as giving Evangelicals a powerful say in the Church of England and so, from the chair, expressed his dissent from Lloyd-Jones' view.[34] The divergence became permanent, with Lloyd-Jones drawing more people into the Fellowship of Independent Evangelical Churches, and Anglicans under Stott's leadership turning towards fuller participation in Anglican counsels. Likewise Baptists underwent a serious schism in the early 1970s over an address to the Baptist Union Assembly that called into question the divinity of Christ, with many of the most conservative leaving the denomination.[35] The Evangelical Alliance, revitalized under Clive Calver during the 1980s, did a good deal to reverse the trend against unity, but the process proved inexorable. The main polarization was now between those who saw doctrinal fidelity as the primary responsibility of Evangelicals and those who, in their vigorous quest for conversions, were less insistent on vocal defense of orthodoxy.[36] The line of fission therefore ran within rather than between denominational groups, particularly in the Church of England. On the one hand stood Reform, an organization established in 1993 to advance the gospel through strict adherence to biblical teaching; on the other, the open Evangel-

---

34 David W. Bebbington, *Evangelicalism in Modern Britain: History from the 1730s to 1980s* (London: Unwin Hyman, 1989), 267.
35 Randall, *English Baptists of the Twentieth Century*, 365–82.
36 Rob Warner, *Re-Inventing English Evangelicalism, 1966–2001: A Theological and Sociological Study* (Milton Keynes: Paternoster Press, 2007).

icals who in 2003 formed a body called Fulcrum. But the bifurcation was felt throughout the Evangelical world. Steve Chalke, the enterprising mastermind behind Oasis, a church grouping based in south London that grappled with inner-city deprivation, was denounced in 2003 for apparently dismissing the doctrine of penal substitution in the atonement. For the conservative stalwarts Chalke was a heretic, but for many others he remained a hero.[37] By the end of the period, Evangelicals were moving in different directions.

New Developments

If there was a decline in various features of Evangelical life, there were many aspects in which there were fresh developments. At a time when other sectors of church life weakened or collapsed, Evangelicals held their own much better. According to the figures for England alone produced by MARC Europe/Christian Research, in 1989 9.9 percent of the population went to church on a given Sunday, but by 1998 the figure was down to 7.5 percent.[38] Yet the proportion of churchgoers who were Evangelicals had increased from 30 to 37 percent.[39] In some measure Evangelicals participated in the general decline in attendance, but in this decade they gained a larger share of the whole worshiping community. That was the main pattern throughout the period. Hence Evangelicals were thrust into greater prominence in ecclesiastical affairs. Already by 1986 a majority of residential ordinands of the Church of England were for the first time found in Evangelical institutions. The future seemed to be theirs. Although in 1987 the complaint was heard that the party was represented by only seven diocesan bishops, overall they were receiving a fairer share of preferment in the church.[40] When the queen appointed Maurice Wood to the see of Norwich in 1971, she noticed that he was described as "conservative Evangelical" and so inquired what that was.[41] In later years she would have had no need. Likewise in 1990 the general secretaryship of the Baptist Union fell to a minister, David Coffey, identified with the conservative strand in Evangelicalism to the extent of having heard a call to ministry at a Keswick meeting.[42] The denominations were emerging

---

37 Holmes, *Wondrous Cross*, 127–29.
38 Peter Brierley, *The Tide Is Running Out: What the English Church Attendance Survey Revivals* (London: MARC Europe/Christian Research, 2000), 27.
39 Peter Brierley, *U.K. Christian Handbook Trends No. 2* (London: MARC Europe/Christian Research, 1999), 12.3.
40 Michael Saward, *The Anglican Church Today: Evangelicals on the Move* (London: Mowbray, 1987), 34–35.
41 Owen Chadwick, *Michael Ramsey: A Life* (Oxford: Clarendon Press, 1990), 142.
42 Randall, *English Baptists of the Twentieth Century*, 471–72.

from a period in which Evangelicals had been marginal into an epoch when they were central to the life of their bodies.

The process of rising to prominence within the denominations was associated with a tendency towards broadening. The phrase "conservative Evangelical," a natural label for Wood in 1971, was soon dropped by most adherents of the movement in favor of the simpler "Evangelical." Part of the explanation is that "conservative" had been used to differentiate the more resolute Evangelicals in the Church of England from their liberal colleagues. The Anglican Evangelical Group Movement, a long-standing organization for liberal Evangelicals, was still holding lively conferences during the 1960s.[43] But by the 1970s its adherents had been almost entirely absorbed into the central bloc of opinion within the church. There was no longer a reason for conservatives to use that term. Many of those identified with the Evangelical movement, furthermore, began to dislike the idea that they were conservative rather than in tune with the times. F. F. Bruce, for instance, rejected the term since, as he explained, he held his views "not because they are conservative—still less because I myself am conservative—but because I believe they are the positions to which the evidence leads."[44] In the Church of England, as the proportion of Evangelical clergy grew, many entered parishes where the liturgical patterns they inherited were much higher than those they would have preferred and, out of pastoral sensitivity, they retained some of them rather than sweeping them away. So they might adopt robes Evangelicals had previously repudiated or allow a bell to be rung at the consecration of the elements during communion. There were even shifts in theology, so that, for example, the statement of the 1977 Nottingham Evangelical Anglican Congress, rather than insisting on the traditional substitutionary view of the cross, observed that Evangelicals gave different degrees of emphasis to "the various biblical expressions of atonement."[45] In 1989 and 1998 roughly half of the Evangelical parishes surveyed reported that they were "broad" rather than "mainstream" or "charismatic."[46] Alarm at this phenomenon helped prompt the creation of Reform, whose leaders were once more happy to call themselves "conservative Evangelical," but the general trend was undoubtedly in a broadening direction.

---

43 *CEN*, 3 May 1963, 3; 17 April 1964, 1, 16.
44 Bruce, *In Retrospect*, 309.
45 *CEN*, 22 April 1977, 10.
46 Peter Brierley, *"Christian" England: What the 1989 English Church Census Reveals* (London: MARC Europe/Christian Research, 1991), 165; Brierley, *Tide Is Running Out*, 146.

On ecumenical relations, there was also an opening up. The traditional view of Evangelicals was that true Christians were already spiritually one and so efforts for institutional unity were a superfluous diversion from gospel work. Ecumenical effort might even prove to be a sinister move towards reabsorption by Rome. Anglican Evangelicals were the firmest opponents of the scheme for Anglican-Methodist unity during the 1960s, not because of any aversion to Methodists but because they objected to the implication of the reconciliation service that the previous ministry of Methodists was invalid.[47] Truth was valued above unity. The first cracks in the standard suspicions of the existing ecumenical enterprise came when some began to urge that there were lessons to be learned from others. Letters to the *Church of England Newspaper* in the wake of the Keele Congress took up this theme.[48] Contacts at local levels increased. Candidates for the ministry of the United Reformed Church and the Baptists trained at the Anglican Oak Hill and members of many denominations, including several future leaders, rubbed shoulders at London Bible College.[49] Local Ecumenical Projects (later Partnerships) sprang up, merging denominational traditions. Joint events such as Spring Harvest brought Evangelicals of various stripes into close fellowship. Denominational loyalties faded as families sought congregations with the best facilities, especially for their children. At the same time as institutional plans for church unity foundered, the divisions between Christians healed in various informal ways. Except in the most conservative circles, Evangelicals ceased to be defined in terms of hostility to other Christian bodies.

Theological Trends

There were several new developments in theological opinion. A Reformed movement gradually gathered force during the period. Scottish Presbyterians had never wholly forgotten their Calvinistic roots. The Free Church of Scotland, possessing a college staffed by able scholars, maintained a firm allegiance to the Westminster Confession, and in the Church of Scotland a group of Evangelical ministers led by William Still of Aberdeen, mostly Calvinists, gathered annually in the Crieff Brotherhood. Martyn Lloyd-Jones was the central figure in the revival of Reformed theology in Wales and England,

---

47 James I. Packer, *All in Each Place: Towards Reunion in England* (Abingdon: Marcham Manor Press, 1965).
48 *CEN*, 19 May 1967, 6.
49 Heinze and Wheaton, *Witness to the World*, 206; Price and Randall, *Transforming Keswick*.

sponsoring the annual Puritan Conferences, which by 1962 attracted some 350 attenders.[50] At first they attracted distrust in the Evangelical establishment, Maurice Wood referring two years earlier at Islington to the strain caused by "ultra-Calvinists."[51] The publications of the Banner of Truth Trust, however, were to disseminate their message widely, and J. I. Packer, the copromoter of the Puritan Conferences, was to turn Calvinism in a mild form into the normative Evangelical theology of the world. Agencies emerged that were more or less committed to a distinctively Reformed theology. Chief among them were the Evangelical Ministry Assembly, founded in 1984 by Dick Lucas, rector of St Helen's, Bishopsgate, in the heart of London, which by 2009 attracted nearly a thousand to its gatherings, and the associated Proclamation Trust, established in 1986 to foster expository preaching.[52] The choice of "Reform" as the title of the conservative Evangelical organization reflected its theology as well as its purpose. Calvinism had enjoyed a resurgence.

In parallel there was an upsurge of charismatic renewal. Classic Pentecostalism, though it had created three substantial denominations by the 1920s, had never achieved the triumphs in Britain that it had managed in many other lands. From the 1960s, however, its distinctive practice of speaking in tongues, assisted by the expressive temper of the decade, poured out into other denominations.[53] The Fountain Trust, set up in 1964, helped both to spread charismatic renewal and to direct the flow of the new movement into denominational channels. By the time of the Nottingham Congress in 1977, renewal had become indigenized in the Church of England, by no means exclusively but certainly predominantly in Evangelical parishes. By that year a consultation on "Gospel and Spirit" between the Church of England Evangelical Council and the Fountain Trust had managed to reach a lengthy agreed statement that demonstrated the acceptability of renewal.[54] Among the Free Churches, the Baptists were most affected. When, in 1975, the minister of Durrington Free Church (Baptist) in Sussex urged the congregation to embrace a new experience of the Spirit, nineteen members left but eight years later there were over five hundred members.[55] The largest congregation in the country by the early 1990s was Kensington Temple, a Pentecostal church whose ethos had

50   CEN, 4 January 1963, 3.
51   CEN, 15 January 1960, 3.
52   http://www.proctrust.org.uk, accessed 7 March 2009.
53   Bebbington, *Evangelicalism in Modern Britain*, chap 7. See also 2:16: "The Rise of Charismatic Renewal in Britain."
54   John Baker et al., "Gospel and Spirit: A Joint Statement" (Esher, Surrey: Fountain Trust and Church of England Evangelical Council, 1977).
55   Andrew Kane, *Let There Be Life* (Basingstoke: Marshalls, 1983), 71–72, 76.

been transformed by renewal.⁵⁶ New charismatic churches sprang up, at first in houses but later in cinemas and other large buildings, some cooperating closely with other Evangelicals but others, particularly in the Covenant Ministries, adopting a sternly isolationist approach.⁵⁷ A succession of growing pains afflicted the charismatic world: over "heavy shepherding" in the 1970s, over John Wimber's Signs and Wonders in the 1980s and over the Toronto Blessing in the 1990s. The epicenter in Britain of the Toronto Blessing, a form of intense spirituality marked, among other phenomena, by animal noises, was Holy Trinity, Brompton, which also pioneered the Alpha movement, a remarkably effective form of low-key evangelism based on meetings to discuss the faith after a meal. Charismatic renewal, a novelty of the period, had particular appeal for the young, and among their number were many fresh converts.

Social Changes

A further development on the Evangelical landscape was the emergence of the black majority churches. Immigrants from many New Commonwealth countries brought their faith with them, and though some were absorbed into predominantly white congregations, a sector of churches providing specifically for black residents grew up. Most at first belonged to Pentecostal denominations from the Caribbean, such as the New Testament Church of God. An African and Caribbean Evangelical Alliance began in 1984 as the West Indian Evangelical Alliance, already catering for a constituency of some fifteen hundred congregations. Its general secretary, Joel Edwards, a Jamaica-born pastor, went on in 1997 to become general director of the whole Evangelical Alliance.⁵⁸ Some black majority churches enjoyed extraordinary growth. The Calvary-Charismatic Baptist Church at Plaistow in east London, a largely Ghanaian congregation launched in 1994 by Francis Sarpong, drew in as many as eight hundred members during only its first six years. On 31 December 1999 it held a baptismal service where there were seventy-nine candidates.⁵⁹ By 1998 over 7 percent of Christian worshipers in England were black, with approximately 4 percent of Asian origin.⁶⁰ In the Church of England, where there was a significant black presence in many multiethnic areas, its most visible sign was the rise to become bishop of Stepney, then bishop of Birmingham

---

56 Jack Hywel-Davies, *The Kensington Temple Story* (London: Monarch Books, 1998).
57 Walker, *Restoring the Kingdom*.
58 Ian Randall and David Hilborn, *One Body in Christ: The History and Significance of the Evangelical Alliance* (Carlisle: Paternoster Press, 2001), 288, 345–46.
59 *Baptist Times*, 16 March 2000, 8.
60 Brierley, *U.K. Christian Handbook*, 12.3.

and finally, in 2005, archbishop of York of John Sentamu, a man of Ugandan background. Like almost all the black church leaders of his day, he was Evangelical by conviction.

In an era of adjustment in the relations between the sexes, gender issues inevitably came to the fore during this period. At its opening, women formed a large majority in the pews but were rarely found in the pulpits. An informal poll of Evangelical clergy in 1966 showed them to be divided over the legitimacy of female ordination.[61] It was noticed that there were still no women speakers at the Nottingham Congress eleven years later, but female students were starting to be admitted to Evangelical colleges: Oak Hill took the step in 1984.[62] The first female president of the Baptist Union was appointed in 1978 and some radical charismatic churches regarded themselves as agents of women's emancipation.[63] As the impetus for women's ordination gathered pace in the Church of England, opinion stiffened within the Evangelical ranks in both directions, leading to two "convulsive" years in 1993, when the decision in favor was taken, and 1994, when the first women took priest's orders.[64] One of the reasons for the launch of Reform was to oppose female ordination, though its churches, such as Jesmond, insisted that there was a place for women in pastoral work, but not in preaching ministry.[65] Evangelical women flocked into full-time service. In 1998, 44 percent of entrants to London Bible College were female.[66] By this point another gender issue, homosexuality, was raising its head. Evangelical refusal to countenance homosexual practice, combined with sympathy for the plight of those with gay inclinations, had been reinforced by *The Church and Homosexuality* (1980).[67] Although a few Evangelicals were prepared to countenance faithful same-sex unions, the main division on this question was on how vocal to be in resisting liberalization of church policy. Wallace Benn, bishop of Lewes, saw the subject as a vital test of loyalty to the Bible; others, such as Christina Rees, were averse to "elevating the issue into a Christian orthodoxy."[68] The

---

61   *CEN*, 23 November 1966, 1.
62   *CEN*, 22 April 1977, 1; Heinze and Wheaton, *Witness to the World*, 197.
63   Randall, *English Baptists of the Twentieth Century*, 412; Walker, *Restoring the Kingdom*, 177.
64   *CEN*, 13 January 1995, 7.
65   Munden, *A Light in a Dark Place*, 229.
66   Price and Randall, *Transforming Keswick*, 287.
67   Michael Green, David Holloway and David C. K. Watson, *The Church and Homosexuality* (London: Hodder & Stoughton, 1980).
68   Stephen Bates, *A Church at War: Anglicans and Homosexuality* (London: Hodder & Stoughton, 2005), 20–21, 25.

proposal in 2003 to consecrate Jeffrey John, a champion of same-sex relationships in the church, to the suffragan see of Reading united almost all Evangelicals in opposition, leading to a volte-face by the archbishop of Canterbury, but how to respond to ruptures in the worldwide Anglican communion on the question again split their ranks in the months around the 2008 Lambeth Conference. The two gender controversies proved to be the most divisive questions of the period.

Social concern was also a controversial domain. In the middle years of the twentieth century Evangelical involvement in such areas had fallen under a cloud because of the association of active philanthropy with the social gospel, an apparent diversion from the spiritual gospel. The older tradition of social activism had never died out among Evangelicals, being institutionally maintained by the Salvation Army and practically by many an Evangelical parish. Yet at the National Assembly of Evangelicals in 1966, for example, "some members were suspicious of a return to 'the social gospel' and called for more direct 'witness.'"[69] Norman Anderson led the way in the recovery of social engagement with his *Into the World* (1968).[70] The Shaftesbury Project, designed to explore social questions on a pan-Evangelical basis, and TEAR Fund, aiming to channel giving through Evangelical churches in the Third World, soon followed. John Stott's *Issues Facing Christians Today* (1984; 4th ed., 2006) supplied a compendium of wisdom that became received opinion in the field. Concern for the welfare of society could spill over into the political sphere.[71] The former quietist tendencies of Evangelicalism were overturned by the fundamental shift in moral values of the 1960s. The "permissive society" became a target for Evangelical critique, at first in the largely spontaneous Festival of Light of 1971 and then in its more structured successor, CARE. Something of the initial defensive stance of the Nationwide Festival of Light is suggested by the comment that its first full-time director, Raymond Johnston, was appointed to "stand up to left-wing academics."[72] The most successful venture of Evangelicals into public life was the Keep Sunday Special campaign of 1986, which contrived to defeat the proposals of Margaret Thatcher's government, then at the height of its power, for the relaxation of restrictions on Sunday trading. The triumph was to be reversed under John Major, and, as Clive Calver ruefully remarked, this campaign was "the only clear illustration

69   *CEN*, 28 October 1966, 14.
70   Norman Anderson, *Into the World: The Need and Limits of Christian Involvement* (London: Falcon Books, 1968).
71   John Stott, *Issues Facing Christians Today* (Basingstoke: Marshall Pickering, 1984).
72   *CEN*, 22 February 1974, 1.

of what could eventually be achieved."[73] Nevertheless Calver's Evangelical Alliance saw itself under his successor as turning into a "Movement for Change" so as to achieve social transformation.[74] The shift towards engagement with sociopolitical issues, though less favored in some more conservative circles, had gone a long way during the years since 1959.[75]

A fundamental feature of British society during the later twentieth century was increasing prosperity. Some might disdain it: a young man attending a conference at St John's College, Nottingham, in 1976, "gloried in being so detached from filthy lucre that he never reconciled his bank statements."[76] Yet the possession of a bank account by this Evangelical hippy was itself a sign that he, and the youth culture that he represented, were the fruit of the affluent society. Church income could hugely increase. St Paul's, Hainault, a charismatic congregation, raised its weekly offerings in the early 1970s from £12 to £100 over only three years.[77] With more resources, churches could increase their personnel. Instead of the traditional single minister, perhaps assisted by a curate and a part-time secretary, large urban congregations could employ over a dozen staff. Church leadership became a specialist skill, possessing its own journal of that name. Money could be lavished on previously undreamt-of equipment. A microphone, noticed in a report of 1974 as a curious oddity in church, became an essential tool of a speaker.[78] Technology transformed worship, even in some smaller churches. At churches with thin congregations, taped music could be a crucial reinforcement of the singing.[79] Enterprising Evangelical groups could enter the media. Attractive magazines catered for specific sections of the population, with *Buzz* making a big impact on teenagers in the late 1970s and *Third Way* engaging with cultural issues down the decades. Capital Radio was set up in 1995 as a Christian broadcasting service for London, and five years later its successor Premier Radio was able to sponsor a range of local radio stations that secured temporary licenses for a

---

73 Clive Calver, "Afterword: Hope for the Future," in *Evangelical Faith and Public Zeal: Evangelicals and Society in Britain, 1780–1980*, ed. John Wolffe (London: SPCK, 1995), 208.
74 *Movement for Change: Evangelicals and Social Transformation*, ed. David Hilborn, (Milton Keynes: Paternoster Press, 2004), xii–xiv.
75 Tim Chester, *Awakening to a World of Need: The Recovery of Evangelical Social Concern* (Leicester: InterVarsity Press, 1993).
76 *CEN*, 6 February 1976, 4.
77 *CEN*, 28 June 1974, 7.
78 *CEN*, 28 June 1974, 7.
79 Personal observation. On worship, see 1:16: "Evangelicals and Public Worship, 1965–2005."

month around Pentecost.[80] A rich society, furthermore, could afford to provide extended education for its citizens. The cohort of young people entering higher education mushroomed. Christian Unions followed suit, expanding from 190 in 1958 to 554 in 1978.[81] The result was a steady stream of able candidates for the ministry and a growing body of educated laypeople in the pews. Bible colleges, once designed to produce evangelists with rudimentary skills, gained the power to grant degrees. Evangelicals, rooted in their society, were shaped by it at least as much as they molded it.

Conclusion

The half-century around the foundation of *Anvil* was therefore an eventful time. Although the Evangelical community persistently adhered to its inherited priorities of Bible, cross, conversion and activism, in 2009 it no longer worried about the preoccupations of 1959 such as the wearing of vestments in church. The older ethos, wary of Rome, worldliness, and the signs of the times but strongly committed to the evangelization of the world, had faded away. The newer developments were numerous: they included greater prominence in the denominations, more ecumenical contacts, a fresh sector of black majority churches, enhanced social concern and the consequences of prosperity. Many of the novelties, however, induced a fracturing of the movement, most visible in the Church of England. A broadening of views led to the emergence of a large section of opinion willing to call itself "open;" the Reformed theological revival stiffened a more conservative grouping; and renewal created a novel sector of vibrant charismatic congregations.[82] Although many parishes mingled people of different allegiances, the divergent tendencies were clear. By the twenty-first century the issues that divided Evangelicals most sharply surrounded questions of gender relations, but there were many other contrasts. Open Evangelicals were generally much happier with contemporary approaches to biblical hermeneutics than members of Reform; charismatic churches were more likely to run Alpha courses while Reform favoured Christianity Explored; there was normally a much more structured liturgy in an open than in a charismatic congregation; and so on. Underlying the differences, it may be suggested, was a more fundamental cultural orientation. Reform promoted a logocentric modernity, stressing accurate teaching,

---

80 *Baptist Times*, 17 February 2000, 2.
81 Douglas Johnson, *Contending for the Faith: A History of the Evangelical Movement in Colleges and Universities* (Leicester: InterVarsity Press, 1979), 338.
82 Graham Kings, "Canal, River and Rapids: Contemporary Evangelicalism in the Church of England," *Anvil* 20:3 (2003), 167–84.

efficient ecclesiastical structures and resistance to contemporary fashions for the sake of the gospel. Charismatics embraced a postmodern delight in variety, authenticity and relevance to felt needs. The open grouping welcomed insights from the modern and the postmodern, being deliberately eclectic. Attitudes to cultural change fostered markedly contrasting stances. The former unity of Evangelicalism had been broken.

16

Evangelicals and Public Worship, 1965–2005

Between 1965 and 2005 there was a drastic transformation of public worship among Evangelicals.[1] The change was readily apparent in the Church of England. Down to 1965 the Book of Common Prayer, compiled in the sixteenth century and revised in the seventeenth, was its only approved liturgy. In that year, however, the Church of England gained the right for the first time to devise its own services without further recourse to parliament. Profiting from this momentous liberation, the church was soon experimenting with fresh services labeled "Series II." Other redrafts led to the *Alternative Service Book* of 1980 and eventually to *Common Worship* in 2000. That book encouraged congregations to draw up their own liturgies so long as certain elements were preserved. Evangelicals gladly embraced their freedom, devising orders of service that included, for example, open prayer. There was an end to uniformity of worship in the established church. It is not so widely appreciated that there was as sweeping a process of change among most other Evangelicals in Britain, whether the Nonconformists of England and Wales or the Presbyterians and others of Scotland. In 1965 they still adhered to the traditional forms such as "Thee" and "Thou" in prayer. By 2005 some were singing extraordinarily untraditional songs, including such lines as "Give me gas in my Ford / Keep me trucking." The experience of worship was revolutionized.

This paper explores the developments that took place over the forty-year period. Its purpose is not just to chronicle, but also to analyze and to try to explain. Almost the sole source is a set of notebooks that the author has kept over nearly the whole of the period. During services I have maintained the

---

[1] This paper was delivered as the Laing Lecture at the London School of Theology in February 2006. I am grateful to the principal and college for their invitation and hospitality.

habit of taking notes on what takes place: not only the sermons, but also the setting, the worshipers and every individual item, including its timing. The result is a solid body of field research.[2] There is a problem of reliability with this material. The author clearly states on 16 January 1972 that he has never previously observed members of the congregation saying the grace together at the end of a service, but equally clearly he has already recorded the practice on 24 November 1968. Like all historical sources, this set of notebooks needs to be treated with care. Yet it provides a full account of services attended, usually two per Sunday, but sometimes only one and occasionally three or even four. For the purposes of this analysis, I have excluded services on weekdays, consequently omitting gatherings on Christmas Day and Good Friday, in order to concentrate on Sunday worship. I have also excluded non-Evangelical congregations, though many are recorded in the notebooks. There is a Unitarian service and one in Great St Mary's, Cambridge, when J. A. T. Robinson, bishop of Woolwich, was the preacher; there are Roman Catholic services and a celebration of the Russian Orthodox liturgy to mark the millennium of the introduction of Christianity into Russia; and there are High Church Anglican services including Solemn High Mass for Ascensiontide at All Saints, Margaret Street, in London, in 1998, when the preacher told a memorable anti-Evangelical joke. "Why," he asked, "is the Church of England like a swimming pool?" The answer was that is "because all the noise comes from the shallow end."[3] Within the Evangelical world, I tried to visit most sectors over the years. Because I am a Baptist, most of the services took place in Baptist churches, but there was also worship in Anglican, Methodist, Congregational and United Reformed Church, Church of Scotland and Fellowship of Independent Evangelical Churches congregations together with a few others: Strict Baptist, Scotch Baptist, Brethren, Church of God and so on. So the data is denominationally varied.

In terms of space, only churches in Britain have been selected, although the notebooks also contain information on churches in Ireland, on the continent, in the United States, Canada, South Africa, Australia, New Zealand and Fiji. Because I moved to Scotland in 1976, the majority of services attended since then have been north of the border, but, since I regularly visited the East Midlands and the south of England for family reasons and often traveled elsewhere for historical research, I built up data on many parts of England and Wales. Patterns of worship were similar in many respects, though change often took

2   These notebooks, in the possession of the author, will be cited as S (for Services), with the date. In the originals the date is coded and occasionally inaccurate.
3   S, 21 May 1998.

place earlier in the south of England, and especially round London, than further north.[4] Scotland was distinctive in a number of ways: in often retaining metrical Psalms, sometimes alongside hymns, into the late twentieth century; in congregations repeating the Lord's Prayer not with the word "trespasses," but with "debts;" and in widespread aversion to the congregation saying "Amen" aloud after prayers. Wales was distinctive in elders or deacons in the Nonconformist denominations occupying the "big seat" at the front, following Calvinistic Methodist practice, as well as, of course, as conducting many services in the Welsh tongue. As a general rule, however, there was more contrast within each national unit than between different national units. Thus normally the contrast between rural and suburban congregations was sharper than that between Scottish and English churches. What is taken as central for this study, however, are changes over time. I have therefore selected for close analysis four groups of services at ten-year intervals: 100 each in 1968–70, 1978–80, 1988–90 and 1998–2000. Although other—and particularly later—services have also been considered, these are the periods scrutinized in detail. The special issue is the question of developments. What have been the main trends over the period? Why has there been a transformation of public worship among Evangelicals since 1965?

Traditional Ways

The starting point is the situation in the late 1960s. What do the notes suggest were the predominant features of worship at that juncture? What were the traditional motifs that were only just beginning to change? In the first place, there was the priority of the spiritual. Evangelicalism was about being set apart from the world, about having a zest for spiritual things. Consequently public worship had an aura of sacredness. It was conducted by somebody whose dress marked him out as different. Anglican clergy wore a surplice together with a broad black scarf, the tippet. Nonconformist ministers almost always wore clerical collars—except Martyn Lloyd-Jones, who when I saw him in 1969 wore a round-cornered collar in the pulpit.[5] Leaders of worship, unless they were laymen, were designated as religious specialists by their dress. Services, furthermore, were periods of sacred time. When a new hymn was to be practiced, the rehearsal took place not within the service but beforehand or afterwards. If sung within worship, the hymn had a particular spiritual purpose that practice would undermine. Although the whole service possessed a measure of separation from the profane, that was specially true of the prayers. Stewards

---

4 See 1:4: "Evangelicalism and Cultural Diffusion."
5 S, 26 February 1969.

permitted late entry during hymns, but not during prayers. Approaching God, a distinctly spiritual act, was not to be disturbed.

Communion was particularly sacred. At my home church in Nottingham,[6] as in other gathered churches, the communion service was essentially for members only, and by no means all members attended. Communion was held as a separate event following the ordinary morning or evening service after a break of several minutes. At communion there were items of fellowship news, a special prayer for the fellowship by a deacon and a fellowship offering—for a charitable fund on behalf of the needy of the congregation, a tradition going back to the origins of Dissent in the seventeenth century. All was explicitly designed for the fellowship of believers, who around the Lord's table were most separate from the world. In ordinary services, furthermore, there was a specific spiritual purpose, though it varied according to the time of day. The morning service was adapted to the needs of the saints, to promote their growth in grace: it was for sanctification. The evening service was for sinners, and the gospel was preached: it was for conversion. Until just about 1965, numbers at the evening service were higher than those at the morning service. An evangelistic emphasis in the evening remained evident in the sample of services from 1978–80, though it faded thereafter. It sometimes led to repeated choruses of the type found in *Golden Bells*, the Scripture Union hymn book, or Sankey's *Sacred Songs and Solos*, which was still employed as the evening hymn book at the Baptist church when I moved to Stirling in 1976.[7] There might also be testimonies from converted individuals and appeals such as that at an evening service in 1970 urging members of the congregation to put their faith in Christ "now."[8] Whether morning or evening, whether for sanctification or conversion, services had an aim beyond themselves, to carry people further into the realm of grace. Worship was concerned with the spiritual.

A second characteristic of Evangelical worship in the late 1960s was (as the French philosopher Jacques Derrida would have said) its logocentricity, its concentration on the word. The sermon was the dominant element in worship. It was dominant in esteem, with the music and prayers being regarded as "the preliminaries." It was also dominant in length. In the period 1968–70, the average length of the main constituents of worship was as follows: prayer 10 minutes; congregational hymns 17 minutes; and the sermon 24 minutes. Some

---

6   On this church, see David W. Bebbington, *A History of Queensberry Street Baptist Church, Old Basford, Nottingham* (Nottingham: For the Church, 1977).
7   On this church, see Brian Talbot, *Standing on the Rock: A History of Stirling Baptist Church, 1805–2005* ([Stirling: For the Church], 2005).
8   S, 30 August 1970.

addresses could be significantly longer: the longest in this period recorded in the note books was 38 minutes.[9] At a traditional service in 1979, the preacher caused some dismay when, seven minutes after the opening of a rather dreary sermon, he said that now he wanted "to begin."[10] Ninety-five percent of the sermons in the years 1968–1970 had texts. The distribution was roughly one quarter from the Old Testament and three-quarters from the New—which was exactly the same as the proportions in a comparable survey undertaken in 1896.[11] A three-point structure was common, though not the norm. Where the sermon contained three points, they helped ensure a fairly tight exegesis of a passage. The "message," a term often preferred to the more ecclesiastical "sermon," was the verbal focus of each act of worship.

People followed the sermons in their Bibles, this often being one of the practices that distinguished an Evangelical from a non-Evangelical congregation. There was always at least one Bible reading. The rendering of the Bible most frequently found among Evangelicals was the Revised Standard Version, because its contemporary language (except for prayers to the Almighty) was designed to communicate the gospel more clearly. Yet the Authorized Version was still in common use, for example at two Norwich churches visited on the morning and evening of a Sunday in 1969.[12] The retention of the Authorized Version, as in much of contemporary America, was an indication of a deep-seated loyalty to the text. It was a sign of logocentricity.

Traditional services were, in the third place, notable for their regularity. The standardization of services was most evident in the Church of England. Evangelicals did not merely tolerate the Book of Common Prayer, but rejoiced in it. The tercentenary of the publication of the Prayer Book in 1662 was marked by the Islington Conference, the annual gathering of Anglican Evangelicals, with the whole proceedings celebrating "The Glory of our Liturgy."[13] The fixedness of the Prayer Book, in embodying the Reformation principles of its chief author, Archbishop Cranmer, was a cause for thankfulness. The attachment of Evangelical Anglicans to the Prayer Book as a whole overcame their worries over particular details, though these scruples sometimes showed in worship. Thus at an Evangelical parish church in Bristol in 1978, before the Prayer Book

9   S, 20 July 1969.
10 S, 12 August 1979.
11 *British Weekly*, 26 March 1896, 379. This survey was conducted by readers of the newspaper, mostly Scottish Presbyterians and English Nonconformists, who sent in a note of the length of the sermon and its text on a single Sunday.
12 S, 22 June 1969.
13 *Church of England Newspaper*, 12 January 1962, 1, 16.

intercession for priests, the officiant took pains to explain to the congregation that all believers are in reality priests.[14] Discomfort with tiny points was a small price to pay for a pattern of worship that had functioned for more than a century as a bulwark against Anglo-Catholic liturgical innovations. So long as Prayer Book worship survived, Evangelicalism enjoyed a secure place within the Church of England.

Nonconformists, for all their devotion to free worship, likewise had very predictable services. Prayers normally consisted of an opening item of praise, by no means perfunctory, of two to four minutes; a prayer associated with the offering, which could be perfunctory; and a long prayer before the hymn preceding the sermon. As an example of a long prayer, we may take the one offered by Leith Samuel at Above Bar Church, Southampton, affiliated to the Fellowship of Independent Evangelical Churches, on 31 October 1971. Starting with the ground of approach to God, the sacrifice of Christ on the cross, the prayer went on to cover the individual needs of the members of the congregation. Then the pastor turned to wider affairs, praying that Ulster criminals would be "brought to book." Finally he offered prayer on behalf of a special concern of church and minister, the spiritual welfare of students at Oxford, Cambridge, London and elsewhere, and other young Christians. This was essentially intercessory prayer; and it lasted eight minutes. Similar prayers were usual at other churches, though normally they were more like five minutes long. Hymns were interspersed between other items, so that the pattern was sometimes called a "hymn sandwich." The singing was normally based on a denominational hymn book. From 1965 even the Anglican Evangelicals had their own, *The Anglican Hymn Book*. The congregation uniformly stood to sing, except in Nonconformist communion services, where sitting seemed the right posture for meditation on the work of Christ. It was still the custom in many places in 1965 to sing "Amen" at the end of every hymn, whether or not it was appropriate, though the traditional practice was fading. Apart from scripture reading and sermon, prayers and hymns, other features that usually appeared in a service were, in the morning, a children's address and in all services the notices, the offering and items by a choir. A choir sometimes contributed an introit at the start, usually an anthem in the middle and occasionally a vesper at the end of the evening service. Often under the baton of a conductor, the choir would normally sing in four parts and might reach high musical standards; or might not. Free Church worship was varied each year by the Sunday school anniversary, with much singing by the children, the

---

14   S, 30 July 1978.

harvest festival, with elaborate displays of produce, and (among Methodists) the Covenant Service at the start of January for renewing dedication to the Lord. Ordinary services, however, were little varied. There might be an occasional solo or poem, but many churches were never so bold. Regularity was the order of the day.

Liturgical Renewal

Nevertheless it should not be supposed that worship was immune to change in the 1960s. On the contrary, powerful influences were impinging on the way in which services were conducted. Most of the fresh developments can be summed up under the heading of the liturgical movement. In the Church of England, the roots of liturgical renewal went back to the Anglo-Catholic ritualists of the nineteenth century. Emphasizing the more frequent celebration of the eucharist, they catered for the widespread desire, specially among the middle classes, for color, mystery and awe in worship, the rising tide of feeling unleashed on the world by writers of the Romantic school. By the 1940s there was a widespread desire to harness this impulse to pastoral needs. The result was the Parish and People Movement, starting in 1949, which transformed the face of the Church of England. Instead of morning prayer ("matins"), the main service of the day became parish communion. By the 1960s, a parish communion, targeting the whole community, had become the norm.

Against all this Evangelicals set their faces. Morning prayer, in their view, was suitable for every worshiper, and so they wanted to retain it. Communion was designed for believers only, and so was inappropriate for the whole parish. The chairman of the 1961 Islington Conference still warned of the dangers of parish communion.[15] The tide of change, however, proved irresistible. Elements of the newer idiom crept into Evangelical services. Crucial was the position of the officiating clergyman at the communion service. The traditional Evangelical conviction was that the clergyman should conduct the service from the "north side" of the Lord's table, that is the left from the point of view of the congregation, whose members could then be involved by observing his movements. Evangelicals rejected the view, originally associated with ritualists but normal in the Church of England by the 1960s, that the officiant should adopt the "eastward position," that is stand with his back to the congregation, so symbolizing that he, the priest, represented the people before God. During the 1960s, however, a new option became available, originating in the Church of South India and propagated by adherents of the liturgical movement: the

---

15 *Church of England Newspaper*, 13 January 1961, 3.

"westward position." According to this school of thought, the clergyman should stand behind the Lord's table, facing the congregation. To this there was no intrinsic theological objection among Evangelicals, and so the practice started to spread among them. In 1967 the Keele Congress of Anglican Evangelicals circumspectly recommended "consideration" of the westward position.[16] It rapidly triumphed, the north side position becoming virtually extinct. At the same time liturgical interest became more popular among Evangelicals under the leadership of Colin Buchanan, subsequently bishop of Aston and of Woolwich, a keen advocate of the parish communion.[17] In due course the Grove Booklets on Ministry and Worship, many of them by Buchanan, became the premier guides to liturgical matters for the Church of England as a whole. Liturgical renewal, shorn of its objectionable doctrinal implications, became entirely acceptable to Anglican Evangelicals.

The liturgical movement also made a major impact on the Free Churches. It spread there in diffuse ways, but was already strong by the later 1960s and continued to influence the churches thereafter. Its hallmark was greater formality. Although its tendency towards a higher churchmanship was in some tension with the populist instincts of Evangelical Nonconformity, several aspects were evident in the churches I visited. The first aspect can be summed up as greater structure. One typical reflection of the insistence of the liturgical movement on the solidarity of the people of God in worship was the practice of the congregation standing for the entry of the minister, sometimes preceded by a layperson carrying a Bible to the pulpit. Prayers requiring the congregation to respond by repeating a phrase, which I encountered at a Northampton Baptist church in 1970, were another symptom.[18] Set prayers that were read, rather than extempore prayers, were a more common feature. At two East Anglian Free Churches visited in 1969, for example, the General Confession was read.[19] Denominational publications such as, among the Baptists, E. A. Payne and S. F. Winward, *Orders and Prayers for Public Worship* (1960), encouraged this practice. Repositioning the main prayer after the sermon as a medium of congregational response was another characteristic sign of concern for structure. This, for instance, was the way in which George Beasley-Murray, principal of Spurgeon's College, preferred to conduct services, as I witnessed in Cambridge

16 Christopher J. Cocksworth, *Evangelical Eucharistic Thought in the Church of England* (Cambridge: Cambridge University Press, 1993), 164.
17 Colin O. Buchanan, *Patterns of Sunday Worship*, Grove Booklets on Ministry and Worship, vol. 9 (Bramcote, Nottinghamshire: Grove Books, 1972), 8.
18 S, 27 September 1970.
19 S, 22 June 1969.

in 1968.[20] Liturgical renewal also led to more distinctive "High Church" customs infiltrating into Nonconformity. In some churches there was a formal offertory, in which the elements for communion were taken in procession together with the people's financial gifts to the minister at the Lord's table, a standard Anglo-Catholic practice at which Evangelical Anglicans baulked.[21] In others, later in the century, there was recitation of the Apostles' Creed, traditionally seen as a fetter on biblical thinking.[22] Although the offertory and creed were items that I observed later, fresh elements of structure were already apparent in churches by the 1960s.

A second feature marking the permeation of the influence of the liturgical movement may be called clericalism. Among Evangelicals, though not in other segments of the church, a higher understanding of the status of the minister was associated with liturgical renewal. The more distinct role for the ordained was expressed in dress. In the Church of England, some Evangelicals, especially of the more open variety, started to wear not the traditional black scarf over the surplice but a colored stole. Some Nonconformists were eventually to copy them, as at New Milton Baptist Church, Hampshire, in 1979.[23] More common, however, was the wearing of a gown, sometimes with academic hood and preaching tabs. Other characteristic expressions were the use of "you" rather than "us" in the benediction, so creating a gulf between minister and people, and raising the hand at the same time, long customary among Methodists and Presbyterians but not in denominations with lower traditions. Most striking over the course of time, however, was the willingness of ministers to pronounce a formal assurance of forgiveness, the equivalent of the Anglican absolution, again addressing the members of the congregation as "you" rather than "us." "Receive forgiveness," declared an Oxford Baptist minister in 1999.[24] "By the authority of our Lord Jesus Christ, be assured that your sins are forgiven," said the minister of a Welsh Presbyterian church in the following year.[25] Ministers were, on this understanding, different from their congregations: they possessed particular "authority." This was a symptom of what may justly be termed "clericalism."

In the third place, as in the Parish and People movement, so among Evangelicals, communion changed its character. It had been normal in the Free

---

20 S, 24 November 1968.
21 S, 18 July 1999.
22 S, 25 October 1998.
23 S, 5 August 1979.
24 S, 18 July 1999.
25 S, 23 January 2000.

Churches since early in the twentieth century, for health reasons, to have separate pieces of bread and individual communion cups. The liturgical movement, however, encouraged the use of a single loaf and a common cup as expressions of unity. They were gradually introduced into the communion service, often alongside rather than replacing the other form. By 2005, for example, there was a single large white loaf at Chichester Baptist Church, though gluten-free wafers were also available.[26] Among Baptists, but not among Congregationalists, it had long been customary for deacons rather than the minister to offer prayers of thanksgiving at the Lord's table. Another change in the observance of communion was therefore the taking over of the task in some congregations by the minister.[27] Most significant, however, was the transformation of communion from a separate service into an integrated part of the main service, a general trend. The new practice was first introduced at Stirling Baptist Church on 1 April 1979, and, though initially it remained exceptional, integrated communion became the sole pattern there from the late 1980s. At first care was taken in many congregations to invite believers to participate, a type of fencing of the table to protect it from unworthy participants. Gradually, however, that limitation was forgotten, and participation was allowed by anyone present, including newcomers with no apparent Christian commitment and the very young. Some churches, though usually those on the broadest fringe of Evangelicalism, frankly accepted this state of affairs by inviting all, and not just believers, to receive the elements. This development totally altered the character of the occasion. From being a closed world for the local fellowship of the strongly committed, communion had become an open event which some ministers, according to the evidence of their exhortations, hoped would be a converting ordinance. Evangelical Nonconformists now observed something very like a parish communion.

Ecumenical contact also allowed the percolation of higher church elements into Evangelical worship. The period coincided with the rise of participation by Evangelicals in the ecumenical movement. Down to the mid-1960s they had commonly looked askance at aspirations after church unity, but, though some remained aloof after 1965, most became cautiously involved, at least in local councils of churches. At joint services Evangelicals were exposed to different styles of worship and in discussion they began to see the point of behavior they had once shunned. Churches which had previously ignored the ecclesiastical year gradually began to incorporate certain of its elements. Christmas and Easter had long been recognized, but increasing attention was paid to

26   S, 2 January 2005.
27   S, 7 September 1969.

them. The Easter acclamation, "Christ is risen / Alleluia!," for example, was sometimes introduced.[28] More radical was the steady growth of references to Advent, Epiphany and Lent. The process was fostered by the use of the lectionary, drawn up by the interdenominational Joint Liturgical Group, first established in 1963.[29] Because the lectionary specified scriptural readings in accordance with the church year, it molded themes of worship around the Christian seasons. By the time of the introduction of the *Methodist Worship Book* in 1999, there was provision within it for marking the forehead with ashes on Ash Wednesday and the exaltation of the cross on Good Friday.[30] At the start of the same century these very practices had been denounced as "popish errors" and had sometimes provoked Evangelical riots. Even if few Evangelical congregations now adopted these particular customs, the tendency was to assimilate more of what other Christians had traditionally observed.

A major consequence of ecumenical contact was, in fact, a willingness among Evangelicals to borrow from Roman Catholics. The process started with the vogue around 1970 for *Prayers of Life* by Michel Quoist, a chaplain in the Catholic diocese of Lyons.[31] Simple unadorned expressions of how life really was, these frank texts seemed to breathe fresh life into addressing the Almighty. Prayers by medieval and post-Reformation Catholic saints began to appear: not surprisingly, perhaps, the prayer of St Richard of Chichester at Chichester Baptist Church in 1979; more unexpectedly, the prayer of St Ignatius Loyola, the founder of the Jesuits, at a notably conservative Evangelical Baptist church in Cheltenham the year before.[32] High Church words of administration also crept into communion. By 1990 an Edinburgh Baptist church was using the words "The body of Christ, broken for you" and "The blood of Christ, shed for you," which might naturally be interpreted as implying the real presence of Christ in the elements.[33] Prayers edged towards intercession for the dead, though usually concentrating on giving thanks for the lives of those who had died. The closest to actual prayer for the departed was at a broad-minded Methodist/United Reformed Church in the south of England in 2005. The phrase used was "commending into your eternal care those who

28 S, 4 April 1999.
29 John R. K. Fenwick and Bryan D. Spinks, *Worship in Transition: The Twentieth Century Liturgical Movement* (Edinburgh: T&T Clark, 1995), 92.
30 Norman Wallwork, "Developments in Liturgy and Worship in Twentieth-Century Protestant Nonconformity," in *Protestant Nonconformity in the Twentieth Century*, ed. Alan P. F. Sell and Anthony R. Cross (Carlisle: Paternoster Press, 2003), 129.
31 S, 29 March 1970; 7 November 1971.
32 S, 7 January 1979; 23 July 1978.
33 S, 12 August 1990.

have died."[34] By then there were many other indications of the assimilation of Catholic influence: the anthem *Ave Verum Corpus* at a Cornish Methodist church; holding up Mary the mother of Christ as an example in a Scottish Baptist church; and prayer there for Catholics on the death of Pope John Paul II.[35] Inherited anti-Catholic inhibitions were steadily eroded. Direct ecumenical contact reinforced the thrust of the liturgical movement, pushing Evangelical worship towards a higher churchmanship.

Informal Tendencies

The fascination of the period, however, lies partly in the circumstance that this trend, largely in the direction of formality, coincided with an even stronger impulse in the opposite direction, towards informality. This process was what may be called an expressive revolution, a dimension of a wider process in society at large that has been described by that phrase.[36] Instead of keeping their feelings to themselves, worshipers increasingly expressed themselves in services. This trend has roots in the so-called Expressionism that remolded Western art and literature in the early twentieth century—as in the architecture of the Modern movement or the fiction of Kafka. In Britain its pioneers were the Bloomsbury Group, and the novels of Virginia Woolf well illustrate its ethos. This cultural mood, originally confined to a small elite, first became a popular phenomenon in the 1960s, represented at the extreme by the unrestrained self-expression of drug, sex and rock 'n' roll. Individuals were called on to "let it all hang out," to display the undifferentiated mixture of thought and feeling that seethes beneath the surface of the human personality. The tide of postmodernism in the late twentieth century can legitimately be seen as the intellectual formulation of this social phenomenon. This fresh idiom, reinforced by other changes, affected all spheres of life in Britain, including worship. Evangelical churches were encouraged by a succession of organizations—Church Growth, Willow Creek, Saddleback—to put as few obstacles as possible in the path of potential converts, and so to adapt to contemporary culture. Deliberate action by many churches therefore hastened what was in any case happening, an accommodation of worship to prevailing idioms in the host culture.

A clear instance was the spread of informal dress. Suits, white shirts and ties were still normal church wear for men in the 1960s. By the 1990s even stewards taking the offering had discarded the suit and tie in favor of open neck

---

34   S, 24 July 2005.
35   S, 10 July 2005; 13 December 1998; 3 April 2005.
36   Bernice Martin, *A Sociology of Contemporary Cultural Change* (Oxford: Basil Blackwell, 1981), chap. 2.

and shirt sleeves. Young men were allowed to sport baseball caps and other headgear in church, a shocking breach of the dress code of their elders. On 4 July 2004 the minister in a distinguished English Baptist church wore a ring in his left ear. Another, and generally earlier, phenomenon was the disappearance of the use of the seventeenth-century language of "Thee" and "Thou" in prayer. This alteration was a natural corollary of the adoption of modern-language Bibles, but the sacredness of prayer dictated the retention of the customary form of address in many churches for a considerable time. I was still noting "You" as relative rarity in 1969; but by 2000 "Thou" had become very uncommon indeed. Contemporary language in prayer was also fostered by liturgical renewal, and it has to be recognized that some of the developments in worship were equally the results of the liturgical movement and of the expressive revolution. Both, for example, encouraged the laying on of hands. The act was a formal recognition of the proper ecclesiastical channels for the transmission of spiritual influence, an imitation of High Church practice. At the same time it was a way of seeking the blessing of the Holy Spirit, an expression of the deepest feelings of all concerned. In general, however, the expressive revolution pointed in fresh directions, away from the structured and the traditional and towards the casual and the novel. What were its dimensions?

Aspects of Change

In the first place there was social change. The late twentieth century witnessed a transformation in the role of women. Inevitably the churches were deeply affected. At the start of the period Free Church communion services provided a reminder of the balance of authority between the sexes. A row of exclusively male deacons in sober suits would assemble alongside the minister facing the congregation. Any women deacons, such as the two out of ten at Broadmead Baptist Church, Northampton, in 1969, were an exception.[37] Hats were still common for women in the late 1960s. There was an intriguing survival of this custom at a Carmarthen chapel in 1990, when, on Sisterhood Sunday, a woman appeared in the pulpit as the preacher wearing a black felt hat.[38] There were, however, signs of a growing awareness of the changing role of women. In 1978 an intercessory prayer at Stirling was devoted to women.[39] In 1990 Simon the Pharisee was denounced in an Edinburgh sermon (by a woman) as a "sexist."[40] In 1998 motherhood was treated at Stirling as an exemplification of

37 S, 7 September 1969.
38 S, 8 July 1990.
39 S, 26 November 1978.
40 S, 12 August 1990.

the spiritual journey.[41] Gender-inclusive language came into fashion. The need to avoid male pronouns for human beings in general was one of the salient changes between the *Alternative Service Book* of 1980 and *Common Worship* of 2000 in the Church of England. The Methodists went so far as to refer to "God our Mother" at one point in their *Worship Book* of 1999.[42] Feminist consciousness had made headway in the churches.

The actual role of women in the services made equivalent advances. They already occasionally read the notices and offered prayer in the late 1960s, but both practices became much more common as the century wore on. Reading the scripture lesson became almost a female prerogative. On five successive Sundays during the summer of 1998 at different Free Churches in England and Wales, a woman took the Bible reading. A crucial breakthrough came with the ordination of women to priest's orders in the Church of England in 1994. Previously, women could be prominent, but had their limitations. Thus at a Bristol parish church in 1978, a woman dressed in surplice and stole led the whole service, but at the absolution referred to "us," not "you." She lacked the authority of a presbyter to pronounce that the sins of others were forgiven. By 2005, however, nearly one-fifth of Anglican clergy were women, and, notwithstanding the principled resistance from the conservative Evangelicals of Reform, many were Evangelicals. There had, of course, long been female ministers in the Free Churches, but they had been far less likely to be welcomed to congregations than their male counterparts. Although that feeling still lingered in certain places at the end of the period, women were coming forward for ministry in large numbers. In 1998, 44 percent of the first-year intake at London Bible College were female.[43] Evangelical women could increasingly express themselves in worship.

A second factor, parallel to the coming forward of women, was the rise to prominence of young people and their culture. In an earlier day, churches had looked askance on the young. In 1960, for instance, the deacons of an East Midlands Baptist Church approved a youth weekend "with the proviso that skiffle should not be used at Sunday services."[44] The prominence of pop music in the lives of many of the younger generation, however, meant that if they were to be reached in evangelism, there had to be concessions to their preferences. Occasional youth services, often using the Church Pastoral

---

41 S, 13 December 1998.
42 Wallwork, "Liturgy and Worship," 129.
43 Ian Randall, *Educating Evangelicalism: The Origins and Development of London Bible College* (Carlisle: Paternoster Press, 2000), 287.
44 Bebbington, *Queensberry Street*, 51.

Aid Society's *Youth Praise* (1966), were launched. *Youth Praise*, for example, replaced the denominational hymn book at a Congregational evening service in Southampton in 1971.[45] Churches started to permit their own pop groups, choruses from *Youth Praise* began to infiltrate into ordinary services and the compositions of Graham Kendrick became popular. Children, too, enjoyed choruses. At annual services marking their summer holiday clubs, simple upbeat songs were tolerated that would have been unacceptable on other occasions.[46] From these initial footholds, a new musical idiom gradually gained ground in the churches.

As the young of the 1960s became the middle-aged of the 1980s and after, they naturally wanted their own taste to occupy a more prominent place in worship. Older guitar players, as at Knutsford Methodist Church, Cheshire, in 2004, led the singing.[47] The new mode was consolidated in fresh song books such as *Mission Praise* (1983), which actually drove out the denominational hymn book in many an Evangelical congregation. Organ playing and singing in parts faded away. Choirs were disbanded or else confined to those eligible for Saga holidays. Thus at Redruth Methodist Church in Cornwall in 2004 there were as many as twenty-seven choir members, but all except one were over the age of fifty.[48] Younger people had in most places won the battle for the song against the hymn, the guitar against the organ. It was significant that when the worship leader at Stirling Baptist Church in 2005 announced that the congregation was about to sing a "Golden Oldie," he meant not a classic hymn by Watts or Wesley but "At your feet we fall," composed in 1982.[49]

Technological change, in the third place, created alterations in the style of services. In many churches, though not in some of the poorer congregations, technical innovations facilitated the process of musical adaptation. The earliest instruments other than organs were normally basic guitars, as strummed by folk singers. That was true of the accompaniment to a duet sung at an Oxford Baptist church in 1969.[50] Other instruments could be added, as at Stirling in 1980, when a group of five musicians consisted of two singers together with a guitarist, a pianist and a player of the castanets.[51] During the 1980s, however, electric instruments were often introduced: electric guitars and keyboards.

45 S, 31 October 1971.
46 E.g. S, 12 August 1990.
47 S, 14 November 2004.
48 S, 28 November 2004.
49 S, 3 April 2005.
50 S, 7 December 1969.
51 S, 19 March 1980.

Drums frequently joined them, and sometimes flute, violin or saxophone. To amplify the music, elaborate sound equipment was often bought. The sound booth could become a focus for male bonding within a congregation, for it was a last field in which men generally possessed the upper hand. The result was a huge increase in the volume of the music, often to the discomfort of the elderly. A further consequence was a change in the style of praise. The worship group at the front, equipped with instruments and microphones, represented the performers. The congregation, as at a pop concert, might sing along or not, according to its whim. At many services congregational participation in the singing became minimal.

Technical change had other dimensions, however, affecting the visual as well as the aural. The first use of overhead projectors in worship, as opposed to their employment at other church events, that I observed was in 1978, at Queensberry Street Baptist Church, Old Basford, Nottingham.[52] Soon screens were acquired, often to the aesthetic detriment of the building. Overheads were eventually, in the richer congregations, superseded by Powerpoint. With either, the words of the songs could be read by members of the congregation when they raised their eyes. There were two crucial consequences. There was no longer any need for a hymn or song book, whether denominational or other; and the hands of worshippers were free, so that they could be used for self-expression. Technical change also ushered in tape/slide presentations, videos and films. Promotional visual material from TEAR Fund, missionary societies or Alpha, which once would have been deployed outside a service, was increasingly located within an act of worship. The visual could also be used for notices, sermon outlines and themes for meditation. New technical aids, furthermore, were not confined to large congregations. Taped music was invaluable for reinforcing singing in small churches, as in a city-center congregation of only fifteen in Preston, Lancashire, in 2004.[53] Technology, then, made an enormous impact during the period, greatly enhancing the variety of worship.

Change in spirituality, fourthly, was a major agent of transformation. One of the most potent motors of development in worship was the charismatic movement. 1965 was the year when the first British charismatic periodical, *Renewal*, started to appear.[54] Where charismatic experience remolded a congregation,

---

52 S, 13 August 1978.
53 S, 10 October 2004.
54 David W. Bebbington, *Evangelicalism in Modern Britain: A History from the 1730s to the 1980s* (London: Routledge, 1989), 230. See also 2:16: "The Rise of Charismatic Renewal in Britain."

worship was revolutionized. Most obviously, hands were raised in worship. It was intriguing to visit a Baptist church in Nottingham regularly and watch the increase in the number of individuals raising their hands: 2 in 1978, 8 in 1988, 20 at the start of 1989 and 30 at the end of the year.[55] Renewal never took over the whole church, and the number of hands raised fell away afterwards. Elsewhere there were other distinctive fruits of charismatic renewal. At a chapel in Wales in 1989 there was singing in the Spirit, the gentle use of tongues for congregational adoration.[56] At a Scottish church in 2003 there was a word of knowledge. The pastor explained that he knew there were individuals present with particular problems—a fear of death, bowel cancer and so on—that needed prayer counseling.[57] Renewal brought ways all its own.

The growth of charismatic phenomena was propagated by a succession of agencies: the Fountain Trust, Dales Week, John Wimber and his Vineyard churches. Perhaps most influential, however, was Spring Harvest, a weeklong training conference that from 1979 brought together charismatics and non-charismatics. It ensured that styles of worship associated with renewal penetrated far beyond the movement's immediate constituency. A local preacher at a Penzance Methodist church in 2004 referred to being asked at Spring Harvest what gives us the "wow" factor.[58] Many Evangelicals brought back to their home congregations the "wow" factor that they had discovered at the conference. Consequently noncharismatic churches were encouraged to change their ways. An Edinburgh Baptist church, for example, had specific prayer to the Holy Spirit at its evening service in 1988.[59] Without the influence of renewal, that invocation would have been unthinkable. So there was sanction in transformed spirituality for much of the alteration that took place during the period.

Cultural change, in the fifth place, ushered in new developments. The shift towards informality of the late twentieth century reflected the broader remolding of Western civilization during the period. Whether in the media or in historiography, the use of the body moved to the center of popular preoccupations. It was so in worship too. The raising of the hands, for example, was a symptom of the fresh stress on the physical. The posture of the body, too, was modified. Since at least the early nineteenth century the standard custom had been to stand for song and to sit or kneel for prayer. In the 1970s and 1980s,

55   S, 13 August 1978; 10 July 1988; 1 January 1989; 31 December 1989.
56   S, 2 July 1989.
57   S, 16 March 2003.
58   S, 21 November 2004.
59   S, 13 November 1988.

however, with the introduction of many choruses, it became common to ask the congregation to remain seated for some of them. Eventually, as the new technology was brought in, it became usual again to stand for most or all of the singing, but in a different way from what had been customary. The new pattern consisted of blocs of music, which I first noted in 1978, in which the worshipers remained standing for several songs at a stretch.[60] During these periods, the body was free to respond to the rhythm, the content and the spirit of the music. Prayer, which was often interspersed between the songs, was now undertaken while the congregation stood. Other physical expressions came into vogue: dance, mime, humorous skits and greetings by handshake and hug. Actions, and specially clapping, were frequently started first with the children, who were allowed to behave differently, but then were taken up by the whole congregation. The body as well as the mind was drawn into the worship experience.

Another way in which a concern with the physical came to the fore related to people's sense of a lack of wholeness. Healing services were introduced, specially where charismatic influence was strong. Those who were suffering from illness were encouraged to seek a cure from Christ himself. These occasions were not simply prayers for healing, which had long been common, but rather entailed prayer counseling, that is spiritual guidance with the laying on of hands, usually at the end of services at the front of the worship area. I first witnessed this style at a partly charismatic Nottingham church in 1988, when seven of the eight prayer counselors raised their hands in praise.[61] Often the problems addressed were psychological difficulties as well as physical ailments, for the human being was characteristically treated as a psychosomatic whole. The consequence was to alter the received pattern of Evangelical worship. The traditional mode had assumed the absolute priority of the spiritual over the physical. The newer style rejected that organizing principle, choosing to put much greater emphasis on the physical.

Another feature of the age, sixthly, was the rise of the visual relative to the verbal. Children preferring television to books constituted one telltale symptom, but the rapid progress of information technology strengthened the trend over time. Devotion to the film and the film star was another aspect of the phenomenon in society at large. It was echoed in church by the replacement of sermon allusions to literature, common in the 1960s, by references to films, sometimes entailing the display of clips on screens during services. Much else in worship reflected the change. It is true that two visual features, once

60 S, 13 August 1978.
61 S, 10 April 1988.

excluded from Evangelical buildings as idolatrous, had been admitted well before 1965. Flowers had been generally acceptable since the 1880s, though as late as 1967, when visiting a Strict Baptist chapel in Worthing, I was given, as a teenager, a tract devoted to denouncing flower displays in church. The other acceptable item was a cross (never crucifix) displayed in the building, the first instance of which in a Baptist church was reputedly the one erected at Mare Street, Hackney, immediately after the Second World War.[62] Other visible features, however, made their entrance only in the late twentieth century. Banners bearing pictures or signs in needlework, collage or other media were originally generated by charismatic renewal. Still, in 1990, a charismatic congregation in the East Midlands had two of its four banners referring to the Holy Spirit.[63] By that time, however, banners were common in Evangelical churches of nearly any description. Candles were widely adopted during the 1990s at the same time as they became popular in gift shops. Sometimes, as at a North Welsh Presbyterian church in 2000, they were lit throughout the service to symbolize the light of Christ. Most frequently there were Advent candles, with one lit by a child on each of the Sundays before Christmas, often at considerable fire risk. The sign of the cross, long regarded as Catholic superstition, crept into some quarters, though most Evangelical Anglicans still preferred to avoid it in absolution or benediction. A cross, for example, was traced on the foreheads of infants at dedication services in Stirling Baptist church from 1997. The service had become a dry christening. Other symbolic actions were introduced, especially at the end of the period. At the start of 2005, for instance, members of a Chichester congregation wrote prayers responding to the Indian Ocean tsunami and filed forward to stick them on the front wall of the church. An appreciation of symbol became much more widespread.

Corresponding to the rise of the visual was the decline of the verbal. This process was by no means absolute. According to my samples, the average length of the sermon in the late 1960s was 24 minutes and in the late 1990s was still 23 minutes, virtually unchanged. Nevertheless the sermon was far less of a work of art. It was often delivered not from a pulpit but from a lower platform or reading desk. Preachers were less declamatory and more chatty. And sermons could be broken up into two, three or four sections, no doubt to cater for the assumed shorter concentration span of the hearers. Where the Bible reading was not prescribed by the liturgy, furthermore, it was frequently abbreviated, incorporated within the sermon or else omitted entirely. Likewise at the communion service in the Free Churches the words of institution might

62 Information from the late Rev. C. M. Moore-Crispin, once minister of the church.
63 S, 22 July 1990.

be left out. At the same time tolerance of ungrammatical songs grew. In the popular piece "Lord, I come to you" there occurred the subject phrase "The knowledge of your love as you live in me" without any following verb or complement. Spelling on display screens became erratic. One instance from 2005 was the presentation of "cords of sinfulness" as "chords."[64] Punctuation often disappeared entirely. While this development was primarily a result of declining educational standards, it was also something more. The word had lost part of its sacredness. The visual had risen in esteem but the verbal had declined.

In the seventh place there was the advance of the ideal of authenticity. To be spontaneous, genuine, laying all bare, carried increasing cachet. So the cult of authenticity gained a major place in worship. Its hallmark was the use of the first person singular. Those leading worship, representing the whole congregation, had traditionally used "we" in prayer. In 1989 I registered a deacon at a Nottingham church saying "my" in a prayer at the Lord's table, though this usage may have been little more than a slip. That drop soon turned into a flood. By 1998 it was common for ministers to employ "I." Often associated with an intensification of the voice, it was meant to express ardor of feeling. Lay worship leaders, often lacking experience of taking congregational prayers, did the same even more frequently. The rise of the worship leader can itself be seen as a way of making services more authentic. Instead of a single preacher imposing his ways on the church, members of the congregation could take the initiative in singing and prayer. In the earlier phase of this development, in the 1970s, the worship leader conducted only about one third of the service and was not normally a musician. From the 1980s, however, a musician frequently led nearly all of the service except the sermon slot. Wishing to demonstrate their immersion in the worship experience, and no doubt moved by the music, leaders would often close their eyes, not while praying (as was traditional), but while singing (which could risk collisions with music stands). The congregation, too, was to enjoy a glow of authenticity. Thus separate periods of music began to be provided, distinguished as praise and worship. Praise was loud and celebratory; worship was quieter and more reflective. The congregation could also show its approval of songs or presentations by applause, something totally prohibited by the conventions of the 1960s. The barrier was first breached by applause at the enthronement of Robert Runcie as archbishop of Canterbury in 1980, when the choir broke into clapping and the congregation joined in. Evangelical congregations followed after some delay. At Stirling Baptist Church a superb solo in September 1988 elicited no applause, but a

---

64 S, 20 February 2005.

year later, in September 1989, a duet and trio of lower quality were followed by spontaneous clapping.[65] Other instances of allowing greater license to the congregation included the singing of "Happy birthday to you" to the minister.[66] Worshipers were more able to show how they really felt.

Some of the biggest shifts towards genuineness were in the area of prayer. There was decreasing use, especially by laypeople, of a concluding formula such as "in the name of Jesus Christ" or even, in some cases, "Amen," so that it was difficult to know when a prayer was over. Again, instead of two long prayers of praise and intercession, perhaps three and five minutes respectively, there were often short, sharp prayers, frequently linking musical items. Thus in a service at Stirling in 1998 there were six prayers, but each was tiny, of one minute or less.[67] Such brief contributions were sufficient to express the sentiments of the moment. More formal prayers such as those associated with the offering could disappear entirely. There was a serious consequence of this shift in practice. Intercession often became drastically curtailed. There was frequently no prayer for anyone beyond the bounds of the congregation. At some services there was no intercessory prayer whatsoever. Those with whom there was no personal link ranked low on a scale of priorities determined by spontaneous inclination. The elevation of authenticity had its casualties.

Resistance to Change

There was, then, an expressive revolution that affected much of Evangelicalism in the period. Nevertheless there was also strong resistance within so diverse a movement. Each of the facets of the revolution had its determined opponents who would not change their ways. Thus women were not always given fuller scope. At an independent Brethren meeting at Chester in 2000, the four men sat round a table for open Bible study while the three women occupied seats behind them, singing the hymns but not otherwise uttering a word.[68] Neither were young people consistently given their head. At a Cornish Methodist chapel evening service in a rear hall in 2004, all twelve present except the pianist were elderly. The traditional order of service included prayers with the response, "Lord, keep us faithful."[69] Technology had no impact on some. The assembly of the Church of God in Kirkintilloch, Scotland, observed in 2000 a form of the Lord's Supper that was modeled as far as possible on the details

---

65   S, 4 September 1988; 24 September 1989.
66   S, 25 February 1990.
67   S, 25 October 1998.
68   S, 16 January 2000.
69   S, 21 November 2004.

recorded in the New Testament. The elders of the church's assemblies from all over the world met every two years to ensure that worship conformed to any new light discerned on the teaching of scripture. The oldest pattern of worship was the ideal; new-fangled technology was anathema.[70] Change in spirituality was also resisted. At St Ebbe's Church, Oxford, a bastion of the Reform movement within the Church of England, there was in 2001 an up-to-date atmosphere with an immensely flourishing student ministry, but not a single individual raised a hand. A resolute form of confessional Calvinism prohibited specifically charismatic practices.[71] The physical was not necessarily respected. At Bethel Strict Baptist Chapel, Luton, in 1994, there was a devotion to patterns of Dissenting worship derived from the eighteenth century that emphasized the spiritual nature of the local church. Nobody was allowed to partake of the Lord's Supper who was not a member of the church.[72] Nor was the visual consistently preferred to the verbal. In 2000 a Chester congregation affiliated to the Fellowship of Independent Evangelical Churches possessed a flipchart for writing words rather than drawing illustrations, displayed not banners but posters carrying scriptural texts and recited an extract from the Heidelberg Catechism.[73] And authenticity was not a universal motif. Instead discipline could prevail. At congregations of the Free Church of Scotland, after much debate during the 1990s, it was settled that there must never be more than four sung items in a service; and at that time the sung items continued to be unaccompanied metrical psalms. These cameos illustrate that the process of change could be resisted, and that in some restricted circles it could be resisted successfully.

Conclusion

Notwithstanding the persistence of congregations where change was not embraced, the bulk of the evidence points to sweeping alterations in public worship among Evangelicals between 1965 and 2005. The traditional pattern was already being eroded in the 1960s by the impact of the liturgical movement. Prayer Book worship started to be varied in the Church of England, and there was an injection of elements of greater dignity into Free Church services. This imitation of selected High Church practices continued under the influence of greater ecumenical contact for the rest of the century. More radical, however, was the impact of the expressive revolution, leading for the

---

70   S, 17 December 2000.
71   S, 11 March 2001.
72   S, 7 August 1994.
73   S, 16 January 2000.

most part not towards greater formality but towards less of it. This process had firm social foundations in the second wave of feminism and the spread of youth culture. It drew on new technology and the currents of spirituality associated with charismatic renewal. And it was rooted in the cultural trends of the time, particularly the growing prominence given to the physical, the visual and the authentic. These characteristics largely superseded the leading features of Evangelical worship at the opening of the period. The priority of the spiritual gave way to an equal emphasis on the physical. The logocentricity of earlier times was drastically modified by the rise of the visual. And the old regularity of Evangelical services was undermined by the quest for authenticity. Each aspect of contemporary culture subverted a typical aspect of the older paradigm. The consequence, in most places, was a transition from one style of Evangelical public worship to another.

INDEX

A

Acworth, James, 36, 102, 242
Addison, Joseph, 49
adventism (second coming), 20, 34, 61, 64, 69–70, 84, 124, 142, 151, 155–66, 204, 230, 253, 268, 308, 334, 357, 365
Africa, 16, 40, 133, 138, 140, 144, 227, 255, 277–78, 335, 341, 348
Ahlstrom, Sydney, 280
Aked, Charles, 243
Akenson, Donald, 19
alcohol, 59, 127, 145
Alternative Service Book, 333, 347, 360
American Board of Commissioners for Foreign Missions, 148
American Civil War, 293
American Tract Society, 97
Anderson, Norman, 343
Anglican Evangelical Group Movement (AEGM), 69, 338
Anglicanism, 6, 8, 11, 18, 22, 24, 31–32, 40, 43, 45, 47, 49, 54, 61–62, 66–67, 69–70, 78, 80, 82, 84, 86–87, 96–97, 107, 109–10, 113, 118, 135, 138, 141, 146, 151, 158–60, 166, 169, 196–97, 204, 210, 217, 231, 238–41, 244, 246, 251, 254, 260–63, 270, 272–74, 276, 286, 289, 297, 301–2, 306, 310–12, 316–18, 322, 324–25, 329–32, 336, 338–39, 343, 348–49, 351–52, 354–55, 360, 365
Anglo-Catholicism, 33, 41, 163, 254, 278, 286, 330, 333, 352–53, 355
Angus, Joseph, 102, 108, 112
anthropology, 8, 75
anti-Catholicism, 13, 33, 159–60, 248, 250, 254–55, 263, 265, 286, 298, 332–33, 358
antislavery, 79
Anvil, 329, 345
Aquinas, Thomas, 312
Ariès, Philippe, 209
Aristotle, 109
Arminianism, 39, 47, 87, 101, 103–4, 109–10, 122–23, 125, 136, 139–40, 152, 169, 186, 188, 199, 221, 240–41, 249, 254, 314
Arminian Magazine, 51
Arminius, Jacobus, 199
Arnold, Thomas, 32, 63
Arthur, William, 201
Asbury, Francis, 276
assurance, 6, 13–14, 54–55, 187–88, 194, 198, 222, 355
Astronomical Discourses (Chalmers), 61, 310
astronomy, 304, 307, 309, 311, 317
Atkins, Gareth, 8
atonement, 1, 5–6, 37, 65, 98, 100, 104, 123, 137–38, 145, 147, 150, 180–81,

194, 216, 213, 316–17, 323, 325, 331, 337–38
Augustanism, 49, 55
Austen, Jane, 76
Australia, 132, 135, 146, 149, 269, 274, 281, 348

B

Bach, Johann Sebastian, 67, 76
Bacon, Francis, 143, 310, 320
Baines, Edward, 218, 224, 230
Banner of Truth Trust, 113, 196, 198, 261, 340
baptism, 38, 62, 116, 136, 171–73, 341
Baptist Historical Society, 270
Baptist Home Missionary Society, 186, 335
Baptist Magazine, 37, 149, 167, 170–71, 177, 212, 231
Baptist Missionary Society (BMS), 82, 100, 335
Baptist Union, 34, 37, 336–37, 342
Baptists, 5, 7, 18, 24, 39–40, 47, 62, 69–70, 80–82, 90–91, 97–103, 108, 112–13, 116, 130, 136, 138, 140, 144–46, 150, 163, 166–67, 170–73, 178, 180, 183, 188–89, 191, 195–96, 203, 211, 216, 218, 220–23, 225–27, 231–32, 237–38, 242–43, 246–47, 258, 270, 273, 275–76, 280–82, 286, 289, 302, 308, 310, 316–17, 320, 330, 335–42, 348, 350, 354, 356–63; Free Baptists, 152, 293; General Baptists, 35, 37, 168, 174–75, 179, 185–86, 199, 321; Particular Baptists, 86, 99, 102, 168, 179; Scotch Baptists, 348; Strict Baptists, 86, 102, 122, 245, 254, 365, 368; Welsh Baptists, 36, 215, 217, 228–30
Barclay, Oliver, 262
Barnes, Albert, 144
Baxter, Richard, 106, 215
Beck, Jakob Sigismund, 105
Belich, James, 267,
Bellamy, Joseph, 98, 102
Benn, Wallace, 342

Bennet, John, 59
Bible, 3–5, 19, 25, 35–37, 41, 44, 52, 61, 65, 75, 82, 102, 104, 115, 18, 123–24, 128–29, 133, 136–37, 139, 145, 147, 152, 164, 172, 179–80, 191, 195, 205, 207, 214–15, 230, 232, 241, 252, 261, 272, 282–83, 285, 301–5, 310, 314, 317–18, 330–31, 334–35, 342, 345, 351, 354, 359–60, 365, 367; *see also* biblicism
Bible and Medical Missionary Fellowship, 335
Bible Christians, 110, 241
Bible Churchmen's Missionary Society, 272, 335
biblicism, 4, 12, 180, 182
Bickersteth, Edward, 110
Binfield, Clyde, 275
black majority churches, 41, 341–42
Bonar, Andrew, 119
Bonar, Horatius, 195
Book of Common Prayer, 347, 351
Booth, William, 38, 293
Boyle, Robert, 310, 313
Boys' Brigade, 149
Brekus, Catherine, 293
Brethren, 10, 14, 29, 39, 64–65, 69–70, 81, 118, 124, 151, 158, 163–64, 166, 189, 267, 275, 282, 286, 307, 329, 334, 336, 348, 367
Brewster, Sir David, 306, 310–11, 317–18
Bridges, William, 29, 31
Bristol Baptist Academy, 98, 100, 112
British and Foreign Bible Society, 40, 62, 82, 147–49
British Broadcasting Corporation (BBC), 273
Broad Churchmanship, 32, 63, 65, 67, 111, 135, 193, 204, 231, 267, 301, 324
Brooke, John Hedley, 22, 296, 313–14
Brooks, Thomas, 198
Brown, Ford K., 290
Bruce, Alexander Balmain, 325
Bruce, Frederick Fyvie, 269, 282, 329, 338
Buchanan, Colin, 354

Buchman, Frank, 70, 81, 206
Buchmanites, 71; *see also* Oxford Group
Buckland, William, 306
Bugg, George, 304, 306, 310
Bunyan, John, 106, 216
Burke, Edmund, 50
Bushnell, Horace, 37
Butler, Josephine, 17
Buzz, 344

C

Cadman, William, 161
Calcutta, 30, 219, 223, 225, 239, 303
Calver, Clive, 336, 344
Calvin, John, 237–66
Calvinism, 1, 5, 39, 46–48, 68, 86–87, 97–109, 111–13, 122–25, 136, 139–40, 152, 168–70, 179, 184–89, 196–201, 206–7, 221–22, 237–66, 283–85, 296, 298, 314, 339–40, 349, 368
Cambridge Inter-Collegiate Christian Union (CICCU), 281
Cambridge University, 53, 68–69, 109, 117, 129, 144, 260, 269, 273, 281, 297, 304, 306–7, 320, 322, 325, 348, 352, 354
Cambuslang Revival, 23, 169, 175, 177
Campbell, John McLeod, 65, 83, 106, 111, 211
Canada, 135, 139, 149, 271, 275, 279, 280, 289, 348
Capital Radio, 344
CARE, 342
Carey, George, 206
Carey, William, 98, 139, 148, 195
Carlile, Wilson, 132
Carlyle, Thomas, 242, 246, 249–50
Carter, Jimmy, 279
Cashdollar, Charles, 19
Catholicism (Roman), 11, 32–33, 248, 251, 254, 274
Chalke, Steve, 5, 337
Chalmers, Thomas, 33, 61–62, 107–8, 111, 113, 143, 188, 238, 304, 306, 310–21, 314–19, 325

Chambers, Robert, 319
charismatic movement, 11–12, 41, 72–73, 76, 79, 81, 89, 156, 196, 205–7, 251, 288–89, 332, 334, 338, 340–42, 344–46, 350, 353–54, 362–65, 368–69
Charles I, 109
Chavasse, Christopher, 37
chemistry, 304, 307
Chicago Evangelization Society, 117
China, 148
China Inland Mission (CIM), 65, 148, 151, 338
Christian Advocate, 140
Christian Observer, 169, 302, 306, 314–15, 317, 319
Christian Witness, 212, 231
Churches of Christ, 267
Church Missionary Society (CMS), 40, 110, 138, 336
Church of England: *see* Anglicanism
Church of England Newspaper, 329–31, 339
Church of God, 341, 348, 367
Church of Scotland, 35, 60–63, 68, 78, 84, 107, 111, 151, 250, 257, 264, 303, 309, 339, 348
Church Pastoral Aid Society, 360
civil rights movement, 293–94
Clapham Sect, 246, 290, 304
Clark, Manning, 274
Clarke, Adam, 36, 142, 310, 312, 314
Coates, Gerald, 206
Coffey, David, 337
Coffey, John, 22, 126
Cohen, Charles L., 176
Cokelers, 29–32, 41
Coleridge, Samuel Taylor, 36, 66, 84, 151, 204, 308–9
Colley, Linda, 295
Common Worship, 347, 360
Compendium of Christian Theology (Pope), 240
Conforti, Joseph A., 95
Congregationalist, 231

Congregationalists, 68, 80, 87–88, 95–96, 103–7, 111–13, 116, 130, 134–37, 140, 142, 144, 150, 152, 166, 194, 196, 211, 214–21, 224, 227–29, 242, 244, 250, 260, 267, 270, 275, 305, 311, 324, 356, 361–68
Conservatives (political), 126, 263, 280
conservatives (theological), 4, 11, 17, 24, 35, 69, 74, 84, 122, 130, 132, 150–52, 162–63, 165–66, 198, 202, 204, 207, 253–54, 256, 262, 265, 268, 280–81, 332, 336–40, 344–45, 357, 360
conversion, 1, 3, 6–7, 12–13, 19, 25, 38–39, 41, 44–45, 54, 59, 65, 115, 122, 128, 138–40, 145, 155, 161, 168–91, 193–94, 197, 200, 207, 216, 220, 267, 301, 305, 325, 331, 333, 336, 345, 350
Conybeare, William Daniel, 306
Cowper, William, 49
Crieff Brotherhood, 339
Cromwell, Oliver, 245–46, 250–52, 254
Crosslinks, 335
crucicentrism, 3, 12, 217; *see also* atonement
Cunningham, William, 108, 239, 316
Currents in World Christianity (1999), 16, 277

D

Dale, Robert William, 112, 188
Darby, John Nelson, 19–20, 64, 124, 151, 163–64
Darwin, Charles, 22, 61, 143, 252, 319–20
Darwinism, 22, 61, 320–24, 326; social Darwinism, 320
Dayton, Donald, 31
Dearmer, Percy, 251
Death and the Enlightenment (McManners), 209
de Gaulle, Charles, 329
Dependents, Society of: *see* Cokelers
Derrida, Jacques, 350
Descartes, René 262

de Wette, Wilhelm Martin Leberecht, 105
Dick, Thomas, 317
dispensationalism, 20, 34, 64, 124, 151, 164, 334
Dissenters, 11, 18–22, 30–31, 40, 43, 48–49, 60, 62, 82, 107, 170–71, 173, 197, 193, 196, 198, 237, 240, 246–47, 260, 285, 306, 336, 350, 368; *see also* Nonconformists
Dixon, Amzi C., 145
Dochuk, Darren, 12
Dr Williams's Centre for Dissenting Studies, 18–19, 285
Drummond, Henry, 6, 120, 130–31, 276, 309, 324
Drummond, Lewis, 276
Duncan, John, 108–9

E

East India Company, 178
Ecclesiastical History Society, 24, 268, 295
Eclectic Society, 307
ecumenism, 285–86, 298, 339, 345, 356–58, 368
education, 51–52, 80, 129, 132, 147–49, 160, 173, 185, 195, 27, 280, 308, 345, 366
Edwards, Joel, 341
Edwards, Jonathan, 15, 47, 82, 95–113, 116, 188, 238, 268, 277
Eliot, George, 54, 77
Eliot, Philip Frank, 30, 32, 41
empire, 6, 16, 18, 109, 149, 278, 281, 335
English Church Census (1989), 34
Enlightenment, 9–10, 12, 21, 43–56, 59–65, 71–72, 74, 79, 97, 141–43, 45, 150–52, 157, 173, 185, 190–91, 198–99, 201–2, 207, 241–42, 248, 265, 274–75, 287, 307–9, 312, 325
entire sanctification, 83, 87, 140–41, 199, 201–2
Erdozain, Dominic, 7
Erskine, John, 55, 98, 107
Erskine, Thomas, 65, 111

Evangelical Alliance, 5, 40, 134, 143, 245, 335–36, 341
Evangelical Coalition for Urban Mission, 335
Evangelical Magazine, 83, 187
Evangelical Quarterly, 256
Evans, Caleb, 100
Evans, James Harington, 220, 230
Expressionism, 8–9, 11–12, 70–74, 358

F

Faber, George Stanley, 206
Fairbairn, Andrew, 240
Falding, F. J., 106
Fellowship of Independent Evangelical Churches, 336, 252, 368
feminism, 292, 360, 369
Festival of Light, 342
Fides et Historia, 281, 283
Finney, Charles, 140, 186, 189–90
First World War, 24, 67, 89, 13, 164, 203, 252
Fisher, Geoffrey, 330
Fisher, Linford D., 13
Fleming, John, 306, 313, 317
Fletcher, John, 54, 276
Foster, Frank H., 112
Foster, John, 302, 317
Fountain Trust, 205–6, 340, 363
Free Church of Scotland, 33, 65, 78, 107–8, 118–19, 122, 129, 146, 149–50, 193, 198, 239–40, 242–43, 247, 256–59, 265, 275, 277, 316, 325, 339, 368
Free Churches, 68, 90, 140, 250–51, 340, 354–56, 359–60, 365
Freedom of the Will (Edwards), 99–100, 103–4, 107, 109, 111
French Revolution, 62, 85, 156, 256
Freud, Sigmund, 71, 207
Fulcrum, 337
Fuller, Andrew, 99–104, 113, 140, 188–89, 238, 208, 310, 316
Fundamentalism, 4, 16, 24–25, 35–37, 65, 81, 131, 152, 162–65, 253, 269, 280, 288

Fyfe, Aileen, 22

G

Gadsby, William, 247
Garden City movement, 66
Gaskell, Elizabeth, 1
Gaskell, William, 1, 26
gender, 121, 176–77, 212, 292–93, 299, 342–43, 345, 360
General Baptist Magazine, 61
General Baptist Repository, 171
Gentleman's Magazine, 52
geology, 104, 304, 306, 309, 312, 317
Germany, 11, 60, 63, 95, 98, 150, 255
Gesenius, Wihelm, 105
Gibbard, Noel, 23
Gibbon, Edward, 43–44
Gibraltar, 137
Gill, John, 101
Gisborne, Thomas, 312, 314, 316
Gladstone, William Ewart, 248
Glasgow Tent Hall, 119, 127
Glorious Revolution (1688), 254, 256
Goode, John, 198
Goode, William, 194
Gorer, Geoffrey, 210
Graham, Billy, 38, 120, 336
Gramberg, Carl Peter Wilhelm, 105
Grass, Timothy, 19
Great Awakening, 55, 77, 273, 289
Gribben, Crawford, 19
Grimshaw, William, 6, 53–54
Groser, William Howse, 57, 73
Groves, Anthony Norris, 64
Guelzo, Allen C., 95
Guest, Mathew, 11

H

Haeckel, Ernst, 322
Hall, Catherine, 16, 292
Hall, Robert, 47
Hamilton, Sir William, 108
Hammond, Geordan, 6
Handy, Robert, 271
Hardy, Thomas, 58
Harper, Michael, 206

Hartman, Karl Robert Eduard, 105
Harvard University, 280
Hastings, Adrian, 278
Hatch, Nathan, 282, 291
Haweis, Thomas, 47–49, 302, 305, 311
Hawker, Robert, 48, 197
Heidelberg Catechism, 368
Helmstadter, Richard, 22
Hempton, David, 275
hermeneutics, 345
Higginbotham, Evelyn Brooks, 294
High Churchmanship, 30, 32–33, 41, 65, 67, 111, 135, 193, 204, 251, 267, 283, 311, 313, 324, 332, 348, 350, 354–55, 356–59, 368
Hill, George, 107
Hilton, Boyd, 5, 21, 278
Hindmarsh, Bruce, 6, 10, 20–21
Hinton, John Howard, 189
Hitler, Adolf, 71
Hodge, A. A., 106
Holifield, E. Brooks, 95
holiness movement, 10, 18, 29, 37, 48, 66, 80, 118, 124–25, 140–41, 151, 165, 193–207, 220–21, 253, 262, 280, 288, 333
Holmes, Janice, 17
Holy Spirit, 12, 23, 38, 125, 189, 203, 213, 217, 282, 293, 359, 363, 365
homosexuality, 342
Hopkins, Evan, 203, 253
Hopkins, Mark, 11, 297
Houlbrooke, Ralph, 209
house churches, 72, 205–6
Howe, John, 215
Hughes, Hugh Price, 7, 277
Hudson, Winthrop, 271
Hume, David, 9, 43, 55, 60, 315
Huntingdon, Countess of, 50, 302
Hutchinson, Mark, 14
Hutchinson, William, 280, 310–11, 313
Huxley, Thomas Henry, 322
hymns, 18, 29, 52, 68, 70, 140, 182, 200, 215, 232, 288, 349–50, 352, 367

I

Independents: *see* Congregationalists
India, 105, 139, 195, 287, 353
inerrancy, 4, 35–36
infallibility, 162
Institutes (Calvin), 241, 252, 260–62
Interserve, 335
Inter-Varsity Fellowship of Christian Unions, 204, 262, 280–81
InterVarsity Press, 287, 334
Iredale, John, 54
Ireland, 23, 34, 130, 135, 178, 248, 255, 289, 295, 348
Irons, Joseph, 247
Irons, William, 309
Irving, Edward, 10, 19, 63–64, 84, 151, 155–58, 309
Islington Conference, 30–32, 38, 40, 82, 329, 340, 351, 353
Israel, 65
Israel, Jonathan, 9
Issues Facing Christians Today (Stott), 262, 343
itinerant preaching, 6, 119, 172, 185, 243

J

Jalland, Pat, 18, 210–12, 217
James, John Angell, 142, 188–90
Jay, William, 215
Jeffrey, Kenneth, 23
Jenkins, Philip, 278
Jesus, 31, 34, 37–38, 48, 61, 64, 68, 133, 137–38, 155–56, 162, 188, 215, 218, 222, 226, 230, 253, 275, 334–35, 355, 367
John, Jeffrey, 343
Johnson, Dale A., 21
Johnson, Paul E., 290
Johnson, Samuel, 50, 85
Johnston, Raymond, 343
Johnston, William, 137, 142
Jones, Bryn, 80
Jones, David Ceri, 6
Jones, Robert Tudur, 23, 95, 135, 295
Joyce, James, 71
Judaism, 19, 133, 162, 214, 224, 230
Jung, Carl, 71, 207

Juster, Susan, 293
justification by faith, 6, 106, 138, 194, 200, 305

K

Kafka, Franz, 358
Kant, Immanuel, 189
Keele National Evangelical Congress (1967), 331–32, 339, 354
Keep Sunday Special campaign, 343
Kent, John, 22, 126
Keswick Movement, 66–67, 69–70, 74, 80, 124–25, 151, 196, 202–4, 206–7, 253, 262, 288, 333, 335, 337
Kevan, Ernest, 34, 39
Kidd, Thomas, 12, 289
Kinnaird, Lord, 126
Kirby, Gilbert, 31
Kloes, Andrew, 14
Knox, John, 239, 249
Knox, Ronald, 66
Kuyper, Abraham, 255–56

L

Labour Party, 66, 82, 258
Ladies' Home Journal, 131
Laing, Sir John, 330
Laqueur, Thomas, 78
Larsen, Timothy, 8
Latourette, Kenneth Scott, 273
Lausanne Covenant, 34, 332
Leeds Mercury, 224
Lewis, Donald M., 14, 20
Lewis, Thomas, 213
liberals (theological), 11, 17, 19, 22, 25, 32–33, 37, 44, 65–70, 74, 80, 96, 111–13, 123, 136, 150, 152, 160, 162, 165, 229, 242–43, 247, 251–53, 258, 260, 265, 278, 301, 318, 324
Lidgett, John Scott, 65
Life of Faith, 202
Linder, Robert D., 281
Lindsell, Harold, 283
Livingstone, David, 144
Lloyd, Jennifer, 17

Lloyd-Jones, Martyn, 25, 84, 113, 196, 260–65, 284, 336, 339, 349
Locke, John, 45, 60, 141–42
London Bible College, 3, 34, 339, 342, 360
London Missionary Society (LMS), 40, 48, 105–6, 168, 215
London Quarterly Review, 317
lovefeasts, 185
Low Churchmanship, 33–34, 36
Lucas, Dick, 304
Luther, Martin, 240, 242–43
Lux Mundi, 324
Lyell, Charles, 318

M

Macdonald, William, 85
Mackenzie, John, 142, 238, 241
MacLaren, Allan, 77, 291
Major, John, 343
Making of the English Working Class (Thompson), 290
Manton, Thomas, 198
MARC Europe/Christian Research, 337
Marsden, George, 277, 280, 282, 284, 288
Marty, Martin E., 280
Martyn, Henry, 110, 272
Marx, Karl, 66, 77, 291–92, 299
materialism, 64, 322
Mathers, James, 132
Maurice, Frederick Denison, 65, 111, 252
McCheyne, Robert Murray, 108, 119
McGrath, Alister, 263–64
McIntire, C. T., 284
McLeod, Hugh, 290
McManners, John, 209
Mead, Sidney, 271
Methodist Magazine, 83, 211–12, 231, 261, 312–13, 315
Methodists, 6, 24–25, 38–39, 43–44, 46–47, 50, 52, 54, 58–59, 67–68, 83, 85, 87, 88, 98, 108, 110, 113, 122–23, 136–41, 145, 150–52, 158, 160, 166, 170–71, 178–79, 185–86, 195–96, 199, 201–2, 215, 221–23, 240, 249, 270–72, 274–76, 286–88,

291, 295, 308, 310, 312, 315, 317, 329, 339, 348–49, 353, 355, 357–58, 360–61, 363; Free Methodists, 24; Primitive Methodists, 36–37, 38–39, 83, 168–69, 182, 290; Wesleyan Methodists, 7, 36, 104, 125, 175, 177, 211–12, 231; *see also* Bible Christians
Meyer, Frederick Brotherton, 35, 125, 163–64
Micklem, Nathaniel, 68, 260
Mildmay Conference, 40, 117–18, 125
millennialism, 20, 46–47, 155–61, 164–66, 348; *see also* postmillennialism; premillennialism
Miller, Hugh, 33, 306, 318–19
Milner, Isaac, 53, 307
Milner, Joseph, 310
missions: foreign, 15–16, 39–40, 48, 51, 62–65, 75, 84, 97–100, 105, 108, 110, 113, 133, 135, 138, 142, 144, 148, 150–51, 156, 164, 178, 185, 195, 198, 218–19, 221, 223, 227, 268, 272–74, 277–79, 287, 294, 298, 314, 335–36, 362; home, 7, 51, 53, 59, 68, 113, 118–19, 121–22, 126–27, 129–30, 132, 139, 152, 212, 331, 335–36, 362
Modernism, 11, 70, 72, 81, 253
Moody, Dwight L., 7, 15, 23, 88, 115–32, 140, 151, 277
Moody Bible Institute, 132
Moorhouse, Henry, 118, 123
Moral Rearmament, 70–71; *see also* Oxford Group
Moravians, 14, 136
More, Hannah, 50, 85, 194
Morgan, Richard Cope, 118, 120
Morley, John, 251
Morris, Dinah, 54
Moule, Handley, 203
Movement for Change, 344
Mozart, Wolfgang Amadeus, 76
Müller, George, 151
Murray, Andrew, 125
Murray, Iain, 261, 284–85, 334

N

Native Americans, 97, 116, 294
Natural Law in the Spiritual World (Drummond), 324
natural theology, 21–22, 60–61, 63, 143, 301–7, 309, 312–26
New Zealand, 82, 135, 148–49, 267, 248
Newman, John Henry, 32
Newman, William, 101
Newton, Sir Isaac, 60, 307, 309–12, 314, 320, 325
Newton, John, 20, 45–46, 49, 53, 109, 187, 197, 302–7
Nichols, William, 172
Nietzsche, Friedrich, 71
Noll, Mark, 7, 77, 95, 269, 275, 260, 280, 282, 294–95
Nonconformists, 2, 6–9, 11, 17–18, 21, 41, 59, 68–69, 86–88, 96, 158, 160, 175–77, 191, 196, 206, 209–33, 246–48, 250, 267, 270, 273, 285–86, 288, 297, 319, 347, 349, 352, 354–56; *see also* Dissenters
North Atlantic Missiology Project (1996), 16, 277
Northamptonshire Baptist Association, 98
Northfield Conferences, 123–25, 130, 151
Northumberland, Seventh Duke of, 158
Nottingham Evangelical Anglican Congress (1977), 354

O

Oasis Charitable Trust, 337
Oldstone-Moore, Christopher, 7
Orchard, William Edwin, 69
Origin of Species (Darwin), 319, 321
Orr, James, 259, 318, 321–24, 326
Osborn, George, 172
Owen, John, 198
Oxford Group, 11, 70–72, 81, 205
Oxford Movement, 34, 63–64, 68, 78, 96, 156, 204, 248, 286

Index 379

Oxford University, 35, 129, 189, 250, 252, 260, 273, 275, 280, 282, 288, 306, 311, 352

P

Packer, James Innell, 261, 265, 284, 333, 340
Paine, Thomas, 9, 316
Paley, William , 61, 313, 315, 321, 323
Palmer, Phoebe, 151, 201
Parker, Joseph, 123, 242
Parker, Thomas Henry Lewis, 263
Pankhurst, Christabel, 17, 162
parliament, 66, 75, 127, 145, 224, 246, 251, 261–62, 330, 347
Payne, Ernest, 354
Payne, George, 106
Peculiar People, 29, 31
Pennefather, William, 40, 118
Pentecostalism, 41, 166, 193, 205, 267, 275, 286, 329, 340–41
Peto, Sir Samuel Morton, 144
Pew Charitable Trust, 277
Pierard, Richard V., 281
philanthropy, 39, 127, 145, 292, 343
Philip, John, 264
physicotheology, 312–14, 325
Pilgrim's Progress (Bunyan), 216
Plymouth Brethren: see Brethren
politics, 82, 127, 244, 247, 251, 263
Pollard, Christian Samuel, 36–37
Pollock, John, 276
Pope Innocent III, 248
Pope John XXIII, 329
Pope John Paul II, 358
Pope Pius IX, 160
Pope, William Burt, 240, 320
postmillennialism, 34, 61–62, 64, 142–43, 151–52, 157, 161, 278, 334–35
Postmodernism, 72, 206–7, 297–99, 346
Poussin, Nicholas, 76
Pratt, John Henry, 306, 313
Pratt, Josiah, 110
Premier Radio, 344

premillennialism, 10, 12, 20, 64–65, 69, 74, 78, 86, 124–25, 151, 157–59, 161–66, 204, 253, 268, 292, 334–35
Presbyterians, 19, 24, 59, 68, 86, 96–98, 102, 107–9, 118, 135–36, 139–40, 149–50, 152, 166, 179, 188–89, 195–97, 224, 237–38, 240, 242, 247, 249–50, 252, 257–58, 265–67, 270, 275, 280, 291, 321, 339, 347, 355, 360, 365; *see also* Church of Scotland; Free Church of Scotland; United Presbyterians; United Free Church of Scotland
Proclamation Trust, 340
Proby, W. H. B., 33
Protestant Reformation Society, 333
Public Worship Regulation Act (1874), 30
Puritanism, 1, 13, 45–46, 102, 106, 109, 116, 170, 176, 183–84, 187, 190, 196, 198, 237–38, 242, 245, 250, 259, 261, 277, 334, 340

Q

Quakerism, 136, 137, 138, 270

R

Rack, Henry, 276
Radcliffe, Reginald, 138
Ragged School Society, 195
Randall, Ian, 18, 289
Rank, J. Arthur, 85
Rattenbury, John, 37, 39
Raven, Charles, 22, 325
Rawlyk, George, 289, 292
Reardon, Bernard, 96, 296–97
Record, 141
Rees, Christina, 342
Reformation, 19, 30, 146, 159, 237, 239, 242, 248, 257–58, 263, 330, 332–33, 351, 357
Reformed theology: *see* Calvinism
Regions Beyond Missionary Union, 164
Reid, Thomas, 60, 141, 311, 315
Religious Tract Society (RTS), 22, 40, 82, 96, 147, 172

Research Scientists' Christian Fellowship, 22
Restoration magazine, 334
revivalism, 13, 50, 120–21, 126, 189, 274, 280, 289
Reynolds, Joshua, 50
Rios, Christopher, 22
Rippon, John, 183–84, 215
Riso, Mary, 18
ritualism, 30, 146, 254
Roberts, Evan, 87
Roberts, John, 103–4
Roberts, Oral, 277
Rodgers, Richard, 72
Rogers, Henry, 96–97, 106–7, 112, 311
Roman Catholicism: *see* Catholicism (Roman)
Romanticism, 8–12, 63–64, 66, 71, 74, 151, 157, 165, 265, 309
Rooker, William, 217
Rupp, Gordon, 273
Ryland, John, 47, 98, 100–101, 307
Ryle, John Charles, 66, 110, 146, 196–98, 202, 239

S

Salvation Army, 38, 199, 293, 343
sanctification, 48, 125, 194, 196–200, 203, 206–7, 220, 253, 272, 333, 350; entire, 83, 87, 140–41, 199, 201–2
Sankey, Ira D., 88, 91, 115, 118–22, 350
science, 4, 21–22, 45, 60–61, 82, 111, 143, 147, 152, 190, 296, 301–26
Scofield, Cyrus Ingerson, 124
Scofield Bible, 164, 334
Scotland, 19, 23, 33, 35, 55, 60–63, 68, 78, 84–86, 96–97, 107–8, 111, 113, 188, 122, 127, 135–36, 146, 149–51, 169, 186, 189, 183, 196, 237, 239, 242–43, 248–53, 255–57, 264–65, 267, 277, 296, 302–3, 306, 309–10, 315, 325, 339, 347–49, 367–68
Scotland, Nigel, 290
Scott, Thomas, 109, 156, 308
Scott, Sir Walter, 63
scriptural geology, 304–6

Scroggie, Graham, 203
Seaman's Friend Society, 148
second coming: *see* adventism
Second Great Awakening, 295
Second World War, 34, 164, 256, 258–59, 280, 324, 365
Sedgwick, Adam, 306
Sell, Alan, 285
Sentamu, John, 342
Servetus, 245, 259
Shaftesbury Project, 262, 343
Shaftesbury, Seventh Earl of, 20, 126, 139, 157, 274
Simeon, Charles, 32, 49, 109, 156, 194, 196–97, 241
Sinners in the Hands of an Angry God (Edwards), 96
Sirgood, John, 29, 41
slavery, 47, 109, 145
Smith, Hannah Pearsall, 202
Smith, John Pye, 22, 104–5, 111, 133, 305–6, 311, 313–14, 317, 319
Smith, Mark, 7
Smith, Robert Pearsall, 202
Smith, William, 246
Smith, William Robertson, 65
Smithies, T. B., 36
Smout, Thomas C., 175, 177
social gospel, 7, 127–28, 145, 258, 277, 279, 343
Society for the Propagation of the Gospel (SPG), 111
Society of Friends: *see* Quakerism
Socinianism, 50, 60, 179, 246
Sovereign Grace Union, 254–56, 258, 265
Spence, Martin, 20
Spencer, Herbert, 320, 322, 324
Spinoza, Baruch, 9, 105
Spurgeon, Charles Haddon, 39, 81, 102, 116, 122, 138, 195, 229, 247, 276, 289, 292, 320, 345
Stanley, Brian, 16, 278
Steadman, William, 100
Steele, Anne, 18–19
Stewart, Dugald, 311, 315

Still, William, 339
Stock, John, 173
Stokes, George, 322–23
Storr, Vernon, 325
Stott, John, 25, 36, 84, 262, 330–31, 334, 336, 343
Stout, Harry S., 269, 284–85
Stubenrauch, Joseph, 20–21
Student Christian Movement (SCM), 130
Student Volunteer Missionary Union (SVMU), 130
Student Volunteer Movement for Foreign Missions, 161
Sumner, John Bird, 303, 306, 310, 314
Sunday school, 52, 57, 78, 83, 117, 147–48, 171, 185, 225–26, 352, 354
Sunday School Union, 57, 147–48
Sweet, William Warren, 271
systematic theology, 102, 105–6, 189–90
Smyth, Charles, 273
Smyth, Edward, 240

T

Tawney, Richard Henry, 258
Taylor, Dan, 37
Taylor, Isaac, 109
Taylor, James Hudson, 65, 151
Taylor, Nathaniel W., 189
Taylor, William, 138, 150
TEAR Fund, 343, 362
temperance, 39, 59, 82, 85, 88, 127, 145, 160
Thatcher, Margaret, 343
Third Way, 344
Tholuck, Friedrich, 139
Thompson, Edward Palmer, 58, 290–91
Thomson, Alexander, 239
Thomson, G. T., 258
Thomson, James, 149
Tillotson, John, 38
Tindal, Matthew, 55
Toland, John, 9
Tongue of Fire (Arthur), 201
tongues, speaking in, 64, 84, 205, 329, 340, 363
Toplady, Augustus, 215

Tractarianism, 146, 309; *see also* Oxford Movement
Tyndale House, Cambridge, 269

U

Unitarians, 52, 133, 193, 245, 270, 301
United Free Church of Scotland, 249, 257, 259, 321
United Presbyterians, 118, 150, 242
United Reformed Church, 275, 285, 287, 339, 348, 357

V

Valenze, Deborah, 178
Van Til, Cornelius, 283–84
Vater, Johann Severin, 105
Vatican II, 263, 285, 332
Venn, Henry, 46, 48, 54
Venn, John, 304, 307
Victoria Institute, 22
Villiers, Henry Montagu, 157
Voltaire, 9, 43, 60

W

Wales, 2, 39, 55, 68, 81, 84, 86, 89, 96–97, 101–4, 108, 113, 140, 149, 178, 188, 193, 196, 211–12, 240, 261, 264, 267, 295, 296, 336, 339, 347–49, 360, 363
Walker, Samuel, 48, 272
Walls, Andrew, 16, 75, 277–78, 287
Ward, William, 178–79
Warner, George, 83
Warner, Rob, 11
Warwick, John Montgomery, 291
Watts, Isaac, 140, 215, 361
Watts, Michael, 11, 169–70, 175–76, 181–83, 191
Wearmouth, Robert, 271
Webber, Robert Eugene, 282–83, 297
Wellings, Martin, 21–22
Welsh Revival, 23, 87
Wesley, Charles, 37, 68, 200, 219
Wesley, John, 6, 9, 32, 35–36, 45–56, 68, 98, 101, 110, 115, 124, 136, 185, 195, 197, 199–203, 207, 215, 224, 240,

270–72, 276, 308–9, 311, 317, 326, 361
Wesleyan Methodist Magazine, 211–12, 231
Westminster Assembly, 198, 237, 242, 264
Westminster Chapel, 196, 260–61, 336
Westminster Confession, 150, 339
westward position, 354
Whale, John Seldon, 260, 263
Wheaton College, Illinois, 282, 286–87
Wheeler, Michael, 210, 228
Whewell, William, 306
White, Barrie, 282
Whitefield, George, 6–7, 32, 38, 47–51, 68, 285, 308
Wilberforce, William, 8, 79, 85, 110, 145, 246, 276, 290, 294, 314–15
Williams, Edward, 87, 103–6, 108, 113, 188, 238
Williams, Raymond, 76
Williams, T. Rhondda, 68
Wilson, Daniel, 30, 239, 303
Wilson, Linda, 17–18, 176, 210, 219

Wimber, John, 341, 363
Winter, Cornelius, 49, 308
Winward, Stephen F., 354
Wolffe, John, 14, 23, 286
women, 17–18, 39–40, 50, 54, 58, 116, 121, 129, 132, 136, 147, 162, 174, 176–78, 180–81, 185, 202, 212, 216–20, 223–25, 292–94, 342, 359–60, 367
Wood, Maurice, 329, 332, 337, 338, 340
Woolf, Virginia, 358
Wordsworth, William, 63, 66, 67, 204

Y

Young, George Malcolm, 273, 278
Young Life Campaign, 69
Young Men's Christian Association (YMCA), 7, 130, 148
youth culture, 11, 83, 176, 205, 344, 360–66, 369
Youth Praise, 361

www.ingramcontent.com/pod-product-compliance
Lightning Source LLC
Chambersburg PA
CBHW021815300426
44114CB00009BA/190